First World War
and Army of Occupation
War Diary
France, Belgium and Germany

34 DIVISION
Headquarters, Branches and Services
Commander Royal Artillery
6 January 1918 - 18 July 1919

WO95/2442

The Naval & Military Press Ltd
www.nmarchive.com
Published in association with The National Archives

Published by

The Naval & Military Press Ltd

Unit 10 Ridgewood Industrial Park,

Uckfield, East Sussex,

TN22 5QE England

Tel: +44 (0) 1825 749494

www.naval-military-press.com

www.nmarchive.com

This diary has been reprinted in facsimile from the original. Any imperfections are inevitably reproduced and the quality may fall short of modern type and cartographic standards.

Contents

Document type	Place/Title	Date From	Date To
Heading	34th Division C. R. A. 1918 Jan-1919 Jly		
Heading	War Diary Of H Q R A 34 Division January 1918 Vol 25		
Miscellaneous	This File Is Only Issued As A Cover To Army Form C 2118 (War Diary)		
War Diary	Boileux Au Mont	06/01/1918	29/01/1918
Operation(al) Order(s)	34th Divisional Artillery Operation Order No. 125 App. 1	06/01/1918	06/01/1918
Operation(al) Order(s)	34th Divisional Artillery Operation Order No. 126 App. II	15/01/1918	15/01/1918
Heading	War Diary H.Q.R.A. 34th Division February 1918 Vol 26		
War Diary	Gomiecourt 57c N W	10/02/1918	10/02/1918
War Diary	Rebreuviette (Lens 1/100000)	11/02/1918	11/02/1918
War Diary	Rebreuve (Lens)	16/02/1918	16/02/1918
Miscellaneous	34th Divisional Artillery March Orders. App I	05/02/1918	05/02/1918
Miscellaneous	March Table		
Miscellaneous	Billetting Table (Table "B")		
Miscellaneous	Table "C" Supply Arrangements Shewing Refilling Points From Which Supplies Will Be Drawn On Dates Stated For Consumption Following Day		
Miscellaneous	Amendment No. 1 To 34th Divisional Artillery March Orders	07/02/1918	07/02/1918
Operation(al) Order(s)	34th Divisional Artillery Operation Order No. 127. App II	16/02/1918	16/02/1918
Miscellaneous	34th, Divisional Administrative Instructions No. 1	16/02/1918	16/02/1918
Miscellaneous	R.A. Entrainment Statement Showing Composition Of Each Train		
Heading	War Diary C. R. A. 34th Division March 1918		
Heading	General Staff 34th Division War Diary March, 1918		
War Diary	Rebreuve Chateau 51c. 1/40,000	01/03/1918	01/03/1918
War Diary	Gomiecourt 51B. 1/40,000	03/03/1918	21/03/1918
War Diary	Ayette 57D. 1/40,000	23/03/1918	23/03/1918
War Diary	Adinfer 51c 1/40,000	25/03/1918	25/03/1918
War Diary	Le Cauroy 51c 1/40,000	26/03/1918	26/03/1918
War Diary	Auxi-Le-Chateau	27/03/1918	27/03/1918
War Diary	Merville 36A 1/40,000	31/03/1918	31/03/1918
Operation(al) Order(s)	34th Divisional Artillery Operation Order No. 128. App I	28/02/1918	28/02/1918
Miscellaneous	34th Divisional Artillery March Orders App II	28/02/1918	28/02/1918
Miscellaneous	March Table Table "A"		
Miscellaneous	Billeting Table Table "B"		
Miscellaneous	Narrative Of Operations (34th Divisional Artillery) During March 21st., 22nd. And 23rd. 1918 App III	30/03/1918	30/03/1918
Heading	34th Divisional Artillery War Diary C. R. A. 34th Division April 1918		
War Diary	Merville (36a 1/40000)	03/04/1918	09/04/1918
War Diary	Lesart (36a 1/40000)	09/04/1918	09/04/1918
War Diary	Neuf Berquin (36a)	09/04/1918	09/04/1918
War Diary	Merville (36a)	09/04/1918	09/04/1918

War Diary	La Motte (36a)	11/04/1918	11/04/1918
War Diary	Le Grand Hazard (36a. D.8.d)	12/04/1918	12/04/1918
War Diary	Le Grand Hazard (36a)	15/04/1918	22/04/1918
Miscellaneous	32nd Div. No. G.S. 1710/4/5. App I	31/03/1918	31/03/1918
Miscellaneous	O C 152 160 Bdes App II		
Miscellaneous	O.C. 152 160 F A Bdes	02/04/1918	02/04/1918
Miscellaneous	March Table For 5th April App III		
Miscellaneous	O.C. 160 F A Bde		
Miscellaneous	O.C. 152 F A Bde App IV	05/04/1918	05/04/1918
Miscellaneous	March Table For 6th April		
Miscellaneous	34th Divl. Arty. No. SC/M/5 App V	06/04/1918	06/04/1918
Miscellaneous	March Table For 7th April		
Miscellaneous	Amendment No. 1 To 34th Divisional Artillery Relief Orders App VI	07/04/1918	07/04/1918
Miscellaneous	34th Divisional Artillery Relief Orders	07/04/1918	07/04/1918
Miscellaneous	36th Divisional Artillery Location Statement	04/04/1918	04/04/1918
Miscellaneous	Narrative Of 34th Divisional Artillery From 9th April To 17th April 1918 App VII		
Operation(al) Order(s)	34th Divisional Artillery Operation Order No. 1	15/04/1918	15/04/1918
Operation(al) Order(s)	34th Divisional Artillery Operation Order No. 2	16/04/1918	16/04/1918
Miscellaneous	Ammunition Expended By 34th Divisional Artillery		
Miscellaneous	Detail Of Moves Of 160th Brigade RFA. From 9th To 14th April 1918 Inclusive	14/04/1918	14/04/1918
Miscellaneous	Detail Of Moves Of 152nd Brigade RFA. From 9th To 14th April Inclusive	14/04/1918	14/04/1918
Operation(al) Order(s)	34th Divisional Artillery Operation Order No. 1 App VIII	15/04/1918	15/04/1918
Miscellaneous	34th Divisional Artillery Operation Order No. 2 App IX	16/04/1918	16/04/1918
Miscellaneous	34th Divisional Artillery Location Statement 17th April 1918. App X	17/04/1918	17/04/1918
Miscellaneous	34th Divisional Artillery Location Statement 22nd April 1918. App XI	22/04/1918	22/04/1918
Heading	War Diary For May 1918 34th Divisional Artillery Vol 29		
War Diary	Le Grand Hazard D.8.d. Sheet 36a	01/05/1918	08/05/1918
War Diary	Le Grand Hazard	08/05/1918	08/05/1918
War Diary	Steenbecque	09/05/1918	31/05/1918
Miscellaneous	34th Division Artillery Location Statement 1st May 1918 App I	01/05/1918	01/05/1918
Miscellaneous	5th Divisional Artillery No. HBM/29/1 App II	07/05/1918	07/05/1918
Miscellaneous	5th Divisional Artillery No. HBM/29/3 App III	15/05/1918	15/05/1918
Miscellaneous	O.C. 152nd Brigade RFA	14/05/1918	14/05/1918
Miscellaneous	5th Divisional Artillery No. HBM/29/2	14/05/1918	14/05/1918
Miscellaneous	34th Divisional Artillery Location Statement 16th May 1918 App IV	16/05/1918	16/05/1918
Miscellaneous	5th Divisional Artillery No. HBM/15/28 App V	19/05/1918	19/05/1918
Miscellaneous	5th Divisional Artillery No. HBM/15/25 App V	15/05/1918	15/05/1918
Miscellaneous	5th Divisional Artillery No. HBM/15/24	15/05/1918	15/05/1918
Miscellaneous	A Form Messages And Signals App VI		
Miscellaneous	Headquarters, 34th Divisional Artillery	25/04/1918	25/04/1918
Miscellaneous	Headquarters, 31st Division "Q"	25/04/1918	25/04/1918
Miscellaneous	34th Div. Arty. No. G/605	12/05/1918	12/05/1918
Heading	War Diary June 1918 Vol 30		
War Diary	Steenbecque 36A 1/40,000	01/06/1918	01/06/1918
Miscellaneous	War Diary July 1918 Vol 31		
War Diary	Steenbecque (36a. 1/40000) C.29.d.	03/07/1918	03/07/1918

War Diary	Rubrouck (Hazebrouck 5a, 1/100000)	04/07/1918	04/07/1918
War Diary	Couthove Chateau. F.21.a. (27, 1/40000)	05/07/1918	06/07/1918
War Diary	Couthove Chateau (27, F.21.a)	07/07/1918	15/07/1918
War Diary	Proven	16/07/1918	16/07/1918
War Diary	Senlis (Beauvais 1/100000)	17/07/1918	18/07/1918
War Diary	Senlis	18/07/1918	19/07/1918
War Diary	Largny (Soissons-1/80000)	20/07/1918	20/07/1918
War Diary	Vivieres (Soissons-1/80000)	21/07/1918	22/07/1918
War Diary	Vivieres	22/07/1918	23/07/1918
War Diary	Chavigny Farm (Soissons 1/80000)	23/07/1918	25/07/1918
War Diary	Chavigny Farm	25/07/1918	28/07/1918
War Diary	Fe. d'Edrolle (Oulchy-Le-Chau 1/20000)	29/07/1918	29/07/1918
War Diary	Fme. d'Edrolle	29/07/1918	31/07/1918
War Diary	Geromesnil Farm	31/07/1918	31/07/1918
Miscellaneous	Warning Order App I	29/07/1918	29/07/1918
Operation(al) Order(s)	34th Divisional Artillery Operation Order No. 5 App IV	05/07/1918	05/07/1918
Miscellaneous	Table "A" Attached To 34th D.A.O.O. No. 5		
Operation(al) Order(s)	34th Divisional Artillery Operation Order No. 3 App II	02/07/1918	02/07/1918
Operation(al) Order(s)	34th Divisional Artillery Operation Order No. 4 App III	03/07/1918	03/07/1918
Miscellaneous	34th Divisional Artillery Instructions No. 1 App V	07/07/1918	07/07/1918
Miscellaneous	App VI		
Diagram etc			
Miscellaneous	List Of Artillery Positions To Be Occupied App VII	11/07/1918	11/07/1918
Miscellaneous	34th Divisional Artillery Instructions No. 2 App VIII	12/07/1918	12/07/1918
Operation(al) Order(s)	34th Divisional Artillery Operation Order No. 6. App IX	12/07/1918	12/07/1918
Miscellaneous	34th Div. Arty. No. O/400. App X	11/07/1918	11/07/1918
Operation(al) Order(s)	34th Divisional Artillery Operation Order No. 7 App XI	15/07/1918	15/07/1918
Miscellaneous	34th Div. Arty. No. G/401. App XII	12/07/1918	12/07/1918
Miscellaneous	Artillery Defence Scheme To Come Into Force 23rd July At 4 a.m. App XIII	24/07/1918	24/07/1918
Miscellaneous	Artillery Arrangement To Come Into Force At 9 p.m. On 25th July App XIV	25/07/1918	25/07/1918
Miscellaneous	34th Divisional Artillery Night Firing 26/27th July	26/07/1918	26/07/1918
Operation(al) Order(s)	34th Divisional Artillery Operation Order No. 7 App XV	26/07/1918	26/07/1918
Miscellaneous	34th Div. Arty. No. G/643. App XVI	24/07/1918	24/07/1918
Operation(al) Order(s)	34th Divisional Artillery Operation Order No. 8 App XVII	20/07/1918	20/07/1918
Miscellaneous	Amendment No. 2 To March Table "A" & "B" (Accompanying 34th D.A. O.O. No. 9) App XVIII	22/07/1918	22/07/1918
Miscellaneous	Amendment To March Table "A" And "B" (Accompanying 34th D.A. O.O. No. 9)	22/07/1918	22/07/1918
Operation(al) Order(s)	34th Divisional Artillery Operation Order No. 9	21/07/1918	21/07/1918
Miscellaneous	March Table "A" , To Accompany 34th Divisional Artillery Operation Order No. 9		
Miscellaneous	March Table "B" To Accompany 34th D.A. O.O. No. 9		
Miscellaneous	34th Division Location Report App Xix	25/07/1918	25/07/1918
Miscellaneous	Order No. 24 App XX		
Operation(al) Order(s)	34th Divisional Artillery Warning Order No. 4 App XXI	26/07/1918	26/07/1918
Miscellaneous	34th Divisional Artillery Arrangements No. 3 App XXII	26/07/1918	26/07/1918
Operation(al) Order(s)	To Be Acknowledged By Wire 34th Division Operation Order No. 235 App XXIII	26/07/1918	26/07/1918
Miscellaneous	App XXIV		
Operation(al) Order(s)	Order Operations No. 35 App XXIV		

Miscellaneous	Note De Service App XXV		
Miscellaneous	F.C.A.D. le 27 Juillet 1918 App XXVI		
Operation(al) Order(s)	34th Divisional Artillery Operation Order No. 8. App XXVII	27/07/1918	27/07/1918
Miscellaneous	G.S. 286/50 App XXVIII	27/07/1918	27/07/1918
Miscellaneous	A Form Messages And Signals App XXIX		
Operation(al) Order(s)	To Be Acknowledged By Wire 34th Division Operation Order No. 256 App XXX	27/07/1918	27/07/1918
Miscellaneous	A Form Messages And Signals App XXXI		
Miscellaneous	Artillery Plan. App XXXII	28/07/1918	28/07/1918
Miscellaneous	To Be Acknowledged By Wire 34th Division Instructions No. 1 App XXXIII		
Miscellaneous			
Operation(al) Order(s)	To Be Acknowledged By Wire 34th Division Operation Order No. 238	28/07/1918	28/07/1918
Miscellaneous	Message By Special D.R.		
Operation(al) Order(s)	To Be Acknowledged By Wire 34th Division Order No. 237	28/07/1918	28/07/1918
Miscellaneous			
Miscellaneous	Plan d Employ App XXXIV		
Diagram etc	Calque pour la designation et le report des objectifs		
Operation(al) Order(s)	Order No. 26 App XXXV		
Miscellaneous	O.C. 152nd F.A. Bde. App XXXVI	28/07/1918	28/07/1918
Miscellaneous	O.C. 152nd F.A. Bde App XXXVII	28/07/1918	28/07/1918
Miscellaneous	Officer Commanding, 34th D.A.C. App XXXVIII	28/07/1918	28/07/1918
Miscellaneous	A Form Messages And Signals App XXXIX		
Operation(al) Order(s)	Order No. 27 App XXXX		
Diagram etc			
Operation(al) Order(s)	34th Divisional Artillery Operation Order No. 10	29/07/1918	29/07/1918
Miscellaneous	G.S. 286/70	29/07/1918	29/07/1918
Operation(al) Order(s)	To Be Acknowledged By Wire 34th Division Operation Order No. 239	29/07/1918	29/07/1918
Operation(al) Order(s)	34th Divisional Artillery Operation Order No. 5 App XXXXI	30/07/1918	30/07/1918
Diagram etc			
Miscellaneous	A Form Messages And Signals App XXXXII		
Miscellaneous	A Form Messages And Signals		
Operation(al) Order(s)	To Be Acknowledged By Wire 34th Division Operation Order No. 240	30/07/1918	30/07/1918
Diagram etc			
Operation(al) Order(s)	34th Divisional Artillery Operation Order No. 11 App XXXXIII	31/07/1918	31/07/1918
Miscellaneous	101st Infantry Brigade App XXXXIV	31/07/1918	31/07/1918
Operation(al) Order(s)	To Be Acknowledged By Wire 34th Division Operation Order No. 241	31/07/1918	31/07/1918
Miscellaneous	To Be Acknowledged By Wire 34th Division Special Instruction No.1	31/07/1918	31/07/1918
Miscellaneous	To Be Acknowledged By Wire 34th Division Special Instructions No. 2	31/07/1918	31/07/1918
Miscellaneous	To Be Acknowledged By Wire. 34th Division Special Instructions No.3	31/07/1918	31/07/1918
Miscellaneous	Reference Para. 13 Of 34th Division Operation Order No. 241 Dated 31.7.18	31/07/1918	31/07/1918
Diagram etc	Calque pour la de'signation		
Miscellaneous	Plan d' Emploi De l' Artilleries App XXXXV		

Miscellaneous	To Be Acknowledged By Wire 34th Division Special Instructions No. 2 App XXXXVI	31/07/1918	31/07/1918
Miscellaneous	34th Division Artillery Instructions App XXXXVII	31/07/1918	31/07/1918
Heading	War Diary For August 1918 Vol 32		
War Diary	Geromenil Farm (Sheet, Oulchy-Le Chateau)	01/08/1918	01/08/1918
War Diary	Geromenil Farm (Oulchy Le Chateau)	02/08/1918	02/08/1918
War Diary	Geromenil Farm (Sheet Oulchy Le Chateau)	03/08/1918	03/08/1918
War Diary	Farm D'Edrolle (Sheet, Oulchy Le Chateau)	03/08/1918	04/08/1918
War Diary	Nanteuil (Sheet, Soissons 1/80,000)	04/08/1918	05/08/1918
War Diary	Esquelbecq (Sheet, 27, 1/40,000)	07/08/1918	07/08/1918
War Diary	Couthove Chateau (27/F.21.a.)	12/08/1918	12/08/1918
War Diary	La Lovie Chateau (Sheet, 27 1/40,000)	22/08/1918	23/08/1918
War Diary	Couthove Chateau (27/F.21.a.)	29/08/1918	31/08/1918
Miscellaneous	Narrative Of 34th Divisional Artillery App I	22/07/1918	22/07/1918
Operation(al) Order(s)	34th Divisional Artillery Operation Order No. 7/2. App V	01/08/1918	01/08/1918
Operation(al) Order(s)	34th Divisional Artillery Operation Order No. 12 App IX	03/08/1918	03/08/1918
Operation(al) Order(s)	34th Divisional Artillery Operation Order No. 13 App X	03/08/1918	03/08/1918
Operation(al) Order(s)	34th Divisional Artillery Operation Order No. 14 App XI	04/08/1918	04/08/1918
Miscellaneous	Training Table		
Miscellaneous	34th Divisional Artillery Administrative Instructions Issued In Conjunction With 34th D.A. O.O No. 14 Today	04/07/1918	04/07/1918
Miscellaneous	34th Divisional Artillery Location Report App XII	07/08/1917	07/08/1917
Operation(al) Order(s)	34th Divisional Artillery Warning Order No. 6. App XIII	10/08/1918	10/08/1918
Operation(al) Order(s)	34th Divisional Artillery Warning Order No. 6 App XIV	11/08/1918	11/08/1918
Miscellaneous	Observation Foots		
Miscellaneous	34th Div. Arty. No. 1205/A	11/08/1918	11/08/1918
Miscellaneous	Reference 34th D.A. Warning Order No. 7. App XV	16/08/1918	16/08/1918
Operation(al) Order(s)	34th Divisional Artillery Warning Order No. 7	15/08/1918	15/08/1918
Miscellaneous	34th Divisional Artillery Location Statement	15/08/1918	15/08/1918
Operation(al) Order(s)	34th Divisional Artillery Operation Order No. 15	17/08/1918	17/08/1918
Miscellaneous	34th Divisional Artillery Location Statement. App XVI	23/08/1918	23/08/1918
Miscellaneous	34th Div. Arty. No. O/409. App XVIII	26/08/1918	26/08/1918
Miscellaneous	A Form Messages And Signals App XIX		
Miscellaneous	A Form Messages And Signals		
Miscellaneous	34th Divisional Artillery Location Statement No. 2. App XX	31/08/1918	31/08/1918
Operation(al) Order(s)	34th Divisional Artillery Operation Order No. 15	17/08/1918	17/08/1918
Map	Oulchy-Le-Chateau		
Map			
Heading	War Diary For September 1918 H.Q.R.A. 34th Division Vol 33		
War Diary	Couthove Chateau (27/F.21.a)	01/09/1918	02/09/1918
War Diary	Douglas Camp, (27/L.14.a.2.0)	03/09/1918	08/09/1918
War Diary	27/K.24.c.2.3	08/09/1918	10/09/1918
War Diary	27/L.36.c.5.5	16/09/1918	30/09/1918
Operation(al) Order(s)	34th Divisional Artillery Warning Order No. 8 App I	31/08/1918	31/08/1918
Operation(al) Order(s)	34th Divisional Artillery Operation Order No. 16 App II	31/08/1918	31/08/1918
Operation(al) Order(s)	34th Divisional Artillery Operation Order No. 17 App III	31/08/1918	31/08/1918

Diagram etc			
Diagram etc	Identification Trace For Use With Artillery Maps		
Operation(al) Order(s)	34th Divisional Artillery Operation Order No. 18 App IV	01/09/1918	01/09/1918
Miscellaneous	34th Divisional Artillery Location Statement No. 3 App V	03/09/1918	03/09/1918
Operation(al) Order(s)	34th Divisional Artillery Warning Order No. 9 App VI	03/09/1918	03/09/1918
Operation(al) Order(s)	34th Divisional Artillery Operation Order No. 19	03/09/1918	03/09/1918
Miscellaneous	34th Divisional Artillery Instructions No. 1	08/09/1918	08/09/1918
Operation(al) Order(s)	34th Divisional Artillery Operation Order No. 22	08/09/1918	08/09/1918
Miscellaneous	34th Div. Arty. No. 1441/A. App VII	04/09/1918	04/09/1918
Miscellaneous	34th Divisional Artillery Location Statement No. 4. App VIII	05/09/1918	05/09/1918
Map	Wytschaete		
Miscellaneous	34th Divisional Artillery Location Statement No. 5	05/09/1918	05/09/1918
Operation(al) Order(s)	34th Divisional Artillery Operation Order No. 20 App IX	05/09/1918	05/09/1918
Operation(al) Order(s)	34th Divisional Artillery Operation Order No. 21	05/09/1918	05/09/1918
Miscellaneous	34th Division Artillery Location Statement App X		
Miscellaneous	34th Division Artillery Location Statement App XI	13/09/1918	13/09/1918
Miscellaneous	34th Division Artillery Location Statement App XII	16/09/1918	16/09/1918
Miscellaneous	34th Division Artillery Location Statement App XIII	21/09/1918	21/09/1918
Miscellaneous	34th Divisional Artillery Instructions No. 1 App XIV	27/09/1918	27/09/1918
Miscellaneous	34th Divisional Artillery Instructions No. 1	27/09/1918	27/09/1918
Miscellaneous	34th Divisional Artillery Instructions No. 1	25/09/1918	25/09/1918
Miscellaneous	34th Divisional Artillery Instructions No. 2 App XV	26/09/1918	26/09/1918
Miscellaneous	34th Divisional Artillery Instructions No. 3 App XVI	26/09/1918	26/09/1918
Diagram etc	Trace For Use With Artillery Maps		
Miscellaneous	Addendum No. 1 To 34th Div. Arty. O.O. No. 22 App XVII	26/09/1918	26/09/1918
Miscellaneous	34th Divisional Arty Operation Order No. 22 Table "A"	27/09/1918	27/09/1918
Operation(al) Order(s)	34th Divisional Artillery Operation Order No. 22	26/09/1918	26/09/1918
Miscellaneous	Table "A"		
Miscellaneous	34th Divisional Artillery Operation Order No. 23. App XVIII	27/09/1918	27/09/1918
Operation(al) Order(s)	34th Divisional Artillery Operation Order No. 23.	26/09/1918	26/09/1918
Miscellaneous	101 Bde App XIX		
Miscellaneous	C Form Messages And Signals App XX		
Miscellaneous	101 Bde App XXI		
Miscellaneous	101 Bde App XXII		
Miscellaneous	101 Bde. App XXIII		
Miscellaneous	Urgent Operation Priority To X Remainder Priority App XXIV		
Miscellaneous	Priority. App XXV		
Miscellaneous	Priority App XXVI		
Miscellaneous	C Form Messages And Signals		
Miscellaneous	C R A		
Miscellaneous	A Form Messages And Signals App XXVIII		
Miscellaneous	Priority App XXIX		
Miscellaneous	101 Bde App XXX		
Miscellaneous	101 Bde App XXXI		
Heading	War Diary H.Q.R.A. 34th Division Vol 34 October 1918		
War Diary	Sheet 28 O.6.a.4.7	02/10/1918	16/10/1918
War Diary	Sheet 29 O.6.a.4.7	17/10/1918	17/10/1918
War Diary	Artoishoek 28/K.30	17/10/1918	19/10/1918

War Diary	Sheet 28. O.6.a.4.7	19/10/1918	20/10/1918
War Diary	Belleghem	23/10/1918	26/10/1918
War Diary	Lauwe	27/10/1918	27/10/1918
War Diary	Beveren	28/10/1918	28/10/1918
War Diary	Beveren Sheet 29, C.25	29/10/1918	31/10/1918
Operation(al) Order(s)	34th Divisional Artillery Operation Order No. 25 App I	01/10/1918	01/10/1918
Operation(al) Order(s)	34th Divisional Artillery Operation Order No. 24	30/09/1918	30/09/1918
Operation(al) Order(s)	Extract From 34th Division O.O. 272	01/10/1918	01/10/1918
Miscellaneous	By Special D.R.		
Miscellaneous	Location Statement App II	04/10/1918	04/10/1918
Operation(al) Order(s)	34th Divisional Artillery Order No. 1 App III	07/10/1918	07/10/1918
Miscellaneous	34th Divisional Artillery Instructions No. 1. App IV	07/10/1918	07/10/1918
Miscellaneous	34th Division "G"	05/10/1918	05/10/1918
Operation(al) Order(s)	Extract From 34th Division Operation Order No. 274	05/10/1918	05/10/1918
Operation(al) Order(s)	34th Division Artillery Operation Order No. 30	04/10/1918	04/10/1918
Miscellaneous	O.C. 2/4th Somerset L.I. (Pioneers)	15/10/1918	15/10/1918
Miscellaneous	O.C. 207th Field Co. R.E.	15/10/1918	15/10/1918
Operation(al) Order(s)	34th Division Artillery Operation Order No. 31. App V	07/10/1918	07/10/1918
Miscellaneous	34th Division Artillery Location Statement No. 1 App VI	08/10/1918	08/10/1918
Miscellaneous	34th Division Artillery Location Statement No. 2	08/10/1918	08/10/1918
Miscellaneous	34th Division Artillery Operation Instructions No. 1. App VIII	11/10/1918	11/10/1918
Operation(al) Order(s)	34th Division Artillery Operation Order No. 32 App VIII	11/10/1918	11/10/1918
Miscellaneous	34th Division Artillery Operation Order No. 32. Addendum No. 1. App IX	11/10/1918	11/10/1918
Miscellaneous	34th Divisional Artillery Operation Instructions No. 2 App X	12/10/1918	12/10/1918
Operation(al) Order(s)	34th Divisional Artillery Operation Order No. 33 App XI	12/10/1918	12/10/1918
Operation(al) Order(s)	34th Divisional Artillery Operation Order No. 34 App XII	12/10/1918	12/10/1918
Miscellaneous	Original		
Operation(al) Order(s)	34th Divisional Artillery Operation Order No. 35 App XIII	12/10/1918	12/10/1918
Miscellaneous	34th Divisional Artillery Operation Instructions No. 3 App XIV	12/10/1918	12/10/1918
Miscellaneous	101st Inf. Bde. App XV	13/10/1918	13/10/1918
Miscellaneous	34th Divisional Artillery Operation Instructions No. 1. App XVI		
Miscellaneous	34th Division		
Miscellaneous	Urgent Operation Priority App XXXII		
Miscellaneous	Urgent Operation Priority To 102 Bde App XXXIII		
Miscellaneous	C. R. A.		
Miscellaneous	U.O.P To 102nd Bde App XXXIV		
Miscellaneous	A Form Messages And Signals App XXXV		
Miscellaneous	A Form Messages And Signals App XXXVI		
Miscellaneous	Urgent Operation Priority App XXXI		
Operation(al) Order(s)	To Be Acknowledged By Wire 34th Division Operation Order No. 282 App XXX	17/10/1918	17/10/1918
Miscellaneous	Messages And Signals App XXIX		
Miscellaneous	A Form Messages And Signals		
Miscellaneous	101 Bde		
Miscellaneous	A Form Messages And Signals		
Miscellaneous			

Miscellaneous	Priority To 10 Corps		
Miscellaneous	Urgent Operation Priority To Remainder Priority	16/10/1918	16/10/1918
Miscellaneous	App XXVIII		
Operation(al) Order(s)	To Be Acknowledged By Wire 34th Division Operation Order No. 281. App XXVII	16/10/1918	16/10/1918
Miscellaneous	Urgent Operation Priority. App XXV		
Miscellaneous	App XXVI		
Operation(al) Order(s)	34th Division Operation Order No. 280. App XXIV	15/10/1918	15/10/1918
Operation(al) Order(s)	To Be Acknowledged By Wire 34th Division Operation Order No. 279. App XXIII	15/10/1918	15/10/1918
Miscellaneous	To Be Acknowledged By Wire. Addendum No. 2 To 34th Division Operation Order No. 279	15/10/1918	15/10/1918
Miscellaneous	Urgent Operation Priority	15/10/1918	15/10/1918
Operation(al) Order(s)	To Be Acknowledged By Wire. 34th Division Operation Order No. 278 App XXII	14/10/1918	14/10/1918
Miscellaneous	E. R.E. & Pioneers	10/10/1918	10/10/1918
Operation(al) Order(s)	34th Division Artillery Operation Order No. 36 App XVII	13/10/1918	13/10/1918
Miscellaneous	Urgent Operation Priority To. App XIX		
Miscellaneous	Urgent Operation Priority To. App XXX		
Miscellaneous	C. R. A.		
Operation(al) Order(s)	To Be Acknowledged By Wire. 34th Division Operation Order No. 277. App XXI	14/10/1918	14/10/1918
Operation(al) Order(s)	34th Divisional Artillery Operation Order No. 36	18/10/1918	18/10/1918
Miscellaneous	34th Division Operation Instruction No. 2 App XVII		
Map			
Diagram etc			
Miscellaneous	App XXXVII		
Operation(al) Order(s)	34th Divisional Artillery Operation Order No. 37 App XXVIII	24/10/1918	24/10/1918
Operation(al) Order(s)	34th Divisional Artillery Operation Order No. 37	24/10/1918	24/10/1918
Miscellaneous			
Miscellaneous	34th Divisional Artillery Operation Order No. 37. Addendum No. 2	24/10/1918	24/10/1918
Miscellaneous	34th Divisional Artillery Operation Order No. 37. Addendum No. 3	24/10/1918	24/10/1918
Miscellaneous	Amendment No. 2 To 34th Divisional Artillery Operation Order No. 37	24/10/1918	24/10/1918
Miscellaneous	34th Divisional Artillery Operation Order No. 37 Amendment No. 1	24/10/1918	24/10/1918
Map	Belgium And Part Of France		
Miscellaneous	34th Division Operation Instructions No. 1. App XXXIX	24/10/1918	24/10/1918
Operation(al) Order(s)	To Be Acknowledged By Wire 34th Division Operation Order No. 269 App XXXX	24/10/1918	24/10/1918
Diagram etc			
Miscellaneous	App XXXXI		
Miscellaneous	C R A		
Miscellaneous	To Be Acknowledged By Wire. Addendum No. 1 To 34th Division Operation Order No. 290. App XXXII	26/10/1918	26/10/1918
Operation(al) Order(s)	34th Divisional Artillery Operation Order No. 38. Appendix XXXXIII	26/10/1918	26/10/1918
Miscellaneous	To Be Acknowledged By Wire. Addendum No. 2 To 34th Division Operation Order No. 290. App XXXXIV	27/10/1918	27/10/1918
Miscellaneous	Table "A"		

Miscellaneous	34th Divisional Artillery Location Statement No. 5 App XXXV	26/10/1918	26/10/1918
Miscellaneous	General Staff 34th Division		
Operation(al) Order(s)	34th Divisional Artillery Operation Order No. 39. App XXXXVI	26/10/1918	26/10/1918
Operation(al) Order(s)	34th Divisional Artillery Operation Order No. 81 App XXXXVII	29/10/1918	29/10/1918
Miscellaneous	34th Divisional Artillery Instruction No. 1. App XXXXVIII	29/10/1918	29/10/1918
Miscellaneous	34th Divisional Artillery Location Statement No. 3. App XXXXIX	29/10/1918	29/10/1918
Operation(al) Order(s)	34th Divisional Artillery Operation Order No. 40	27/10/1918	27/10/1918
Operation(al) Order(s)	34th Divisional Artillery Operation Order No. 42	30/10/1918	30/10/1918
Diagram etc	34th Divnl Artillery Barrage Map		
Diagram etc	34th Divnl. Artillery H.A. Tasks		
Diagram etc	34th Divnl. Artillery 4.5 How Targets		
War Diary	Beveren Sheet 29, C. 25. Cent	01/11/1918	02/11/1918
War Diary	Moorseele, Sheet 28	03/11/1918	12/11/1918
War Diary	Moorseele	12/11/1918	15/11/1918
War Diary	Wattripont Sheet 29, W. 29.c.4.9	16/11/1918	16/11/1918
War Diary	Lessines	16/11/1918	17/11/1918
Miscellaneous	App I		
Operation(al) Order(s)	To Be Acknowledged By Wire 34th Division Operation Order No. 298	02/11/1918	02/11/1918
Miscellaneous	Appendix "I" To Accompany 34th Division Operation Order No. 298		
Miscellaneous	Table "A"		
Miscellaneous	34th Divisional Artillery Location Statement. App II	05/11/1918	05/11/1918
Miscellaneous	Headquarters, 103rd Infantry Brigade App III		
Miscellaneous	34th Divisional Artillery Narrative Of Operations Since 26th October, 1918 App IV	05/11/1918	05/11/1918
Operation(al) Order(s)	34th Divisional Artillery Order No. 1 App V	06/11/1918	06/11/1918
Miscellaneous	34th D.A.C.	06/11/1918	06/11/1918
Miscellaneous	34th Divisional Artillery Location Statement	09/11/1918	09/11/1918
Operation(al) Order(s)	34th Divisional Artillery Operation Order No. 44 App VI	11/11/1918	11/11/1918
Miscellaneous	34th Division Location Report No. 26	09/11/1918	09/11/1918
Operation(al) Order(s)	34th Divisional Artillery Operation Order No. 45 App VII	13/11/1918	13/11/1918
Miscellaneous	34 D.A., OO/45a.	14/11/1918	14/11/1918
Map	Minutes Of Second Corps Conference, Held 10 am., 13th November 1918.	13/11/1918	13/11/1918
Miscellaneous	Minutes Of Second Corps Conference, Held 10 am., 13th November, 1918	13/11/1918	13/11/1918
Miscellaneous			
Operation(al) Order(s)	34th Division Operation Order No. 303	14/11/1918	14/11/1918
Operation(al) Order(s)	34th Divisional Artillery Operation Order No. 46. App VIII	14/11/1918	14/11/1918
Miscellaneous	March Table To Accompany 34th Divisional Operation Order No. 304		
Operation(al) Order(s)	34th Division Operation Order No. 304	15/11/1918	15/11/1918
Miscellaneous	34th Division Amendment No. 1 To Operation Order No. 305	17/11/1918	17/11/1918
Miscellaneous	Reduction Of Batteries To Four Guns. App VIII	15/11/1918	15/11/1918
Miscellaneous	34th Division App IX		
Miscellaneous	Addendum No. 1	17/11/1918	17/11/1918

Operation(al) Order(s)	34th Divisional Artillery Operation Order No. 47. App X	17/11/1918	17/11/1918
Miscellaneous	March Table "A" To Accompany 34th Division Operation Order No. 305		
Operation(al) Order(s)	34th Divisional Artillery Operation Order No. 48. App XI	17/11/1918	17/11/1918
Miscellaneous	34th Div. Arty. No. G. 784. App XIII	19/11/1918	19/11/1918
Miscellaneous	34th Divisional Artillery Location Statement. App XII	19/11/1918	19/11/1918
War Diary	Lessines	01/12/1918	01/12/1918
War Diary	Soignies	12/12/1918	14/12/1918
War Diary	Courcelles	16/12/1918	17/12/1918
War Diary	Chatelet	18/12/1918	18/12/1918
War Diary	Profondeville	19/12/1918	31/12/1918
Operation(al) Order(s)	34th Divisional Artillery Operation Order No. 48 App I	08/12/1918	08/12/1918
Miscellaneous			
Operation(al) Order(s)	34th Divisional Artillery Operation Order No. 49. App II	11/12/1918	11/12/1918
Miscellaneous			
Operation(al) Order(s)	34th Divisional Artillery Operation Order No.51 App III	15/12/1918	15/12/1918
Miscellaneous	March Table Attached To 34th D.A. O.O. 51 D/15-12-18	15/12/1918	15/12/1918
Operation(al) Order(s)	34th Divisional Artillery Operation Order No. 52 App IV	16/12/1918	16/12/1918
Miscellaneous	March Table "G" Attached To 34th D.A. O.O. No. 52		
Operation(al) Order(s)	34th Divisional Artillery Operation Order No. 53. App V	16/12/1918	16/12/1918
Miscellaneous	March Table "H" To 34th D.A. O.O. No. 52		
Operation(al) Order(s)	34th Divisional Artillery Operation Order No. 54 App VI	17/12/1918	17/12/1918
Miscellaneous	March Table "I" Attached To 34th D.A. O.O. No. 54 D/17-12-18		
War Diary	Profondeville	01/01/1919	25/01/1919
War Diary	Siegburg	27/01/1919	04/02/1919
War Diary	Siegburg Germany	00/03/1919	03/05/1919
War Diary	Siegburg	04/05/1919	30/05/1919
War Diary	Siegburg Germany	18/06/1919	30/06/1919
War Diary	Siegburg	02/07/1919	18/07/1919

34TH DIVISION

C. R. A.

~~JAN 0 6 1918~~

1918 JAN — 1919 JLY

Vol 25

WAR DIARY

HQRA 34 DIVISION

~~152~~ BDE RFA

~~160~~ BDE RFA

~~34~~ D.A.C.

~~34~~ DTMO.

JANUARY 1918

This file is only issued as a cover to
Army Form C 2118 (War Diary).

Army Form C. 2118.

Instructions regarding War Diaries and Intelligence Summaries are contained in F. S. Regs., Part II. and the Staff Manual respectively. Title pages will be prepared in manuscript.

WAR DIARY
or
INTELLIGENCE SUMMARY.

Month of January 1918 (Erase heading not required.) H.Q.R.A. 34th Division Page 1

Place	Date	Hour	Summary of Events and Information	Remarks and references to Appendices
BOILEUX AU MONT	Jany 6		A/14. Battery R.F.A. withdrew to its Wagon lines	App I
"	7		68th Battery R.F.A. withdrew to its Wagon lines	App I
"	9		The 14th Army Brigade R.F.A. marched to BAPAUME under orders of the 4th Corps.	App I
"	16		Batteries of the 26th Army Brigade R.F.A. withdrew to their Wagons lines and ceased to be under orders of C.R.A. 34 Division	App II
"	29	10am	H.Q.R.A. 3rd Division relieved HQRA. 34th Division in the line. H.Q.R.A. 34 Division moved to GOMIECOURT. 57C N.W. 1/20000.	

A5834 Wt. W4973/M687 750,000 8/16 D. D. & L. Ltd. Forms/C.2118/13.

App I

SECRET. Copy No. 9....

34th. DIVISIONAL ARTILLERY OPERATION ORDER No. 125.

Ref. Sheet 51B S.W. 1/20,000. 6th. January, 1918.

1. The 14th. Army Brigade RFA will be withdrawn to its Wagon Lines, (BOISLEUX ST. MARC) by the night of 7/8th. January 1918 and will march to BAPAUME on the 9th. January under orders of IVth. Corps.

2. A/14 Battery RFA will withdraw to its Wagon Lines tonight (6/7th. January).

A/178 Battery RFA will move into the positions vacated by A/14 Battery RFA tonight, night (6/7th. January).

68th. Battery RFA will withdraw to its Wagon Lines night 7/8th. January.

Positions thus vacated become re-inforcing positions Right Group. Telephone lines belonging to these positions will be left down and ammunition up to 200 Rounds per gun will be left under weather proof cover in these positions. Surplus ammunition will be gradually transferred as required by O.C. Right Group.

O.C. Right Group will arrange for a warden for each of these positions.

Map-Boards, maps, aeroplane photographs, etc. of outgoing Batteries will be collected by O.C. Right Group.

3. O.C. Right Group will arrange all details of relief between A/14 and A/178 Batteries RFA.

4. For the night 6/7th. January the front of the Right Group will be covered by 68th. Battery, B/178, C/178 and D/178 Batteries. From night 7/8th. January onwards by 178th. Brigade RFA (A, B, C and D Batteries).

O.C. Right Group will arrange his Normal S.O.S. Lines from night 6/7th. January onwards as follows:-

6-18-pr Guns - U.1.c.92.64 to U.1.d.28.30.
12 " " - U.7.b.98.28 to U.1.d.40.05.

These co-ordinates are approximate - Barrages will be placed as near our front line as safety permits.

4.5" Howitzers - U.1.d.72.95.
U.1.d.98.60.
U.2.c.18.14.
U.8.a.50.55.
U.8.c.98.95.) On return of
U.14.b.5.5.) detached Section.

Special Concentrations for local attacks will be:-

S.O.S. RIGHT. 3-18-pr Batteries. U.14.b.15.25/ - U.8.c.80.15- - U.8.c.50.30 - U.8.c.2.9 - U.8.a.23.15 - U.7.b.75.40.

1-4.5 How. Bty. U.9.c.15.20 , U.8.c.98.95, U.8.d.20.00, U.8.a.05.55, U.2.c.18.14, U.1.b.80.32.

S.O.S. LEFT. 3-18-pr Batteries. U.8.a.23.15 - U.7.b.75.40 - U.1.d.2.4 - U.1.b.55.65.

1-4.5 How, Bty. U.9.c.15.20, U.8.c.98.95, U.8.a.28.68, U.2.c.18.14, U.1.d.98.60, U.1.b.80.32.

Mutual..........

Mutual Support given by O.C. Right Group will be:-

To Left Group 40th. D.A.
4 guns Barrage U.14.b.5.4 - U.14.b.7.0.
2 Hows Points U.14.b.5.5, U.14.b.6.2.

To Centre Group 34th. D.A.
4 guns Barrage U.1.b.62.18 - 38.62.
2 Hows.Points U.1.b.62.18, U.1.d.78.90.

5. Batteries of 14th. Brigade RFA will withdraw with echelons full.

6. Completion of relief tonight will be reported by telephone to H.Q.R.A. by code word "DONE".

7. O.C. Right Group will acknowledge.

Major,
Brigade Major.R.A.
34th. Divisional Artillery.

Issued at 12 noon.

Copies to: 1-3. Right Group.
4. Centre Group.
5. S.C.R.A. 34th. Div.
6. 34th. Div. "G".
7. H.Q.R.A. VIth. Corps.
8. H.Q.R.A. 40th. Div.
9-10. War Diary.
11. File.

App II

S E C R E T.

Copy No. 18....

34th. DIVISIONAL ARTILLERY OPERATION ORDER No. 126.

15th. January 1918.

1. In accordance with VIth. Corps Order No. 265. The Batteries of the 26th. Army Brigade RFA at present in action on 34th. Division front will withdraw to their Wagon Lines on evening of 16th. instant.

2. On withdrawing from positions the above Batteries will cease to be under orders of C.R.A. 34th. Division.

3. All map boards, aeroplane photographs, log-books and documents relating to Defence of 34th. Division Front will be handed over to Os.C. Centre and Left Groups who will return the map boards to D.A.H.Q..

4. Camouflage and telephone lines and Trench Stores will be left in situ. Ammunition will be handed over to Os.C. Centre and Left Groups. Further instructions re disposal of this ammunition will be issued later.

5. Particular care will be taken that positions vacated are left clean and all empties, tins, etc. removed. Os.C. Groups will satisfy themselves that these points have been complied with.

6. Os.C. Groups will make the necessary arrangements for the care of the positions vacated.

7. O.C. Centre Group will make the necessary adjustment of S.O.S. and Counter-Preparation Barrages and report changes to this Office.

8. ACKNOWLEDGE.

Percy Knolson [signature]
Major,
A/Brigade Major.R.A.
34th. Divisional Artillery.

Issued at 6 p.m.

Copy: 1-3. Centre Group.
4-5. Left "
6. 26th. A. Bde.RFA.
7. D.T.M.O.
8. 34th. D.A.C.
9. 34th. Div. "G".)
10. RA. VIth. Corps.)
11. HA. " ")
12. 101st. Infy. Bde.) For information.
13. 102nd. " ")
14. 103rd. " ")
15. RA. 4th. Div.)
16. RA. 40th. ")
17. 39th. H.A.G.)
18-19. War Diary.
20. File.

Vol 26

WAR DIARY

HQ R.A 34th DIVISION

~~152 BRIGADE~~ RFA

~~160 BRIGADE~~ RFA

~~34th D.A.C.~~

~~34th D.T.M.O.~~

FEBRUARY. 1918.

Instructions regarding War Diaries and Intelligence Summaries are contained in F. S. Regs., Part II. and the Staff Manual respectively. Title pages will be prepared in manuscript.

Army Form C. 2118.

WAR DIARY

~~or~~

~~INTELLIGENCE SUMMARY.~~ H.Q.R.A.

34 Division

Month of February 1918 (Erase heading not required.)

Place	Date	Hour	Summary of Events and Information	Remarks and references to Appendices
	Feb.			
COMIECOURT 57 C N W	10		H.Q.R.A. moved to REBREUVIETTE ————	App I
REBREUVIETTE (LENS 1/100000)	11		H.Q.R.A. moved to REBREUVE CHATEAU.	
REBREUVE (LENS)	16		Provisional March and Entraining Orders issued ————	App II

A5834 Wt. W4973/M687 750,000 8/16 D. D. & L. Ltd. Forms/C.2118/13.

App I

SECRET. 34th.Div.Arty.No. O/345. Copy No. 23

34th. DIVISIONAL ARTILLERY MARCH ORDERS.

1. Brigades of 34th. Divisional Artillery will come under the orders of C.R.A. 34th. Division on completion of relief on night 8/9th. inst.

2. The 34th. Divisional Artillery will march to WAMIN Area as shown on attached Table "A". The route from Wagon Lines to ADINFER will be direct via HENDECOURT and not via AYETTE as previously ordered.

3. The 34th. Divisional Artillery will be in G.H.Q. Reserve from 12 noon on 9th. February.

4. All Units will march with full echelons with following exceptions:-
D.A.C. will dump 756 rounds 18-pdr. 50% A.X.
" " " 792 " 4.5 How. B.X.
" " "984000 " S.A.A.
(All above from G.S. wagons) and will leave a Guard under an N.C.O. until this ammunition is taken over by 59th. D.A.C. on 12th. inst. This party will be rationed for consumption on 13th. inst. 34th. D.A.C. will take over similar amounts from Guard of 59th. D.A.C. at GROUCHES on 12th. inst.

5. Trench Mortar personnel will move by Lorry on 9th. and 10th. inst. to CANETTEMONT. T.M. Lorries will enter CANETTEMONT via REBRUEVE and HONVAL. 2" Mortars and Stores will be handed over to 59th. Division at MORY on the 8th. inst. D.T.M.O. 34th. Division will take over corresponding stores from 59th. Division at IVERGNY on 10th. inst. (Receipts to be obtained and given. D.A.C. will provide 3 G.S. Wagons and teams for transport of these stores from IVERGNY to CANETTEMONT.

6. Transport. 34th. D.A.C. will provide, as complete turnouts, 3 G.S. Wagons per battery and 2 G.S. Wagons per Brigade Headquarters. These will be attached to batteries on the 7th. inst and will remain with them until 10 a.m. 12th. inst. They will be rationed by batteries for consumption on the 9th. and will join with rations and forage for the 7th. and 8th.
Arrangements are being made for the transport of heavy baggage. Os.C. Brigades will be notified later as to arrangements made.

7. H.Q. Coy. Train will march under their own arrangements and will be billetted as shown on attached Billetting Table "B". Supply Wagons will join D.A.C. by 8 a.m. on 7th. inst. Baggage Wagon Horses and Drivers will join D.A.C. by 8 a.m. on 7th. and batteries by 6 p.m. 9th. and will remain with Batteries until completion of march.

8. Refilling will be as shown on attached Table "C".

9. R.A. Headquarters will close at GOMIECOURT at 10 a.m. on the 10th. and will open at REBREUVE or REBREUVIETTE(exact place will be notified later) at 2 p.m. on the 10th. inst.

10. Brigades, D.A.C., D.T.M.O. and H.Q.Coy. Train ACKNOWLEDGE.

[signature]
Captain,
Brigade Major.R.A.
34th. Divisional Artillery.

5th. February 1918.

P.T.O.

DISTRIBUTION:- 1-5. 152nd. Bde. RFA.

6-10. 160th. " "

11-14. 34th. D.A.C.

15. D.T.M.O.

16. H.Q.Coy.Train.

17. 34th. Div. "G".

18. " " "Q".

19. VIth. Corps R.A.

20. 3rd. Div. Arty.

21. 59th. " "

22. S.C.R.A.

23-24. War Diary.

25. File.

26-27. Spare.

MARCH TABLE. (TABLE "A")

Serial No.	Date Feby.	Unit.	From.	To.	Route.	Remarks.
1.	7th.	34th. D.A.C.	Wagon Lines.	SOUASTRE.	HENDECOURT-ADINFER-MONCHY au BOIS-BIENVILLERS.	To march under orders of O.C., D.A.C. Not to enter BIENVILLERS before 11 a.m.
2.	8th.	34th. D.A.C.	SOUASTRE	ETREE-WAMIN.	COUTURELLE - SUS ST. LEGER - BEAUDRICOURT.	Times of march to be arranged by O.C. D.A.C.
3.	10th.	160th. Bde. RFA.	Wagon Lines	BERLES & POMMIER	HENDECOURT-ADINFER - MONCHY au BOIS.	To be clear of Wagon Lines by 9-30 a.m.
4.	10th.	152nd. Bde. RFA.	Wagon Lines.	BIENVILLERS	- ditto -	To be clear of Wagon Lines by 10-30 a.m.
5.	11th.	160th. Bde. RFA.	BERLES & POMMIER.	REBREUVIETTE.	SAULTY-GRAND BULLECOURT-LIENCOURT-FREVENT Road.	To be clear of POMMIER by 8-15 a.m.
6.	11th.	152nd. Bde. RFA.	BIENVILLERS.	WAMIN.	- ditto -	To march at 8-30 a.m. & be clear of BIENVILLERS at 9 a.m.

BILLETTING TABLE. (TABLE "B")

Unit.	Date.	From whom obtained.	Billetting parties report at.	Area.
34th.D.A.C.	7th.	Area Commandant SOUASTRE.	Area Commandant's Office 10 am.	SOUASTRE.
34th.D.A.C.	8th.	Billet Warden REBREUVIETTE.		ETREE WAMIN.
34th. T.Ms.	9th & 10th.	- ditto -		CANETTEMONT.
160th.Bde.RFA. 152nd.Bde.RFA.	10th. 10th.	Area Commandant BERLES - ditto -	Area Commandant's Office 9-30 am. - ditto -	BERLES & POMMIER. BIENVILLERS.
160th.Bde.RFA. 152nd.Bde.RFA.	11th. 11th.	Billet Warden REBREUVIETTE. - ditto -	Billet Warden's Office 10 am. - ditto -	REBREUVIETTE. WAMIN, BROUILLY ROZIERE.
H.Q. Coy. Train.	10th. 11th.	Area Commandant BERLES Billet Warden REBREUVIETTE.	Billet Warden's Office 10 a.m.	POMMIER. REBREUVIETTE.

TABLE "C".

Supply Arrangements shewing refilling points from which supplies will be drawn on dates stated for consumption following day.

Unit	6th.	7th.	8th.	9th.	10th.	11th.
34th. D.A.C.	H.Q.Coy.Train Camp BOISLEUX au MONT.	Train Camp.	WAMIN (dumped by lorry).	WAMIN (drawn under ASC arrangements from FREVENT)	WAMIN.	WAMIN.
34th. T.M.Bs.	Train Camp.	Train Camp.	Train Camp.	Train Camp.	WAMIN.	WAMIN.
152nd. Bde. RFA.	Train Camp.	Train Camp.	Train Camp.	Train Camp.	Train Camp.	WAMIN.
160th. Bde. RFA.	As for 152nd. Brigade RFA.					
R.A.H.Q.	ERVILLERS.	ERVILLERS.	ERVILLERS.	ERVILLERS.	WAMIN.	WAMIN.

NOTES:-

1. From 11th. inclusive refilling point for all Units will be WAMIN.
2. Times for refilling will be notified direct to Units by Supply Officer.
3. Supply railhead in new area will be FREVENT.

SECRET. 34th.Div.Arty.No. 0/345/1.

AMENDMENT NO. 1. to

34th. DIVISIONAL ARTILLERY MARCH ORDERS.

Reference para. 9. - R.A.H.Q. 34th. Division will open at REBREUVIETTE at 2 p.m. 10th. inst.

Close at REBREUVIETTE 10 a.m. 11th. inst.

Re-open at REBREUVE CHATEAU 12 noon 11th. inst.

Captain,
Brigade Major.R.A.
34th. Divisional Artillery.

7th. Feby. 1918.
Copy to all recipients of 0/345.

War Diary

App II

S E C R E T.   Copy No. 23.

34th. DIVISIONAL ARTILLERY OPERATION ORDER NO. 127.

Ref: Sheet LENS 1/100,000.   16th. February 1918.

1. During the time the Division is in G.H.Q. Reserve, it must be prepared to move at short notice.

2. The Division will move by rail, either in Strategical or Tactical Trains. In the former case the Divisional Artillery will be conveyed by Rail, in the latter case proceed by March Route.

3. Entrainment for a move by Strategical Train will be carried out by Groups, under the orders of Group Commanders.
   R.A. Group.
   R.A. Units and No. 1 Coy. Train under C.R.A.

4. The arrangements for move by Strategical Trains are given in 34th. Divisional Artillery Administrative Instructions No. 1 issued simultaneously with this Order.
   In the event of a move by Tactical Trains being ordered the Divisional Artillery will move as may be directed.

5. The Routes to the Entraining Stations will be as follows:-

152nd. Brigade RFA and D.A.C.	to FREVENT via REBREUVIETTE & GRAND BOURET to PETIT HOUVIN & ST. POL via HOUVIN-HOUVIGNEUL & BUNEVILLE.
160th. Brigade RFA.	to all Stations via GRAND BOURET.
T.M. Batteries	with No. 3 Section D.A.C.
No. 1 Coy. Train	via GRAND BOURET & FREVENT.

6. All Units will at once prepare provisional Movement Orders.

7. ACKNOWLEDGE.

[signature]

Captain,
Brigade Major.R.A.
34th. Divisional Artillery.

Issued at 4.30 pm.

Copies: 1-5. 152nd. Bde. RFA.
6-10. 160th. " "
11-15. D.T.M.O.
16-19. 34th. D.A.C.
20. No. 1 Coy. Train.
21. 34th. Div. "G".
22. VIth. Corps RA.
23-24. War Diary.
25. File.
26-28. Spare.

SECRET.

34th, DIVISIONAL ADMINISTRATIVE INSTRUCTIONS NO. 1.

16th. February 1918.

Reference 34th. Divisional Artillery Operation Order No. 127.

1. The following instructions will be followed in the event of the move being by Strategical Train.

2. The entrainment will be carried out in the order given in Table "A". The entrainment must be completed half-an-hour before the Scheduled hour of departure of the train. The hour of departure of the first train will be notified to all concerned by telegram. Trains will follow each other at an interval of about 4 hours.

3. On receipt of this telegram each Unit will send an Officer to reconnoitre the Route as laid down in para. 5 of above quoted order and also to reconnoitre the Entraining Station and ascertain the arrangements as regards forming up places, Watering Places, etc.,

4. Officers as detailed below will go to each Entraining Station to be there half-an-hour before the first R.A.Unit arrives, as representatives of R.A.H.Q. These Officers will take with them a statement, which will be issued from this office, showing the order of entrainment of the Group and composition of each train.

FREVENT.	An Officer detailed by 160th, F.A.Bde.
PETIT HOUVIN.	" " " " D.T.M.O.
ST POL.	" " " " D.A.C.

5. The above Officers will report by wire at noon each day of their entrainment, to Staff Officer, 34th. Division, C/o. R.T.O. FREVENT, the progress of entrainment of their Group, showing by Units the departures between noon and noon, A final report being forwarded when the last train is ready to start.

6. Each Unit will furnish the R.T.O. at its Entraining Station with an accurate state giving the number of Officers, O.R., animals and Vehicles to proceed in each Train (Detached Companies, vide Table "A" will be required to send on a similar state). This state must reach the R.T.O. quarter of an hour before any portion of the Unit reaches the Station.

7. No Troops or Transport will enter the Station Yard until permission of the R.T.O. is received.

8. Units must be at their entraining Stations 3 hours before the time of departure of their Train.

9. LOADING AND UNLOADING PARTIES. O's. C. Trains will tell off the necessary parties before arrival at the Entraining Station. These parties will work under the instructions of the R.T.O.

Continued.

10. **SUPPLIES.** Supply Wagons will travel loaded and will accompany Units on the Train. Unless otherwise ordered Supply Wagons will proceed to Group Refilling Points and pick up one day's rations, join their Units, and move with them to the Entraining Station.

11. **BAGGAGE.** On receipt of orders to entrain the Officer Commanding Divisional Train will arrange to despatch Baggage Wagons to Units.

If time allows, Lorries for the conveyance of blankets and extra stores to the entraining Station, will be arranged for by D.H.Q. If time does not allow, blankets and stores which cannot be carried on War establishment Transport, are to be stacked in present Billeting area and left under a guard, Guards to be provided with 7 days' rations. Arrangements for picking up of these blankets and stores will be made by D.H.Q. as soon as circumstances permit.

12. **ADVANCE PARTIES** for taking over Billets or Camps will travel in the first train of each Unit, i.e.

152nd. F.A.Bde.	Train No.	22.
160th. " "	" "	27.
D.A.C., D.T.M.O. and No. 1. Coy. Divl. Train	" "	20.

13 **VACATING OF BILLETS.** Units will make every endeavour to leave their Billets in a clean and Sanitary condition.

14. **AREA STORES** should be handed over to the Billet Warden or left with the extra baggage.

15. **CLAIMS.** O's. C. Units must endeavour to obtain from Maires of Villages, before leaving, a statement of claims for damage. Such claims as are admitted should be countersigned and returned to the Maire.

Captain.
A/Staff Captain.
34th. Divisional Artillery.

R.A. Entrainment Statement showing composition of each Train.

FREVENT.

Serial Number.	Composition.	Offrs.	O.R.	L.D.	H.D.	AXLES.
22	A/152. Bty.	5	191	164		38
	Divl. Train.		5	1	4	4
	D.A.C. No. 1.	1.	23	32		10.
		6	219	197	4	52
25	D/152. Bty.	5	191	164		38
	Divl. Train.		5	1	4	4
	D.A.C. No. 1.	1.	23	32		10.
		6	219	197	4	52.
28	B/160. Bty.	5	191	164		38
	Divl. Train.		5	1	4	4
	D.A.C. No. 2.	1	23	32		10.
		6	219	197	4	52
31	D/160. Bty.	5	191	164		38
	Divl. Train.		5	1	4	4
	D.A.C. No.2.	1	23	32		10.
		6	219	197	4	52.

PETIT HOUVIN.

Serial Number.	Composition.	Offrs.	O.R.	L.D.	H.D.	AXLES.
20	H.Q.D.A.C.	3	39	32		12
	H.Q. Divl. Train.	8	103	24	76	83
		11	142	56	76	95.
23	B/152. Bty.	5	191	164		38
	Divl. Train.		5	1	4	4
	D.A.C. No. 1.	1	23	32		10
		6	219	197	4	52
26	D/152. Bty.	5	191	164		38
	Divl. Train.		5	1	4	4
	D.A.C. No. 1.	1	23	32		10
		6	219	197	4	52.

(Continued)

PETIT HOUVIN (Continued).

Serial No.	Composition.	Offrs.	O.R.	L.D.	H.D.	AXLES.
29	160. Bde. H.Q.	5	27	17		2
	No. 2 Sec. D/A.C. less 4 G.S. wagons & 16 L.G.S. & teams.		122	145		30
	Divl. Train.		13	1	12	12
		5	162	163	12	44
32	½ No. 3. Sec. D.A.C.	2	81	98		40
	Y & Z T.M.Btys.	4	46			
	Divl. Train.		5	1	4	4
		6	132	99	4	44

ST POL.

Serial No.	Composition.	Offrs.	O.R.	L.D.	H.D.	AXLES.
24	152. Bde. H.Q.	5	27	17		2
	No. 1 Sec. D.A.C. less 4 G.S.Wagons & 16 L.G.S.& teams.		122	145		30
	Divl. Train.		13	1	12	12
		5	162	163	12	44
27	A/160. Bde.	5	191	164		38
	Divl. Train.		5	1	4	4
	D.A.C. No.2.	1	23	32		10
		6	219	197	4	52
30.	C/160. Bty.	5	191	164		38
	Divl. Train.		5	1	4	4
	D.A.C. No.2.	1	23	32		10
		6	219	197	4	52
33	½ No.3.Sec.D.A.C.	2	81	98		40
	X & V T.M.Btys.	5	89			
		7	170	98		40

WAR DIARY

C. R. A.

34th DIVISION.

MARCH 1 9 1 8

Attached :- Operation Orders
Narrative of Operations 21st-23rd

Part of APPENDIX 'C'

GENERAL STAFF

34th DIVISION

W A R   D I A R Y

MARCH, 1918

Copies of messages and orders received and issued during Operations, March, 1918.

Instructions regarding War Diaries and Intelligence Summaries are contained in F. S. Regs., Part II. and the Staff Manual respectively. Title pages will be prepared in manuscript.

Army Form C. 2118.

WAR DIARY
or
INTELLIGENCE SUMMARY.
(Erase heading not required.)

MARCH 1918.

H.Q.R.A. 34th. Division.
Page 1.

Vol 27

Place	Date	Hour	Summary of Events and Information	Remarks and references to Appendices
	March.			
REBREUVE CHATEAU. 51c. 1/40,000.	1.		H.Q.R.A. moved to GOMIECOURT. 51B. 1/40,000. --	APP. 1.
GOMIECOURT. 51B. 1/40,000	3.		March 2nd. and 3rd. Divisional Artillery marched from the WAMIN AREA to the 40th. Divisional Artillery Wagon Lines, Vide, March Table. ------------------	APP.11.
	3.	10 a.m.	Command of Centre Sector, VIth. Corps passed to 34th. Division,	APP.1.
	4.		On nights March 3rd./4th. and 4th./5th. 34th. Divisional Artillery batteries relieved 40th. Divisional Artillery in the line.	APP.1.

Army Form C. 2118.

WAR DIARY
or
INTELLIGENCE SUMMARY.
(Erase heading not required.)

Instructions regarding War Diaries and Intelligence Summaries are contained in F. S. Regs., Part II. and the Staff Manual respectively. Title pages will be prepared in manuscript.

MARCH 1918.

H.Q.R.A. 34th. Division.

Place	Date	Hour	Summary of Events and Information	Remarks and references to Appendices
	March.			
GOMIECOURT 51B. 1/40,000.	21.	5 a.m.	Hostile bombardment commenced. Vide, "Narrative of Operations".	APP.111.
AYETTE. 57D. 1/40,000.	23.	2 p.m.	Command of Centre Divisional Artillery VIth. Corps passed to C.R.A. 31st. Division. H.Q.R.A. 34th. Division moved to ADINFER in the evening keeping in close touch with C.R.A. 31st. Division.	
ADINFER. 51c. 1/40,000.	25.		H.Q.R.A., less Staff Captain R.A., moved to LE CAUROY. 51^{c} 1/40,000. Staff Captain R.A., established headquarters with 34th. D.A.C.	

A5834 Wt. W4973/M687 750,000 8/16 D. D. & L. Ltd. Forms/C.2118/13.

Army Form C. 2118.

Instructions regarding War Diaries and Intelligence Summaries are contained in F. S. Regs., Part II. and the Staff Manual respectively. Title pages will be prepared in manuscript.

WAR DIARY
or
INTELLIGENCE SUMMARY.
(Erase heading not required.)

MARCH 1918.

H.Q.R.A. 34th. Division.

Page 3.

Place	Date	Hour	Summary of Events and Information	Remarks and references to Appendices
	March.			
LE CAUROY. 51^c 1/40,000.	26.		H.Q.R.A. moved to AUXI -LE - CHATEAU (LENS sheet).	
AUXI - LE - CHATEAU.	27.		H.Q.R.A. moved to MERVILLE 36^a 1/40,000 XVth. Corps. Reserve Area. First Army. C.R.A. and Brigade Major by car. Transport by road. Remainder of personnel by rail. Entraining Station FREVENT, 51^c 1/40,000.	
MERVILLE. 36A. 1/40,000	31.		C.R.A. joined the Divisional Artillery in the VIth. Corps Third Army. [signature] Lieut. R.A. for C.R.A. 34th. Division.	

A5834 Wt W4973/M687 750,000 8/16 D. D. & L. Ltd. Forms/C.2118/13.

War Diary APP I

SECRET. Copy No. 17.

34th. DIVISIONAL ARTILLERY OPERATION ORDER No. 128.

28th. February 1918.

1. The 34th. Divisional Artillery will relieve the 40th. Divnl. Artillery in the line in the Centre Sector of the VIth. Corps Front.
2 Sections per Battery on night 3/4th. March.
1 Section " " " " 4/5th.
The 152nd. Brigade RFA will relieve the 178th. Brigade RFA, Lt. Col. W.F.PARSONS. D.S.O. (Left Group). Headquarters St. LEGER MILL, T.28.a.1.9.
The 160th. Brigade RFA will relieve the 181st. Brigade RFA, Lt.Col. The Hon. H.R.SCARLETT, D.S.O. (Right Group). Headquarters B.4.d.4.9. (South edge of St. LEGER.).
The 34th. Division Trench Mortars will relieve the 40th. Divn. Trench Mortars in the line during the 3rd. and 4th. March. Headquarters D.T.M.O. in ST. LEGER.
34th. D.A.C. will relieve 40th. D.A.C. Detailed orders for D.A.C. will be issued later.

2. All reliefs to be completed by 8 p.m. 4th. March and reported to this Office by telephone, by Code word "PIP PIP". Command of Groups will pass at this hour.

3. Ammunition, Map Boards, Photographs, Log Books and telephone lines will be taken over "in situ" and copies of receipts forwarded to this Office.
Trench Mortars of 40th. Division will be taken over "in situ" and the 8 Mortars now in possession of 34th. Division will be handed over to 40th. Division.

4. One Officer and a proportion of Signallers per Brigade H.Qrs. and Battery will proceed direct to 40th. Division Wagon Lines on 2nd. March and will proceed to gun positions on morning of 3rd. March.

5. O.C. 152nd. Brigade RFA will arrange to collect the three guns under overhaul from I.O.M. on afternoon of 3rd. March.

6. Headquarters R.A. will close at REBREUVE Chateau at 10 a.m. on March 1st. and will re-open at COMMIECOURT at 6 p.m. same date.

7. Command of Sector will pass to 34th. Division at 9 a.m. on March 3rd. at which hour Left Group 59th. Division will become Right Group 34th. Division and Right Group 3rd. Division will become Left Group 34th. Division.

8. ACKNOWLEDGE.

[signature]
Major,
Brigade Major R.A.
34th. Divisional Artillery.

Issued at 1 p.m.

Copies:
1. 152nd. Bde. RFA.
2. 160th. " "
3. 34th. D.A.C.
4. D.T.M.O.
5-6. 34th. Div. "G".
7. " " "Q"
17-18. War Diary.
8. S.O.R.A. 34th. Div.
9. VIth. Corps R.A.
10-12. 3rd. D.A. (1 for Rt.Group)
(1 for DTMO 40th.Div).
13-14. 59th.D.A. (1 for Left Group).
15-16. 40th.DA. (1 for 40th.D.A.C.)
19-20. File.

War Diary App II

Secret

34th. Div. Arty. No. O/347.

34th. DIVISIONAL ARTILLERY MARCH ORDERS.

1. The 34th. Divisional Artillery will march to forward Area as shown on attached table "A".

2. All units will march with full echelons.

3. Trench Mortar personnel will move by lorry to ST. LEGER on the 2nd. and 3rd. March.

4. 5 Lorries per Brigade will report at each Brigade H.Q.'s at 8 a.m. on the 2nd. March. 4 Lorries for T.M.B's will report at CANETTEMONT at 8 a.m. on the 2nd., and the same on the 3rd. March.

5. H. Q. Coy. Train will march under their own arrangements and will be billotted as shown on attached table "B", and will rejoin Div. Train on 3rd. March.

6. Rations for 2nd. and 3rd. March will be carried. Rations for 4th. March will be delivered on arrival at Wagon Lines.

7. 500 Yards distance will be maintained on line of march between batteries and sections of D.A.C.

[signature]
Major,
Brigade Major R.A.
34th. Divisional Artillery.

28-2-18.

Copies to:-

152nd. Brigade RFA.
160th. Brigade RFA.
34th. D.A.C.
D.T.M.O.
H.Q. Coy. Train.
34th. Div. "G".
34th. Div. "Q".
VI Corps R.A.
3rd. D.A.
59th. D.A.
40th. D.A.

MARCH TABLE   TABLE "A"

Serial No.	Date.	Unit	From	To	Route	Remarks
1.	2nd.	152nd. Bde. RFA.	Billets WAMIN etc.	COUIN COIGNEUX HENU	BEAUDRICOURT SUS-ST-LEGER SOMBRIN SAULTY SOLERNEAU GAUDIEMPRE	To be clear of Cross Roads ETREE-WAMIN Stn. at 9-30 a.m.
2.	2nd.	D.A.C.	Billets ETREE-WAMIN	SOUASTRE	ditto	Head of Columns to move off from ETREE-WAMIN S Stn. at 10 a.m.
3.	2nd.	160th. Bde. RFA.	Billets REBREUVIETTE etc	GAUDIEMPRE ST. AMAND.	ditto	Head of Column to pass REBREUVIETTE Church at 10-30 a.m.
4.	3rd.	D.A.C.	SOUASTRE	Wagon Lines between HAMELINCOURT & MOYENNEVILLE S.28.d, 29c, 30c.	BIENVILLERS MONCHY-au-BOIS ADINFER AYETTE.	To be clear of SOUASTRE by 8 a.m.
5.	3rd.	160th. Bde. RFA.	GAUDIEMPRE & ST. AMAND.	Wagon Lines HAMELINCOURT A.5, 6 & 11.	POMMIER BIENVILLERS MONCHY-au-BOIS ADINFER AYETTE.	Head of Column to move off from POMMIER at 9-15 a.m.
6.	3rd.	152nd. Bde. RFA.	COUIN COIGNEUX HENU	Wagon Lines ARGYLL Camp S.17.c & [illegible].	BIENVILLERS MONCHY-au-BOIS ADINFER BOISLEUX-au-MONT.	Head of Column to move off from SOUASTRE at 10 a.m.

BILLETTING TABLE. Table "B"

Unit	Date	Billetted at	Billeting parties to report to
152nd. Bde. 2 Batteries 1 Battery 1 " H.Qrs.	Night 2/3rd March. " " "	COIGNEUX COUIN HENU HENU or COUIN	Billet Warden COUIN at 11-30 am.
160th. Bde. H.Qrs & 3 batteries 1 Battery	" "	GAUDIEMPRE ST. AMAND.	Sub-Area Commandant GAUDIEMPRE. at 11-30 a.m.
34th.D.A.C.	"	SOUASTRE	Area Commandant SOUASTRE at 11-30 a.m.
H.Q. Coy. Train	"	GAUDIEMPRE or ST. AMAND	Sub-Area Commandant GAUDIEMPRE.

App III

NARRATIVE OF OPERATIONS (34th. DIVISIONAL ARTILLERY) DURING

MARCH 21st., 22nd. and 23rd. 1918.

1. GENERAL ACTION OF ARTILLERY.

21st. The Hostile Bombardment commenced at 5 a.m. It was very heavy and there was much Gas Shelling chiefly directed against the 1st. System and areas in which Batteries were sited. MAIDA VALE was heavily shelled as well as CROISELLES and the S. end of HENIN HILL where A/152 and C/160 were situated. Back area villages were shelled by H.V. guns during the early part of the morning.

Telephone communication between Right Group and A & D/160 was cut early in the bombardment, and was never re-established with the advanced sections of these Batteries which were situated East of the ECOUST-CROISILLES Railway.

Observation was impossible throughout the greater part of the morning owing to mist.

Between 3-30 and 4 p.m. large numbers of the enemy advanced north-westwards over the ridge N.W. of ECOUST. The main positions of A & D/160 were in the direct line of this advance and came under heavy rifle and M.G. fire. The guns were run out and fired over open sights together with the Lewis Guns of the Battys until the enemy were close on them when Major YOUNG (Comdg D/160) took over command of both batteries, O.C., A/160 having being wounded by M.G. fire, sent the breech-blocks to the rear and organised the detachments into a firing party with rifles and Lewis Guns and fell back fighting.

During the morning's bombardment a section of C/160 in CROISELLES had both guns put out of action by shell fire and the detachments killed or wounded; Lieut TALBOT, the Officer in charge, being killed while actually firing one of his guns.

At 6 p.m. teams were brought up by Lieut WALKER and the 2 guns removed under rifle fire, the enemy being then in possession of the S.E. portion of the village.

B/160, a silent battery in action 1,000 yards S.E. of ST. LEGER engaged very good targets throughout the day from the time observation became possible. During the late morning, with observation from the Ridge W. of ECOUST, the enemy's Infantry were engaged advancing from BULLECOURT.

From 3-30 p.m. onwards this battery fired continuously at short ranges on the enemy in MAIDA VALE and on the ECOUST and ST. LEGER - CROISILLES Spurs. During the afternoon 4 of the 6 guns were put out of action by shell fire, the 2 remaining guns firing until our Infantry fell back to the trench line in rear of the battery when the detachments withdrew, taking the breech-blocks with them. The detachments of these 2 guns returned later and re-opened fire for a short time.

During the night teams were brought up and removed all 6 guns to the Wagon line, were the damaged ones were repaired and all brought into action on the 22nd.

At 2 p.m. the 23rd. Battery (3rd. Division) was placed under the orders of C.R.A. 34th. Division and ordered to report to O.C. Right Group in ST. LEGER. This battery came into action in the evening W. of ST. LEGER in B.2.d. where it was joined during the night 21/22nd. by C/160 which had been made up to 6 guns from the Workshops at COURCELLES-le-COMTE. This battery (23rd) did much good work and engaged good targets whilst attached to the 34th. Division.

About dusk the H.Q. Right Group withdrew from ST. LEGER and proceeded to H.Q. Left Group at ST. LEGER MILL. It was subsequently ordered to withdraw to the Wagon Lines at HAMELINCOURT during the night 21/22nd.

Contd.........

The 34th. Divisional Artillery was then formed into one Group under Lieut.Col. W.G.THOMPSON, as follows:-
A, B, C & D Batteries 152nd. Brigade RFA.
C/160 Brigade and 23rd. Battery.
During the night 21/22nd. the advanced section of B/152 was withdrawn to its main position and all guns of A, C & D/152 were withdrawn at intervals to positions 1,000 yards E. of BOYELLES.
Group H.Q. moved to HENIN with H.Q. 101st. Infantry Brigade and established telephonic communication with all batteries.
The situation of our front line was communicated to O.C. Group and a general S.O.S. Line ordered 300 yards east of this for the night. O.C. Group was told to be prepared to fire S.O.S. on any portion of the front from old N. boundary to opposite the E. corner of ST. LEGER WOOD.

22nd. About noon on the 22nd, as the occupation of HENIN HILL by the enemy appeared imminent, B/152 was ordered to withdraw and join the remainder of the Brigade E. of BOYELLES. C/152 withdrew to the railway between HAMELINCOURT and MOYENNEVILLE. B/160 having repaired their guns came into action alongside, but later moved up to the positions E. of BOYELLES.
O.C. Group moved with H.Q. 101st. Infantry Brigade to H.Q. M.G. Battalion in BOYELLES.
At 3-45 p.m. orders were received from VIth. Corps that the 155th. Army Brigade RFA. had been placed under orders of C.R.A. 34th. Division and was proceeding to DOUCHY-lez-AYETTE. The O.C. of the Brigade reported at GOMIECOURT during the evening and was allotted positions near ARGYLE CAMP to cover the front of the 2nd . Guards Brigade. The 155th. Brigade came into action during the night but was placed under the 3rd. Division and passed out of the control of C.R.A. 34th. Division.
During the night 22/23rd. the remainder of the 34th. Divnl. Artillery plus 23rd. Battery RFA. were gradually withdrawn to positions E. of the railway in rear of HAMELINCOURT and reformed into 2 Groups as follows:-

Right Group. Lt. Col. WARBURTON.
H.Q. HAMELINCOURT.
B/160, C/160, 23rd. Battery.
Reinforced during 23rd. by A/160 with new guns received from Army Gun Park.

Left Group.
Lt. Col. THOMPSON.
H.Q. HAMELINCOURT.
A, B, C, & D Batteries 152nd. Brigade RFA.
About 7 p.m. H.Q.R.A. 34th. Division moved from GOMIECOURT to AYETTE.

23rd. At 6 a.m. on the 23rd. Os.C. 165 and 170 Brigades RFA. (31st. D.A.) reported at AYETTE and the following instructions were issued to them:-
O.C. 165 Brigade to reconnoitre positions in the valley S. of MOYENNEVILLE in A.4.d. H.Q. in MOYENNEVILLE.
O.C. 170 Brigade to reconnoitre positions E. or N. of GOMIECOURT as the situation at the time demanded, H.Q. in GOMIECOURT Chateau. Both Brigades to come into action as soon as possible to cover the Right half of the Divisional Front.
These Brigades came into action during the afternoon of the 23rd.
The H.Q. of 152nd. Brigade and 160th. Brigade were ordered to move back to N. end of MOYENNEVILLE during the afternoon.
During the morning of the 23rd. O.C. Left Group moved one section of C/152 forward to a position E. of BOYELLES. This section did good work throughout 23rd. and 24th. firing with observation on parties of the enemy who were endeavouring to establish themselves on the ST. LEGER - HENIN Road.

Contd...........

Command of the 34th. Divisional Artillery was handed over to C.R.A. 31st. Division at 2 p.m. 23rd. and H.Q.R.A. 34th. Division moved to ADINFER in the evening keeping in close touch with C.R.A. 31st. Division.

2. OUR FIRE.

During the night 20/21st. Counter Preparation "B" was put down by all guns at following times:-

2-10 to 2-15 a.m.
2-45 to 2-50 "
3-20 to 3-25 "
4-5 to 4-15 "
4-45 to 4-55 "

From 5 a.m. to 6-30 a.m. batteries fired Counter-Preparation "A".

At 6-30 a.m. orders were issued to slow down to 1 round per gun per minute and to change on to Counter Preparation "B".

At 10 a.m. 21st. Right Group fired S.O.S. on Left of 59th. Division front.

Up to 3-30 p.m. fire was kept up at varying rates and on various areas and targets as reports from Ground observers and Aeroplanes were received.

From 3-30 p.m. 21st. onwards the situation changed so quickly that all control of fire was left in the hands of Group and Battery Commanders, Groups being kept informed of the situation as far as it was known and S.O.S. lines being ordered from Div. H.Q. for each night.

At 10-20 a.m. on the 22nd. a heavy bombardment of CROISILLES was commenced in which the H.A. were asked to co-operate. The village was reported to be used as an assembly point by the enemy. This bombardment was repeated shortly afterwards and reports subsequently received stated that this fire had cleared the enemy out of the village.

At 6 p.m. 22nd. an S.O.S. call on the front of 3rd. Division was answered by all guns that could be brought to bear.

3. AMMUNITION SUPPLY. Was well maintained by ammunition wagons removing ammunition from evacuated positions, from A.R.P. near BOYELLES until empty, and from positions unlikely to be occupied. The dumps at rear positions proved of great value.

As far as can be ascertained very little ammunition fell into the hands of the enemy, being almost entirely fired or removed, except in the case of re-inforcing positions for the 1st System, which were never occupied and from which it was not possible to remove ammunition.

After the A.R.P. near BOYELLES was abandoned and a new one opened at BOIRY ST RICTRUDE the supply was not so good. This was due to the congestion of traffic on the roads in rear and to the arrival of re-inforcing Brigades, all clamouring for ammunition. More A.R.Ps. should have been provided so as to avoid congestion.

4. WATER SUPPLY. The water supply at HENDECOURT and DOUCHY-les-AYETTE broke down badly. This was a serious matter and took some time to get right and seriously hampered the supply of ammunition by horse transport.

5. HEAVY ARTILLERY. Liaison between H.A. and Divisional Artillery was not good. The Liaison Officer with 34th. Divisional Artillery was not kept informed of the H.A. situation by his own Brigade and was rarely in communication with them. Requests for assistance had usually to be made through B.M. VI Corps H.A. and took a very long time.

I am convinced that the H.Q. of an affiliated Brigade of H.A. should be with Div. H.Q., otherwise the affiliation is a dead letter.

Contd.........

6. COMMUNICATIONS.
Direct lines from C.R.As. of Divisions to G.O.C.R.A. Corps are most necessary, it took anything from 30 minutes to 1 hour to get through to Corps R.A. with the Corps H.Q. line which was the only one available.

[signature]

Brigadier-General,
C.R.A., 34th. Division.

30th. March 1918.

34th Divisional Artillery

C. R. A.

34th DIVISION

APRIL 1918

Appendices attached:-

Narrative of Operations 9th-17th
Operation Orders.
March Tables
Moves
Locations.
Ammunition Expenditure

Army Form C. 2118.

Instructions regarding War Diaries and Intelligence Summaries are contained in F. S. Regs., Part II. and the Staff Manual respectively. Title pages will be prepared in manuscript.

WAR DIARY
or
INTELLIGENCE SUMMARY.
(Erase heading not required.)

Month of April, 1918.

H.Q.R.A., 34th. Division.

Page 1.

VII 28

Place	Date	Hour	Summary of Events and Information	Remarks and references to Appendices
	April			
MERVILLE (36a 1/40000	3		Batteries withdrew to Wagon Lines on nights April 2nd./3rd., 3rd./4th.	Ap.p. I
,,	3		(1) Preparatory to rejoining the 34th Division, 34th. Divisional Artillery assembled on the night, April 3rd., as follows:- 152nd. Bde., R.F.A., at GOUY-EN-ARTOIS. 160th. Bde., R.F.A., and H.Q. Coy. 34th. Divisional Train at BARLY. 34th. D.A.C., 34th. T.M. Batteries and part of H.Q.R.A. with the Divisional Artillery at BAVINCOURT.) Sheet LENS 11. (2) Under the orders of respective C.O.'s, Wagon Lines and 34th. D.A.C. marched on the 3rd. April to above locations. Gun limbers remained to pull out guns on completion of relief, and marched direct to the Billeting Area.	Ap.p.II

(A7092). Wt. W12839/M1293. 75,0.0. 1/17. D. D. & L., Ltd. Forms/C.2118/14.

Army Form C. 2118.

Instructions regarding War Diaries and Intelligence Summaries are contained in F. S. Regs., Part II. and the Staff Manual respectively. Title pages will be prepared in manuscript.

WAR DIARY
or
INTELLIGENCE SUMMARY.
(Erase heading not required.)

Month of April, 1918.

H.Q.R.A., 34th. Division,
Page 2.

Place	Date	Hour	Summary of Events and Information	Remarks and references to Appendices
	April			
MERVILLE.	5		34th. Divisional Artillery moved from the GOUY-EN-ARTOIS, BARLY, BAVINCOURT area to the	
(36a 1/40000			GAUCHIN-VERLOINGT, HERNICOURT, RAMECOURT Area (Sheet LENS 11).	Ap.p.III
,,	6		March continued to the ECQUEDECQUES, BOURECQ, ST.HILAIRE Area (Sheet HAZEBROUCK 5a).	Ap.p.IV
,,	7		March continued to the HAVERSKERQUE Area (Sheet HAZEBROUCK 5a).	Ap.p.V
,,	8		Relief of the 38th. Divisional Artillery on the ARMENTIERES Front commenced.	Ap.p.VI
			One section per battery relieved on the night 8th./9th.April.	
,,	9	5 am.	Hostile attack began.	
			Vide "34th. Divisional Artillery Narrative of Operations from 9th. April to 17th. April, 1918."	Ap.p.VII

(A7092). Wt. W12839/M1293. 75,000. 1/17. D. D. & L., Ltd. Forms/C.2118/14.

Instructions regarding War Diaries and Intelligence Summaries are contained in F. S. Regs., Part II. and the Staff Manual respectively. Title pages will be prepared in manuscript.

Army Form C.

WAR DIARY
or
INTELLIGENCE SUMMARY.

(Erase heading not required.)

H.Q.R.A., 34th. Division.

Month of April, 1918.

Page 3.

Place	Date	Hour	Summary of Events and Information	Remarks and references to Appendices
	April			
LESART. (36a 1/40000)	9	9 am.	H.Q.R.A. established a report centre at LE SART (36a).	
NEUF BERQUIN (36a)	9	10.20 a.m.	H.Q.R.A. was established at NEUF BERQUIN (36a).	
MERVILLE. (36a)	9	3 pm.	H.Q.R.A. moved from NEUF BERQUIN and joined the H.Q. 50th. Division at K.22.a.5.0 (Sheet 36a).	
LA MOTTE. (36a)	11	12 noon	H.Q.R.A. moved to K.15.d.2.7 (36a), and to LE MOTTE Chateau (36a) about 7 p.m., where C.R.A. was in touch with G.O.C.'s 29th., 31st. and 50th. Divisions.	
LE GRAND HAZARD (36a.D.8.d.)	12	10 pm.	H.Q.R.A. moved from LA MOTTE to LE GRAND HAZARD (36a).	

(A7092). Wt. W12839/M1293 75,000. 1/17. D. D. & L., Ltd. Forms/C.2118/14.

Instructions regarding War Diaries and Intelligence Summaries are contained in F. S. Regs., Part II. and the Staff Manual respectively. Title pages will be prepared in manuscript.

WAR DIARY
or
INTELLIGENCE SUMMARY.
(Erase heading not required.)

Army Form C. 2118.

Month of April, 1918.

H.Q.R.A., 34th. Division,

Page 4.

Place	Date	Hour	Summary of Events and Information	Remarks and references to Appendices
	April			
LE GRAND HAZARD (36a.)	15		34th. Divisional Artillery consisted of two Groups covering the front on either side of the boundary between the XI and XV Corps.	App. VIII
,,	16		Group Boundaries re-adjusted.	App. IX.
,,	17		Location Statement, vide	App. X.
,,	17 to 30		The enemy carried out no further attacks on the Divisional Artillery front. Batteries put down harassing fire by night, and by day when observation was impossible.	
,,	22		Location Statement, vide	App. XI.

C Thompson Lieut RA.
for C.R.A. 34 Division

(A7092). Wt. W12839/M1293. 75,0.0. 1/17. D. D. & L., Ltd. Forms/C.2118/14.

App I

SECRET.

C.R.A.	D.A.D.V.S.
C.R.E.	A.P.M.
14th Inf.Bde.	Camp Comdt.
96th Inf.Bde.	Divl. Train.
97th Inf.Bde.	Div.M.T.Coy.
32nd Dn.M.G.C.	VI Corps.
16th High.L.I.	31st Division.
Div.Signal Co.	41st Division.
A. & Q.	Guards Divn.
A.D.M.S.	34th Divl. Artillery.

32nd Div.No,G.S.1710/4/5.

Reference Addendum No. 1 to 32nd Div. Order No.168.

The 32nd Divisional Artillery will relieve the 34th Divl. Artillery on nights April 2nd/3rd and April 3rd/4th and NOT on nights April 1st/2nd and April 2nd /3rd as therein stated.

The relief will be carried out under orders to be issued by C.R.A., 32nd Division.

G.I.McKenzie.

Lieut-Colonel,
General Staff,
32nd Division.

31st March 1918.

OCs 152 160 Bdes

O/C do. Wagon Lines

OC. 34 DAC. DTMO.

OC HQ. 34 Divnl Train.

APP II

S.C.M. 1

Moves

1. a) On night of 3rd inst the 34 Divnl Arty. will assemble preparatory to rejoining 34 Divn as follows:-

152 Bde — GOUY EN ARTOIS

160 Bde + HQ Coy 34 Divnl Train } BARLY

34 DAC and 34 TM Batteries RA. HQ. } BAVINCOURT.

b) Wagon Lines and DAC will march to above locations on ~~afternoon of~~ 3rd inst. under the orders of respective C.O.s. Gun limbers will remain to pull out guns on completion of relief and march direct to new billeting area.

(c) Billets will be obtained from respective Town Majors. Billeting parties should be sent in advance as there are already a certain number of troops in these villages.

Transport 2 (a) 5 DAC wagons complete turnouts will remain with each Bde..

b) 5 lorries are allotted to each Bde
6 " " " " DTMO.
1 lorry is " " HQ DAC.
These lorries will be at
La Bazèque on Gaudiempré
rd at V 27 central (sheet 51 (C)) at 11 am
on 3rd inst.
Each Bde, DAC & DTMO will
send an officer to take over.
Thereafter lorries will move with
Units who will be responsible for rationing
drivers.
c) All echelons will be EMPTY of
amm.

Miscellaneous 3(a) All DAC amm wagons now
attached six to each Bty will rejoin
DAC by midnight 2/3rd inst.
All TM personnel incldg Lts COX &
BLYTHE will rejoin DTMO by mid-
night 2/3rd inst.

(b) DTMO will draw rations separately for T.M. batteries on 3rd inst. for consumption 4th inst. HQ. DAC. will provide transport for this purpose

(c) It is probable that the march will be resumed on 4th inst. and further orders as to this will be issued as soon as possible.

(d) O.C. HQ Coy. 34 Divl Train is allotted 14 lorries for supplies.

4. Acknowledge.

Copies HQRA 32nd Div
SCRA VI Corps.

OC. 152 160 FA. Bdes

" OC 34 DAC. " " Wagon Lines

DTMO.

HQ Coy 34 Divnl Train.

Further to this office SCM 1 yesterday:-

1. All tents must be handed over to relieving Units.

2. Receipts will be taken for amm on charge.

3. There are no restrictions as to route to-morrow.

3x. All G.S. wagons, attached to batteries, will not march with batteries but as a separate Brigaded convoy. None are to ride on G.S. wagons.

4. The march will be resumed on 5th inst to St POL

SC.

2/4/18

App III

March Table for 5th April.

Unit	MOVE. From	To.	ROUTE.	Billeting Area	Remarks.
152nd Bde.	GOUY EN ARTOIS	GAUCHIN VERLOINGT.	BARLY - AVESNES - GIVENCHY - TERNAS - ROELLECOURT. ST POL.	GAUCHIN.	To march from GOUY at 9 A.M.
160th Bde.	BARLY	HERNICOURT	As for 152nd Bde.	HERNICOURT and S. end of WAVRANS.	To march from BARLY at 9 A.M.
34th D.A.C.	BAVINCOURT	RAMECOURT	ETREE WAMIN MONCHEAUX HERLIN	RAMECOURT	To march from BARLY at 9.30 A.M.
34th T.M. Btys	-do-	-do-	As for D.A.C.	RAMECOURT & S.E. Suburbs of ST POL.	To be clear of BAVINCOURT by 9 A.M.
H.Q. Arty 34th Divn.	BARLY	-do-	As desired.	RAMECOURT. O.C. 34th D.A.C. to allot	To march from BARLY at 8 A.M.

25/11/[illegible]

O.C. 152 Bde
O.C. 160 Bde
O.C. 34 DAC
" D.T.M.O.
" HQ Coy Train

1 34 Div Artillery will move to [illegible] on 5th instant in accordance with attached March Table.

2 Billeting Parties should be sent well in advance as billeting [illegible] in advance [illegible]. 160 Bde will expand to the "block" [illegible] South end of WAVRANS area including RATHONVAL and BRIAS if desirable. 152 Bde should get the personnel of at least 2 Batteries into Physical & Bayonet Training Schools (now empty) just E of Railway [illegible] at GAUCHIN. The area is controlled by Area Comdt, ST POL whose office is near the station. There will be a billet warden in each village [illegible] arrival.

3 Each Bde, DAC, DTMO & Train Coy will send a mounted or cyclist orderly to DAHQ RAMECOURT station on arrival tomorrow, to receive orders for next day's march to [illegible] area via PERNES.

4 Supply wagons will be sent to railheads at HERNICOURT, GAUCHIN or RAMECOURT [illegible] for refilling [illegible] those [illegible]. [illegible] will at once send guides for these wagons directly their billets are known.

5 100 yard intervals to be maintained between Batteries & sections DAC.

6 O.C. [illegible] [illegible] will [illegible] Brigade Armoury

7 There is a Veterinary [illegible] Post at RAMECOURT

[illegible]/11/18

8 Acknowledge.

[illegible]
[illegible] 34 Div

SC/M/14. App IV

O.C. 152 F.A.Bde.
O.C. 160 F.A.Bde.
O.C. 34 D.A.C.
D.T.M.O.
O.C. H.Q. Coy 34 Div. Train

1. 34 Div Arty will move to LILLERS Area on 6th instant, in accordance with attached March Table.

2. Paras 5 and 6 of this Office No SC/M/13 of yesterday hold good.

3 Supply Wagons of various Units in that area to ECQUEDECQUES BOURECQ - ST HILAIRE Churches. Guides to be sent to collect, directly Units arrive in the Area.

4 D.A.H.Q. tomorrow night will be at MERVILLE.

[illegible]
Captain,

5 Apl '18. S.C. R.A. 34th Division

March Table for 6th April

Unit	Move		Route	Billeting Area	Remarks
	From	To			
152 Bde.	GAUCHIN	ECQUEDECQUES	ST. POL. PERNES. PERFAY LIERES FANCQUENHAM.	ECQUEDECQUES. Billets from Town Major LILLERS. Billeting Parties to report to him at 12 NOON	March at 9.30 A.m. not to enter PERNES before 11.30 A.m.
160 Bde.	HERNICOURT	BOURECQ.	WAVRANS HESTRUS PERNES. PERFAY LIERES	BOURECQ. Billeting Parties to meet Staff Capt. Bde. (NORRENT FONTES AREA) at 12 noon at Road Junction of ST HILAIRE - LIERES. ST HILAIRE - BOURECQ Roads	March at 9.15 A.m. To be clear of PERNES by 11.30 A.m.
3rd D.A.C.	RAMECOURT	ECQUEDECQUES and BOURECQ.	ST. POL. PERNES. PERFAY. LIERES	No 1 Sec. ECQUEDECQUES Billets as for 152 Bde. H.Q. & No 2 Sec. BOURECQ and ST. HILAIRE Billeting Parties as for 160 Bde.	To march at 10.A.m.
3rd T.M. Bty.	HERLIN	ST HILAIRE.	As for 3rd D.A.C.	ST HILAIRE Billeting Parties as for 160 Bde.	To march at 9.30 A.m.
H.Q. Coy 3rd Div Train	RAMECOURT	ECQUEDECQUES	As desired	ECQUEDECQUES As for 152 Bde.	To march at 8 A.m.

APP V

SECRET. 34th. Divl. Arty. No. SG/M/5.

O.C. 152nd. F.A. Brigade.
O.C. 160th. " "
O.C. 34th. D.A.C.
D.T.M.O.
O.C. H.Q. Coy. 34th. Divl. Train.

---

1. 34th. Divisional Artillery will continue the march to HAVERSKERQUE Area on 7th. in accordance with attached march table.

2. Billeting parties will report at Sub-Area Commandants office. HAVERSKERQUE at 10 a.m. on 7th. The Area Commandant will then allot billets to a representative officer from each Brigade, D.A.C., D.T.M.O., and Train Coy.

3. Lorries will be parked on St. Venant - HAVERSKERQUE - MERVILLE Road.

4. 34th. Divisional Artillery will relieve 38th. Divisional Artillery in the line on 8th. & 9th. insts., under orders to be issued later.

Captain.
Staff Captain.
34th. Divisional Artillery.

6th. April 1918.

MARCH TABLE FOR 7th. APRIL.

UNIT.	Move.		Route.	Billeting Area.	Remarks.
	From	To			
152. Bde.	ECQUEDECQUES.	HAVERSKERQUE.	LILLERS -ST. VENANT.	HAVERSKERQUE. (Croix Marraisse.)	March at 9-15 a.m. To be clear of LILLERS by 10-15 a.m.
160. Bde.	BOURECQ.	HAVERSKERQUE.	do	South part of HAVERSKERQUE.	March at 10 a.m.
34. D.A.C.	ECQUEDECQUES & BOURECQ.	do	do	HAVERSKERQUE. (LE CORBIE.)	March at 10-45 a.m.
34. T.M.B.	ST.HILAIRE.	do	do	HAVERSKERQUE. (LA MALADERIE.)	March at 8-30 a.m.
H.Q. Coy. 34.Divl.Train.	ECQUEDECQUES.	do	do	HAVERSKERQUE. (LE CORBIE)	March at 8 a.m.

War Diary

APP VI

S E C R E T. 34th. Div. Arty. No. O/379/1.

AMENDMENT No. 1 to 34th. DIVISIONAL ARTILLERY RELIEF ORDERS.

Delete para. 3. Substitute new para. as follows:-

"Units will take their own guns into action".

[signature]
Major,
Brigade Major. R.A.
34th. Divisional Artillery.

7-8-18.

Copies to all recipients of O/379.

War Diary 24

S E C R E T. 34th.Div.Arty.No. 0/378.

34th. DIVISIONAL ARTILLERY RELIEF ORDERS.

1. The 34th. Divisional Artillery will relieve the 38th. Divnl. Artillery in the line on the nights of 8/9th and 9/10th. April.
One Section per Battery will relieve on night 8/9th, two Sections per Battery on night 9/10th.

2. 160th. Brigade RFA will take over the Right Group H.Q. H.17.b.15.80, relieving the 121st. Brigade RFA.
152nd. Brigade RFA will take over the Left Group H.Q. B.30.d.1.6 relieving the 122nd. Brigade RFA.

3. ~~Guns will be exchanged.~~ Units will take their own guns into action.

4. Telephone Lines, map boards, log books, maps, aeroplane photos and Documents relating to defence of the line will be taken over.

5. The 34th. D.A. will march from the HAVERSKERQUE area to the Wagon Lines of 38th. D.A. as follows:-
(a) 8th. April. 2 guns with F.B. Wagons only, 1 officer, detachments, 1 signalling N.C.O. and 3 signallers per battery. To move off at 8 am. 160th. Brigade RFA. leading.
H.Q. and No. 1 and 2 Sections D.A.C., head of column to move off at 8-30 a.m.
(b) 9th. April. Remainder of 34th. D.A. 160th. Brigade RFA. leading, head to move off at 8 a.m.
Os. i/c Brigade Signalling Sections should proceed to new Group H.Qrs. on the 8th.

6. Route in all cases will be MERVILLE, ESTAIRES, CROIX du BAC.
500 yards distance will be maintained between batteries and Sections of D.A.C.

7. Trench Mortar personnel will march with D.A.C.
D.T.M.O. & necessary signallers will proceed to H.Q. D.T.M.O. 38th. Divn. on the afternoon of the 8th. to take over telephone lines.
Instructions will be issued later as to the disposal of Trench Mortars and beds of 38th. D.A.

8. Location Statement of Gun Positions and Wagon Lines is attached.

9. H.Q.R.A. 34th. Division will move to STEENWERCK onthe 9th. inst.

10. Command will pass on completion of relief on night 9/10th.

11. ACKNOWLEDGE.

[signature]
Major,
Brigade Major.R.A.
34th. Divisional Artillery

7th. April 1918.

Copies: 1-5. 152nd. Bde.
6-10. 160th "
11-13. 34th D.A.C.
14-16. D.T.M.O.
17-18. 34th. Div. "G".
19. " " "
20. XVth. Corps R.A.
21. R.A. 40th. Div.
22. R.A. 25th. Div.
23-24. War Diary.
25. File.

S E C R E T. COPY R.A. 38th.Div.H. G.S.1586/27.

38th. DIVISIONAL ARTILLERY.
LOCATION STATEMENT.

Unit	Headquarters	Gun Position	No of guns	Wagon Lines	Remarks.
38th. Div.Arty.	STEENWERCK				
RIGHT GROUP.					
121 Bde.	H.17.b.15.80			A.30.c.4.1.	
A/121	H.12.d.05.09.	A.11.d.73.61	1	H.3.b.7.9.	
		H.11.d.73.67	1		
		H.12.c.90.52	1		
		H.12.c.90.60	1		
		H.12.c.89.71	1		
		H.12.c.88.75	1		
B/121	H.12.c.8.9.	H.12.b.10.10.	3	B.27.d.7.8.	5 guns silent
		H.18.d.88.75	1		
		H.12.b.33.61	1		
	X	I. 9.c.30.65	1		
C/121	I.7.d.35.15	I. 7.d.70.50	2	B.27.d.7.8.	1 gun at I.O..
		I.7.b.20.20.	2		
		I.7.b.80.45	1		
D/121	H.17.d.4.3.	H.18.a.2.1.	4	B.26.d.3.1.	4 How's silent.
		I.13.c.55.05.	2		
LEFT GROUP					
122 Bde.	B.30.d.1.6.			A.30.c.3.4.	
A/122	C.19.b.35.60.	C.19.b.12.03.	1	H.1.b.50.90	1 gun at I.O.M.
		C.14.c.88.90	1		
		C.14.c.87.82	1		
		C.19.b.18.42	1		
		C.19.b.17.52	1		
B/122	B.30.b.60.75	B.30.b.23.68	6	H.1.d.5.4.	
C/122	B.30.c.90.40	C.18.c.30.70	2	H.1.b.6.5.	
		B.30.d.13.65	2		silent
	X	I.2.b.45.53	1		
D/122	C.19.c.4.2.	C.19.c.35.10.	4	A.30.c.4.8.	2 How's silent
		B.23.b.60.25.	2		

38th. D.A.C.H.Q. A.28.b.7.4.
No. 1 Section B.23.c.4.5.
" 2 " B.19.c.4.7.
" 3 " Moved with Division.

38th. D.T.M.O. H.4.c.3.3.
X/38th T.M.B. C.27.b.55.95.
Y/38th T.M.B. I.1.d.62,66.

POSITIONS OF 6" (NEWTON) TRENCH MORTARS IN ACTION.

LOTHIAN I.10.c.25.50.
------- C.12.c.95.90.
SALONICA C.22.d.10.70.
WILLOW WALK C.28.d.60.30.
S.P.X. I.4.b.40.40.

X Anti-Tank Guns.

4-4-18.

(Sd) J.A.MARSTON, Major. R.A.
Brigade Major. 38th. Divisional Artillery.

App VII

NARRATIVE OF 34th. DIVISIONAL ARTILLERY

from 9th. April to 17th. April 1918.

1. The 34th. Divisional Artillery was withdrawn from action in the VIth. Corps (near ADINFER WOOD) on the evening of the 3rd. April.

The march to First Army area commenced on the 5th. and all batteries and sections D.A.C. reached HAVERSKERQUE by noon on the 7th.

One section per battery and the D.A.C. marched to Wagon Lines of 38th. D.A. near CROIX DU BAC and ERQUINGHEM on the morning of the 8th. and the 2 guns with detachments and 2 Officers per battery relieved corresponding sections of 38th. D.A. in action in ARMENTIERES and south of the town on the evening of the 8th. Brigade Signalling Officers and Adjutants or Orderly Officers had proceeded to forward area on the 7th. The Reconnaissance Officer and O.C. R.A.H.Q. Signals were at STEENWERCK having been lent to 38th. D.A.

Three 18-pdrs and 2 4.5" Hows. were condemned on the 7th, and of these two 18-pdrs and one 4.5" How. were sent to No. 14 & 21 Workshops near STEENWERCK and DOULIEU on the morning of the 8th.

R.A.H.Q. remained in MERVILLE and Brigade H.Qrs. in HAVERSKERQUE during the night 8th/9th.

According to original plan the remaining sections of batteries and all H.Qrs. were to move into forward area on the 9th. moving off at 8 a.m. and picking up new guns at Workshops en route.

2. At 6-30 a.m. on 9th. a Staff Officer of XV Corps brought a written message to the effect that B.Cs. of 34th. D.A. should be collected as soon as possible and should remain with the 4 guns of batteries. Batteries were not to move E. of MERVILLE but were to remain on HAVERSKERQUE - MERVILLE road until further orders. Head of Column at LE SART. C.R.A. 34th. Division to see G.O.C. 57th. Division as soon as possible, the 4 guns per battery to be prepared to go into action in support of Portuguese or 57th. Divn. Arty

On receipt of above C.R.A. 34th. Division proceeded to CROIX DU BAC by car, and Brigade Major to LE SART where B.Cs. were met on the road and given necessary instructions, orderlies being sent back to turn Ammunition Wagons back to fill with Ammunition from Dump on HAVERSKERQUE - ST. VENANT road. A Report Centre was opened at LE SART and at 9-50 a.m. it was reported to XV Corps that H.Q, 10-18-pdrs and 3 4.5" Hows of 152nd. Brigade RFA and H.Q., 12-18-pdrs and 4-4.5" Hows. of 160th. Brigade RFA were at LE SART.

At 10-20 a.m. following message was received from XV Corps

"(1) The enemy are reported in our Support Lines on part of the front of the Right Brigade of the Right Divn and to be attacking the Portuguese.

(2) 34th. D.A. will move as soon as Amm. Echelons are full to area TROU BAYARD (G.19.) CUL DU SAC Farm (G.8.d) CRUSEO BEAU (G.2) and PT. DU PETIT BOIS (L.17) via LE SART Rd Junct. K.28.b & NEUF BERQUIN.

(3) 34th. D.A. H.Qrs. will be established in NEUF BERQUIN.

(4) 34th. D.A. will be ready at short notice to place 2-18-pdr Btys in action stride the LA BASSEE - ESTAIRES Rd near CARTER'S Post in M.2.c, and 1-18-pdr Bty and 1-4.5" How. Bty in positions S. of FERME DE BRETAGNE (G.26.b & 21.c.)

(5) Please report completion of move to area given in para. 2 and when H.Qrs. is established at NEUF BERQUIN.

(6) After move of D.A. to TROU BAYARD area A.. refilling point will be DOULIEU Church."

(7) Later, enemy are reported in N.3.

April 9th. At 10-25 a.m. the following message was sent to 38th. D.A. "Please direct sections and all Officers and men of 34th. D.A. as soon as ready to proceed to DOULIEU Church and await orders. Echelons full if possible. R.O., Signalling Officer and Detachment to proceed to NEUF BERQUIN where H.Q. 34th. D.A. will be."

At 11-20 a.m. following message was received from XV Corps "(1) One Bde of 34th. D.A. will move into action in positions about FERME BRETAGNE (G.20 & 21) as soon as possible. The other Bde will remain in reserve near CUL DU SAC Ferme (G.8.c) or CRUSEO BEAU (G.2)
(2) The Sections of 34th. D.A. which are at present at the Wagon Lines of 38th. D.A. will move at once to rejoin remainder of 34th. D.A. in the CRUSEO BEAU - CUL DU SAC area.
(3) 34th. D.A. will report when this order is carried out.
(4) On coming into action about FERME BRETAGNE, 1 Bde of 34th. D.A. will come under command of 57th. D.A."

On receipt of above message Brigades were ordered forward, the 160th. Brigade to go into action and come under command of 57th. D.A. This Brigade came into action in Squares G.19, 14 & 8 at 3 p.m.

Batteries were clear of LE SART at 12-30 p.m.

At 12-45 p.m. following message was received from XV Corps:- "The O.C. of the Artillery Bde of 34th. Div. which comes into action first will get into touch as soon as possible with G.O.C. Infantry Bde. of 50th. Divn at G.19.d.2.6. C.R.A. 34th. Divn. will get into touch as soon as possible with G.O.C. 50th. Divn (H.Q. MERVILLE-LA MOTTE Road, ½ mile N.W. of MERVILLE).
The 2nd. Bde. of 34th. D.A. will move into action as soon as possible and will come under orders of 57th. D.A."

152nd. Bde. RFA was ordered into action in accordance with above and was in position in squares L.16 & 17 at 3-15 p.m. in support of 151st. Infy. Bde.

The personnel of sections from ARMENTIERES with guns of 38th. D.A. rejoined batteries at 3 p.m., the guns at workshops were picked up and all batteries went into action complete with 6 guns.

Nos. 1 and 2 Sections of 38th. D.A.C. were placed under orders of C.R.A. 34th. Division, corresponding sections of 34th. D.A.C. being under 38th. D.A.

At 4-50 p.m. orders were received from XV Corps that 152 and 160 Bdes were to come under orders of C.R.A. 34th. Divn. and cover 50th. Division Infantry. O.C. 152nd. Bde. was ordered to get into touch with and cover front of 151st. Infy. Bde. and O.C. 160th. Bde. to cover fronts of 149th and 150th. Infy.Bdes. (C.R.A. reported to G.O.C. 50th. Division at once).

R.A.H.Q. 34th. Divn. moved from NEUF BERQUIN during the afternoon and joined H.Q. 50th. Divn. at K.22.a.5.0.

April 10th.
3. At 7-35 a.m. a message was received by telephone from Liaison Officer with 151st. Infy. Bde. that enemy were holding PONT LEVIS (ESTAIRES). Ordered Brigades to being all possible fire on Bridge and on roads S.E. of it.

This Bridge was reported to be again in our hands at 8-45 am

At 1-5 p.m. 152nd. Bde. report line as follows:- L.30.c.9.5 - L.34.b.3.9 - L.34.c.6.6 - L.33.c.0.2 - R.2.d.7.0 - R.8.d.7.0 - R.15.central.

At 2-22 p.m. message was received from 160th. Bde. stating that a retirement had taken place on their left about 12-40 p.m. but that 149 and 150 Infy. Bdes were confident of holding the enemy. Front was being reinforced from Bde. H.Q. A later message stated that at 1-20 p.m. our line ran through G.15.c and G.20.b. and that a counter-attack had been ordered. All of ESTAIRES less 60 yards near Bridge clear of enemy.

Later report received at 3-50 p.m. stated that enemy had recaptured ESTAIRES.

April 10th. contd.

Message received from 160th. Bde. at 4.30 p.m. that Infantrywere withdrawing to line L.29.d.6.2 - L.29.b.8.0 - along road to L.23.d.5.4.

At 6.15 p.m. enemy reported to be bringing up guns across PONT LEVIS in ESTAIRES; this was repeated to XV Corps H.A.

Message received 6.25 p.m. from Liaison Officer with 151 Infantry Brigade. Gives line held at 5 p.m. as follows:-
L.29.b.1.1 - L.29.d.6.5 - L.35.a.3.8 - L.34.b.1.8 - L.29.c.2.3
L.34.b.3.5 - L.33.d.1.9 - L.34.c.3.5 - L.32.d.8.2 - R.8.c.1.8
R.14.b.6.7 - also a few men on line L.34.c.6.3 - R.4.a.2.4.

At 10.10.p.m. the following dividing line was allotted to Groups for the night:-
L.29.b.8.0 - L.23.d.5.5.

At 10.55 p.m. message from 160th. Bde. timed 9.15 p.m. stated our line to be:-
A.16.c.6.9 - along road to G.c.3. Enemy are holding STEENWERCK.

April 11th.
4.

The following locations of our line were received at times shown:-
6.20 a.m. from 152nd. Bde.,- L.29.a.2.8 - L.28.c.7.4 - L.27.d.5.5
L.33.a.2.2 - R.8.b.5.5.
8.20 a.m. from 160th. Bde.,- L.23.c.0.0.- L.24.c.9.4 - PT. de POIVRE - along S.E. of road to G.8.d.8.6.
3.30 p.m. from 87th. Infy.Bde., - L.18.c. - G.7 - G.8 central - E. of DOULIEU.

H.Q.R.A. moved to K.15.d.2.7 about noon, and to LA MOTTE Chateua about 7 p.m., where 34th. D.A. was in touch with G.O.C.s 29th., 31st. and 50th. Divisions.

April 12th.
5.

Following message from 50th. Divn. G. to 29th. Divn. G, timed 1.50 a.m.,
"Line now formed from K.35.a.2.7 along W. bank of stream to bridge at K.29.a.4.8; thence to W. bank opposite LES PURESBECQ AAA Parties of our men are definitely established about R.16.b.5.1, in K.18.a and K.12.d AAA and attempt is being made to make this line as continuous as possible AAA Right is in touch with 61st. Divn. AAA Understand from 31st. Divn. that Guards' Bde. are advancing from about VIEUX BERQUIN with right direction on PURESBECQUES, and left on L.7.central AAA."

Following message from Liaison Officer (160th. Bde.) received at 2.45 a.m. (message timed 11.45.p.m.):-
"Message from Liaison Officer timed 11.45.p.m. 11.4.18 AAA During the night the Infantry will withdraw to the following line (at about 2.30 a.m.:-
149 Bde., VIERHOECK, K.12.central, L.7.a.3.8.
86th. Bde., L.7.a.3.8 along road to L.3.a.13.99.
87th. Bde., L.3.a.13.99, L.3.central, L.4.a.0.0. to cross Roads L.4.a.9.2.
92nd. Bde., L.4.a.9.2, F.28.central, F.22.central,
This Brigade will probably take up its H.Q. on the main NEUF BERQUIN Road near LA COURONNE.

At 5.a.m. O.C. 152nd. Bde. was ordered to open steady rate of fire on roads in K.29.b, being careful to keep W. of stream in K.29.a and c., which we hold.

All available guns were kept on MERVILLE, and N. exits during morning up to 10.45 a.m., Heavies being asked to co-operate.

At 10.45.a.m. 160th. Bde. were taken off MERVILLE and their fire turned on to front of 149th. Infy. Bde. and left of 4th. Guards' Bde., including VIEUX MOULIN - NEUF BERQUIN road add NEUF BERQUIN Church.

April 12th. contd.

At the same time 152nd. Bde. reported that Guards' Bde. request a ten-minutes barrage at 11.a.m. along MERVILLE - NEUF BERQUIN Road to support counter-attack,(leaving two Hows. on MERVILLE).

At 11.30.a.m., 31st. Divn. reported that left of 29th. Divn. was being forced back to line F.19.b. - F.17.central.

At 12.45.p.m., 160th. Bde. reported the 4th. Guards' Bde. advancing with left at K.6.d.9.7. 50th. Divn. left at K.16.c.0.0. 29th. Divn. just in front of LA COURONNE and through F.26.d.

At 4.15. p.m., reports of enemy massing in K.28.a at 3.5 p.m. were received from 11th. Corps.

In addition to Infantry targets, batteries of 152nd. Bde. engaged hostile guns in the open with direct observation and good effect as follows:-
10.a.m., field guns in K.13.d, noon, field guns L.1.c.2.1, K.6.d.95.05, on road in K.18.b. In some cases the detachments were observed to be driven away.

H.Q.R.A. moved from LA MOTTE to LE GRAND HASARD about 10.p.m.

April 13th. 6.

160th. Bde. reported at 9.45.a.m. Line to be:-
5th. Divn., K.15.d.5.9 - to K.16.b.1.9.
4th. Guards' Bde., K.16.b.1.9 to LA COURONNE.
12th. K.O.Y.L.I. through FME. LABIS to MERRIS.
Two Australian Battalions digging in on line K.14.d.7.0 - E.28.c.1.1 - E.17.a.9.8.

From 10.a.m. onwards throughout the day, very heavy fighting took place all along the front of the forest.

Barrages and concentrations were put down at request of Infantry or by direct observation of enemy massing as follows:-
10.a.m., Both Brigades, K.16.c.8.5 - K.12.b.0.9 (10 minutes).
11.a.m., 152nd. Bde., K.9.d, E.27.d.
11.25.a.m., 152nd. Bde., K.16.c.3.4 to K.17.a.0.3.
11.50.a.m., 160th. Bde., F.19.c - F.25.a (two batteries).
K.1.c.7.2 - E.30.d.7.0 (one battery).
152nd. Bde., K.11.d.5.3 - K.6.c.6.2 (one battery).
2.30.p.m., 152nd. Bde., VIERHOUCK to K.6.b.5.9 (10 minutes).
160th. Bde., N. and S. line through E.24.d.
3.45. p.m., 160th. Bde. & D/152) VIEUX BERQUIN, S. of N. edge of E.24.c.
5.5.p.m., 160th. Bde., above concentration to extend N. as far as and including Church. (15th.Corps H.A. asked to co-operate and endeavour to knock out church).
5.30.p.m., 160th. Bde., K.5.a.4.2, E.29.central, E.23.d.central - Church. Thickest near Church.
5.33 p.m., 152nd. Bde., E.17.a.central - L'EPINETTE - K.5.a.4.2 and E. of E.17.a.central.
6.25.p.m., rate of fire reduced to 1 r.p.g.p.m.
8.30.p.m., 160th. Bde., area shoot on VERTE RUE.

During the day the following reports were received of position of our Infantry:-
11.50 a.m. from 160th. Bde., K.26.b.5.7 - K.21.b.5.4 - K.15.c.6.5 K.15.b.central - K.9.d.2.0 - K.10.a.6.1 - K.10.b.5.5 - L'EPINETTE as before to FME LABIS.
12.15 p.m., from 160th. Bde. Gaps in our line in K.5.b and K.11.a, but re-inforcements going up.
12.45.p.m. from 92nd. Infy.Bde. E.6.b.central - E.6.d.1.1 - 200 yards W. of lower edge of wood - FME. LYNDE - FME. LABIS - LA COURONNE.
2.p.m. from 152nd. Bde., 29th. Divn. fallen back to E.23.d.5.0 E.23.b.5.9.
3.15.p.m., from 152nd. Bde. line of 95th. Infy. Bde. runs K.15.b.4.0 - K.9.d.4.0 - K.10.c.2.0 - K.10.d.0.8 - K.10.d.0.3 - K.5.d.0.8. Left not in touch with Guards.

April 13th.
contd. 4.34.p.m., 31st. "G" ordered 4th. Guards (via 160th. Bde.) to fall back to Australian line.
5.p.m. from 152nd. Bde. ARREWAGE - K.4.central - Australian line on W.edge of wood. 92nd. Infy. Bde. are trying to throw back their flank to E.17.b to join with Australian line.
6.25.p.m. from 4th. Guards' Bde. timed 4.35.p.m. Posts between K.5.b and ARREWAGE line N. runs E.17.central - E.12.c.8.0 - E.12.b.4.2.
6.55 p.m. from 160th. Bde. Guards now report line K.15.d.3.9 - K.10.a.3.2 - K.10.a.9.5 - E.28.c.3.2 - E.17.a.8.8.
10.25.p.m. from 152nd. Bde. 95th. Bde. line - K.15.b.3.0 - K.9.d.4.0 - K.10.c.9.9 - K.4.a.8.6 - E.28.c.2.2 - E.22.c.9.2 - to RUE DU BOIS.

At 12.15 p.m., 152nd. Bde. reported Enemy attempting to attack had been caught by rifle and artillery fire. The attack had been broken up and many casualties inflicted particularly in K.6.c.

The following boundaries were given to Groups:-
12.25.p.m. 152 Bde., Right Boundary, - LA MOTTE - MERVILLE Road inclusive.
Inter-Bde. Boundary is E.28.a.4.0 - L.7.c.0.0.
160 Bde Left Boundary E.11.c.7.3, F.13.c.2.6, F.20.a.0.0.
7.55.p.m. 152 Right Boundary, K.9.a.0.4, K.16.central.
Inter-Bde. Boundary, E.22.c.0.0., E.29.d.0.0.
160 Bde. Left Boundary, E.17.b.0.8., F.13.c.5.0.

Harassing Fire at 30 rounds per piece on approaches in Group Zones ordered at 8.p.m., and SOS Lines to be 500 Yards E. of our front posts.

April 14th.
7.

At 7.30.a.m., 160 Bde. R.F.A. reported the enemy to have assembled about LA COURONNE and to be attacking N.W. towards LA BECQUE (E.23.)
152 Bde.R.F.A. and H.A. turned on.
160 Bde. R.F.A. already firing SOS.
The attack was repulsed with heavy casualties, the Australians allowing the enemy to get close before opening fire.
The 119th. Bde A.F.A. came under the control of the C.R.A. 34th. Division at 9.a.m. when the Divnl Artillery was organised as under:-

Brigade.	Liaison.	Front covered.
152nd. Bde. D.17.c.5.9, Right Group,	95th.Inf.Bde. K.1.c.5.2.	Right Bdy., K.9.c.0.4, to K.16 cen Inter-Grp.Bdy. E.22.c.0.0 to E.29.d.0.0.
119th. Bde. E.8.a.1.2, Left Group.	2nd.Aust.Inf. Bde. D.23.a.2.3.	Inter-Grp.Bdy.E.22.c.0.0. - E.29.d.0.0. Left Bdy. E.9.cent.-E.18.central.
160th.Bde. D.16.b.4.9.	2nd.Aust.Inf. Bde. D.23.a.2.3.	Superimposed over the Divisional Artillery Front.

At 12 noon the enemy resumed the attack about VERTE RUE and VIEUX BERQUIN. Up to 2.30.p.m., no organised attack developed. Batteries and H.A. fired concentrations on enemy assembling.
(1) E.29.central, E.24.c., 12 noon,
(2) VERTE RUE and K.6.b, 1.20.p.m.
(3) VERTE RUE in E.28.d, E.29.c.1.38.p.m.
At 2.33 p.m., the enemy pressed hard from line VIEUX BERQUIN - VERTE RUE. Brigades and H.A. fired SOS concentration on this sub-sector. At 3.12.p.m., artillery Liaison Officer, 2nd. Aust. Infantry Brigade reported there was no change in the line.
Occasional bursts were fired on VIEUX BERQUIN during the

April 14th. Contd. afternoon, large numbers of enemy on road in E.17, E.24 and E.23.b. were scattered; Infy. targets in K.16.a., K.10.d, and mounted troops on road K.16.b. engaged.

7-45 p.m. Artillery Liaison Officers with Infy. Bdes reported our line - VERTE BOIS, N, K.20.b & c, along edge of wood K.15.d.4.4, Bridge in K.15.a, K.15.b.10.85, K.10.a.8.4, K.4.central, E.28.c.05.15, E.28.c.18.20, E.28.c.4.2, E.28.a.35.10, E.22.b.05.05, E.22.b.35.12, E.23.a.05.12, E.23.a.02.32, E.16.38.20, E.17.a.15.25. Two posts were lost at E.17.c.10.05, E.23.a.15.90.

S.O.S. Lines based on this front line were arranged with Infy. Bde. Commanders.

Harassing night fire was put down on roads etc and trench being dug K.11.a.1.6 to K.11.a.3.3.

5th. D.A. ordered at 10-30 p.m. new South boundary E - W Grid Line between K.11. and K.17.

April 15th. 8. During the day batteries carried out sniping of movement.

1-15 p.m. Brigades fired bursts on movement on N - S road in K.5.b & d.

7-55 p.m. enemy concentration at K.5.b.2.7 engaged with 10 rounds G.F. from 152nd. Bde.

Prisoners captured morning 16th. stated 200 enemy preparing to attack were caught by this fire and broken up.

At request of Infantry this was repeated at midnight.

12-55 p.m. Liaison Officer with 2nd. Aust. Infy. Bde. reported line of posts K.4.c.5.8 - K.4.a.45.40 - E.28.c.50.10 - E.28.c.60.40 - E.28.c.30.75 - E.28.a.60.65 - E.28.a.60.90.

Harassing fire was kept up during the night.

From 6 p.m. the 34th. D.A. was reorganised into 2 subgroups forming a group under 5th. Division but covering the front on either side of the Army junction (See O.O. No. 1 attached).

April 16th. 9. Few "living" targets were observed . The enemy no longer exposed himself and no hostile sniping was reported. Enemy posts to hold about 8 men each have been dug in depth.

152nd. Bde. RFA. put down demonstration fire in support of operations carried out by the French on the Left.

10 rounds G.F. from 2 batteries were fired on much movement in K.12.a & c at 5-40 p.m.

Harassing fire was maintained.

O.C. 79th. Bde. RGA. reported to C.R.A. 34th. Division under whose control the Brigade passed as it came into action.

<u>8-50 p.m.</u> 174th. Siege Battery reported in action D.22.a.75.55.

<u>10-5 p.m.</u> 14th. Siege Battery " " " D.21.d.4.3(3 Hows) D.21.d.48.50 (3 Hows).

C.R.A. 5th. Division subsequently ordered this Brigade to fire mainly on the XI Corps front and to take up S.O.S. lines between S of K.16 and K.17 and VIERHOUCK.

New Zones were allotted to Groups from 6 p.m. (See O.O.No.2 attached).

April 17th. 10. 9-50 a.m. S.O.S. reported E.11.b. and E.17.c. Left Group fired on S.O.S. lines.

79th. Bde. RGA bombarded road junctions E.17.d.8.0, E.24.a.1.4 and road F.13.a.5.3 to MERRIS.

Concentrations were fired by Divisional Artillery and 79th. Bde. RGA. during the day on :-

(1) LA COURONNE - POINT RONDIN road (152 Bde fired 700 rds on this target during the day)
(2) Hostile batteries reported on road F.13 - VIEUX BERQUIN.
(3) Cross Roads K.6.b.
(4) VIERHOUCK and VIERHOUCK -VERTE RUE road.
(5) Road junction L.13.b.

Harassing fire by night and during bad observation continued.

During evening the two 60-pdr Btys of 79th. Bde. RGA came into action as follows:- 1/1 Essex H.B. D.21.d.9.1.
142nd. H.B. D.27.b.08.89.

S E C R E T. Copy No. 28.

34th. DIVISIONAL ARTILLERY OPERATION ORDER No. 1.

15th. April 1918.

1. From 6 p.m. 15th. inst the 34th. Divisional Artillery will consist of two Groups covering the front on either side of the boundary between the XI and XV Corps.

2. The Right Group (160th. Bde. RFA) will cover the Left Front of the Left Brigade 5th. Division (at present 95th. Infantry Bde, H.Q. J.L.a.5.3.)
The Left Group (152nd. Bde. RFA) will cover the Right Front of the Right Brigade 1st. Australian Division (at present 2nd Aust. Infy. Bde. H.Q. D.24.a.8.1.)

3. The following will be Group Boundaries:-
Right Group - South Boundary.
K.14.b.00.35 to L.19.a.0.5.
Left Group - North Boundary.
E.22.c.00.50 to F.25.a.00.00.
Inter-Group Boundary.
Corps Boundary K.5.c.00.95 to L.7.a.0.0.

4. Groups of 34th. D.A. will arrange for their S.O.S. Barrage to extend for 100 yards S. in the case of Right Group and 100 yds N. in the case of Left Group of their outer flank boundaries. The junction of the barrage on the inter-group boundary will be checked under arrangements to be made between Group Commanders.

5. Liaison. O.C. Right Group will detail an Officer to be at H.Q. 95th. Infy. Bde. Direct telephone lines will be maintained from Groups as follows (to be arranged by O.C. 34th. D.A. Signal Detmt).
Right Group (1) to 95th. Infy. Bde (2) to Left Group 5th D.A. 27th. Bde. RFA. H.Q. J.11.a.9.8.
Left Group. (1) to Arty. Liaison Officer with 2nd Aust. Infy. Bde (2) to 11?th. Army Bde. RFA (H.Q. D.10.d.5.5.)
In addition lateral communication will be maintained between Groups of 34th. Div. Arty.

6. S.O.S.
The exact line for the S.O.S. Barrage will be arranged between Group Commanders and G.Os.C. Infantry Brigades (in the case of 152nd. Bde. RFA the S.O.S. line will be communicated to O.C. 152nd. Brigade by Arty. Liaison Officer with 2nd. Aust. Infy. Bde.
The line so arranged will be communicated to 34th. R.A.H.Q.
The following are the S.O.S. Signals :-
XI Corps Front. Succession of GREEN Very lights until answered.
1st. Aust. Div. Front. As above until 8 p.m. 15th. inst when it will be changed to Rifle Grenade bursting into RED over GREEN over YELLOW.

7. All batteries will answer all "LL" calls within their range with 10 rounds Gun Fire.
Zones for "GF" calls are allotted as follows:-
Right Group. S. Boundary. E and W Grid Line through K.15 and K.18. central.
Left Group. N. Boundary. E and W Grid Line through E.22.c.0.0. and F.19.c.0.0.

8. ACKNOWLEDGE.

[signature]
Major,
Brigade Major. R.A.
34th. Divisional Artillery.

Issued at 6 p.m.
Distribution overleaf.....

Copy: 1-5. 152 Bde. RFA.
6-10. 160th. "
11-14. 1st. Aust Div. Arty.
15-18. 5th. D.A.
19. R.A. XI Corps.
20. R.A. XV Corps
21. B.G.R.A. 34th. Div.
22. Signal Officer 34th. D.A.
23-24. War Diary.
25. File.
26-28. Spare.

S E C R E T. Copy No. 28.

34th. DIVISIONAL ARTILLERY OPERATIONORDER No. 2.

16th. April 1918.

1. From 6 p.m. to-night 16th. inst, the Group boundaries of 34th. Divisional Artillery will be readjusted as follows:-

Right Group Southern Boundary will be E. & W. Grid Line between K.10. and K.16. squares.
Inter-Group Boundary E. & W. line through K.4.c.8.4. (le CORNET PERDU inclusive to Left Group)
Left Group North Boundary E. & W. line through SECLIN (K.22.c.0.5)

2. The point of junction for Group S.O.S. Barrages will be K.4.d.4.4.

3. The Right Sub-sector is covered by 160th. Brigade RFA only, no Brigade of 5th. D.A. being super-imposed.

4. Zones for "GF" etc calls will be as follows:-
Right Group Southern Boundary as above. NorthernBoundary E. & W. Grid Line through K.4.central.
Left Group Southern Boundary E. & W. Grid Line through K.4.central.
NorthernBoundary E. & W. Grid Line between K.23. and K.29. squares.

5. Liaison will remain as in Operation Order No 1. of 15-4-18.

6. ACKNOWLEDGE (by wire)

[signature]
Major,
Brigade Major.R.A.
34th. Divisional Artillery.

Issued at 4-15 p.m.

Copy: 1-5 152nd. Bde. RFA.
6-10 160th. Bde. RFA.
11-14 1st. Aust D.A.
15-18 5th. D.A.
19 R.A. XI Corps
20 R.A. XV Corps
21 C.C.R.A. 34th. Div.
22 Signal Officer 34th. D.A.
23-24 War Diary.
25 File
26-28 Spare.

AMMUNITION EXPENDED BY 34th. DIVISIONAL ARTILLERY.

	18-Pdr.	4.5"How.
3 p.m. 9th. to 12 noon 10th.	2400	350
12 noon 10th. " " " 11th.	3300	550
" " 11th. " " " 12th.	5700	515
" " 12th. " " " 13th.	3000	900
" " 13th. " " " 14th.	8200	2100
" " 14th. " " " 15th.	7000	1700
" " 15th. " " " 16th.	3500	1050
" " 16th. " " " 17th.	3800	1050
" " 17th. " " " 18th.	4000	1200.

Ammunition was drawn from undermentioned places between following times:-

DOULIEU CHURCH from afternoon 9th. to afternoon of 10th.

VIEUX BERQUIN " " 10th. " " " 11th.

STRAZEELE " " 11th. " night " 12th.

GRAND HASARD " morning 13th. " afternoon " 17th.

MORBECQUE " 17th. to date.

-.-.-.-.-.-.-.-.-

All Ammunition was brought up to Gun Positions by D.A.C. and Battery Ammunition Wagons.

Detail of Moves of 160th. Brigade RFA. from 9th. to 14th. April 1918 inclusive.

April 9th. Brigade went into action at 2-30 p.m. in support of 149th. and 150th. Infantry Brigades.

B.H.Q. G.3.b.5.8.
A/160 G.14.b.2.8.
B/160 G.14.c.6.4.
C/160 G.8.d.7.3.
D/160 G.14.a.1.3.

7 p.m. C/160 moved to G.3.a.5.8.
D/160 " " G.3.a.8.2.
11 p.m. A/160 " " A.26.c.8.0.
B/160 " " G.3.d.0.4.

April 10th. 1-30 a.m. B.H.Q. moved to F.27.b.2.4.

1-30 a.m. to 5-0 a.m.
(A/160 moved to L.5.c.5.0.
(B/160 " " L.11.b.1.3.
(C/160 " " G.1.d.4.2.
(D/160 " " L.4.b.0.3.

4 p.m. to 6 p.m.
(A/160 moved to F.27.d.7.0.
(B/160 " " L.4.a.8.4.
(C/160 " " L.4.b.5.5.

April 11th. 9 a.m. to 12 noon.
(B.H.Q. moved to F.19.b.8.9.
(B/160 " " F.26.d.6.1.
(C/160 " " F.27.a.6.9.
(D/160 " " F.26.d.5.5.

6 p.m. to 8 p.m.
(B.H.Q. moved to E.15.b.4.8.
(A/160 " " E.29.d.4.5.
(B/160 " " E.22.b.5.3.
(C/160 " " E.16.a.6.4.
(D/160 " " E.16.a.2.3.

10-30 p.m. A/160 " " E.9.c.6.3.

April 12th. 4 p.m. to 6 p.m.
(B.H.Q. moved to D.6.d.0.7.
(A/160 " " E.7.c.5.4.
(B/160 " " E.8.b.4.2.
(C/160 " " D.12.c.2.8.
(D/160 " " D.18.b.8.2.

April 13th. 6 a.m. to 8 a.m.
(B.H.Q. moved to D.16.b.4.8.
(B/160 " " D.18.d.0.6.
(C/160 " " D.24.b.6.7.

Detail of moves of 152nd. Brigade RFA. from 9th. to 14th. April inclusive.

April 9th. Brigade went into action at 3-15 p.m. in support of 151st. Infantry Brigade:-

B.H.Q. L.11.d.1.1.
A/152. L.17.d.3.8.
B/152. L.17.d.5.9.
C/152. L.16.d.3.4.
D/152. L.16.c.8.6.

and remained there until

" 10th. 7 a.m. B.H.Q. moved to L.9.d.6.0.
2 a.m. A/152 " " L.10.c.3.9.
6 a.m. B/152 " " L.9.b.6.6.
7 a.m. C/152 " " L.9.b.2.5.
8 a.m. D/152 " " L.9.c.2.4.

" 11th. 1-30 p.m. B.H.Q. moved to L.9.b.2.5.
2-0 p.m. A/152. " " K.17.a.9.9.
3 -0 p.m. B/152 " " K.12.a.1.2.
5-0 p.m. C/152 " " K.12.a.5.3.
4 p.m. D/152 " " K.18.central.

4 p.m. B.H.Q. moved to K.10.d.5.7. Very soon afterwards batteries retired again between 5 and 7 p.m. to:-
A.Bty.E.27.d.8.2. C.Bty. K.4.c.1.5.
B. " K.4.c.3.7. D. " K.4.c.3.8.
At 8 p.m. B.H.Q. moved to E.28.d.1.3. FME BEAULIEU.

" 12th. 1 a.m. B/152 moved to E.22.c.9.1.
4 a.m. C/152 " " and bivouaced in E.22.a. and want into action in E.16.c.8.2. at 8 a.m. (13th inst)
4 a.m. D/152 moved to and bivouaced in E.22.a. and went into action in E.22.c.4.2. at 8 a.m.
4 p.m. B.H.Q. moved to E.22.a.3.2.

Between 4 p.m. and 6 p.m. batteries moved back in turn as follows:-
A/152 E.19.d.2.8.
B/152 E.20.a.8.8.
C/152 E.20.b.2.9.
D/152 E.20.c.3.9.
9 p.m. B.H.Q. moved to LE TIR ANGLAIS, D.17.c.5.9.

" 13th. Between 5 p.m. and 8 p.m. batteries moved in turn as follows:-
A. Bty. D.28.b.8.8. C. Bty. D.23.b.8.7.
B. " D.23.a.1.1. D " D.23.b.8.1.

" 14th. 6 p.m. C/152 moved to D.23.a.1.1. alongside B/152.

War Diary App VIII

S E C R E T.

34th. DIVISIONAL ARTILLERY OPERATION ORDER No. 1.

15th. April 1918.

1. From 6 p.m. 15th. inst the 34th. Divisional Artillery will consist of two Groups covering the front oneither side of the boundary between the XI and XV Corps.

2. The Right Group (160th. Bde. RFA) will cover the Left Front of the Left Brigade 5th. Division (At present 95th. Infantry Bde, H.Q. J.5.a.5.3.)
The Left Group (152nd. Bde. RFA) will cover the Right Front of the Right Brigade 1st. AustralianDivision (At present 2nd Aust. Infy. Bde. H.Q. D.24.a.8.1.)

3. The following will be Group Boundaries:-
Right Group - South Boundary.
K.14.b.00.35 to L.19.a.0.8.
Left Group - North Boundary.
L.22.c.00.50 to F.25.a.00.00.
Inter-Group Boundary.
Corps Boundary K.3.c.00.95 to L.7.a.0.0.

4. Groups of 34th. D.A. will arrange for their S.O.S. Barrage to extend for 100 yards S. in the case of Right Group and 100 yds N.in the case of Left Group of their outer flank boundaries. The junction of the barrage on the inter-group boundary will be checked under arrangements to be made betweenGroup Commanders.

5. Liaison. O.C. Right Group will detail an Officer to be at H.Q. 95th. Infy. Bde. Direct telephone lines will be maintained from Groups as follows (to be arranged by O.C. 34th. D.A. Signal Detmt).
Right Group (1) to 95th. Infy. Bde (2) to Left Group 5th D.A. 27th. Bde. RFA. H.Q. J.11.a.9.8.
Left Group. (1) to Arty. Liaison Officer with 2nd Aust. Infy. Bde (2) to 119th. Army Bde. RFA (H.Q. D.10.d.6.5.)
In addition lateral communication will be maintained between Groups of 34th. Div. Arty.

6. S.O.S.
The exact line for the S.O.S. Barrage will be arranged between Group Commanders and G.Os.C. Infantry Brigades (in the case of 152nd. Bde. RFA the S.O.S. line will be communicated to O.C. 152nd. Brigade by Arty. Liaison Officer with 2nd. Aust. Infy. Bde.
The line so arranged will be communicated to 34th. R.A.H.Q.
The following are the S.O.S. Signals :-
XI Corps Front. Succession of GREEN Very lights until answered.
1st. Aust. Div. Front. As above until 9 p.m. 15th. inst when it will be changed to Rifle Grenade bursting into RED over GREEN over YELLOW.

7. All batteries will answer all "LL" calls withintheir range with 10 rounds Gun Fire.
Zones for "GF" calls are allotted as follows:-
Right Group. S. Boundary. E and W Grid Line through K.15 and K.18. central.
Left Group. N. Boundary. E and W Grid Line through E.22.c.0.0. and F.19.c.0.0.

8. ACKNOWLEDGE.

[signature]
Major,
Brigade Major. R.A.
34th. Divisional Artillery.

Issued at 6 p.m.

Distribution overleaf....

Copy: 1-5. 152 Bde. R.A.
6-10. 160th. " "
11-14. 1st. Aust Div. Arty.
15-18. 5th. D.A.
19. R.A. XI Corps.
20. R.A. XV Corps
21. S.C.R.A. 34th. Div.
22. Signal Officer 34th. Div.
23-24. War Diary.
25. File.
26-28. Spare.

App IX

S E C R E T.   Copy No. 23

34th. DIVISIONAL ARTILLERY OPERATION ORDER No. 2.

16th. April 1918.

1. From 8 p.m. to-night 16th. inst, the Group boundaries of 34th. Divisional Artillery will be readjusted as follows:-

<u>Right Group Southern Boundary</u> will be E. & W. Grid Line between K.10. and K.16. squares.
<u>Inter-Group Boundary</u> E. & W. line through K.4.c.2.4. (le CORNET PERDU inclusive to Left Group)
<u>Left Group North Boundary</u> E. & W. line through SECLIN (K.22.c.0.3)

2. The point of junction for Group S.O.S. Barrages will be K.4.d.4.4.

3. The Right Sub-sector is covered by 160th. Brigade RFA. only, no Brigade of 5th. D.A. being super-imposed.

4. Zones for "GF" etc calls will be as follows:-
<u>Right Group</u> Southern Boundary as above. Northern Boundary E. & W. Grid Line through K.4.central.
<u>Left Group</u> Southern Boundary E. & W. Grid Line through K.4.central. Northern Boundary E. & W. Grid Line between [illegible] and E.29. squares.

5. Liaison will remain as in Operation Order No 1. of 15-4-18.

6. ACKNOWLEDGE (by wire)

[signature]
Major,
Brigade Major.R.A.
34th. Divisional Artillery.

Issued at 4-15 p.m.

Copy: 1-5 152nd. Bde. RFA.
6-10 160th. Bde. RFA.
11-14 1st. Aust D.A.
15-18 5th. D.A.
19 R.A. XI Corps
20 R.A. XV Corps
21 C.R.A. 34th. Div.
22 Signal Officer 34th. D.A.
23-24 War Diary.
25 File
26-28 Spare .

APP X

S E C R E T. Ref. Sheet 36A.

34th. DIVISIONAL ARTILLERY LOCATION STATEMENT.

17th. April 1918.

Unit	Location.	Front covered.	WagonLines.
H.Q. 34th. D.A.	D.14.b.2.5.	K.9.d.4.0-E.22.d.2.3.	
Right Group.			
160th.Bde.RFA.	D.16.b.5.8.	K.9.d.4.0-K.4.c.7.4.	
A/160.	E.7.c.4.5.		C.16.d.3.2.
B/160.	D.16.d.9.6.		C.16.d.9.9.
C/160.	D.24.b.6.8.		C.16.b.4.5.
D/160.	D.16.b.8.1.		C.16.d.9.9.
Left Group.			
152nd.Bde.RFA.	D.17.c.5.8.	K.4.c.7.4-E.22.d.2.3.	
A/152.	D.28.b.8.8.		C.22.b.1.6.
B/152.	D.23.a.0.0.		C.23.b.0.9.
C/152.	D.23.a.2.2.		C.23.b.1.5.
D/152.	D.24.c.6.7.		C.23.c.1.9.
79th. Bde.RGA. (attached)	D.14.b.0.4.	S of E & W Grid Line through F.25.c.0.0.	
14th.Siege Bty. 6-6" Hows.	D.21.d.5.5(3) D.21.d.4.3(3)		
174th.Siege Bty 6-6" Hows.	D.22.a.6.5.		
1st S Essex H.B. 6-60 prs	D.21.d.9.1.		C.11.c.7.3.
142nd. H.B. 6-60 prs	D.27.b.1.9.		C.30.a.6.1.
38th. D.A.C.			D.14.c.3.1.
A.R.P.	D.14.c.8.4.		

[signature]

Major,
Brigade Major.R.A.
34th. Divisional Artillery.

Distribution.: 152nd. Bde. RFA (6)
160th. " " (6)
79th. B.A.G. (6)
5th. D.A. (2)
1st. A.D.A. (2)
RA, XI Corps (2)
RA, XV Corps (2)
S.C.R.A. (1)
War Diary (2)
File (1)
Spare (2)

App XI

SECRET. REF. Sheet 36A.

34th. DIVISIONAL ARTILLERY LOCATION STATEMENT.

22nd. April 1918.

Unit	Location	Front covered	Wagon Lines.
H.Q. 34th D.A.	D.14.b.2.5.	K.9.d.4.0-E.28.a.54.60.	
Right Group.			
160th.Bde.RFA.	D.16.b.5.8.	K.9.d.4.0-K.4.c.52.45.	
A/160.	J.5.a.9.5.		C.16.d.3.2.
B/160.	J.5.b.4.9.		C.16.d.9.9.
C/160.	D.28.b.8.8.		C.16.b.4.5.
D/160.	D.23.d.7.1.		C.16.d.9.9.
Left Group.			
152nd.Bde.RFA.	D.17.c.5.8.	K.4.c.52.45-E.28.a.54.60	
A/152.	D.24.b.42.75.		C.22.b.1.6.
B/152.	D.24.b.0.8.		C.23.b.0.9.
C/152.	D.23.b.8.7.		C.23.b.1.5.
D/152.	D.24.c.6.7.		C.23.c.1.9.
79th.Bde.RGA. (attached)	D.14.b.0.4.	S of E & W Grid Line through F.25.c.0.0.	
14th.Siege Bty. 6-6" Hows.	D.21.d.5.5.(3) D.21.d.4.3.(3)		
174th.Siege Bty. 6-6" Hows.	D.22.a.6.5.		
1st S Essex H.B. 6-60-pdrs.	D.21.d.9.1.(4) D.16.b.25.60(2)		C.11.c.7.3.
142nd. H.B. 6-60-pdrs.	D.27.b.1.9.		C.30.a.6.1.
38th. D.A.C.			C.18.b.5.9.
D.R.P.	D.14.c.8.4.		

[signature]
Major,
Brigade Major.R.A.
34th. Division al Artillery.

Distribution: 152 Bde RFA. (6)
160 Bde RFA. (6)
79th Bde RGA (6)
5th. D.A. (2)
57th.D.A. (2)
1st A.D.A. (2)
RA, XI Corps (2)
RA, XV Corps (2)
S.C.R.A. (1)
War Diary (2)
File (1)
Spare (2)

95/29

WAR DIARY. for. MAY. 1918.

34TH. DIVISIONAL ARTILLERY.

H.Q. R.A. 34. Div.
152nd. BRIGADE. R.F.A.
160th. BRIGADE. R.F.A.
34th. Div. Ammn. Col.
34th. Divl. T.Ms.

Instructions regarding War Diaries and Intelligence Summaries are contained in F. S. Regs., Part II. and the Staff Manual respectively. Title pages will be prepared in manuscript.

Army Form C. 2118.

WAR DIARY
or
~~INTELLIGENCE SUMMARY~~

(Erase heading not required.)

H.Q.R.A., 34th. Division.

Month of May, 1918.

Page 1.

Place	Date	Hour	Summary of Events and Information	Remarks and references to Appendices
	May			
LE GRAND HAZARD D.8.d. Sheet 36a.	1		Location Statement, vide --------	App. I.
do.	8		34th. D.A.C., H.-Qrs., and Nos. 1 and 2 Sections marched from POPERINGHE area, and relieved the 38th. D.A.C. at MORBECQUE, during the 7th. May and 8th. May.	
			No. 3 Section, 34th. D.A.C. remained under the control of the Headquarters, 34th. Division.	
	8		The 152nd. Brigade, R.F.A., was relieved in the line by the 38th. Army Brigade, R.F.A.,- 1 section per Battery on night 7th./8th. May, 2 sections per Battery on the morning of 8th. May.	
			During the 8th. May, the Brigade marched to rest area at WITTES (36a).	

(A7092). Wt. W12839/M1293. 75,000. 1/17. D. D. & L., Ltd. Forms/C.2118/14.

Army Form C. 2118.

Instructions regarding War Diaries and Intelligence Summaries are contained in F. S. Regs., Part II. and the Staff Manual respectively. Title pages will be prepared in manuscript.

WAR DIARY
or
INTELLIGENCE SUMMARY.

(*Erase heading not required.*)

H.Q.R.A., 34th. Division.

Month of May, 1918.

Place	Date	Hour	Summary of Events and Information	Remarks and references to Appendices
	May			
LE GRAND HAZARD	8		At 9 p.m., the control of the 160th. Brigade, R.F.A., in the line, was taken over by the C.R.A., 5th. Division.	
			The 5th. Divisional Artillery was organised as under:-	
			Right Group, 15th. Brigade, R.F.A., 84th. Army Brigade, R.F.A.,	
			Left Group, 27th. Brigade, R.F.A., 160th. Brigade, R.F.A. --------	App. II.
STEENBECQUE	9	10 am.	H.Q.R.A. moved to BRASSERIE, D.25.c.3.4 (36a).	
do.	10		34th. D.A.C. moved to STEENBECQUE area.	
			H.Q., I.5.b.5.3; No. 1 Section, I.5.a.9.8; No. 2 Section, C.30.c.4.4.	
do.	13		Headquarters, 34th. Division, moved from the POPERINGHE area to NIELLES-LEZ-BLEQUIN, (HAZEBROUCK 5A).	

(A7092). Wt. W12839/M1293. 750,000. 1/17. D. D. & L., Ltd. Forms/C.2118/14.

Army Form C. 2118.

Instructions regarding War Diaries and Intelligence Summaries are contained in F. S. Regs., Part II. and the Staff Manual respectively. Title pages will be prepared in manuscript.

WAR DIARY
or
INTELLIGENCE SUMMARY.
(Erase heading not required.)

H.Q.R.A., 34th. Division.

Month of May, 1918. Page 3.

Place	Date	Hour	Summary of Events and Information	Remarks and references to Appendices
	May			
STEENBECQUE	16		The 152nd. Brigade, R.F.A., relieved the 27th. Brigade, R.F.A. (5th. Division) in the line on the nights 14th./15th. May and 15th./16th. May. One Section per Battery relieved on the first night, and two Sections per Battery on second night.	
			A/152 relieved 119th. Battery at D.30.c.2.2,	
			B/152 ,, 120th. ,, ,, J.5.c.3.0,	
			C/152 ,, 121st. ,, ,, J.10.b.6.0,	
			D/152 ,, 37th. ,, ,, J.11.c.0.5, ----------	App.III.
do.	16		Location Statement, ---------	App.IV.
do.	21		5th. Divisional Artillery concentration, vide ---------	App. V.
do.	22		H.Q.R.A. moved to C.30.b.5.2 (36a).	
	27		H.Q.R.A. moved to C.29.d.4.0 (36a).	
	31		Congratulations received by 34th. Divisional Artillery, vide ---------	App.VI.

C Thompson
Lieutenant, R.A.,
for C.R.A., 34th. Division.

(A7092). Wt. W12839/M1293. 75 ,0.0. 1/17. D. D. & L., Ltd. Forms/C.2118 14.

APP I

SECRET.

Ref Sheet 36A.

34th. DIVISIONAL ARTILLERY LOCATION STATEMENT.

1st. May 1918.

Unit	Location	Front covered	Wagon Lines.
H.Q. 34th. D.A.	D.14.b.2.5.	K.9.d.4.0-E.22.d.0.1.	@
Right Group.			
160th.Bde.RFA.@	D.22.c.10.90.	K.9.d.4.0-K.4.c.52.45.	
A/160. @	J.5.a.7.3.		C.16.d.3.2.
B/160. @	J.5.b.0.6.		C.16.d.9.9.
C/160.	D.28.b.8.8.		C.18.c.1.1. @
D/160.	D.23.d.7.1.		C.16.d.9.9.
Left Group.			
152nd.Bde.RFA.@	D.16.b.45.86.	K.4.c.5 2.45-E.22.d.0.2.	@@
A/152. @	D.24.b.44.72.		C.22.b.1.6.
B/152. @	D.18.c.72.10.		C.23.b.0.9.
C/152. @	D.23.b.80.82.		C.23.d.8.1.
D/152.	D.24.c.6.7.		C.23.c.1.9.
38th. D.A.C.			C.18.b.5.9.
A.R.P.	D.14.c.9.4.		

@ Alterations since issue d/22-4-18.

Percy Knowles [signature]
Major,
Brigade Major.R.A.
34th. Divisional Artillery.

152 Bde RFA (6)
160 Bde RFA (6)
79 Bde RGA (6)
5th. D.A. (2)
57th D.A. (2)
1st A.D.A. (2)
RA, XI Corps (2)
RA, XV Corps (2)
S.S.R.A. (1)
War Diary (2)
File (1)

SECRET. 5th Divisional Artillery No. HBM/ 39/1.

App II

1. From 9.0 P.M. on May 8th, 160th Brigade R.F.A. will form a Sub-group under Lieut. Colonel BERKELEY. D.S.O. Commanding 27th Brigade R.F.A.

2. From 9.0 P.M. May 8th, the Field Artillery covering the 5th Division front will be grouped as follows :-

RIGHT GROUP. H.Q. J.26.a 6/0.	- Lieut. Col. HAWKES. D.S.O. 15th Brigade R.F.A. 84th Army Brigade RFA.
LEFT GROUP. H.Q. J.9.d 8/4.	- Lieut. Col. BERKELEY. D.S.O. 27th Brigade R.F.A. 160th Brigade R.F.A.

3. On withdrawal to Wagon Lines, 152nd Brigade R.F.A. will be prepared to come into action to cover the Left/Inf. Brigade 5th Division, and will be kept in readiness to move at 2 hours notice.

4. Acknowledge. 241

Headquarters.
R.A. 5 Divn.
7th May, 1918.

[signature]
Major R.A.
Brigade Major Royal Artillery 5th Division.

Copies to :- 34th Divnl Art'y.
160th Brigade RFA.
27th -----"------
15th -----"------
84th -----"------
V Div G
RA XI Corps

-----------X-X-X-X-X-X-X-X-----------

160 Bde.

For information.

H.Q. RA. 34th Div will close at LE GRAND HASARD on the ~~afternoon~~ morning of the 9th and will be established at C.30 d. 8.1. but will not exercise tactical control after 9 p.m. 8th.

152 Bde. are moving to rest billets in WITTES area. on evening of 8th & morning of 9th.

0/393/1

App III

5th Divisional Artillery No. HBM/29/3.

SECRET.

1. 84th Army Brigade R.F.A. will march from present Wagon Lines at 9.0 A.M. May 16th, under Orders of O.C. 84th Army Brigade, to the Rest Billets vacated by 152nd Brigade R.F.A. at WITTES.

2. 152nd Brigade R.F.A. Wagon Lines will move to 27th Brigade R.F.A. present Wagon Lines at 9.0 A.M. May 16th., under Orders of O.C. 152nd Brigade R.F.A.

3. 27th Brigade R.F.A. Wagon Lines will move to 84th Army Brigade R.F.A. Wagon Lines at 9.0 A.M. May 16th., under Orders of O.C. 27th Brigade R.F.A.

4. Acknowledge.

J Wallace
Major R.A.

Headquarters.
R.A. 5 Divn.
15th May, '18.

Brigade Major R.A. 5th Division.

Copies to :- 84th Army Brigade RFA.
27th Brigade RFA.
152nd Brigade RFA (Left Group).
34th Div. Arty.
5th Division 'G'.
" 'Q'.
XI Corps R.A.
15th Brigade RFA.

SECRET.   34th.Div.Arty.No. 0/395.

Arw

O.C. 152nd. Brigade RFA.

Reference 5th. Divisional Artillery No. HBM/29/2.

1. On the 14th. and 15th. gun teams only will march to the 27th. Brigade Wagon Lines.

2. The 27th. Brigade RFA are vacating their Wagon Lines on the morning of the 16th. inst., when the 152nd. Brigade RFA will take them over.

3. The following are the locations:-

119th.	Battery	Wagon	Lines......	I.5.c.5.4.
120th.	,,	,,	,, ...	I.12.a.3.5.
121st.	,,	,,	,, ...	~~I.7.c.9.4.~~ I.6.c.9.4.
37th.	,,	,,	,, ...	I.5.d.6.5.

G. Thompson Lt
for. Major,
Brigade Major.R.A.
34th. Divisional Artillery.

14th. May 1918.

Copies to:- 5th. Div. Arty.
O.C. No. 1 Coy. Train 34th. Divn.
S.C.R.A. 34th. Divn.

SECRET. 5th Divisional Artillery No.HBM/29/2.

34 Divl Arty

Bar

1. 84th Army Brigade R.F.A. will be withdrawn to Wagon Lines :-
   152nd Brigade, R.F.A. will relieve 27th Brigade R.F.A.
   27th.Brigade, R.F.A. will relieve 84th. Army Bde. R.F.A.

2. Reliefs will take place on the nights 14th/15th. May and 15th/16th. May, one section per battery being relieved on the first night and two sections per battery on the 2nd. night. On each night sections of 27th. Brigade will not move to relieve sections 84th. Brigade until they have been relieved by sections 152nd. Brigade. Reliefs by 152nd. Brigade batteries will be completed not later than 10-30p.m.

3. Reliefs will be as follows -

A/152.	relieves	119th.	119th.	relieves	A/84.
B/152.	"	120th.	120th.	"	B/84.
C/152.	"	121st.	121st.	"	C/84.
D/152.	"	37th.	37th.	"	D/84.

Hqrs. 152 Bde. relieves Hqrs. 27th. Bde.
Hqrs. 27th. Bde. relieves Hqrs. 84th. Bde.

4. On completion of relief the artillery covering the 5th. Division Front will be grouped as follows -

RIGHT GROUP. Lieut-Col. HAWKES, D.S.O., 15th. Brigade R.F.A.
15th. Brigade R.F.A.
27th. Brigade R.F.A.

LEFT GROUP. Lieut-Col. ALLCARD, D.S.O., 152nd. Brigade R.F.A.
152nd. Brigade R.F.A.
160th. Brigade R.F.A.

5. Command of battery positions will pass on completion of reliefs. Command of LEFT Group will pass to Lieut-Col. ALLCARD at 6 p.m. May 15th.

6. All photographs, intelligence maps, artillery boards, ammunition, back positions etc. will be handed over to relieving units.

7. Positions at present are -

27th. Brigade R.F.A.	Hqrs.	J.9.d.8/5.	
	119th.Bty.	D.30.c.2/2.	
	120th Bty.	J.5.c.3/0.	
	121st Bty,	J.10.b.6/0.	(4 guns)
		J.12.a.3/7.	(2 guns)
	37th Bty.	J.11.c.0/5.	
84th Army Bde.R.F.A.	Hqrs.	J.26.b.45/50.	
	A/84 Bty.	J.33.c.9/8.	
	B/84 Bty.	P.5.b.3/8.	
	C/84 Bty.	J.29.c.6/8.	
	D/84 Bty.	J. 15.d 6/6.	(4 Hows.)
		J.10.c.9/4.	(2 Hows.)

J Wallace
Major, R.A.
14th May, 1918. Brigade Major, 5th Divisional Artillery.

Copies to:-

34th Divisional Artillery	(8 copies)
27th Brigade, R.F.A.	(5 ---"---)
84th Army Bde.R.F.A.	(5 ---"---)
15th Brigade, R.F.A.	(1 copy)

App IV

SECRET.

Ref: Sheet 36A.

34th. DIVISIONAL ARTILLERY LOCATION STATEMENT.

16th. May 1918.

Unit	Location.	Wagon Lines.
H.Q. 34th. D.A.	D.25.c.3.4.	
152nd. Bde. RFA.	J.9.d.8.5.	
A/152.	D.30.c.2.2.	I.5.c.5.4.
B/152. (5 guns)	J.5.c.3.0.	I.12.a.3.5.
(1 gun)	K.14.b.3.7.	
C/152. (4 guns)	J.10.b.8.0.	I.6.c.9.4.
(2 ")	J.12.a.3.7.	
D/152.	J.11.c.0.5.	I.5.d.6.5.
160th. Bde. RFA.	D.22.c.1.9.	
A/160.	J.5.a.66.29.	C.16.d.3.2.
B/160.	J.5.a.90.49.	C.16.d.9.9.
C/160.	D.28.b.45.32.	C.28.d.9.4.
D/160. (4 Hows)	J.5.b.38.78.	C.16.d.9.9.
(2 Hows)	D.23.d.51.11.	
34th.D.A.C., H.Q.		I.5.b.5.3.
No. 1 Section.		I.5.a.9.8.
No. 2 Section.		C.30.c.4.4.
A.R.P.	C.30.d.0.6.	
No. 1 Coy. Train, 34th. Divn.	I.15.a.1.9.	

G Thompson Lt.
for Major,
Brigade Major.R.A.
34th. Divisional Artillery.

Distribution:-

152nd .Bde.RFA	(6)	S.C.R.A.	(1)
160th " "	(6)	5th. D.A.	(2)
34th. D.A.C.	(4)	War Diary	(2)
No. 1 Coy.Train	(1)	File	(1)

App V
P.C.W.

5th Divisional Artillery No. HBM/15/28.

SECRET.

Reference 5th Divnl Art'y No. HBM/15/24 of 15 instant.

para. 1 (h)

Concentration (h) will take place at 2.0 A.M. May 20th and not at 3.30 A.M.

J. Wallace
Major R.A.
Brigade Major R.A. 5th Division.

Headquarters.
R.A. 5 Divn.
19th May, 1918.

COPIES TO :- Recipients of
5th D.A. HBM/15/24.

34 DA.

5th Divisional Artillery No. HBM/15/25.

SECRET.

Reference No. HBM/15/24 para. 1(c)

For "K.21.b 0/2"

Read "K.21.b 85/95".

J. F. Wallace
Major R.A.
Brigade Major R.A. 5th Division.

Headquarters.
R.A. 5th Division.
15th May, 1918.

COPIES TO:- Recipients of HBM/15/24.

5th Divisional Artillery No. HBM/15/24. SECRET.

1. Concentrations will be carried out as follows :-

(a) May 16th. 4.30p.m. Trench from K.21.b 4/4 to K.21.c 7/9. Junction of Groups K.21.b 0/2.

(b) May 17th. 3.15a.m. Left Group. Trench K.26.d 2/5 - K.26.c 6/3.
Right Group. Trench K.32.a 3/7 - K.31.b 95/20.

(c) May 17th. 4.45p.m. Trench and shell-holes from K.16.c 3/3 to K.21.b 50/65. Junction of groups K.21.b 0/2.

(d) May 18th. 3.15a.m. Trench and wire K.16.a 0/9 - K.15.b 55/75 - K.15.b 7/5 - K.15.b 5/1. Junction of groups K.15.b 55/75.

(e) May 18th. 5.30p.m. Same as (b).

(f) May 19th. 3.40a.m. Same as (d).

(g) May 19th. 2.0 p.m. Area K.33.a 30/85 - K.33.a 9/9 - K.33.b 0/6 - K.33.a 4/4.

(h) May 20th. 3.30a.m. Same as (d).

2. 4.5" Howitzers will use 106 fuze for these Concentrations. 18pounders will use H.E.

3. Rates of fire :-

18-POUNDERS. 4 rounds per gun per minute.

4.5" HOWS. 2 rounds per gun per minute.

4. Each Concentration will last 5 minutes.

5. Each group will employ two 4.5" How. Batteries and two 18-pounder batteries for each concentration, except (b) and (e).

For (b) and (e) Left Group will employ two 4.5" How. batteries.

and Right Group will employ two 4.5" How. batteries and 4 18-Pdr batteries, of which latter two will be employed on the Left Group target.

6. Time will be sent out by telephone from these H.Q. 1½ hours before each concentration.

7. ACKNOWLEDGE.

Headquarters.
R.A. 5 Divn.
15th May, 1918.

J Wallace
Major R.A.
Brigade Major R.A. 5th Division.

DISTRIBUTION OF COPIES. :-

Left Group (10)	5th Division 'G' (1).
Right Group (10)	13th, 15th, 95th Inf. Bdes (1 each).
34th D.A. (1)	XI Corps R.A. (1).
CBSO XI Corps (1).	---"---- H.A. (1).

"A" Form. Army Form C. 2121.
(In pads of 100.)

MESSAGES AND SIGNALS.

No. of Message..............

Prefix........Code........m	Words.	Charge.	This message is on a/c of:	Recd. at ....m.
Office of Origin and Service Instructions.	Sent		..................Service.	Date..............
	At..........m.			From..............
	To..............			
	By..............		(Signature of "Franking Officer.")	By..............

TO 34th D.A. **App VI**

Sender's Number.	Day of Month.	In reply to Number.	AAA
* R.A. 139.	14th		

95th	Brigade	report	as
follows	aaa	The	barrage
put	down	by	the
152	Brigade	RFA	on
my	left	Battalion	front
this	morning	was	entirely
responsible	for	the	complete
failure	of	the	German
attack	It	was	splendid
aaa	The	G.O.C.	5th
Division	wishes	to	congratulate
the	152	Brigade	

From C.R.A. 5th Div.
Place
Time

The above may be forwarded as now corrected. (Z) [signature] B.G. C.R.A. 5th Div.

Censor. Signature of Addressor or person authorised to telegraph in his name.

* This line should be erased if not required.

(3796.) Wt. W 492/M1647. 650,000 Pads. 5/17. H. W. & V., Ld. (E. 1187.)

Headquarters,

34th Divisional Artillery.

The 31st Division has been mentioned in the Commander-in-Chief's despatches.

The Divisional Commander wishes you to inform the Officers and men of your Artillery, who were covering part of this Division's front on both occasions, that he considers their cooperation played a great part in gaining this honour.

W. H. Annesley

Lieut. Colonel,

25.4.18. A.A. & Q.M.G., 31st Division.

Headquarters,
31st. Division "Q"

34th. Divisional Artillery are most grateful to G.O.C., 31st. Division for the kind way he has associated them with the well deserved mention received by the Division.

The entente established between the 34th. D.A. and 31st. Division in March at AYETTE, more especially with the 4th. Guards Brigade, was renewed on April 11th. at LA MOTTE much to our gratification.

The confidence inspired in the Gunners by having such Infantry in front of them lightens our task immensely and all ranks will remember this happy association.

R.C. Walthall

Brigadier-General,
C.R.A., 34th. Division.

25-4-18.

34th.Div.Arty.No. G/605.

O.C. 152nd. Bde. RFA.
O.C. 160th. Bde. RFA.
34th. D.T.M.O.

The following extracts from a letter from G.O.C.,R.A. XVth. Corps to C.R.A. 34th. Division are circulated - "I am sending you a line to tell you how sorry we are to be losing you from this Corps. We should have been in a perilous state on April 9th. without your timely assistance and so would the 50th. Division. Your Brigades did splendid and valuable work and I only wish you were remaining with us".

C. Thompson Lt
for
Major,
Brigade Major.R.A.
34th. Divisional Artillery.

12-5-18.

Vol 35

WAR DIARY.

JUNE 1918.

Headquarters, 34th. DIVISIONAL ARTILLERY,

~~152nd. B~~rigade, ROYAL FIELD ARTILLERY,

~~160th. B~~rigade, ROYAL FIELD ARTILLERY,

~~34th. D~~IVISIONAL AMMUNITION COLUMN,

~~34th. D~~IVISIONAL TRENCH MORTARS.

Instructions regarding War Diaries and Intelligence Summaries are contained in F. S. Regs., Part II. and the Staff Manual respectively. Title pages will be prepared in manuscript.

WAR DIARY
or
INTELLIGENCE SUMMARY.
(Erase heading not required.)

Headquarters. R.A.
34th Division.

Army Form C. 2118.

Month of June 1918.

Page I.

Place	Date	Hour	Summary of Events and Information	Remarks and references to Appendices
STEENBECQUE. 36A. 1/40,000.	June 1.		Location Statement :- (Reference Sheet 36A.)	

		Location.	Wagon Lines.
H.Q. 3 4th D.A.		C.29.d.5.0.	
152nd Bde. R.F.A.	H.Q.	J.9.d.8.5.	
"A" Battery.		D.30.c.3.3.	I.5.c.5.4.
"B" "		J. 5.c.3.0.	I.12.a.3.5.
"C" "	4 guns.	J. 10.b.6.0.	
	2 "	J. 10.b.4.3.	I.6.a.9.4.
"D" "		J. 11.c.0.5.	I.5.d.6.5.
160th Bde. R.F.A.	H.Q.	D.22.c.1.9.	
"A" Battery.		J.5.a.66.29.	C.16.d.3.2.
"B" "		J.5.a.90.49.	C.16.d.9.9.
"C" "		D.28.b.6.5.	C.28.d.9.4.
"D" "	4 Hows;	J.5.b.38.78.	C.16.d.9.9.
	2 "	D.29.d.85.40.	
34th D.A.C.	H.Q.	I.5.b.5.3.	
No 1.Section.		I.5.a.9.8.	
No 2. "		C.30.c.4.4.	
A. R. P.		C.30.d.0.6.	
No 1.Coy,34th Div. Train.		I.15.a.1.9.	

During the month the Brigades in action remained under the command of the C.R.A.,5th Division.
The 5th Divisional Artillery was organised as under :-

Right Group.	15th Brigade R.F.A.	27th Brigade. R.F.A.
Left Group.	152nd Brigade.R.F.A.	160th Brigade. R.F.A.

C Thompson

Lieut. R.A.
for C.R.A.; 34th Division.

(A7092). Wt. W12839/M1293. 75,0.0. 1/17. D. D. & L., Ltd. Forms/C.2118/14.

~~HQ 34 D~~
HQ RA 34 D
9 WO 31
July 1918

WAR DIARY

H.Q.R.A. 34th Division.

152nd Brigade R.F.A.

160th Brigade R.F.A.

34th D.A.C.

D.T.M.O.

17

This file is only issued as a cover to
Army Form C 2118 (War Diary).

Army Form C. 2118.

Instructions regarding War Diaries and Intelligence Summaries are contained in F. S. Regs., Part II. and the Staff Manual respectively. Title pages will be prepared in manuscript.

WAR DIARY
or
INTELLIGENCE SUMMARY.

(Erase heading not required.)

Month of July, 1918.

Head Quarters, Royal Artillery, 34th. Division.

Page 1.

Place	Date	Hour	Summary of Events and Information	Remarks and references to Appendices
	1918 July			
STEENBECQUE (36a, 1/40000) C.29.d.	3rd.		The 34th. Divisional Artillery was relieved in the line by the 59th. Divisional Artillery. One section per battery was relieved on each night,- 1st./2nd. July, 2nd./3rd. July, 3rd./4th. July.	App. I
RUBROUCK (HAZEBROUCK - 5a, 1/100000)	4th.		34th. Divisional Artillery marched from Wagon Lines in STEENBECQUE area to billets in the RUBROUCK area.	
			Head-quarters, R.A., moved to RUBROUCK.	App. II
COUTHOVE Chateau. F.21.a. (27, 1/40000)	5th.		34th. Divisional Artillery marched from RUBROUCK to Wagon Lines in the HAANDEKOT area, E.4.d, Sheet 27.	
			Head-quarters, R.A., moved to COUTHOVE Chateau, F.21.a.	App.III
,,	6th.		One section per battery took up positions covering the EAST POPERINGHE or BLUE Line, as per	App.IV

(A7092). Wt. W12839/M1293 75,0.0. 1/17. D. D. & L., Ltd. Forms/C.2118/14.

Army Form C. 21

Instructions regarding War Diaries and Intelligence Summaries are contained in F. S. Regs., Part II. and the Staff Manual respectively. Title pages will be prepared in manuscript.

WAR DIARY
or
INTELLIGENCE SUMMARY.
(Erase heading not required.)

Month of July, 1918

H.Q.,R.A.,
34th. Division.

Place	Date	Hour	Summary of Events and Information	Remarks and references to Appendices
	July			
COUTHOVE Chateau. (27, F.21.a)	7		34th. Divisional Artillery Instructions No. 1; vide	App. V
,,	8		S.O.S. Lines for the Defence of the EAST POPERINGHE or BLUE Line; vide	App.VI
,,	10		G.O.C., 34th. Division, inspected the 152nd. Brigade, R.F.A., and the 160th. Brigade, R.F.A., in drill order; also the Trench Mortar Batteries in their Camp, 27,E.16.d.2.7.	
,,	11		30th. (American) Division relieved the 34th. (British) Division in the Defence of the EAST POPERINGHE Line.	
			The C.R.A., 3 4th. Division, established liaison with the 30th. (American) Division.	
,,	11		In the event of an enemy attack, and the occupation of the EAST POPERINGHE Line by the 30th. (American) Division, the C.R.A., 34th. Division, would command the artillery supporting the Division.	
,,	11		List of artillery positions to be occupied by British Artillery if the Belgian Army only be attacked; vide	App.VII
,,	11		34th. Division now in G.H.Q. Reserve; vide	App. X

(A7092). Wt. W12839/M1293. 75 ,000. 1/17. D. D. & L., Ltd. Forms/C.2118 14.

Instructions regarding War Diaries and Intelligence Summaries are contained in F. S. Regs., Part II. and the Staff Manual respectively. Title pages will be prepared in manuscript.

WAR DIARY
or
INTELLIGENCE SUMMARY.
(Erase heading not required.)

Army Form C. 2118.

Month of July, 1918.

H.Q., R.A.,
34th. Division.

Place	Date	Hour	Summary of Events and Information	Remarks and references to Appendices
	July			
COUTHOVE Chateau, (27, F.21.a)	12		34th. Divisional Artillery Instructions No. 2 issued;	App.VIII
,,	12		Provisional Orders for Entrainment whilst in G.H.Q. Reserve; vide	App. IX
,,	12		List of O.P.'s for the EAST POPERINGHE Line, ...	App. XII
,,	15		Orders for the 34th. Divisional Artillery to take part in the practice of the occupation of the WEST POPERINGHE Line; vide 34th. Divisional Artillery Operation Order No. 7; ...	App. XI
PROVEN	16		Head-quarters, R.A., entrained at PROVEN (Hazebrouck, 5a).	
SENLIS (BEAUVAIS - 1/100000)	17		Head-quarters, R.A., proceeded by train via DUNKIRK, CALAIS, BOULOGNE, NOYELLES, CHARS, PONTOIS, detrained at CHANTILLY, and marched to SENLIS (BEAUVAIS Sheet, 1/100000).	
,,	18		34th. Division came under the command of French Reserve Army.	

(A7092). Wt. W12839/M1293. 75,0:0. 1/17. D. D. & L., Ltd. Forms/C.2118/14.

Instructions regarding War Diaries and Intelligence Summaries are contained in F. S. Regs., Part II. and the Staff Manual respectively. Title pages will be prepared in manuscript.

Army Form C. 2118.

WAR DIARY
or
INTELLIGENCE SUMMARY.

(Erase heading not required.)

Month of July, 1918.

H.Q., R.A.,
34th. Division.

Sheet 4.

Place	Date	Hour	Summary of Events and Information	Remarks and references to Appendices
	July			
SENLIS	18		<u>LOCATION STATEMENT</u>:- (BEAUVAIS Sheet, 1/100000) H.Q., R.A., ... SENLIS. 152nd. Bde., R.F.A., ... VEMARS. 160th. Bde., R.F.A., ,,. LA CHAPELLE. 3 4th. D.A.C., ... SURVILLIERS.	
,,	19		H.Q., R.A., moved to LARGNY (SOISSONS Sheet, 1/100000). Brigades and D.A.C. marched to the area of FRESNOY (BEAUVAIS Sheet, 1/100000).	
LARGNY (SOISSONS - 1/80000)	20		During the night 20th./21st., Brigades and D.A.C. marched to area of LONGAVESNES and VIVIERES (SOISSONS, 1/80000)	App.XVII
VIVIERES (SOISSONS - 1/80000)	21		H.Q., R.A., moved from LARGNY to VIVIERES (SOISSONS, 1/80000).	
	22		160th. Brigade, No. 2 Section and S.A.A. Section, D.A.C., marched from LONGAVESNES and VIVIERES to Wagon Lines in the area of LONGPONT (SOISSONS, 1/80000)	App.XVIII

(A7092). Wt. W12839/M1293. 75,0.0. 1/17. D. D. & L., Ltd. Forms/C.2118/14.

Instructions regarding War Diaries and Intelligence Summaries are contained in F. S. Regs., Part II. and the Staff Manual respectively. Title pages will be prepared in manuscript.

WAR DIARY
or
INTELLIGENCE SUMMARY.
(Erase heading not required.)

Army Form C. 2118.

Month of July, 1918. H.Q., R.A., 34th. Division. Page 5.

Place	Date	Hour	Summary of Events and Information	Remarks and references to Appendices
	JULY			
VIVIERES	22		During the night, 22nd./23rd., under orders of the 38th. Divisional Artillery (French), the 160th. Brigade moved into action in positions covering the 34th. Division in the line in the TIGNY-HARTENNES Sector (OULCHY-LE-CHATEAU, 1/20000).	
,,	23		160th. Brigade, R.F.A., supported a minor attack by the 34th. Division.	
CHAVIGNY FARM (SOISSONS-1/80000)	23		H.Q., R.A., moved to CHAVIGNY Farm. 152nd. Brigade, No. 1 Section and Head-quarters, 34th. D.A.C., moved to Wagon Lines in the area of LONGPONT	App.XVIII
,,	23		During the night, 23rd./24th., 152nd. Brigade R.F.A., moved into action under orders of the 38th. (French) Divisional Artillery;	App.XVIII
,,	23		Artillery Organisation;	App.XIII
,,	25		34th. Division Location Statement;	App. XIX

(A7092). Wt. W12839/M1293. 750,000. 1/17. D. D. & L., Ltd. Forms/C.2118/14.

Army Form C. 2118.

WAR DIARY
or
INTELLIGENCE SUMMARY.
(Erase heading not required.)

Instructions regarding War Diaries and Intelligence Summaries are contained in F. S. Regs., Part II. and the Staff Manual respectively. Title pages will be prepared in manuscript.

Month of July, 1918.

H.Q., R.A., 34th. Division.

Place	Date	Hour	Summary of Events and Information	Remarks and references to Appendices
	July			
CHAVIGNY Farm	25	9 pm	C.R.A., 34th. Division assumed command of the artillery covering the 34th. Division, comprising:- 152nd. Brigade, R.F.A., 160th. Brigade, R.F.A., 41st. Regement of Artillery (French), 5e Groupe du 110 d'Artillerie (French).	App.XIV
,,	25		L'A.D./38 (French) came under orders of the 20th. C.A. No. 1 Groupe, 32/A.D. withdrew to the Wagon Lines.	App. XX
,,	26		Harassing night fire and counter-preparation orders;	App.XV
,,	26		Explanatory notes for use of French Meteor Wire;	App.XVI
,,	26		Warning Order No. 4;	App.XXI
,,	26		Heavy Artillery (French) supporting the 34th. Division;	App.XXII
,,	26		Preliminary orders for operations to be carried out by the 34th. Division as Right Division of 30th. Corps;	App.XXIV

Instructions regarding War Diaries and Intelligence Summaries are contained in F. S. Regs., Part II. and the Staff Manual respectively. Title pages will be prepared in manuscript.

WAR DIARY
or
INTELLIGENCE SUMMARY.

(Erase heading not required.)

Army Form C. 2118.

Month of July, 1918.

H.Q., R.A.,
34th. Division.

Page 7.

Place	Date	Hour	Summary of Events and Information	Remarks and references to Appendices
	July			
CHAVIGNY Farm	26		Heavy Artillery covering the 30th. Corps Front;	App.XXV
,,	27		Reconnaissances of routes to the new area;	App.XXIII
,,	27		Plan d'Emploi:	App.XXVI
,,	27		34th. Divisional Artillery was withdrawn from the line in the night 27th./28th., and moved to a position of concentration in the BUISSON DE HAUTWISON area;	App.XXVII
,,	27		34th. Division G.S./286/50;	App.XXVIII
,,	27		From the time of arrival in bivouac to-night all units are to be ready to move at an hour's notice;	App.XXIX
,,	27		The 3 4th. Division was relieved in the line by French troops on the night July 27th./28th.	App.XXX
,,	28		Reconnoitring of positions in the new area carried out;	App.XXXI
,,	28		34th. Divisional Artillery plan for the attack on July 29th.;	App.XXXII
,,	28		34th. Division instructions No. 1, and Operation Orders No. 237 and No. 238; ...	App.XXXIII

(A7092). Wt. W12839/M1293 75 ,o.o. 1/17. D. D. & L., Ltd. Forms/C.2118/14.

Army Form C. 2118.

WAR DIARY
or
INTELLIGENCE SUMMARY.
(Erase heading not required.)

Instructions regarding War Diaries and Intelligence Summaries are contained in F. S. Regs., Part II. and the Staff Manual respectively. Title pages will be prepared in manuscript.

Month of July, 1918.

H.Q., R.A., 34th. Division.

Place	Date	Hour	Summary of Events and Information	Remarks and references to Appendices
CHAVIGNY Farm	July 28		Plan d'Emploi of Artillery covering the 34th. Division;	App.XXXIV
,,	28		Ordre No. 26;	App.XXXV
,,	28	noon	Location Statement;	App.XXXVI
,,	28		Warning Order to Brigades and D.A.C.	App.XXXVII
,,	28		34th. D.A.C. ordered to move forthwith to ROZET Wood;	App.XXXVIII
Fe.d'EDROLLE	28		H.Q., R.A., moved to Fme. d'EDROLLE, one mile W. of BILLY-SUR-OURCQ.	
(OULCHY-LE-Chau.1/20000)	29		Zero hour for attack, 4.10 a.m.;	App.XXXIX
,, n	29	6 am	152nd. Brigade, R.F.A., report; "103rd. Infantry Brigade believed to have captured their objective. Supporting battery will not move until the situation is more clear."	
		7.15 am	Message from 103rd. Infantry Brigade, timed 6.55 a.m.; "Have reached objective and now re-forming. Have about 60 or 70 prisoners."	

(A7092). Wt. W12839/M1293. 75 ,o.o. 1/17. D. D. & L., Ltd. Forms/C.2118/14.

Army Form C. 2118.

Instructions regarding War Diaries and Intelligence Summaries are contained in F. S. Regs., Part II. and the Staff Manual respectively. Title pages will be prepared in manuscript.

WAR DIARY
or
INTELLIGENCE SUMMARY.
(Erase heading not required.)

Month of July, 1918.

H.Q., R.A., 34th. Division.

Place	Date	Hour	Summary of Events and Information	Remarks and references to Appendices
	July			
Fme.d'EDROLLE	29	8.05 am	To deal with hostile M.G. fire from BERGNEUX, the 34th. Divisional Artillery fired a concentration on the village and Hill 158, 8.5 a.m. to 8.45 a.m.	
		9.55 am	160th. Brigade, R.F.A., report; "Heavy fighting in progress in BERGNEUX. Believe we hold the wood 600 yards due W. of BERGNEUX."	
		11.15 am	152nd. Brigade, R.F.A., Liaison Officer reports; "101st. Infantry Brigade are consolidating in the G.M.P. Line. The left flank of the 103rd. Infantry Brigade is being refused to conform to this movement."	
		2.35 pm	152nd. Brigade, R.F.A., have established an O.P., which is in communication, in BOIS DE MONTCEAU.	
		4.10 pm	152nd. Brigade, R.F.A., Liaison Officer with 101st. Infantry Brigade reports; "Our Infantry hold GRAND ROZOY-BEUGNEUX Road as far as just N. of "B" in BERGNEUX."	
		4.55 pm	152nd. Brigade, R.F.A., reports; "At 3 p.m., the G.M.P. line was strongly held, but there were no troops E. of it."	

Army Form C. 2118.

Instructions regarding War Diaries and Intelligence Summaries are contained in F. S. Regs., Part II. and the Staff Manual respectively. Title pages will be prepared in manuscript.

WAR DIARY
or
INTELLIGENCE SUMMARY.
(Erase heading not required.)

H.Q., R.A.,
34th. Division.

Place	Date	Hour	Summary of Events and Information	Remarks and references to Appendices
	July			
Fme.d'EDROLLE	29		Orders for lifting of S.O.S. barrage as the Infantry push on during the night ...	App.XXXX
,,	30		34th. Divisional Artillery Warning Order No. 5, ...	App.XXXXI
,,	30		Heavy Artillery carried out a bombardment of BERGNEUX in support of an operation by 103rd. Infantry Brigade;	App.XXXXII
,,	31		34th. Divisional Artillery Operation Order No. 11;	App.XXXXIII
,,	31		34th. Division Operation Order No. 241;	AppXXXXIV
,,	31		Plan d'Emploi de l'Artillerie, ...v	App.XXXXV
,,	31		34th. Division Special Instruction No. 2;	App.XXXXVI
,,	31		34th. Divisional Artillery Instruction;	App.XXXVII
GEROMESNIL FARM.	31	10 pm	Head-quarters, R.A., moved to GEROMESNIL FARM (OULCHY-LE-CHATEAU, 1/20,000).	

P.C. Walthall

Brigadier-General,
Commanding Royal Artillery, 34th. Division.

SECRET.   34th.Div.Arty.No. O/396.

App I

WARNING ORDER.

1. The 34th. Divisional Artillery will be relieved in the line by the 59th. Divisional Artillery.

2. One Section of each Battery will be relieved on the night of the 1st/2nd July.

3. Remaining two Sections on the nights of the 2nd/3rd & 3rd/4th July.

4. 34th. Divisional Artillery will march from present Wagon Lines on the 3rd. July to rejoin the Division in the llnd. Corps area.

Captain,
Brigade Major.R.A.
34th. Divisional Artillery.

29th. July 1918.

Copies to:- 152nd. Bde. RFA (5)
160th. Bde. RFA (5)
34th. D.T.M.O.
34th. D.A.C. (3)
S.C.R.A.
File.

"A" Form
MESSAGES AND SIGNALS.
Army Form C. 2121
(in pads of 100).
No. of Message..........

War Diary

APP V 21

S E C R E T. Copy No. 21..

34th DIVISIONAL ARTILLERY OPERATION ORDER No. 5.

Ref: Sheet 27 N.E.) 28 N.W.) 1/20,000.

5th. July 1918.

1. One Sections per battery will take up positions covering the EAST POPERINGHE or BLUE Line as per attached Table "A".

2. Sections to be in action by 12 noon 6th. inst.

3. Personnel - Only 2 N.C.Os. and 4 gunners per section need remain with the guns to fire them in case of necessity.

4. An Officer per battery will be on duty at the Wagon Lines and hold himself in readiness to proceed to the section in action and take command if required.

4. Routes to BLUE line positions should be made known to all Officers and senior N.C.Os. as soon as possible.

5. H.Q. have been selected as under -
   152nd. Bde. RFA. in Camp at F.23.a.2.9.
   160th. Bde. RFA. in Camp at F.16.d.9.0.

6. H.Q.R.A. 34th. Division at COUTHOVE CHATEAU, F.21.a.5.4.

7. Resection of positions and Map Boards have been applied for but are not yet available.
   Batteries must therefore prepare their own fighting maps. A tracing showing trenches completed in the BLUE Line will be forwarded shortly.

8. Brigades to ACKNOWLEDGE.

[signature]

Captain,
Brigade Major.R.A.
34th. Divisional Artillery.

Issued at 6 p.m.

Copies: 1-5. 152nd. Bde.RFA.
6-10. 160th. Bde.RFA.
11-14. 34th. D.A.C.
15. S.C.R.A.
16. IInd. Corps RA.
17. 34th. Divn. "G".
18. O. i/c R.A. Sigs.
19. File.
20-22. Spare.

TABLE "A".

attached to 34th. D.A.O.O.No. 5.

Battery.	Position.	S.O.S. Lines.	O.P.
A/152. 2 guns.	BL.1. F.18.c.4.5.	A.29.c.1.3 to G.5.a.10.75.	House A.20.d.37.70.
B/152. 2 guns	BL.2. F.23.b.5.5.	G.4.b.80.15 to G.4.d.65.75.	Tree A.25.b.3.8.
C/152. 2 guns	BL.3. F.22.d.7.9.	Enfilade roads 1 gun-G.4.d.20.40. 1 gun-G.4.d.40.00.	House A.20.d.40.70.
D/152. 2 Hows.	BL.4. F17.d.8.5.	1 how-G.5.a.85.25. 1 " -A.29.d.55.65.	House A.20.d.6.4.
A/160. 2 guns	BL.5. F.17.c.50.75.	A.28.b.25.75 to A.28.b.00.95.	Water Tower A.20.d.60.50.
B/160. 2 guns	BL.6. F.18.a.2.3.	A.28.b.85.30. to A.28.b.60.50	Trench A.20.d.7.1.
C/160. 2 guns	BL.7. F.17.b.6.1.	A.28.d.9.6. A.28.b.8.2.	do
D/160. 2 Hows.	BL.8. F.16.d.8.7.	1 how-A.22.d.95.75. 1 how-A.28.b.75.45.	House A.20.d.33.45.

Army Form C. 2121
(in pads of 100).

"A" Form
MESSAGES AND SIGNALS.

No. of Message............

Prefix.........
Office of Origin

S E C R E T. Copy No. 22

App II

34th. DIVISIONAL ARTILLERY OPERATION ORDER No. 3.

Ref: Map HAZEBROUCK
5A, 1/100,000.

2nd. July 1918.

1. The 34th. Divisional Artillery will march on July 4th. from their present Wagon Lines to billets in the RUBROUCK area.

2. Units will march at the following times:-
   152nd. Brigade RFA........8-30 a.m.
   160th. " " ....9-15 a.m.
   34th. D.A.C...............10-0 a.m.

3. Starting Point LA BELLE HOTESSE.

4. Route - LYNDE.
   EBBLINGHAM.
   LE NIEPPE.
   COIN PERDU.
   LE MENEGAT cross roads.
   RUBROUCK.

5. 500 yards distance will be maintained between batteries and sections D.A.C.

6. 2nd. Line Transport will march in rear of Brigades in charge of an Officer.

7. Billeting parties will meet the Staff Captain R.A. at the Area Commandant's Office RUBROUCK at 11 a.m.

8. 34th. D.A.H.Q. will close at 9-0 a.m. on July 4th. Subsequent communications c/o Area Commandant, RUBROUCK.

9. ACKNOWLEDGE by wire.

[signature]
Captain,
Brigade Major.R.A.
34th. Divisional Artillery.

Issued at 2 p.m.

Copies: 1-5. 152nd.Bde.RFA.
6-10. 160th. " "
11-13. 34th. D.A.C.
14. No. 1 Coy. Train.
15. 59th. D.A.
16. 5th. D.A.
17. XIth. Corps R.A.
18. XVth. Corps R.A.
19. IInd. Corps R.A.
20. File.
21-22. War Diary.
23-24. Spare.

"A" Form
MESSAGES AND SIGNALS.
Army Form C. 2121 (in pads of 100).
No. of Message..........

S E C R E T.   App III   Copy No. 21.

34th. DIVISIONAL ARTILLERY OPERATION ORDER No. 4.

Ref: Sheet 27 1/40,000.   3rd. July 1918.

1. The 34th. Divisional Artillery will march on Ju.y 5th. from RUBROUCK to Wagon Lines in the HAANDEKOT area E.4.d.

2. Units will march at the following times:-
   152nd. Brigade RFA..... 9-30 a.m.
   160th. " " .....10-15 a.m.
   34th. D.A.C. .....11-0 a.m.

3. Starting Point - Cross Roads in H.4.a.

4. Route - WORM HOUDT.
   HERZEELE.
   HOUTKERQUE.
   HAANDEKOT.

5. 500 yards distance will be maintained between batteries and sections D.A.C.

6. Billeting parties to meet the Staff Captain R.A. at the Area Commandant's Office E.16.d.8.6. at 11-0 a.m.

7. H.Q., 34th. D.A. will be at COUTHOVE Chateau, F.21.a. on arrival.

8. Brigades and D.A.C. please ACKNOWLEDGE.

Captain,
Brigade Major.R.A.
34th. Divisional Artillery.

Issued at 11-30 a.m.

Copies: 1-5. 152nd.Bde.RFA.
6-10. 160th. " "
11-13. 34th. D.A.C.
14. No. 1 Coy. Train.
15. XIth. Corps.
16. XVth. Corps.
17. IInd. Corps.
18. 34th. Div. "G".
19. Area Comdt. HAANDEKOT.
20. File.
21-22. War Diary.
23-24. Spare.

"A" Form
MESSAGES AND SIGNALS.
Army Form C. 2121
(in pads of 100).
No. of Message...........

SECRET.   Copy No. 15

WA

34th. DIVISIONAL ARTILLERY INSTRUCTIONS No. 1.

App V

1. Arcs of Fire.
Arrangements must be made so that all guns and howitzers can fire on the whole of the BLUE LINE front liable to be occupied by the 34th. Division viz:- from A.22.central to G.15.d.2.7.
If this cannot be done by enlarging existing pits and platforms fresh ones must be selected.

2. O.Ps. sufficiently close to admit of control by voice should be reconnoitred and marked if available.

3. Dumps. 100 rounds per gun in action must be maintained.

4. Responsibility for other positions in addition to the positions already occupied, Brigades will be responsible for maintenance and improvement of positions as under -

152nd. Brigade RFA.
"F" Brigade.

18-pdrs	(6)	F.29.d.6.3.
"	(2)	F.23.b.87.98.
"	(2)	F.23.b.9.9.
"	(2)	F.17.d.90.01.
"	(4)	L.5.b.20.55.
"	(2)	L.5.b.42.77.
4.5 How.	(6)	F.29.a.77.50.

160th. Brigade RFA.
"G" Brigade.

18-pdr	(6)	A.19.b.45.70.
"	(6)	F.24.c.90.60.
"	(6)	A.19.d.99.25.
4.5 How.	(4)	F.24.a.30.70.
"	(2)	F.24.a.70.40.

5. Brigades to ACKNOWLEDGE.

[signature]
Captain,
Brigade Major.R.A.
34th. Divisional Artillery.

7-7-18.
Copies. 1-5 152nd.Bde.RFA.
6-10.160th. " "
11. 34th. "G".
12. R.A. IInd. Corps.
13. R.A. 39th. Div.
14. File.
15-18. Spare.

"A" Form
MESSAGES AND SIGNALS.
Army Form C. 2121 (in pads of 100).
No. of Message..........

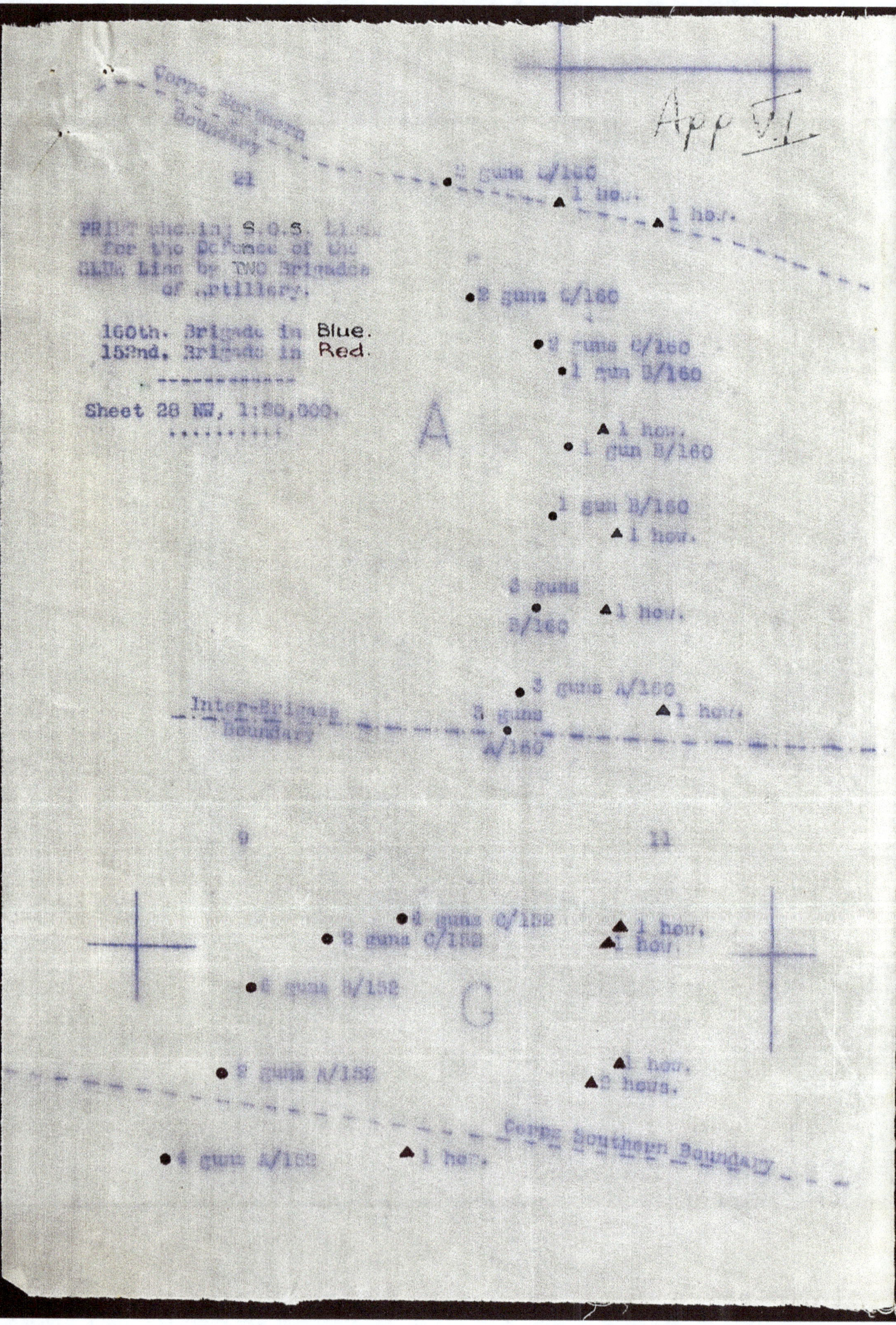

App VI

Corps Northern Boundary

21

PRINT showing S.O.S. Lines for the Defence of the BLUE Line by TWO Brigades of Artillery.

160th. Brigade in Blue.
152nd. Brigade in Red.

Sheet 28 NW, 1:20,000.

2 guns C/160
1 how.
1 how.

2 guns C/160

2 guns C/160
1 gun B/160

A

1 how.
1 gun B/160

1 gun B/160
1 how.

2 guns B/160
1 how.

3 guns A/160
1 how.

Inter-Brigade Boundary
3 guns A/160

9

11

4 guns C/152
1 how.
2 guns C/152
1 how.

4 guns B/152

G

1 how.
2 guns A/152
2 hows.

Corps Southern Boundary

4 guns A/152
1 how.

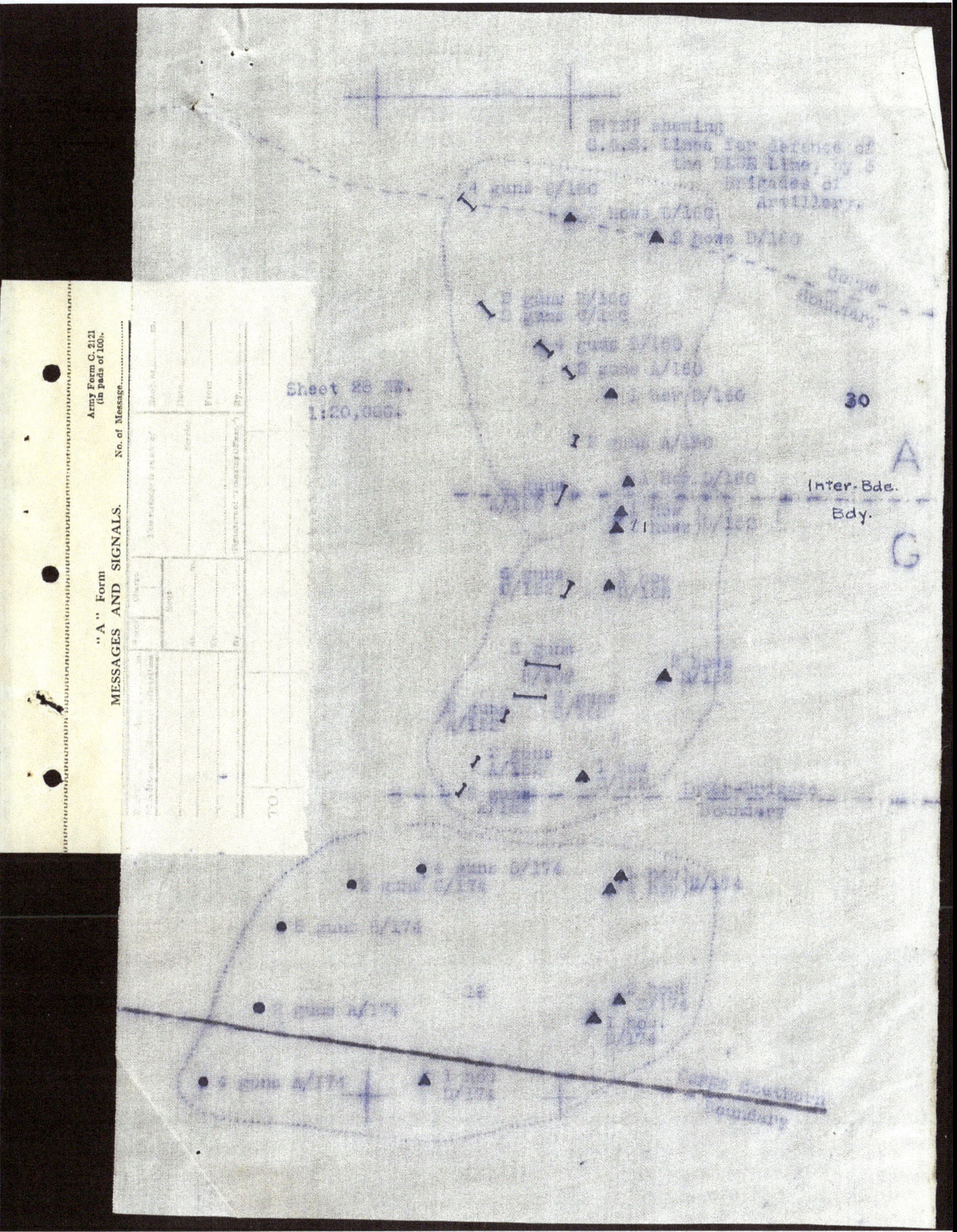

Army Form C. 2121
(in pads of 100).
"A" Form
MESSAGES AND SIGNALS.
No. of Message
TO
Artillery.
Corps
Boundary
Sheet 28 NE.
1:20,000.
30
A
Inter-Bde.
Bdy.
G
Boundary
Corps Southern
Boundary

App VII

Ref: Sheets 27 NE, 28 NW. SECRET

LIST OF ARTILLERY POSITIONS to be occupied

if the Belgian Army only be attacked.

F.2.a.75.20	F.3.c.90.95
F.3.b.50.35	F.3.b.75.45
F.9.b.95.40	F.4.a.95.25
F.4.d.35.10	F.10.a.35.70
F.10.a.65.35	F.10.b.50.45
F.11.d.70.20	F.12.a.65.10
A.1.b.90.27	A.1.d.85.72
A.7.b.50.75	A.7.b.80.20
A.2.a.25.38	A.8.b.30.50.
A.14.b.95.70.	A.14.d.75.80
A.14.d.65.40	A.14.d.85.65
A.3.b.55.30	A.9.d.10.95
A.9.d.30.72	A.16.a.50.10
A.22.a.60.97	

11th. July, 1918.

"A" Form
MESSAGES AND SIGNALS.
Army Form C. 2121
(in pads of 100).
No. of Message..............

App VIII

SECRET.

34th. DIVISIONAL ARTILLERY INSTRUCTIONS No. 2.

Ref: Sheets 27 N.E.) 28 N.W.) 1/20,000.

12th. July 1918.

The 34th. D.A. and one Brigade 39th. D.A. may be called upon
1.(a) in the event of an attack on the Belgian Army only and not on 11 Corps To reinforce the Artillery covering the right of the Belgian Army.
(b) To reinforce the Artillery covering one or both the Divisions in the line in the 11nd. Corps area.
(c) In the case of the 30th. American Division occupying the EAST POPERINGHE LINE to cover the whole of this line in the Corps area.

2. In (a) of above, the two Brigades of the 34th. D.A. will be prepared to occupy all or a portion of the following positions:-

152nd.Bde.RFA.

A Battery	- A.16.a.50.10.	with rear positions about	F.11.d.70.20.
B "	- A.22.a.60.97.	" " " "	F.10.b.50.45.
C "	- A.14.b.95.70.	" " " "	F.9.b.95.40.
D "	- A.14.d.65.40.	" " " "	F.10.a.35.70.

160th.Bde.RFA.

A Battery	- A.8.b.30.50.	" " " "	F.3.b.75.45.
B "	- A.3.b.55.30.	" " " "	F.4.a.95.25.
C "	- A.2.a.25.35.	" " " "	F.4.d.35.10.
D "	- A.9.d.30.72.	" " " "	F.3.b.50.35.

Routes to these positions from present positions and Wagon Lines must be reconnoitred.

3. In case (b), the action of the Artillery will depend entirely on circumstances.

4. In case (c), this will be done either -
(i) by the two Brigades of 34th. D.A. and one Brigade of 39th. D.A. from the positions at present allotted to them.
"H" Group - 152nd. Bde. H.Q. at F.22.b.3.5.
"I" " - 160th. " " " F.16.b.45.15.
"D" " - 174th. " " " F.27.d.4.4.
or
(ii) by the two Brigades of the 34th. D.A. only, from their present position
152nd. Bde. "H" Group.
160th. Bde. "I" Group.

5. S.O.S. Lines for sub-para (i) and (ii) of para. 4 have been issued on separate tracings.

6. Liaison.
(1) When three Brigades are covering the whole front -
174th.Bde. will find one Liaison Officer, not below the rank of Capt. at Right and Right Centre Regimental H.Q. at ZWYNLAND BREWERY, L.21.c.0.4.
152nd.Bde. will find a Liaison Officer (Capt) at Left Centre Regtl. H.Q. at A.26.c.9.7.
160th.Bde. will find Liaison Officer (Capt) at Left Regtl. H.Q. at OOSTHOVE FM. A.20.c.5.5.
(2) Two Brigades only covering the front -
152nd.Bde. will find Liaison Officer with Right & Right Centre Regts.
160th.Bde. will find Liaison Officer with Centre Left & Left H.Q.

P S [signature] Major,
A/Brigade Major.R.A.
34th. Divisional Artillery.

Copies: 152nd.Bde. (5)
160th.Bde. (5)
R.A. 39th.Div.(6)
R.A. 11nd. Corps (1)
34th. Div "G" (1)

App IX

SECRET. Copy No. 21

34th. DIVISIONAL ARTILLERY OPERATION ORDER No. 6.

Reference Sheets:-
27 NE 1:20,000
19 SE 1:20,000
5a HAZEBROUCK 1:100,000

12th. July 1918.

1. During the time that the Division is in G.H.Q. Reserve, it must be prepared to move at short notice. It is possible that the units first for entrainment will be required to commence entraining 8 hours after receiving the order to move.

2. If the Division is ordered to move by rail, Strategical Trains will be used. In that case the whole Division will be conveyed by train.

3. Entrainment for a move by Strategical Trains will be performed under the orders of Group Commanders. Groups will be composed as follows:-

"X" Brigade Group.
Commander G.O.C. Infantry Brigade at CORMETTE.
Entraining Station - ST. OMER.
The Infantry Brigade at CORMETTE.
1 Company Div. Train, S.A.A. Section, D.A.C.

R.A. Group.
Entraining Stations - HEIDEBEEK (19/X.20.c.) PROVEN and WAAYENBURG.
34th. Div. Arty. (less S.A.A. Sec. D.A.C.
No. 1 Coy. Div. Train.

4. The arrangements for move by Strategical Trains are given in 34th. Division Administrative Instructions No. 52 issued simultaneously with this order.

5. Moves to entraining stations will be carried out under the orders of Group Commanders, who will prepare the necessary march orders forthwith.

6. The S.A.A. Section of D.A.C. will march on receipt of orders from this office by the route - WATOU - WINNEZEELE - CASSEL - ZUYTPEENE - CLAIRMARAIS to ST. OMER; where it will come under the orders of G.O.C. "X" Brigade Group.

7. All formations and units will prepare provisional movement orders at once.

8. Brigades and D.A.C. to ACKNOWLEDGE.

P.S. Myburgh Major,
A/Brigade Major.R.A.
34th. Divisional Artillery.

Issued at 7 p.m.

Copies; 1-5. 152nd.Bde.
6-10. 160th.Bde.
11-14. 34th. D.A.C.
15. D.T.M.O.
20-21. War Diary.
16. O i/c R.A. Sigs.
17. R.A. IInd. Corps.
18. 34th. Div. "G".
19. No. 1 Coy. Train.
22. File.

"A" Form
MESSAGES AND SIGNALS.

Army Form C. 2121
(in pads of 100).

No. of Message..........

SECRET.

34th. Div. Arty. No. 0/400.

Appx I

O.C. 152nd. Bde. RFA.
O.C. 160th. Bde. RFA.
O.C. 34th. D.A.C.
D.T.M.O.

As 34th. Division is now in G.H.Q. Reserve, all units will be prepared to move at 24 hours notice.

Orders re entrainment will be issued later.

(Sd) P.S. MYBURGH, Major
A/Brigade Major. R.A.
34th. Divisional Artillery.

11-7-18.

War Diary

App XI

SECRET. Copy No. 15...

34th. DIVISIONAL ARTILLERY OPERATION ORDER NO. 7.

15th. July 1918.

1.

The 34th. D.A. will take part in this practice Scheme by
(i) Reconnoitring positions for the defence of this line.
(ii) Providing Liaison Officers with Brigades and Battalions and making S.O.S. arrangements with the Infantry.

2. Reference (i) of above.

160th. Brigade RFA. will cover the Left Sector from present position in "I" Group but will reconnoitre positions in F.9. to fall back to.

152nd. Brigade RFA. will cover Right Sector. Positions to be reconnoitred in F.19 & 20.

Guns will not be moved.

3. Reference para. (ii) of above.

Os.C. Brigades will get into touch with their corresponding Infantry Brigade as soon as possible after the Brigades move up.

Brigades will supply a Liaison Officer (Captain) who will remain with the Infantry Brigade during their tour in the line.

Battery Commanders will get into touch with the Battalions they cover as soon as possible after they move up and select O.Ps.

Batteries will provide a Liaison Officer with the Battalion they cover, this Officer will remain with the Infantry during their tour in the Line.

F.O.Os. will also get into touch with Company Commanders and Infantry actually holding the line also reconnoitre for forward O.Ps.

4. Orders for the commencement of this Scheme will be issued by telephone as soon as the Infantry orders have been received.

[signature] Major,
a/Brigade Major R.A.
34th. Divisional Artillery.

Issued at 10 am
Copies: 1-5. 152nd. Bde. RFA.
6-10. 160th. " "
11. 34th. Div. "G".
12. 101st. Infy. Bde.
13. 102nd. " "
14. 103rd. " "

S E C R E T. Copy 34th. Div. Arty. No. [illegible]

App XII

O.C. 152nd. Bde. RFA.
O.C. 160th. Bde. RFA.
39th. Div. Arty. (G).
IInd. Corps H.A.

Ref: Sheets 27 N.E. & 28 N.W. 1/20,000.

1. The list of O.Ps. shown in Table "A" attached to 34th. D.A. O.O. No. 3 dated 5th. July 1918 is cancelled.

2. 13 O.Ps. on the list shown below are allotted as follows:-
(a) With 2 Brigades of Artillery covering the Corps Front -
152nd. Bde.RFA. Nos. 8 to 13.
160th. Bde.RFA. Nos. 1 to 7.
(b) With 3 Brigades of Artillery -
174th. Bde.RFA. Nos. 10 to 13.
152nd. Bde.RFA. Nos. 6 to 9
160th. Bde.RFA. Nos. 1 to 5.

3.

No.	Name.	Location.	Description of work required.
1.	[illegible]	A.21.c.12.01.	Two trees.
2.	[illegible]	A.20.d.33.56.	Two trees.
3.	[illegible]	A.20.d.33.47.	Concrete in house.
4.	[illegible]	A.20.d.58.38.	Concrete in house.
5.	HEDGE.	A.26.d.56.08.	Concrete in pill-box in corner of hedge.
6.	BUTT.	A.26.b.30.35.	Concrete pill-box behind hedge.
7.	[illegible]	G.1.b.1.3.	Tower O.P. in Chateau.
8.	[illegible]	G.3.c.30.15.	Tower in Goods shed.
9.	[illegible]	G.8.a.13.17.	Accommodation in Brigade H.Q. in cellars.
10.	[illegible]	G.14.b.80.77.	Concrete in house.
11.	[illegible]	G.15.a.5.1.	Front Line Trench O.P.
12.	SHED.	G.16.a.84.95.	Concrete tunnel on top of pill-box.
13.	[illegible]	L.12.c.05.40.	Chimney in Brewery to be made accessible, and accommodation in cellars of Brigade H.Q.

All O.Ps. are for the use of 1 Field Artillery and 1 Heavy Artillery party, except BUTT, which will be constructed for 2 parties from Heavy Artillery, and SHED, which will be for one Field Artillery party only.

4. Work is being done on these O.Ps. under Corps arrangements.

R S [illegible]
Major,
A/Brigade Major R.A.
34th. Divisional Artillery.

12-7-18.

War Diary

App XIII

SECRET.

38th. Division. (French)
Artillery.

ARTILLERY DEFENCE SCHEME

to come into force 23rd. July at 4 a.m.

1. ORGANIZATION.
Head quarters: CHAVIGNY FARM (09.59)
Brig. Gen. E.C. WALTHALL, C.M.G. D.S.O. C.R.A.
Col. BERANGER. Attached.

Group.	Infantry covered.	Brigades.	O.P.
North.		152nd.	
Lt.Col.SAVILLE		11/32	61.52
Comdg. Group.	102nd. Brigade.	111/32	61.52.
Commt SUTTERLIN		111/41	59.39.
attached.			
South.		160th.	62.39.
Lt.Col.WARBURTON.		1/32	53.43.
Comdg. Group.	101st. Brigade.	1/41	71.39.
Lt.Col.THOUVENOT		11/41	65.37.
attached.			
Howitzers.	Divisional Front.	-	45.45.

R.A.H.Q. 34th. Division control the whole of the Artillery and issue orders direct to English Units and French Groups. Requests for Artillery fire should be made by the Infantry through the English Artillery.

2. The N. & S. Groups normally cover the front of the Infantry Brigade they support.
The Howitzer Group covers the whole Divisional Front. All batteries must however be prepared to turn their fire on to any target within the limit of their range and switch.

3. O.Ps. (Ground)
4 O.Ps. are permanently manned by Officers.
All information is sent to the C.R.A's office (an Intelligence Summary from 6 p.m. to 6 p.m. is rendered at 12 m.n.
Balloon 87. (Capt. de VERTUS) BEAUREPAIRE Farm.
52 Squadron of Aeroplanes. (Lieut REDON) at RUSSY-BEMONT.

4. Liaison.
(a) With Infantry. At each Infantry Brigade H.Q. in the line an English Artillery Officer and a French Artillery Officer with a Liaison detachment of 4 N.C.Os, 3 telephone Detachments, 9 signallers and runners supplying 1 N.C.O., 1 telephone detachment and 3 signallers or runners to each Battn. H.Q. in the line.
(b) Telephones. See Scheme.
(c) Wireless. All Groups and Brigades have wireless masts near their H.Q. The North Group have a transmitting Station.

5. "S.O.S." Barrages.
In each Group two Brigades of 75 mm. form the direct barrage with one Brigade of 18-pdrs superimposed and one Brigade of 75 mm forming a "combing" barrage 200 to 600 metres beyond the direct barrage. The exact line of this barrage to be arranged by Group Commanders and Infantry Brigades and modified from time to time as necessary.
Rate of fire - 4 rds p.g.p.m. for 3 minutes then 1 rd p.g.p.m. for 7 minutes. (One SOS Barrage uses about 2,500 rounds) This barrage should not be called for oftener than twice in one hour, and should be called for by S.O.S. Signals, telephone and wireless.

6..........

6. Counter-Preparation.

Group Commanders arrange with Infantry Brigades the targets and zones for C.P.

Two C.Ps. should be arranged,

(a)one between 500 and 1,200 metres beyond our front line and
(b)one between 1,200 and 2,000 metres from our lines.

Field Guns form a "Combing"barrage, howitzers fire on selected points.

A C.P. offensive consists of a 15 minute shoot, 2 rds p.g.p.m. for guns and 1 rd. p.h.p.m. for howit by 10 minutes at 1 rd. p.g.p.m. for guns and ¼ rd.p.

Generally the first 10 minutes should be C.P.(a 5 minutes C.P.(b)

7. Harassing fire is ordered daily from the C.R.A'

8. Concentrations to be carried out by one Brigade howitzer battery are prearranged and numbered -

No.							
1	12,5.33,5	6	04.38	11	15.37	17	17
2	11,5.37,	7	03.43	12	14,5.40	18	17
3	11.39	8	00.47	13	11.43	19	19
4	10.41,5	9	04,5.41	14	10.26	20	24.
5	06.3 3.	10	10.40.	15	11.27	21	16.
				16	09.33 3	22	10

9. Supply of Ammunition.

75. LONGPONT Station.

18-pdrs, 4.5 Hows & 155. to the West of MAISON FORESTI

P.S. [illegible] Major,
A/Brigade Major.
34th. Divisional Artillery.

24th. July 1918.

War Diary

APP ~~XVII~~ XIV

34th. Div. Arty.

S E C R E T.

ARTILLERY ARRANGEMENTS

to come into force at 9 p.m. on 25th. July.

1. ORGANISATION.
Headquarters - CHAVIGNY FM. (09.59)
Brig.Gen. E.C.WALTHALL, C.M.G. D.S.O. C.R.A.

Group.	Infantry covered.	Brigade.
Left Group. Lt.Col.SAVILLE	102nd. Infy. Bde. (04.51)	152nd.
Right Group. Lt.Col.WARBURTON.	101st.Infy. Bde. (73.47)	160th.
Group Thouvenot. Lt.Col.THOUVENOT.	Divisional Front.	41st. Regt.

2. The Right and Left Groups normally cover the front of the Infantry they support.
Thouvenot's Group covers the whole of the Divisional Front. Requests for its fire should be made to this office.

3. Liaison will be arranged in detail between the Commanders of the Right and Left Groups and the G.Os.C. of the Infantry Bdes they support, reporting such arrangements to this office.
All French Liaison Detachments to be relieved by British personnel by 9 p.m. 25th. July.

4. "S.O.S." Barrages.
In the Right and Left Groups the direct barrage will be formed by the 18-pdrs and will cover the whole divisional front. The exact line of this barrage to be arranged between Groups and Infantry Brigades.
4.5" Howitzers will barrage in their respective group zones on the sunk road, 14.26 to 10.42.
Thouvenot's Group will form a "combing" barrage 600 metres deep beyond the direct barrage.
One sub-group of the 41st. Regt. d'Artillerie from 05.39 to 05.43. The remaining two sub-groups from 09.25 to 08.32.
Rates of fire -
18-pdrs & 75 mm. 4 r.p.g.p.m. for 3 mins and then 1 r.p.g.p.m. for 7 mins.
4.5" Hows....... half the above rates.

5. Counter-Preparation.
(a) 18-pdrs and 75 mms. S.O.S. lines searching back 1000 metres.
4.5" Hows. points in this zone selected by Group Commanders.
(b) 18-pdrs and 75 mms. 1000 metres beyond S.O.S. lines searching back 800metres.
4.5" Hows. Points in this zone selected by Group Commanders.
A C.P. consists of a 15 minute shoot, 5 mins at 2 r.p.g.p.m. followed by 10 mins at 1 r.p.g.p.m.; 4.5" Hows. firing at half these rates.
Generally the first 10 minutes should be C.P.(a) and the last 5 minutes C.P.(b)

P.T.O.

6. Night Harassing Fire will be ordered daily from the C.R.A's office.

7. During the day every opportunity should be taken of engaging enemy movement and suitable targets such as located M.G. positions, dugouts, etc.
A list of theses will be forwarded from time to time.

8. Brigades please ACKNOWLEDGE.

Captain,
Brigade Major.R.A
34th. Divisional Arti

25-7-18.

Copies: 152nd. Bde. RFA (5)
160th. " " (5)
34th. Div. "G". (16)
32 Regt d'Art. (1)
War Diary (2)
File (2)
Spare (2)

19th.French Div. (1)
12th. " " (1)
30th. French Corps (1)

S E C R E T. 34th.Div.Arty.No. O.O./7/1.

34th. DIVISIONAL ARTILLERY

NIGHT FIRING 26/27th. July.

Group TOUSSAINT

Counter-Preparation (for 2 minutes only)

(a) Eloignee
4.5 a.m. to 4.7 a.m.

(b) Rapprochee
4-20 a.m. to 4.22 a.m.

Rate of fire -
1 round per gun per minute.

Captain,
Brigade Major.R.A.
34th. Divisional Artillery.

26-7-18.

SECRET.

App XV

Copy No. 8.

34th. DIVISIONAL ARTILLERY OPERATION ORDER No. 7.

Night Firing 26/27 July.

26th. July 1918

1. HARASSING FIRE from 11-0 p.m. to 3-0 a.m.

Targets:- Left Group - (93.45) 97.47) (94.41) (10.426) (10.416) XXXXXXXX (116.375) (145.408) (15.37)

Right Group - (186.336) (116.326) (130.298) (105.31) (21.345) (205.27)

Group Thouvenot - (21.40) (30.41) (22.35) (26.35) (215.328) (300.28)

Ammunition Expenditure - 100 Rds per battery 18-pdr & 4.5" How.
70 " " " 75 mm.

2. COUNTER-PREPARATION -

4.5 a.m. }
4.20 a.m. } for 2 minutes.

3. ACKNOWLEDGE.

Captain,
Brigade Major.R.A.
34th. Divisional Artillery.

Issued at 5-30 p.m.

Copies: 1-2. 152nd. Bde. RFA.
3-4. 160th. Bde. RFA.
5-6. Thouvenot's Group.
7. 34th. Div. "G".
8. File.

"A" Form
MESSAGES AND SIGNALS.
Army Form C. 2121
(in pads of 100).
No. of Message.................

App XVI

S E C R E T.

34th.Div.Arty.No. G/643.

O.C. 152nd. Bde. RFA. (5)
O.C. 160th. Bde. RFA. (5)

French Meteor wires or "Sondage" are sent by Wireless direct to Groups every four hours.

Brigades should endeavour to take these wires on their masts or at any rate to get a copy from the nearest French Group, translate them and send out to batteries.

An example and translation are attached for guidance.

The following notes will facilitate translation:-

Barometer is given in centimetres.	1 c.m. = .394 inches
Height is given in 100 metres.	100 m. = 328 feet.
Thermometer in Centigrade.	Fahr. = $\frac{9 \times Cent.}{5} + 32$

hence 10 Cent = 50 Fahr.
20 " " 68 "
30 " " 86 "

Direction of wind is given in 10 grades = 9 degrees.
Strength of wind in metres per second.

P S Myburgh Major,
Brigade Major.R.A.
34th. Divisional Artillery.

24-7-18.

EXAMPLE.

SONDAGE du 10me Juillet 1918.
13.3 0 (Time)

MBY (Sender Xth Army).			MAX (Sender VIth Army).		
30	13	17	30	13	17
00	40	03	00	40	53
02	38	06	02	38	56
04	30	05	04	30	55
08	35	10	08	35	60
15	40	02	15	40	52
62	12	18	62	12	68

Notes:-

1. No message is for Artillery unless starting with 30.
2. Message reads and is sent from left to right.
3. The sender MBY is our Army. The sender MAX is the neighbouring Army and adds 50 to speed of wind which should be deducted before translation.
4. Top figure of second column are last 2 figures of barometer reading and the digit 7 must be added and a decimal point put in. In this case 71.3.
5. Top figure of third column is Temperature.
6. Remainder reads 1st Col. Height, 2nd Col. Direction of Wind, 3rd. Col. Speed of Wind.
7. The last line may be disregarded as it refers to very heavy pieces only.

Translation.

Meteor of July 10th 1918. 1-30 p.m. Xth. Army.

R.A. Barometer 28.5 inches. Temperature 62.6 Fahr.

Wind.

0 feet	360°	10 f.s.
656 "	342°	20 "
1312 "	270°	15 "
2624 "	315°	35 "
4920 "	360°	5 "

<u>S E C R E T.</u> App XVII Copy No....

34th. DIVISIONAL ARTILLERY OPERATION ORDER No. 8.
-.-

Ref:- SOISSONS Sheet (French) 1/80,000.

<u>20th. July 1918.</u>

1. The 34th. D.A. less T.Ms. will march to-night to Bivouacs around LONGAVESNE.

2. Probable route (at present being reconnoitred) BONNEUIL EMEVILLE - MDS. FME. - TAILLEFONTAINE - MARIVAL - LONGAVESNE.

3. Starting point - Cross Roads immediately below O in BONNEUIL.

4. Order of March - 152nd. Bde. RFA, 160th. Bde. RFA, D.A.C.

5. March Table -
152nd. Bde. RFA. Head of Column to pass starting point 10 p.m.
160th. " " " " " " " " " 10-25 p.m.
D.A.C. " " " " " " " " " 10-50 p.m.

6. Intervals - 50 yards will be maintained between batteries and Sections D.A.C., 100 yards between Brigades.

7. The object of this march by night is concealment and care must be taken to avoid discovery by air reconnaissance after dawn.

8. H.A.H.Q. will remain at LARGNY tonight, forward Report Centre at VIVIERES.

9. Please ACKNOWLEDGE.

P S Myburgh
Major,
A/Brigade Major.R.A.
34th. Divisional Artillery.

Issued at 6 p.m.
Copies:- 1. 152nd. Bde. RFA.
2. 160th. Bde. RFA.
3. 34th. D.A.C.
4. D.T.M.O.

"A" Form
MESSAGES AND SIGNALS.
Army Form C. 2121 (in pads of 100).
No. of Message..................

App XVIII

SECRET.

AMENDMENT No. 2 to MARCH TABLE "A" & "B"
(accompanying 34th. D.A. O.O. No. 9).

1. H.Q. and No. 1 Section 34th. D.A.C. will march to Wagon Line Wt of LONGPONT at 8 a.m. 23rd. inst.

2. 152nd. F.A. Brigade will march at 10 a.m. 23rd. inst to Wagon Lines S.W. of LONGPONT.

3. Route and other restrictions are unchanged.

4. 152nd. Brigade and D.A.C. to ACKNOWLEDGE.

[signature]

Captain for
Brigade Major.R.A.
34th. Divisional Artillery.

22nd. July 1918.

Copy to all recipients of O.O. No. 9.

SECRET.

AMENDMENT TO MARCH TABLE "A" and "B"
(accompanying 34th. D.A. O.O. No. 9.

1. 160th. Bde. RFA, will move up complete at 2 p.m. to-day 22nd., accompanied by No. 2 Section D.A.C.

2. 152nd. Bde., RFA, will NOT move at all to-day, but will move up complete to -morrow at a time to be notified later.

3. S.A.A. Secti on will move up at 4 p.m., as ordered in March Table "A".

4. Starting Point and Route as per March Table "A".

5. 100 yards interval will be maintained between Batteries.

6. Brigades and D.A.C. ACKNOWLEDGE.

(Signed) C. THOMPSON, Lieut.,
for Major,
a/Brigade- Major, R.A.,
34th. DIVISIONAL ARTILLERY.

22nd. July, 1918.

Copies to all recipients of O.O. No. 9

SECRET. Copy No. 22

34th. DIVISIONAL ARTILLERY OPERATION ORDER No. 9

Ref: Map SOISSONS Sheet
(French) 1/20,000.

21st. July, 1918.

1. 34th. Divisional Artillery will relieve 38th. French Divnl. Artillery in the line on the nights 22nd./23rd. and 23rd./24th. July.

2. 34th. Divisional Artillery will march to-morrow and next day in accordance with attached March Tables A and B.

3. Guides will meet units ½ mile W. of MAISON FORESTIER to guide them to their Wagon Lines, whence Batteries will move up into action after dark under orders of Battery Commanders.

These guides will be posted by S.C.R.A. to-morrow, but on the next day Brigades will be responsible for posting their own guides.

4. Orders will be issued later as to composition of groups in the line.

5. Command will pass on the completion of reliefs on night 23rd./24th. July.

6. ACKNOWLEDGE.

(signed) E.C.WALTHALL,
Brigadier-General,
C.R.A., 34th. Division.

Issued at 12 midnight.

Copies 1-5 152nd. Bde., R.F.A.,
6-10 160th. Bde., R.F.A.,
11-14 34th. D.A.C.,
15 S.C.R.A.,
16 34th. Divn., "G",
17 H.Q., 34th. Divnl Train.,
18 O.i/c R.A. Sigs.,
19-20 War Diary.
21 DTMO.

MARCH TABLE "A", to accompany 34th. DIVISIONAL ARTILLERY OPERATION ORDER No. 9.

Unit.	Starting Point.	Time to pass Starting Point.	Route.	Destination.	Remarks.
160th. Bde., half each A, B, C and D Batteries	Cross Roads on VIVIERS-PUSIEUX Road, ½-mile W. of PUSIEUX.	3 p.m.	REND de la REINE - TOUR REAUMONT - CARREFOUR DU SAUT DUCERF - MAISON FORESTIER.	Wagon Lines.	Intervals 100 yards between half Batteries, and 25 yards between every six vehicles of S.A.A. Section. Strict march discipline to be maintained.
152nd. Bde., half each A, B, C and D Batteries.		3 p.m.			
S.A.A. Section, 34th. D.A.C.		4 p.m.			

MARCH TABLE "B" to accompany 34th. D.A. O.O. No. 9.

Unit.	Starting Point.	Time to pass Starting Point.	Route.	Destination.	Remarks.
H.Q. & remaining ½ Btys 160th.Bde.	As in Table "A".	7 a.m.	As in Table "A".	Wagon Lines.	As in Table "A" with addition of 100 yards interval between Sections D.A.C. and 25 yards between every 6 vehicles of D.A.C.
H.Q. & remaining ½ Btys 152nd.Bde.		8 a.m.			
H.Q. & Nos 1 & 2 Sections 34th. DAC.		9 am.			

"A" Form
MESSAGES AND SIGNALS.
Army Form C. 2121
(in pads of 100).
No. of Message..................

App XIX

S E C R E T. G.S. 39.

34th DIVISION.

LOCATION REPORT.

Ref: Maps OULCHY-LE-CHATEAU 1/20,000.
and SOISSONS 1/80,000. 25th July, 1918.

Serial No.	Formation or Unit.	Location.
1	34 Div HQ (Advanced)	Caves close to CHAVIGNY FERME.
2	34 Div Report Centre	64.44
3	34 Div HQ (Rear)	Main MONTGOBERT - LONGPONT Road 500yds W of LA GRILLE.
4	101st Inf.Bde HQ.	78.84
5	2/4th R.W.Surrey Regt.	97.33
6	4th R. Sussex Regt.	76.83
7	2nd L.N.Lan. Regt.	79.83
8	101st L.T.M.Battery.	
9	102nd Inf.Bde HQ.	64.51
10	1/4th Cheshire Regt.)	
11	1/7th Cheshire Regt.)	about PARCY TIGNY.
12	1/1st Hereford Regt.)	
13	102nd L.T.M.Battery.	Detached from Division.
14	103rd Inf.Bde HQ.	BLANZY.
15	5th K.O.Sco. Bord.	72.43
16	8th Scottish Rifles.	85.28
17	5th Arg.& Suth'd Highrs.	95.16
18	103rd L.T.M.Battery.	Detached from Division.
19	34th Div. Arty. HQ.	Caves close to CHAVIGNY FERME.
20	152nd Brigade R.F.A.	59.53
21	160th Brigade R.F.A.	53.45
22	X/34 T.M.Battery R.A.)	LIGNY.
23	Y/34 T.M.Battery R.A.)	
24	34th Div.Amm.Col.	LA GRILLE Farm (vicinity).
25	34th Div.Engineers HQ.	near CHAVIGNY Fm.
26	207th Field Coy R.E.	MONTBRAMBOEUF Farm.
27	208th Field Coy R.E.	MOULIN DE VILLERS HELON.
28	209th Field Coy R.E.	VIOLAINE.
29	2/4th Somerset L.I.	65.44.
30	34th M.G. Corps.	65.44.
31	34th Div. Signal Coy.	Caves close to CHAVIGNY Fm.
32	A.D.M.S.	Main MONTGOBERT - LONGPONT Road 500 yds W. of LA GRILLE.
33	102nd Field Ambulance. (Div. Rest Station)	VEZ.
34	103rd Field Ambulance. (Clearing operations).	H.Q. & Walking wounded Collecting Post 70.50 - 85.15. Sheet VILLERS COTTERETS 1/20000 A.D. Station 75.85 - 84.50, Sheet OULCHY LE CHATEAU 1/20000
35	104th Field Ambulance (Main Dressing Station)	LARGNY.
36	34th Div. Train H.Q.)	
36(a)	No. 1 Coy.)	Main MONTGOBERT - LONGPONT Road
36(b)	No. 2 Coy.)	500 yds W. of LA GRILLE.
36 (c)	No. 3 Coy.)	
36(d)	No. 4 Coy.)	
37	44th Mob. Vet. Sec.	ditto.
38	D.A.D.O.S.	ditto.
39	D.A.D.V.S.	ditto.
40	231st Employment Coy.	Detached.

P.T.O.

41	A.P.M.	Main MONTGOBERT - LONGPONT Road 500yds. W. of LA GRILLE.
42	D.G.O.	ditto.
43	Railhead.	VILLERS COTTERETS.

[signature] Capt.

for Lieut. Colonel, G.S.
34th Division.

25th July, 1918.

Army Form C. 2121
(in pads of 100).

"A" Form
MESSAGES AND SIGNALS.

No. of Message..........

A. D. / 3 8

P.C.A.D. le 25 juillet 1918

App XX

5152

ORDRE n° 24

L' A.D./38 est mise à partir du 26 juillet 8 heures à la disposition du 20° C.A. - Elle est attribuée à l' A.D./12 (P.C. à BEAUREPAIRE)

I.- L' A.C.D./38 et l' A.L.C./38 cessent à partir du 25 juillet 21 H. leur mission d'appui de la 34° D.I. W. Le Comt.de l' A.C.D. laissera un Officier à la disposition du Colonel SAVILLE jusqu'au 27 , 8 h.

Le I/32 est ramené dans la nuit du 25-26 à ses échelons ; les autres groupes et la S.M.A. restent en place . Le 26 , à 8 h 30 , le Ct. de l' A.C.D. et les Cts de Groupe , le Ct. du VIII/117 seront rendus à la Ferme BEAUREPAIRE pour recevoir les ordres ~~xxxxxx~~ de l' A.D./12 et prescrire les reconnaissances de positions qui seront occupées dans la nuit du 27-28.

Le I/32 prendra sur ses positions son plein de munitions et passera;le reste au III/41 , les autres groupes conserveront les munitions actuellement sur leurs positions . La S.M.A. fera son plein avec les munitions de récupération .

Dans les nuits du 26-27 & 27-28, le I/32 et les 4° du 32, 23° du 117 occuperont leurs nouvelles positions .

Les liaisons du 32° et du VIII/117 avec l' A.D./12 seront établies le 26 avant midi .Leurs liaisons avec l' A.D./38 à CHAVIGNY ne seront interrompues que sur ordre .

II.- Le Ct. du P.A.D./38 rejoindra la S.M.I. à VIEUX-MOULIN le 26; la SMA/38 recevra à partir du 26 les ordres du Ct. du P.A.D/12 (P.C. à VERTEFEUILLE. l' E.R.D. ira à la Ferme de L' EPINE (N.de VIVIERES)

III.- Le Ct. de l' A.D./38 sera le 26 à partir de 16 heures à CUISE-LAMOTTE.

Le Colonel BERANGER, Ct.l'A.D./38

Destinataires:
Grpts. NORD, SUD, A.L.C. P.A.
A.D./34 , A.D./12 - A/30

8

La liaison du 32e du 8/117 et de la SMA/38 avec le PCAD se fera par l'intermédiaire de l'AD/12
Le motocycliste de l'AD/38 passera tous les matins à 8 heures au PC Beaurepaire.

"A" Form
MESSAGES AND SIGNALS.

Army Form C. 2121
(in pads of 100).

No. of Message..............

SECRET.

34th. DIVISIONAL ARTILLERY WARNING ORDER No. 4.

The Division will be relieved in the line tomorrow night 27th. inst. and withdrawn to an area to be notified later.

Batteries will go back to their Wagon Lines for the night 27/28th.

Captain,
Brigade Major, R.A.
34th. Divisional Artillery.

26-7-18.

Copies			
152nd. Bde. RFA.	(5)	No. 1 Coy. Train.	(1)
160th. Bde. RFA.	(5)	H.A. Sect. 34th. M.T.Coy.	(1)
34th. D.A.C.	(4)	War Diary	(2)
D.T.M.O.	(2)	File	(1)

App XXII

S E C R E T.

34th. DIVISIONAL ARTILLERY ARRANGEMENTS No. 3.

Heavy Artillery supporting 34th. Division.

1. DISPOSITION.

Group P.C.
TOURNAIRE 47.46.

Consists of two 155 mm batteries (3 guns each) at 53.45 and 58.37.

2. S.O.S. BARRAGE.

(a) In case of attack on the Divisional Front
(1[illegible].46) (143.40[illegible]) (15.33) (11[illegible].306) (10.3[illegible]) (094.0[illegible]6)

(b) In case of attack on the Left Brigade Front.
(1[illegible].46[illegible]) (146.4[illegible]6) (155.375) (116.41[illegible]) (11.09) (1[illegible].41)

(c) In case of attack on the Right Brigade Front.
(1[illegible].318) (1[illegible].30) ([illegible]60.275) (116.375) (157.506) (117.292)

3. Counter-Preparation.

(a) Approaches
as for (a) in para. 2.

(b) Klaigues

Points	(30.41)	1 How.
	(31.39)	2 Hows.
	(335.38[illegible])	1 How.
	(313.310)	1 How.
	([illegible].280)	1 How.

Captain,
Brigade Major R.A.
34th. Divisional Artillery.

20th. July 1918.
Copies: 152nd. Bde. RFA. (1)
160th. Bde. RFA. (1)
Group TOURNAIRE (3)
34th. Div. "G". (1)

"A" Form
MESSAGES AND SIGNALS.
Army Form C. 2121
(in pads of 100).
No. of Message..................

App XXIII

Copy No. 5

SECRET.

TO BE ACKNOWLEDGED BY WIRE.

34th DIVISION OPERATION ORDER No. 235.

26th July, 1918.

Reference Maps
OULCHY LE CHATEAU 1:20,000
& SOISSONS (Fr) 1:80,000.

1. The Division will be relieved in the line tomorrow night and withdrawn to an area to be notified later.

2. Reconnaissances of routes to the new area will be made tomorrow morning. The following will meet a Staff Officer from Divisional Headquarters at the road junction N.E. exit from VILLERS-HELON, (46,37) at 9 am.

Infantry and Pioneers

Staff Captains of Infantry Brigades and 2 Mounted Officers per Battalion.

Royal Engineers

1 Mounted Officer per Company.

Machine Gun Battalion

1 Mounted Officer per Company.

Royal Artillery

As detailed by C.R.A. S.C. 2 1 O. per brigade & 2 from D.A.C.

Each of these Officers will be provided with a copy of Maps OULCHY LE CHATEAU 1:20,000 and SOISSONS (Fr) 1:80,000.

H. J. Dooner
Lieut. Colonel, G.S.
34th Division.

Issued at 6.15 pm

DISTRIBUTION.

Copy No. 1 G.O.C.
2 101st Infy Bde.
3 102nd Infy Bde.
4 103rd Infy Bde.
5 C.R.A.
6 C.R.E.
7 Signal Coy.
8 "Q" Adv.
9 2/4th Som. L.I.
10 34 Bn M.G.Corps.
11 A.D.M.S.
12 D.A.D.V.S.
13 D.A.D.O.S.
14 "Q" Rear.
15 D.G.O.
16 44th Mob. Vet. Sec.
17 34th M.T. Coy.
18 103rd Field Ambulance.
19 12th French Division.
20 19th French Division.
21 British Liaison Officer with XXX French Corps.
22 G.H.Q. South.

"A" Form
MESSAGES AND SIGNALS.
Army Form C. 2121
(in pads of 100).
No. of Message..................

App XXIV

- 30e C.A. -

Etat-Major

3e Bureau SECRET

N° 93/. P.C.

Q.G. le 28 Juillet 1918

ORDRE D'OPERATIONS N° 48

I.- Le 30e C.A. a pour mission de s'emparer un jour J ultérieurement fixé de la crête : Orme du Grand Rozoy, mamelon 205 (1 km.N. de Beugneux) , en partant d'une base de départ orientée face au N-E, et passant sensiblement par : le ravin de la cote 148 (1 km. Est de Hartimprè), la lisière Est du bois de la Baillette, et le ravin Nord d'Oulchy le Château

L'attaque du 30e C.A. sera précédée d'une opération faite à une date antérieure par le 11e C.A. à l'effet de s'emparer de la butte Chalmont .

II.- LIMITES D'ACTION du 30e C.A.-

Limite Nord.- Point 06.30 sur la [illegible] -Cote 182 -Carrefour 70.3-20 dans le bois de [illegible]- Cote 185 (600 m. N.E. de Villers Hélon) crête Sud du moulin de Villers Hélon.

Limite Sud.- Voir limite Sud indiquée ci- après .

III.- L'attaque sera menée par 2 Divisions accolées :
-25e D.I. à gauche (7 bataillons)
-34e D.I. Britannique à droite .

La 19e D.I. continuera à maintenir la possession de la crête de Plessier-Huleu et assurera la couverture de [illegible] face au bois du Plessier par 2 de ses bataillons.

IV.- OBJECTIFS DES DIVISIONS.-

25e D.I.- Bois de la Terre à l'or - Crête de l'Orme du Grand Rozoy - Mamelon 203 (1 km. N-O de [illegible]

La 25e D.I agira avec son gros au Sud [illegible] de la croupe : Station de Plessier Huleu [illegible] de la Terre à l'or , de façon à déborder [illegible] de flanc de la lisière Sud du Bois du [illegible] elle débordera Grand Rozoy par le Nord [illegible] nettoiera que lorsque la ligne d'attaque [illegible] nettement dépassé .
Grand Rozoy sera à partir de [illegible] soumis [illegible] violente neutralisation d'artillerie [illegible] sera à H + 1h.20 .

34e D.I. Britannique.- Crête du plateau Nord [illegible] entre le mamelon 205 exclu et Servenay [illegible]

La 34e D.I. Britannique étendra l'[illegible] des hauteurs dans la direction de [illegible] jusqu'à la cote 189 (chemin de Beugneux [illegible]

Liaison à gauche vers 203 avec la [illegible] droite avec les troupes du 11e C.A. [illegible] de la Butte Chalmont ont ordre de [illegible] au mouvement de la 34e D.I. Britannique [illegible] s'établir sur le front : Beugneux-[illegible]
Le 2e objectif sera fixé par une instruction ul[illegible]

APP XXIV

- 30° C.A. -
État-Major
3° Bureau
N° 92/3 P.C.

au P.C. le 26 Juillet 1918

SECRET

ORDRE D'OPÉRATIONS N° 35

I.- Le 30° C.A. a pour mission de s'emparer au jour J ultérieurement fixé de la crête : Orme du Grand Rozoy , mamelon 205 (1 km.N. de Beugneux) , en partant d'une base de départ orientée face au N-E, et passant sensiblement par : le ravin de la cote 148 (1 km. Est de Hartimpré), la lisière Est du bois de la Baillette, et le ravin Nord d'Oulchy le Chateau.

L'attaque du 30° C.A. sera précédée d'une opération faite à une date antérieure par le 11° C.A. à l'effet de s'emparer de la butte Chalmont .

II.- LIMITES D'ACTION du 30° C.A.-

Limite Nord.- Point 06.30 sur le G.M.P. -Cote 158 -Carrefour 70,5 -30 dans le bois de Mauloy- Cote 136 (600 m. N.E. de Villers Hélon) croupe Sud du moulin de Villers Hélon.

Limite Sud.- Voir limite Sud indiquée ci- après .

III.- L'attaque sera menée par 2 Divisions accolées :
-25° D.I. à gauche (7 Bataillons)
-34° D.I. Britannique à droite .

La 25° D.I. continuera à maintenir la possession de la crête de Plessier-Huleu et assurera la couverture de son flanc face au bois du Plessier par 2 de ses bataillons.

IV.- OBJECTIFS DES DIVISIONS.-

25° D.I.- Bois de la Terre à l'Or - Crête de l'Orme du Grand Rozoy - Mamelon 205 (1 km. N-O de Beugneux

La 25° D.I agira avec son gros au sud de l'arête de la croupe : Station de Plessier Huleu -Bois de la Terre à l'Or , de façon à échapper aux feux de flanc de la lisière Sud du Bois du Plessier- elle débordera Grand Rozoy par le Nord et ne le nettoiera que lorsque la ligne d'attaque l'aura nettement dépassé .
Grand Rozoy sera à partir de H soumis à une violente neutralisation d'artillerie , qui cessera à H + 1h.20 .

34° D.I. Britannique.- Crête du plateau Nord de Beugneux entre le mamelon 205 exclu et Servenay inclus.

La 34° D.I. Britannique étendra l'occupation des hauteurs dans la direction de Bucy-le-Bras jusqu'à la cote 199 (chemin de Beugneux à Bucy) .

Liaison:à gauche vers 205 avec la 25° D.I. à droite avec les troupes du 11° C.A. qui , partant de la Butte Chalmont ont ordre de se conformer au mouvement de la 34° D.I. Britannique et de d'établir sur le front : Beugneux-Wallée.
Le 3° objectif sera fixé par une instruction ultérieure.

19° D.I.-

- 3 Gr. de 75 (AD/19).

L'A.L. du C.A. comprenant :

- 3 Groupes de 105
-3 Groupes de 155 L. 77
- 2 Groupes de 220 TR
- 2 Groupes de 280
- 1 Groupe de 145

agira en destruction et en contre batterie.

L'Artillerie du 11° C.A. prètera son appui au 30° C.A.
Il sera fait pour neutraliser le bois du Plessier un large emploi d'obus toxiques et fumigènes .

IX.-

L'attaque aura lieu par surprise au peitit jour , sans préparation d'artillerie .

Elle sera précédée d'un barrage roulant d'obus explosifs et fusants très dense qui sera établi à l'heure H sur la voie ferrée.

Vitesse de déplacement : 100 m. en 4 minutes .

Heure de mise en marche du barrage : H + n minutes (sera fixée ultérieurement d'après la distance à laquelle la base de départ se trouvera de la ligne de chemin de fer , compte tenu des progrès réalisés lors de l'opération à faire antérieurement par le 11° C.A. sur la Butte Chalmont .)

X.-

Il sera fait un arrêt sur la ligne marquée par : ligne du G.M.P. entre l'Orme du Grand Rozoy et la lisière Est de Grand Rozoy , Cote 128 (600 m. S-E de Grand Rozoy) cote 118 sur la rû de Chaudey.
jusqu'à H + 2 h.10.

A partir de cette heure H + 2 h.10 le barrage sera levé et les troupes continueront leur mouvement sous la protection de batteries d'accompagnement dont les déplacements seront prévus à l'avance .

X1.- RESERVE DE C.A.

- 1 Bataillon Britannique qui marchera derrière la gauche de sa division , mais qui ne dépassera pas sans ordres du Général Cdt. le C.A. la route de Soissons.

Ce Bataillon aura en permanence une liaison au P.C. de la 34° D.I. Britannique.

X11.- P.C. de Départ .-

30° C.A.- Ferme Nadon

25° D.I.- Bois de la Folie , puis Plessier Huleu .

34° D.I Britan. Ferme Edrelle , puis Ferme Giroménil.

Le Général Cdt. le 30° C.A.
H. PENET

MISSION DE LA 19° D.I.-

- Arrêter net toute contre-attaque ennemie débouchant du Bois du Plessier.

- Neutraliser par ses feux d'artillerie et d'infanterie les lisières de ce bois.

- 1 R.I. d'une Division disponible est demandé à l'Armée; ce régiment sera le jour J dans la région : Bois de Maloy-Blanzy à la disposition du Général Cdt. le C.A. pour étayer en cas de besoin la 19° D.I.

V1.- LIMITES DES ZONES D'ACTION DES DIVISIONS.-

Limite Nord de la 25° D.I. - Ferme Margimpré - Station de Plessier Huleu - Arête de la croupe du bois de la Terre à l'Or - Bois de la Terre à l'Or - Orme du Grand Rozoy - lisière Est du bois de Plantis.

Limite entreles D.I. -

-Corne Nord du bois de la Baillette- Grand Rozoy (à la 25° D.I. - Cote 198 (1.200 m. N. de Beugneux)(à la 34° D.I. Britannique)/

Limite Sud de la 34° D.I. Britannique.- Route Oulchy le Chateau Beugneux - Jusqu'à la cote 183 - Hauteur 158 Sud de Beugneux - Servenay(inclus).

V11.- MISE EN PLACE DES TROUPES D'ATTAQUE.-

Les troupes d'attaque seront mises en place dans la nuit qui précèdera lâattaque , elle devront être en plawe à H - 1 heure.

Il ne sera fait aucune relève ni changement de limite sur le front avant le jour J .

A l'heure H , les troupes d'attaque qui ne seraient pas déjà dans leur secteur normal , dépasseront les unités en ligne pour se porter à l'attaque.

V11.- ARTILLERIE.-

34° D.I. Britannique.-

12 Groupes de 75/77.......... (3 Gr. de 77 organiques
(3 Gr. de 75 du 41° R A C P
(3 Gr. de 75 (d'un R A C P du
(20° C.A.) AD 38
(3 gr. de 75 (demandés à l'Armée)

3 Bies de 105 obusiers....... organiques

2 Gr. de 155 C.Schneider ....(1 Gr. du 20° C.A.
(1 Gr. demandé à l'Armée

25° D.I.

12 Gr. de 75 .... (3 Gr. de 75 organiques
(3 Gr. de 75 de l'A.D.1
(3 Gr. de 75 du 226° R A C P
(3 Gr. de 75 demandés à l'Armée

8Bies de 155 C. Schneider (2 Bies 155C.Schn.(AD/1)
(1 gr. 155 C. Schn.(AD/25 organ.)
(1 gr. 155 C.Schn.(AD/19)

19° D.I.......

App XXV

-30° C.A -
ARTILLERIE
N° 69 P.C.

P.C. le 26 Juillet 1918

NOTE DE SERVICE

-:-:-:-:-:-:-:-

Les 2° , 4° et 5° Groupes du 286° R.A.L. (220 TR)et 280) sont remis à la disposition du 30° C.A.

En outre , un autre groupe de 280 sera très prochainement alloué au 30° C.A.

L'ensemble de ces 4 groupes formera un sous-groupement , commandé par le Lt-Colonel JULLIEN , qui établira son P.C. dans la région Violaine - Louatre - Villers -Hélon , et qui sera sous les ordres du Lt-Colonel Cdt. l'A.L. 30 .

Les emplacements de ces groupes (dont 2 positions de batterie antérieures de 220 Schneider pourront être occupées à nouveau) devront être choisis de façon à pouvoir agir jusqu'au méridien 186 .

Zone d'action pour les 220 TR. :

au Nord , parallèle 283
au sud , parallèle 279

Zone d'action pour les 280 :

au Nord : ouvrages du G.M.P. sur le parallèle 281
au sud: ouvrages du G.M.P. sur le parallèle 278

Des reconnaissances nécessaires et les mises en batteries seront effectuées dans le plus bref délai possible .

Compte rendu sera adressé au Colonel Cdt. l'A/30 , indiquant le moment où les batteries seront en mesure de tirer .

Le Colonel Cdt. l'A/30
FONDEUR

Destinataires:
Général Cdt. le 30°C.A. à titre de C.R.
Lt-Colonel Cdt. l'A.L. 30 pour exécution
Général Cdt. l'A.D. W)
Colonel Cdt. l'A.D. 25) à titre de renseignement.

"A" Form
MESSAGES AND SIGNALS.
Army Form C. 2121 (in pads of 100).
No. of Message

34° Division.

ARTILLERIE.

N° 5202

P.C.A.D. le 27 juillet 1918

App XXVI

PLAN d' EMPLOI SOMMAIRE.

I.- le 30° C.A. a pour mission de s'emparer au jour J ultérieurement fixé de la crête : Orme du Grand Rozoy, mamelon 205 (1 km N. de BEUGNEUX,) en partant d'une base de départ orientée face au N.E. et passant sensiblement par : le ravin de la Cote 148 (1 km. Est de MARTIMPRE) la lisière Est du Bois de la BAILLETTE, et le Ravin Nord d' OULCHY-LE-CHATEAU.

L'attaque du 30° C.A. sera précédée d'une opération faite à une date antérieure par le 11° C.A. à l'effet de s'emparer de la butte CHALMONT.

II.- L'attaque sera menée par 2 Divisions accolées.
25°D.I. à gauche (7 Btns.) 34° D.I. Britannique à droite.

III.

ORGANISATION DE L'ARTILLERIE. (Général WALTHAL / Colonel BERANGER) P.C. : Ferme d' Edrolles.

A) Sous_Groupement NORD_ (Colonel WARBURTON 160° Bde. / Lt. Col. MONOD 5° RAC
Appui de la 101° Brigade

B) Sous_Groupement SUD - (Colonel SAVILLE 152° Bde / Ct. SUTTERLIN 32° RAC
Appui de la 103° Brigade

C) A.L.C. (Ct. VAUCHEY VIII/117 / A.L.C./48
Appui de la 34° D.I. W - P.C. Ferme d' Edrolles.

Emplacements : voir calque ci-joint - Les emplacements doivent permettre l'appui jusqu'au 1er objectif.

Zônes d'action des sous groupements prévues sur le calque ci-joint

IV.- PREPARATION - Sous Groupements A & B : Néant
Sous Groupement C : Tranchées du G.M.P. Bois du Montceau, Bois 36-62, Bois Ouest de Beugneux.

V.- ACCOMPAGNEMENT - S/ Grpts. A & B : barrage roulant depuis le barrage initial jusqu'au barrage devant le 1er objectif (voir calque) Vitesse : 100 m. en 4 minutes. Dans chaque sous groupement, la brigade britannique et deux groupes en barrage roulant, un groupe en ratissage. Dans chaque groupe, 2 batteries en obus explosifs, 1 batterie en obus à balles fusants 100 mètres en arrière.

Les groupes de ratissage auront une batterie pour tirer sur objectifs fugitifs.

S/ Groupement C. Barrages demi-fixes levés quand l'infanterie arrive à 500 mètres.

Au delà du 1er objectif, l'accompagnement de l' attaque est assuré par les groupes d'accompagnement.

Mise en place et ravitaillement.

Mise en batterie dans la nuit du 28 au 29.

Les batteries doivent avoir deux jours de feux sur les positions le 30 au matin.

Garder les coffres pleins.

La S.M.A./33 à la disposition du Grpt. SUD, la S.M.A./48 à la disposition du Grpt. NORD.

DEPLACEMENT - Fera l'objet d'un ordre ~~xxxx~~ ultérieur. Il commencera dès H + 1 h.

Le Colonel BERANGER, Ct l' A.D.

Destinataires :
5° RAC - 32° RAC -
A.D./34 (3) VIII/117
A.L.C./48 - A/30

Army Form C. 2121 (in pads of 100).
No. of Message.....
"A" Form
MESSAGES AND SIGNALS.

App XXVII

SECRET. 27th. July, 1918.

34th. DIVISIONAL ARTILLERY OPERATION ORDER No. 8.

1. 34th. Divisional Artillery will be withdrawn from the line to-night, and will move to a position of concentration in the BUISSON de HAUTWISON area.

2. Brigades will march this evening to BUISSON de HAUTWISON area, via LONGPONT and CORCY, 152nd. Bde. at 6.0 p.m., and 160th. Bde. at 5.0 p.m.

3. Gun Limbers, F.B. Wagons and first-line wagons will be emptied at the A.R.P. as soon as possible, and will remain in their present Wagon Lines till required to go up and re-fill at the gun positions.

4. Brigade Commanders will commence re-filling their echelons and withdrawing their guns as soon as darkness permits, and will move them direct to new Wagon Line area via VILLERS HELON and LOUATRE.

5. H.Q. and Nos. 1 and 2 Sections, D.A.C., will remain in their present Wagon Lines during the night 27th./28th., and will move under the orders of O.C. to the new area on the 28th.

6. Nos. 1 and 2 Sections, D.A.C., will be responsible for clearing the battery positions of all ammunition during the night of 27th./28th., and returning it to the A.R.P. They will not leave their Wagon Lines to do this before 10. p.m.

7. The S.A.A. Section will move complete at 4.0 p.m. to new area.

8. Wagon Lines in the new area will be pointed out by the Officers who accompanied the S.C.R.A. this morning.

9. The A.R.P. will remain in its present position.

10. Brigades and D.A.C. please acknowledge.

Major, R.A.,
Brigade-Major,
34th. Divisional Artillery.

Distribution:-
152 H.Q. 5
W.L. 5
160 H.Q. 5
W.L. 5
D.A.C. 1
Div."G" 1
War Diary 2 ✓
File 1

1 to Bdes + DAC. App XXVIII

SECRET.

G.S. 266/50.

G.O.C. 101st Infantry Brigade. (4)
G.O.C. 102nd Infantry Brigade. (4)
G.O.C. 103rd Infantry Brigade. (4)
C.R.A. (4)
C.R.E. (4)
O.C. 2/4th Somerset L.I. (1)
O.C. 34th Bn. M.G. Corps. (5)
A.D.M.S. (4)
O.C. Div. Train. (1)
"Q". (2)

The Divisional Commander wishes to impress the extreme importance of the following points with regard to the forthcoming operations.

1. The success or failure of the operations will very largely depend upon the rapid and efficient co-operation of Infantry and Artillery. The closest liaison must be maintained between Infantry Brigadiers and Artillery Group Commanders and all ranks, both of Artillery and Infantry, must be thoroughly conversant with the prescribed Light Signals. The Infantry must also be thoroughly conversant with the Light Signals and panels prescribed for communication with aeroplanes.

2. The Infantry advance is a long one and there is sure to be a certain amount of straggling. All tendency to this must be checked with a firm hand and unwounded men must be kept in the ranks. No unwounded soldier is to accompany a wounded man to the rear, except in cases of absolute necessity.

It must be impressed on all ranks, that it is in the highest degree unsoldierlike for any wounded man who can walk to abandon his arms and equipment.

Battle Straggler Posts must be established in rear of all Brigades in action.

3. The supply of both Artillery and Infantry ammunition will be difficult. It is therefore necessary that all Small Arm Ammunition is taken from killed and wounded men and that all routes are left free for the passage of Artillery and Small Arm Ammunition limbers. Pack transport of S.A.A. must be freely used.

4. Finally the Divisional Commander wishes it to be impressed on all ranks that the operations in which the Division is about to take part, will, if successful, have a great and possibly decisive effect in this area, and that they will be fighting side by side with French troops whose operations during the last few days have enhanced the glory of the French Army. The Divisional Commander therefore relies upon all ranks doing their duty thoroughly and gallantly to the utmost of their power in order to defeat the enemy and uphold the honour of the British Army.

Every advance must be made with dash, every position taken must be held at all costs and every success must be exploited to the utmost.

27th July, 1918.

J. G. Dill [signature]
Lieut. Colonel, G.S.
34th Division.

"A" Form
MESSAGES AND SIGNALS.
Army Form C. 2121 (in pads of 100).
No. of Message..........

"A" Form
MESSAGES AND SIGNALS.

Army Form C. 2121 (In pads of 100.)

No. of Message............

Prefix............Code............m. | Words 67 | Charge

Office of Origin and Service Instructions

MCD

PRIORITY

Sent
At ....m.
To ....
By ....

App XXIX

This message is on a/c of:
............Service.
(Signature of "Franking Officer")

ARMY TELEGRAPHS YCD 27.VII.18.

Recd. at........m.
Date............
From............
By............

TO	101 Bde 102 " 103 "	C.R.A. C.R.E. 2/4th Somerset L.I.	34th M.G. Bn. Signal Coy.	Train A.D.M.S. "Q"

Sender's Number.	Day of Month.	In reply to Number.	AAA
G. 95	27		

The French have taken FERE EN TARDENOIS AAA All units must be held in readiness to move at an hour's notice from the time of arrival in bivouac tonight AAA Reconnaissances in connection with the operations already outlined must be carried out as early as possible tomorrow morning AAA ACKNOWLEDGE

If	is	possible	that
these	operations	may	take
place	morning	29th	AAA

ACKNOWLEDGE

From	34 Div.
Place	
Time	10.15 pm

The above may be forwarded as now corrected. (Z)

....
Censor.

H. Brown Lt.Col. GS
Signature of Addressor or person authorised to telegraph in his name

* This line should be erased if not required.

Order No. 1625. Wt. W3253/ P 511 27/2 H. & K., Ltd. (E. 2634).

"A" Form
MESSAGES AND SIGNALS.
Army Form C. 2121 (in pads of 100).
No. of Message............

App XXX

Copy No. 5.

S E C R E T.

****

TO BE ACKNOWLEDGED BY WIRE.

34th DIVISION OPERATION ORDER No. 232.

****

Ref. Maps :
OULCHY LE CHATEAU 1:20,000
SOISSONS S.E. 1:50,000

27th July, 1918.

---

1. The Division will be relieved by French Troops on the night July 27th/28th as follows -

From the Southern Boundary to Point 99.30, (on PARIS Defence Line) by troops of the 19th French Division taking over from the 101st Brigade.
From Point 99.30 to Northern Boundary by troops of the 12th French Division taking over the remainder of the line held by 101st Brigade and all that of the 102nd Brigade.
The numbers of the Regiments have not yet been notified.

2. Reconnaissances will be made by officers of relieving French Units today. All arrangements as to guides will be made mutually between G.Os.C. Brigades and Colonels Commanding relieving French Units.

3. (a) The area in which the Division will concentrate after relief is -

BOIS DU BOEUF - BOIS DE NADON - BUISSON DE HAUT WISON.

(b) Destinations of units.

101st Brigade & 1 Coy M.G.Bn.	- BOIS DU BOEUF Northern End.
102nd Brigade	- BOIS DE NADON Eastern End.
103rd Brigade & 1 Coy M.G.Bn.	- BOIS DU BOEUF Southern End.
Field Coys R.E. 2/4th Somerset L.I. M.G. Battalion (less 2 Coys)	- BOIS DE NADON Western End.
R.A.	.. BUISSON DE HAUT WISON (SOISSONS S.E. 1:50,000) Western edge of Sheet, between meridians 280,281.

4. Routes on relief -

101st Brigade by main road HARTENNES ET TAUX to St REMY BLANZY.
102nd Brigade by road passing Eastern edge of BOIS DE MAULOY - BLANZY.
103rd Brigade 2 Battalions as for 101st Brigade.
1 Bn. & M.G.Coy as for 102nd Brigade.
Field Coys R.E. VILLERS-HELON - LOUATRE.
2/4th Somerset L.I. VILLERS-HELON - LOUATRE.
Machine Gun Bn. - Coys in line as per Brigades they are in the line with.
H.Q. & Coy not in the line as for R.E.
R.A. .. VILLERS-HELON - LOUATRE.

THESE ROUTES ARE LIABLE TO ALTERATION.

5. Units of the 103rd Brigade will be moved into the new area directly light permits and will be clear of Point 132 West of BOIS DE LA FOLIE as early as possible.

6.....
P.T.O.

"A" Form MESSAGES AND SIGNALS. Army Form C. 2121 (in pads of 100). No. of Message..........

6. Officers detailed in para. 2 of Operation Order No. 235 of 28th inst. will reconnoitre the routes given in para. 4 above, the best approaches to them on leaving the line, and, from them into the area allotted to each unit, and will be prepared to guide their units on relief.

7. A.D.M.S. will arrange to withdraw the Advanced Dressing Station on the morning of July 28th.

8.(a) Destinations of Field Ambulances, Divisional Train, Mobile Vet. Section, M.T. Coy and Div. Employment Coy. will be notified later.
(b) H.Q. and No. 1 Section Signal Coy. will move with Divisional H.Q.

9.(a) All stores handed over by the French on taking o
Sector will be handed back on relief.
(b) All British ammunition and stores will be remove
area by units in whose charge they now are.

10.(a) Command of Brigade Sectors will pass at 2 am. J
(b) Command of the Divisional Sector will pass at 4

11. Completion of reliefs will be reported by wire.

12. Divisional H.Q. will remain in its present locat
further orders.. It will eventually open at FERME D'

J. G. Dormer

Lieut Colonel,
34th Division

Issued at 5 am.

Copy No. 1 G.O.C.
2 101st Infy Bde.
3 102nd Infy Bde.
4 103rd Infy Bde.
5 C.R.A.
6 C.R.E.
7 Signal Coy.
8 "Q" Adv.
9 2/4th Somerset L.I.
10 34th Bn.M.G.Corps.
11 A.D.M.S.
12 D.A.D.V.S.
13 D.A.D.O.S.
14 "Q" Rear.
15 D.G.O.
16 A.P.M.
17 44th Mob. Vet. Sec.
18 34th M.T.Coy.
19 103rd Field Ambulance.
20 12th French Division.
21 19th French Division.
22 British Liaison Officer XXX Fr.Corps.
23 G.H.Q. South.

Army Form C. 2121
(in pads of 100).

"A" Form
MESSAGES AND SIGNALS.

No. of Message..................

Prefix............Code..............m. Office of Origin and Service Instructions.	Words / Charge. Sent At.............m. To............ By............	This message is on a/c of .... Service. (Signature of "Franking Officer.")	Recd. at..........m. Date.......... From .... By..........

APP XXXI

TO 168th Bde

Sender's Number.	Day of Month.	In reply to Number.	AAA
* BM	27		

Brigade commanders accompanied by one officer prepared to go at once to reconnaitre will meet C.R.A. at FONTAINE ALIX FARM (57. 01) at 8.30 a.m. tomorrow morning. Brigades must be prepared to go into action tomorrow night. Please ACKNOWLEDGE.

From BM RA 34th Div
Place
Time

The above may be forwarded as now corrected. (Z)

Censor. Signature of Addressor or person authorised to telegraph in his name

* This line should be erased if not required.

Wt. W492/M1647 100,000 pads. 4/17. W. & Co., Ltd. (E. 1187.)

Army Form C. 2121
(in pads of 100).
"A" Form
MESSAGES AND SIGNALS.
No. of Message..................

34th. Division.  SECRET.

ARTILLERY PLAN.

1. The Division will attack on the 29th. at an hour H to be notified later.

2. Organization of the Artillery.
H.Q. Brig. Gen. WALTHALL, C.M.G. D.S.O.) Command Post
Colonel BERANGER.) Fme d'EDROLLES.

(A) Northern Group.
Supporting 101st. Infy. Bde.
Lt.Col. WARBURTON. D.S.O. 160th.Bde.) Command Post
Lt.Col. MONOD 5th. Arty.Regt.) Fme GEROMENIL

(B) Southern Group.
Supporting 103rd. Bde.
Lt.Col SAVILE, D.S.O. 152nd.Bde.) Command Post
Comdt. SUTTERLIN. 32nd. Arty.Regt.) BOIS ST. HILAIRE.

(C) Superimposed Group.
Lt.Col. ------ 224th.Arty.Regt.) Command Post ---

(D) Corps Heavy Artillery.
Comdt. VIAL. V111 118
V111 117
A.L.O. / 68

Positions should admit of support up to the Infantry first objective.

3. Preparation.
Groups A, B and C NIL
Group D. During the day of the 28th. Trench destruction of G.M.P. BOIS de MONTCEAU, Wood 36.82 and Wood W. of BEUGMEUX.
The Heavy Artillery of the 30th. Corps will cooperate in the preparation of the G.M.P. and BEUGNEUX.

4. Covering Fire.
Creeping Barrage and Combing Barrage.
In each of Groups A and B two "groupes" and the British Brigade in the creeping barrage. One "groupe" in the "combing" barrage.
In each "groupe" and brigade 2 batteries using H.E., one battery firing shrapnel superimposed on the other 2 batteries and 100 metres beyond their barrage line.
Group C in the combing barrage.
Each of the combing barrage "groupes" in groups A and B will have a battery in readiness to fire on fleeting opportunity targets.
The creeping barrage will come down at H hour and stand till H plus 4 mins. at which time it will commence to creep.
Speed of Barrage 100 metres per 4 mins in lifts of 100 metres.
Rate of Fire. 4 r.p.g.p.m. for the first 8 mins then 1 r.p.g.p.m. except for the lift on to the G.M.P. when the rate will be increased to 4 r.p.g.p.m. for 2 mins.
Combing barrage will keep up a uniform rate of fire of 1 r.p.g.p.m.
The barrage will stop as soon as the infantry reach their first objective.
The barrage will protect the first objective till H plus 1.50 and not until H plus 2.10 as previously stated.

Beyond the objective the attack will be supported by
A/152 and 1 section D/152 under the orders of O.C. A/152.
B/160 " 1 " D/160 " " " " O.C. B/160.
The Os.C. A/152 and B/160 willreport respectively to the G.Os.C. 103rd. Infy. Bde. and 101st. Infy. Bde as soon after H plus 1.50 mins as possible and will come under their orders.

(Contd).

Group D.
Standing barrage lifted when the Infantry are within 500 metres. First Standing Barrage on the trenches of the G.M.P. and BOIS de MONTCEAU.
4.5" Hows. will similarly carry out standing barrage on points selected by the Bde. Commander and lift off these points when the Infantry arrive within 500 metres.

5. Liaison.
All Infantry Liaison will be found by 34th. D.A.
One Officer of the rank of Captain and a sufficient party of signallers will be detailed by each Brigade as liaison with the Infantry Brigade they support.
The H.Q. of both Infantry Brigades at the commencement of operations will be in the S.W. corner of the BOIS de BAILLETE (13.76

6. Observation Party.
Brigade Commanders will each detail an Observation party consisting of 1 officer and as many signallers, runners, etc. as may be considered necessary.
The role of these parties will be to watch the progress of the Infantry and indicate targets to the batteries.
After H plus 1.50 the closest possible touch with the Infantry must be maintained.

7. Orders for the forward movement of batteries will be issued later.

8. Watches will be synchronised by telephone.

9. Brigades please ACKNOWLEDGE.

Captain,
Brigade Major.R.A.
34th. Divisional Artillery.

28-7-18.
7-30 p.m.
Copies: 152nd. Bde. RFA.
160th. Bde. RFA.
34th. Dv. "G".
32nd Regt d' Artillerie
War Diary.

File
App XXXIII

Copy No. 14

SECRET
****

TO BE ACKNOWLEDGED BY WIRE

34th DIVISION

INSTRUCTIONS No. 1

GENERAL SCHEME

1. The Division will carry out an attack on the enemy at an early date (afterwards referred to as "H" day) in conjunction with troops of the 11th French Corps on the Right and the 25th French Division on the Left.

TROOPS

2. The attack will be carried out by the 103rd Infantry Brigade plus 1 Company 34th Bn. M.G. Corps on the Right and the 101st Infantry Brigade plus 1 Company 34th Bn. M.G. Corps on the Left.

3. The 102nd Infantry Brigade (less 1 Battalion) 2/4th Somerset Light Infantry, 207th, 208th and 209th Field Coys. R.E. and 34th Bn. M.G. Corps less 2 Companies will form a Divisional Reserve. The Field Coys. R.E. and 2/4th Somerset Light Infantry (Pioneers) will be under the command of the C.R.E.

4. 1 Battalion of the 102nd Infantry Brigade will be detailed as Corps Reserve. It will be in position in the ravine at the N.W. corner of the BOIS DE BAILLETTE and direct telephonic communication is being arranged by O.C. Div. Signal Coy.

5. The Artillery of the 34th Division supplemented by 2 Regiments of French Field Artillery (total 108 field guns and 56 howitzers) supplemented by Heavy Artillery, will support the attack.

STARTING LINE, BOUNDARIES and OBJECTIVES

6. The approximate line from which the attack will start is shown in dotted BLUE on the attached map.

The actual line will depend on the result of an operation which will be carried out by the 11th French Corps on H minus 1 day with the object of capturing the BUTTE CHALMONT.

7. The limits of the front of the Division are shown in BLUE and the dividing line between Brigades in BLUE DOTTED CHAIN.

8. The first objective is shown in BROWN. With reference to this line it should be understood that the line is only intended to show approximately the line which has to be reached and on which a main line of resistance should be formed.

A second objective will be ordered as and when circumstances permit.

ACTION OF TROOPS ON FLANKS

9. (a) The 25th French Division will attack on the Left of the 34th Division. The line from which its attack will start is approximately from the N.E. corner of the BOIS DE LA BAILLETTE along the ravine running through Point 148 (1 kilometre S.E. ...

S.E. of MARTIMPRE FARM).

(b) This Division, keeping in touch on its Right with the 34th Division, will attack with its left on the general line:- station of PLESSIER HULEU - BOIS DE LA TERRE A L'OR - ORME DU GRAND ROZOY. It will take as much advantage of ground as possible to avoid enfilade fire from the BOIS DU PLESSIER. It will skirt GRAND ROZOY on the North and mop up the village when the line of advance has reached a line to the North of the village.

(c) The first objective of this Division is to gain the line:- BOIS DE LA TERRE A L'OR - ORME DU GRAND ROZOY - Point 203 - the Northern Boundary of the 34th Division zone on the Eastern end of the feature 203.

(d) A second objective will be ordered according to circumstances.

10. The 11th French Army Corps, on the right of the 34th Division, will attack from the BUTTE CHALMONT, with its left in touch with the 34th Division and will establish itself on the line WALLÉE (1,500 yards East of the BUTTE CHALMONT) - BEUGNEUX (exclusive).

PLAN OF ATTACK

11. The Infantry of the 101st and 103rd Infantry Brigades and the Machine Gun Coys. attached to them will be assembled during the night of the H minus 1/H day in their attack formations with the leading wave as close to the existing front line East and South of the BOIS DE BAILLETTE as possible.

The position of assembly for the Divisional Reserve will be in the BOIS DE BAILLETTE.

12. The Artillery action will be as follows :-

(a) 1st Phase - The barrage will open at H hour on the line of the railway East of the BOIS DE BAILLETTE. It will lift from that line at H plus N minutes. (The number of minutes represented by N depends upon the distance of the front line from the railway.)

N=4

The barrage will advance by lifts of 100 yds. every 4 minutes and will continue at this rate until the leading waves of Infantry have reached the line shown GREEN on the map.

The barrage will remain East of that line until H plus 2 hours 10 minutes when it will cease.

During this pause of the barrage at least 2 Batteries of field guns and 2 sections field howitzers (British) will move forward to advanced positions, which must be previously reconnoitred. This artillery will then come under the command of G.O.C. 101st and 103rd Infantry Brigades, 1 Battery field guns and 1 Section of howitzers to each Brigade.

(b) 2nd Phase - The Infantry will continue their advance at H plus 2 hours 10 minutes and the rôle of the field artillery will then be to cover and assist the advance of the Infantry, Batteries being moved forward as opportunity offers under orders from Divisional Headquarters.

13. The Infantry action will be as described below :-

(a) The disposition of Battalions is left to Brigadiers but troops should be disposed in depth, the principle that each Commander has a Reserve under his hand being observed.

The density ...

14. (a) The Action of the Divisional Reserve cannot be accurately forecasted. It will be moved into the BOIS DE BAILLETTE and subsequently to the line of the road BEUGNEUX - GRAND ROZOY. There will be held in readiness to capture the village of SERVENAY, to resist counter-attack or exploit success. The 2/4th Somerset Light Infantry will be held in readiness to be attached to the 102nd Infantry Brigade instead of the Battalion detailed as Corps Reserve.

The Battalion of the 102nd Infantry Brigade detailed as Corps Reserve will be placed in the rear of the Left of the Division but will not pass the SOISSONS - CHATEAU THIERRY Road without orders from the Corps Commander which will be issued through Divisional Headquarters.

(b) The 34th Bn. Machine Gun Corps less the two Coys. attached to the 101st and 103rd Infantry Brigades will be handled as opportunity offers.

Those Companies may be used during the pause between the 1st and 2nd phases to deal with counter-attack during the pause and with hostile opposition as soon as the Infantry advance is resumed.

In the 3rd phase a proportion of guns may be detailed to occupy defensive positions to cover the line consolidated.

It must be borne in mind that the ammunition supply will be difficult and that every gun must be brought as far forward as possible before it is brought into action throughout.

J.G. Dooner

Lieut. Colonel, G.S.
34th Division.

Issued at 1.30 pm
28 July 1918

	Copies numbered
G.O.C..	1
101st Infantry Brigade	2 - 5
102nd " "	6 - 9
103rd " "	10 - 13
C. R. A.	14 - 16
C. R. E.	17
2/4th Somerset L.I.	18
M.G. Battalion	19 - 23
Signal Coy.	24
A.D.M.S.	25
"Q"	26
A.P.M.	27
30th French Corps	28
25th French Division	29

The density of the leading waves must depend upon the amount of opposition met with. These waves must be fed from those in rear.

(b)
<u>1st Phase</u>

(i) The advance will commence at H hour, troops passing through the Infantry holding the line. The leading waves will follow the barrage, which will consist entirely of H.E., as closely as possible.

(ii) Special parties must be told off beforehand to mop up the trench line which runs Southwards from GRAND ROZOY and which the leading waves must pass over without a pause.

(iii) GRAND ROZOY is inclusive to the 25th French Division. It will be neutralised by Heavy Artillery throughout the advance and will be encircled and attacked by that Division from the North. The G.O.C. 101st Infantry Brigade will, however, detail a flank guard to deal with any attack debouching from the village on his flank. This flank guard must keep well away from the village to avoid the neutralising fire.

(iv) On reaching the line marked GREEN on the map the leading waves will halt and all Units will reorganise under the cover of the protective barrage which will remain down for about 50 minutes. During this pause every effort must be made to replenish supplies of ammunition and push forward machine guns. The neutralising fire on GRAND ROZOY will probably continue during this phase and all troops must be warned that this is our fire and not that of the enemy even though it may be behind them.

(c)
<u>2nd Phase</u>

(i) The advance will be resumed at H plus 2 hours 10 minutes and will proceed as before but without the creeping barrage. It is during this period that the closest liaison should be maintained between Infantry and Artillery Commanders so that full use may be made of the available Artillery support.

(ii) The village of BEUGNEUX and the Woods to the West of it constitute the most formidable positions in this phase.
Frontal attacks on these positions must be avoided. The G.O.C. 103rd Infantry Brigade will detail a special party to occupy the Hill 158 at the Southern end of the village and will endeavour to encircle the village either by the West using the copse running South from the road as a screen for the movement, or by both flanks using Hill 158 as a pivot of manoeuvre for movement S.E. of the village. The 101st Infantry Brigade will manoeuvre to turn the Western flank of the Woods.

(d)
<u>3rd Phase</u>

On reaching approximately the line marked BROWN upon the map a defensive position will be selected and consolidated as quickly as possible. <u>At</u> the same time G.O.C. 103rd Infantry Brigade will push out a strong advance guard in the direction of the BOIS DE BUIS D'ARCY and Point 192 South of SERVENAY. The G.O.C. 101st Infantry Brigade will similarly push out advanced guards in the direction of Point 199 and BURY LE BRAS FARM and also along the spur running N.E. from Point 198.

14. ....

SECRET
****

Copy No. 5

TO BE ACKNOWLEDGED BY WIRE.

34th DIVISION OPERATION ORDER No. 238
****

Reference Sheets
OULCHY LE CHATEAU) 1:20,000.
FERE EN TARDENOIS)

29th July 1918

---

1. Advance to first objective will be resumed at 2.30 pm. 103rd Brigade and one company Machine Gun Battn on right, 102nd Brigade on left.

Starting line - A line from Southern Div. Boundary through the two houses on the road S.W. of BEUGNEUX along the Northern Border of Wood West of BEUGNEUX to Northern Div. Boundary. Initial barrage line will be 150 yards E. of above line.

2.(a) Leading troops of attacking Brigades must be on the starting line at 2.28 pm. Barrage will lift off initial line 2.30 pm and advance at the rate of 100 yards in four minutes to the line 203, 194 S.W. Corner of SERVENAY. 102nd Brigade will push through to the objective detailing one or two Coys. to attack BEUGNEUX from the N.W.

(b) All available Heavy Artillery is now bombarding the positions to be attacked and will continue to do so until the troops get within 500 yards when it will lift to other targets.

3. One Battalion will be kept in Brigade Reserve. Close touch must be kept with the French on their left who will be attacking at the same time.

4. 103rd Infantry Brigade will turn BEUGNEUX by the South and push through to the objective. Special troops to be detailed to attack BEUGNEUX from E. and N.E. Close touch must be kept with the French troops on the right who will be advancing at the same time.

5. As soon as the 102nd Brigade has passed through the 101st Brigade in the old PARIS LINE, the latter will be reorganised and take up a position of readiness in the old PARIS LINE and BOIS DU MONTCEAU.

6. 1/4th Cheshires will move at once to West side of BOIS DU MONTCEAU and come under the orders of the Divisional Commander who will issue them through G.O.C. 101st Brigade who will get into touch with them forthwith.

J.G. Dooner
Lieut. Colonel, G.S.
34th Division.

Issued at 1.30 pm

Copy No. 1 G.O.C.
2 101 Inf. Bde.
3 102 " "
4 103 " "
5 C.R.A.
6 C.R.E.
7 34th Bn. M.G. Corps
8 Signal Coy.
9 "Q"
10 A.D.M.S.
11 A.P.M.
12 XXX French Corps
13 25th French Division

MESSAGE BY SPECIAL D.R.

C.R.A.
C.R.E.
101 Bde
102 Bde
103 Bde
34th M.G.Bn

G 124 29th

On reaching objective, 101 and 103 Bdes will consolidate on line of heights SERVENAY (exclusive) Point 199-Hill 205 to Divisional boundary aaa The 101 Bde will then push an Advanced Guard in the direction of BUCY-LE-BRAS FARM ready to proceed to FERME D'ARSON N.E. of MAAST - ET - VIOLAINE on receipt of further orders aaa The 25th French Div will hold the line from Hill 205 facing North and will continue the advance in the direction of LES CROUTTES and VIOLAINE aaa On receipt of orders, the 102 Bde will move to the BOIS LE MT JOUR and keep touch with the 25th French Div on its left and 101 Bde on its right aaa ~~ACKNOWLEDGE by~~ bearer

FROM:- 34th Division

Time:- 10 am

J.G. Dower

Lieut. Colonel G.S.
34th Division

P.1

Copy No. 5

SECRET
****

TO BE ACKNOWLEDGED BY WIRE

34th DIVISION OPERATION ORDER No. 237
****

Reference Sheets
OULCHY LE CHATEAU) 1:20,000.
FERE EN TARDENOIS)

28th July, 1918.

---

1. The enemy has been pushed across the OURCQ at FERE EN TARDENOIS which is now held by French troops.
This morning he has been pushed back along the BUTTE CHALMONT as far as the PARIS DEFENCE LINE of Trenches. Our line runs along these trenches as far as Point 123, thence along the stream to Point 122 South of the Railway Station 1 kilometre S.W. of GRAND ROZOY. The enemy resistance was slight but his artillery retaliation on the captured line has been heavy. BEUGNEUX is reported to be strongly held.

2. (a) The XXXth French Corps, with the 34th Division on the right and the 25th French Division on the left, assisted by the co-operation of the XIth French Corps on its right, will attack the enemy in accordance with the plan detailed in "Instructions No. 1" issued to-day.

(b) The 2nd Battalion, 16th Infantry Regiment will be on the left of the 101st Infantry Brigade. 1 Company will be in close liaison with the left of the 101st Infantry Brigade and will have an English speaking Officer with it.

3. The 34th Division will attack the enemy according to the plan given in "Instructions No. 1."

4. The actual line from which the attack will start is the line of the stream from where it cuts the Southern Divisional Boundary to where it meets the Railway (Pt. 122), thence along the Railway to the Northern Divisional Boundary.

5. Troops will be formed up by 1 a.m. to-morrow in rear of the line as follows -

(a) 103rd Infantry Brigade and 1 Machine Gun Coy. on the right.
101st Infantry Brigade and 1 Machine Gun Coy. on the left
These Brigades will be formed up in their attack formation with the leading waves close up to the line.

(b) 102nd Infantry Brigade and 2/4th Somerset Light Infantry in the Western end of the BOIS DE BAILLETTE.

(c) Field Coys. R.E. on the reverse slope West of GEROMENIL Farm immediately North of Point 161.

6. Routes to forming-up places as follows. Separate orders have been given regarding guides.

(a) 103rd Brigade and Machine Gun Coy.

FONTAINE ALIX FERME - Point 181 - Point 174 - BILLY SUR OURCQ - Point 165 East of GEROMENIL Farm - S. end of OULCHY LA VILLE.

P.T.O. .....

(b) 101st Brigade and Machine Gun Coy.

ST. REMY-BLANZY - Point 142 - FERME DE FRONTENY - Point 189 - Northern end of OULCHY LA VILLE

(c) 102nd Brigade, 2/4th Somerset Light Infantry and 34th Machine Gun Battalion less 2 Coys. will follow the 101st Brigade in that order.

(d) R.E. Coys. will follow the Machine Gun Battalion as far as cross roads at Point 184 and proceed independently to their destination.

(e) The head of the 101st Brigade will pass the centre of ST. REMY-BLANZY village at 10 p.m. by which hour French troops will be clear of it. The head of the 103rd Brigade will pass FONTAINE ALIX FERME not later than 9 pm.

(f) 2 troops, 3rd French Dragoons, will be at Divisional Headquarters at 4 a.m. They will march independently.

7. The 52nd Escadrille, French Flying Corps, will co-operate with the Division. All ranks will be warned to give immediate response to calls to show position. The signal is a light bursting into 6 white lights. Troops in the front line only will respond to the signal.

8. The attack will commence at Zero hour which will be notified as soon as possible.

9. (a) The line of the initial barrage which will commence at Zero will be 150 metres East of the starting line (vide para. 4). The barrage will remain on this line until Zero plus 4 when it will advance as described in "Instructions No. 1." The barrage will halt 250 metres East of the line shown on the map at Zero plus 1.50.

(b) The infantry advance will begin at Zero hour, the leading waves getting as close as possible to the barrage before it lifts. The attack will proceed as described in "Instructions No. 1" except that the 2nd Phase will begin at Zero plus 1.50.

(c) The left flank of the 101st Brigade will keep 300 metres to the South of GRAND ROZOY and the G.O.C. 101st Brigade will detail a special party to block the Eastern entrance.

1 Company of the 2/16th French Infantry Regiment will be on the immediate left of the 101st Brigade and will attack the village from the South.

10. Divisional Battle Straggler Posts will be established at BILLY SUR OURCQ and ST. REMY-BLANZY.

11. Prisoners' Cage will be established at EDROLLE FARM, 2,000 yards West of VILLE SUR OURCQ.

12. (a) An Advanced Dressing Station will be established in the neighbourhood of BILLY-SUR-OURCQ.
(b) The Main Dressing Station will be established in the neighbourhood of CHOUY.
(c) The Walking Wounded Collecting Post will be at the Main Dressing Station.

13. The following roads are allotted to the Division for use during the operations :-

(a) Horse Transport

Route DU PENDU* - Route LONGPONT* - CORCY - Route de la VALLEE DE NADON - FERME NADON - FONTAINE ALIX.

(b) Motor Transport

(i) Following the circuit - VILLERS COTTERETS - CORCY - LONGPONT - Carrefour MONTGOBERT.

(ii) In common with IIth French Corps - Route CORCY* - MAUCREUX CHATEAU* - CHOUY - BILLY-SUR-OURCQ - FERME GEROMENIL.

(* See VILLERS COTTERETS Sheet, 1:20,000)

14. (a) Advanced Divisional Headquarters has opened at EDROLLE FARM.
(b) An Advanced Report Centre will open at GEROMENIL FARM at 3.30 am.
(c) Rear Divisional Headquarters remain in their present location.

[signature]
Lieut. Colonel, G.S.
34th Division.

Issued at
7 pm

Copy No. 1 G.O.C.
2 101st Infantry Brigade
3 102nd " "
4 103rd " "
5 C. R. A.
6 C. R. E.
7 2/4th Somerset L.I.
8 34th Bn. M.G. Corps.
9 Signal Coy.
10 A.D.M.S.
11 "Q"
12 A.P.M.
13 XXXth French Corps
14 25th French Division.
15 3rd French Dragoons

"A" Form
MESSAGES AND SIGNALS.
Army Form C. 2121 (in pads of 100).
No. of Message........

Au delà du 1er objectif , l'accompagnement de l' attaque sera assuré par des groupes qui se déplaceront .

Sous groupement D : Barrages demi-fixes levés quand l' Infanterie arrive à 500 mètres .

Premier barrage demi-fixe sur tranchées du G.M.P. et Bois de MONTCEAU

V. - LIAISONS .- Toutes les liaisons auprès de l' Infanterie sont fournies par l' Artillerie Britannique .

Les Groupements détacheront un Officier de liaison monté et un agent de liaison monté au P.C.A.D.

Liaisons téléphoniques - Voir schéma . Le Groupement C se reliera à la Ferme d' Ecrolles .

T. S . F . Chaque Groupe et chaque Groupement sont munis d'une antenne réceptrice .

Indicatif de l'avion de la 34° Division : K U

VI.- OBSERVATION :

O. T. A déterminer par les Commandants de Groupe et de Groupement .

O. A . Escadrille 52
Ballon 45

VII.- MISE EN PLACE : Toutes les batteries doivent être en place dans la nuit du 28 au 29 , une pièce en batterie avant la nuit effectuera un accrochage .

VIII.- RAVITAILLEMENT :

Les batteries doivent conserver leurs coffres pleins .
Avoir deux jours de feu (y compris les munitions des coffres) le 29 au matin .

Dépôts de munitions au Bois de PRINGY pour le 32° et le 117° et britanniques .

Les autres éléments se ravitaillent au dépôt du 11° Corps .

IX.- DEPLACEMENT DES BATTERIES .-

Fera l'objet d'un ordre ultérieur .

P. le Général WALTHAL , Ct. l'AD/ 34
le Colonel BERANGER.

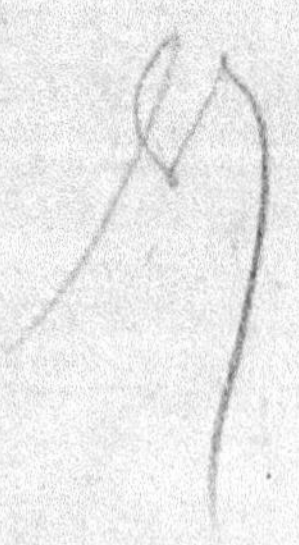

Destinataires :

Groupements A	(4)
" B	(4)
" C	(4)
" D	(3)
34° D.I. W	(1)
A.D./34	(3)
A/30	(1)
D.I. voisines	(2)
Aviation	(1)

34ᵉ Division .

ARTILLERIE .

N°

P.C.A.D le 28 juillet 1918

APP XXXIV

P L A N d ' E M P L O I

I.- l' attaque prévue au Plan d' Emploi du 27 juillet aura lieu le 29 à une heure H qui sera fixée ultérieurement

II.- ORGANISATION DU COMMANDEMENT

Général WALTHAL) P.C. : Ferme d' Edrelles .
Colonel BERANGER)

A.- Sous Groupement NORD
Colonel WARBURTON 160ᵉ Bde) P.C. : Ferme Geremenil
Lt.Col. MONOD 5ᵉ RAC)
Appui de la 101ᵉ Brigade

B.- Sous Groupement SUD
Colonel SAVILLE 152ᵉ Bde.) P.C.: Bois St. Hilaire
Comt. SUTTERLIN 32ᵉ RAC)
Appui de la 103ᵉ Brigade

C.- Sous Groupement de superposition :
Lt. Col. X... 224ᵉ RAC P.C. : ....

D.- A.L.C.
Ct. VIAL : VIII/118 -
VIII/117
A.L.C./68

EMPLACEMENTS : Doivent permettre l'appui jusqu'au 1er objectif .

III.-PREPARATION :

Sous Groupements A, B, C, : Néant

Sous Groupement D : Dans la journée du 28 , tirs de destruction sur les tranchées du G.M.P. , Bois du Monteau, Bois 35-82, Bois ouest de BEUGNEUX.

L' A.L./30 coopère à la préparation sur le G.M.P. et BEUGNEUX.

IV.- ACCOMPAGNEMENT .-

Barrage roulant et ratissage .

Dans chacun des sous groupements A et B , deux groupes et la brigade britannique en barrage roulant , un groupe en ratissage.

Dans chaque Groupe : 2 batteries en obus explosifs , 1 batterie en obus à balles 100 m. en arrière .

Sous Groupement C : en ratissage .

Chacun des 2 Groupes de ratissage des sous groupements A & B a une batterie prête à tirer sur objectifs fugitifs .

Le barrage roulant sera assis à l'heure H et maintenu sur place jusqu'à H + 4 minutes , heure à laquelle il se mettra en mouvement .

Vitesse : 100 m. en 4 minutes par bonds de 100 mètres .

Cadence : 4 coups par pièce minute pendant les 10 premières minutes , puis 1 coups par pièce minute avec renforcement de 4 coup par pièce minute au passage du G.M.P. pendant 2 minutes

Pour le ratissage : cadence uniforme : 1 coup par pièce-minute

Le barrage est éteint dès que l' Infanterie fait connaître qu'elle a atteint son 1er objectif .

L'arrêt primitivement prévu sur le 1er objectif jusqu'à H + 2 h 10' ne durera que jusqu'à H + 1 h 50'

au delà ....

"A" Form
MESSAGES AND SIGNALS.

Army Form C. 2121
(in pads of 100).

No. of Message..................

Calque pour la désignation et le report des objectifs.

25° D.I

Barrage fixe à H+1h50

Limite de Brigades

1er Objectif

Ligne de départ

H+1h04 · +50 · +52 · +48 · H+44

H+4 · +8 · +12 · +16 · +20 · +24 · +28 · +32 · +36 · +40 · +44 · +48

11e C.A.

280 · 279 · 278

184 · 185 · 186

Feuille Oulchy $\frac{1}{20000}$

28/7/18

Les heures indiquées sont celles auxquelles le barrage quitte la ligne

34e Division . W.

ARTILLERIE .

N°

SECRET

P.C.A.D. le 28 Juillet 1918

23 heures 20

App XXXV

£208

ORDRE N° 26

I.- L'heure H est : H = 4h10 (quatre heures dix)

II.- Entre H + 1 heure et H + 1 h 30', chaque brigade britannique déplace une batterie de campagne et 2 pièces de 4 pouces 1/2 à la disposition de l'Infanterie.

Dans chaque sous groupement, un groupe de 75 se portera en avant, par batteries successives pour venir occuper un emplacement dans les boqueteaux au Nord du BOIS de la BAILLETTE (S/ Groupement NORD) et un emplacement au voisinage de la route OULCHY-LA-VILLE - OULCHY-LE-CHATEAU (S/ Groupement SUD)

III.- Le mouvement se continuera ensuite en se conformant au mouvement de l'Infanterie et en n'ayant jamais qu'un groupe de 75 en mouvement, les deux groupes de 75 en position pouvant exécuter les concentrations demandées.

IV.- Le dispositif à réaliser quand l'Infanterie occupera le 2e objectif (cote 205-194 , Servenay) est le suivant :

Artillerie britannique vers le Bois du Monteau - Cote 136.

2 Groupes par groupement pour les sous groupement Nord et Sud au voisinage de la ligne Cote 128 (Vallée du Rû de Chanday) Cote 139 (Est de Bois de la Baillette)

1 Groupe sur les emplacements indiqués au § II.

G: C à l'Est ~~d'Oulchy~~ et à l'ouest d'Oulchy la Ville

V.- ~~A partir de H + 1 h 30', le groupement de superposition devient disponible~~ le groupement C est à la disposition de la 34 DW jusqu'à la fin de l'opération

VI le PC de la 34 DW se portera ultérieurement à la ferme Géromesnil

Le Colonel BERANGER . Ct.1' A.D.

[signature]

AD/34

"A" Form
MESSAGES AND SIGNALS.
Army Form C. 2121 (in pads of 100).
No. of Message.......

App XXXVI

SECRET.

O.C. 152nd F.A.Bde.
O.C. 160th F.A.Bde.
O.C. 34th D.A.C.

Disposition Report noon 28th instant.

152nd and 160th F.A.Brigades N.E. edge of BUISSON de HAUT

BUISSON.

34th D.A.C. Vallée du Gros Chéne

Captain.
Staff Captain.
34th Divisional Artillery.

28th July 1918.

"A" Form
MESSAGES AND SIGNALS.
Army Form C. 2121
(in pads of 100).
No. of Message..................

App XXXVII

"A" Form
MESSAGES AND SIGNALS.
Army Form C. 2121 (in pads of 100).
No. of Message..............

SECRET.

O.C. 152nd F.A.Bde.
O.C. 160th F.A.Bde.
O.C. 34th D.A.C.

W A R N I N G O R D E R.

1.....34th Division will attack to the South of GRAND ROZOY tomorrow morning, 29th instant.

2.....Batteries will be prepared to put all guns in action in OULCHY la VILLE area tonight ready to fire at dawn.

3.....Battery and D.A.C. Echelons will be dumped at guns tonight and refilled immediately afterwards from A.R.P. being established at triangle of roads N. edge of ROZET Wood (59.75 Sheet SOISSONS, S.E., 1/50,000).

4.....Brigades must reconnoitre Wagon Lines today in ROZET Area and North of River OURCQ.

D.A.C. will be in South West part of ROZET Wood near A.R.P.

5.....Brigades must get in touch with D.A.C. and arrange for Sub-Section of D.A.C. to go up into action with each Battery tonight and after emptying rejoin D.A.C. in ROZET Wood.

Captain.
for Brigade Major.
34th Divisional Artillery.

28/7/18

SECRET.

App XXXVIII

Officer Commanding,
34th. D.A.C.

1. 34th. D.A.C. (including S.A.A. Section) will march forthwith to ROZET Wood, sites for bivouacs to be selected by an advance party but to be near A.R.P.

2. Route LONGPONT - VIOLAINE - LOUATRE - CHOUY. Interval 100 yards between every 6 vehicles.

3. When passing BUISSON de HAUTWISON an Officer from each of 1 and 2 Sections will report to 152 and 160 Brigade H.Q. respectively and arrange to comply with para. 5 of this office Warning Order today.

4. R.A.H.Q. and Divisional H.Q. will be at Fe. d'Edrolle 1 mile W. of BILLY - sur - Ourcq.

5. O.C. S.A.A. Section must keep in close touch with 34th. Division "Q" and Infantry Brigades.

6. Report arrival and location to R.A.H.Q.

Captain,
Staff Captain,
34th. Divisional Artillery.

28-7-18.

Issued at 11-45.a.m.

"A" Form
MESSAGES AND SIGNALS.
Army Form C. 2121 (In pads of 100).
No. of Message..........

"A" Form

Army Form C. 2121
(In pads of 100.)

MESSAGES AND SIGNALS.

No. of Message...........

Prefix..............Code..............m. | Words | Charge.

Office of Origin and Service Instructions

Sent

At ....m.

To ....

By ....

This message is on a/c of:

Service.

App XXXIX

(Signature of "Franking Officer")

Recd. at......m.

Date..........

From..........

By..........

TO				
	101	102	103	1 B
	CRA	CRE	MG	BTN
	SIGNALS	Q	ADMS	

Sender's Number.	Day of Month.	In reply to Number.	AAA
GM 3			

H	Hour	will	be
4.10	am	29th	JULY.

From		
Place	34	DIV
Time		

The above may be forwarded as now corrected. (Z) V Hawker Major

....

Censor. Signature of Addressor or person authorised to telegraph in his name

* This line should be erased if not required.

Order No. 1625 Wt. W3253/ P 511 27/2 H. & K., Ltd. (E. 2634)

"A" Form

Army Form C. 2121
(in pads of 100).

MESSAGES AND SIGNALS.

No. of Message..............

34° D.I.W. le 29 Juillet 1918

App XXXX

ARTILLERIE

5217

ORDRE N° 27.

I -. Les 101° et 103° Brigades sont revenues sur la tranchée du C.M.P. où elles se réorganisent avec des postes avancés à l'Est. Elles se reporteront en avant pour occuper au moins la ligne du ruisseau cote 128 et cote 118.

II- les groupes passeront la nuit sur leurs positions actuelles.
Ligne de barrage à fixer avec les commandants de brigade pour s'adapter aux positions de l'infanterie.
En rendre compte ~~xxxxx~~ téléphoniquement par coordonnées chiffrées.

III Tirs d'interdiction pour la nuit du 29 au 30 :
s/Groupement NORD. 47 99,54 08,55 04,51 95.
s/groupement SUD: 55 97,57 95,64 02,65 99.

Tirs de 21 heures à 24 heures et entre 4 heures et 4 heures 30.
Consommation: 1.000 coups par groupement(dont 400 pour les brigades britanniques.)

IV -Continuer le ravitaillement avec la plus grande activité de façon à avoir 2 jours de feu au jour

Le Colonel BERANGER Ct l'A.D.

Destinataires:
s/ groupt NORD
SUD
A.L.C
34° D.I.W.

V. L'infanterie doit, cette nuit, avancer peu à peu et venir occuper les lignes bleues I, II, III du calque ci-joint. A ce moment le barrage sera sur les lignes rouges A, B, C. L'heure du passage d'un barrage à l'autre sera ordonnée par les brigadiers d'infanterie. Ne faire le barrage que sur la demande de l'infanterie.
Tenir compte, s'il y a lieu, de la ligne occupée, pour les tirs d'interdiction

illis sur les objectifs

acer le calque exac-
s mais cela n'est .
arte employée. Ces

Calque pris sur la feuille de ....

à l'échelle de ....

Signature .... Date ....

S E C R E T. *File.* Copy No. *4*...

34th. DIVISIONAL ARTILLERY OPERATION ORDER No. 10.

29th. July 1918.

1. Reference to the Order No. 27 issued by Colonel BERANGER and the tracing accompanying it.

Herewith *34th Div. O.O. No. 239 & G.S. 284/70.*

2. The above tracing is merely a guide.
Group Commanders will, through their Liaison Officers, arrange with the Infantry Brigadiers at what time they will lift, and the exact details of the S.O.S. lines to be taken up in
3. each case.
They will inform this office whenever one of these lifts takes place and the co-ordinates of the lines agreed upon.

3 Brigades please ACKNOWLEDGE.

[signature]
Captain,
Brigade Major.R.A.
34th. Divisional Artillery.

Issued at 10 p.m.
Copy No. 1. 152nd. Bde. RFA.
2. 160th. Bde. RFA.
3. 34th. "G".
4 File.

G.S. 286/70.

SECRET.

101st Infantry Brigade. 102nd Infantry Brigade. 103rd Infantry Brigade. C.R.A. (3 copies) C.R.E. 34th Bn. M.G.Corps.	) For) infor-) mation.	"Q". A.D.M.S. Signal Coy. 30th French Corps. 25th French Division.	) For) infor-) mation.

1. Reference Order dictated by Col. DOONER, reports of the establishment of the front line are to be rendered every hour commencing 9 pm.

2. As soon as this line is established, G.Os.C. Brigades will establish a further line of posts on the general line East, North and North East of BEUGNEUX within their respective zones.

They will arrange the line of the S.O.S. barrage to cover this line with their Os.C. covering Artillery Groups through Liaison Officers.

3. As soon as this line is established they will push out a further line of posts on the general line 65.99 -Pt.122 -Pt.189 to junction with 25th French Division.

Line of S.O.S. barrage for this line will be arranged as before.

The three Brigadiers will endeavour to carry out these successive advances simultaneously so as to avoid breaks in the S.O.S. barrage.

4. Each of these advances will be a distinct operation and will not be undertaken till the line held has been established; but they should follow one upon the other as soon as possible.

5. BEUGNEUX will not be bombarded after the first line of posts is established unless bombardment is called for.

6. As each successive line of posts is pushed out supporting troops must move up accordingly but each Brigade must keep one Battalion in the G.M.P.

7. Liaison with the French Division on the Right will be arranged by Divisional Headquarters according to the information received.

J.G. Dooner
Lieut. Colonel, G.S.
34th Division

29th July, 1918.

SECRET
****

Copy No.

TO BE ACKNOWLEDGED BY WIRE

34th DIVISION OPERATION ORDER No.239.

Reference Sheets
OULCHY LE CHATEAU)
FERE EN TARDENOIS) 1:20,000.

29th July 1918

1. The three Brigades will be reorganised as rapidly as possible -
103rd Brigade on the right.
102nd " " " centre
101st " " " left.

2. Brigade boundaries will be -
(a) Between 103rd and 102nd Brigades
A point on the G.M.P. 100 yards north of the track north of point 123 and running from OULCHY LA VILLE to Point 1.9 - G of BEUGNEUX - S.edge of quarry 200 yards north of Point 148 - Point 172.

(b) Between 102nd and 101st Brigades.
100 yards north of western edge of BOIS DE MONTCEAU - small copse 400 yards N.W. of B. of BEUGNEUX - Point 194 - Point 199.

3. Patrols will be pushed forward at once to establish themselves on the line - 2 houses south of N of BEUGNEUX - B of BEUGNEUX - BEUGNEUX - GRAND ROZOY to our junction with the French on the G.M.P. These patrols will push forward as far as they can in the direction of this line, stay out at the furthest point that they can reach and send back constant reports. They will be supported by other troops sent forward by G.Os.C. Brigades.

4. Each Brigade will keep one reserve battalion in the G.M.P.line. 102nd Brigade is responsible for the BOIS DE MONTCEAU.

5. Brigades on the flanks will be responsible for obtaining and keeping close touch with the French Troops. The left of the 41st French Division is believed to be 400 yards south of Hill 158, whence there is a refused flank to Point 118.

6. 1/4th Cheshire Bn. will, on relief by 102nd Brigade, be withdrawn to Divisional Reserve, ravine about "VERS SOISSONS" under orders to be issued by 101st Brigade. The C.O. this Battalion will detail 4 runners to proceed to H.Q. 101st Brigade who know their way to where Battalion H.Q. will be established.

7. O.C. Machine Gun Bn. will detail 1 coy. to each Brigade. The 1 coy now at BOIS DE MONTCEAU will be relieved under arrangements to be made by 102nd Brigade and will be withdrawn to BOIS DE BAILLETTE and come into Divisional Reserve.

8. S.O.S.Lines. Eastern edge of BEUGNEUX, thence in straight line along northern edge of Wood.

J.G. Dooner
Lieut-Colonel, G.S.,
34th Division.

Dictated to Bde.Majors 101 102 103 Bdes.& MG Bn (at 6.55 pm.
Issued at 9.40 pm.

Distribution overleaf...

"A" Form
MESSAGES AND SIGNALS.
Army Form C. 2121
(in pads of 100).
No. of Message

App XXXXI

SECRET.

34th. DIVISIONAL ARTILLERY WARNING ORDER No. 5.

1. The attack will be resumed tomorrow July 31st. at an hour to be notified later, probably 5 a.m.

2. Attached Tracing shows lines of initial and final barrages and boundaries of divisional and brigade fronts.

3. The attack will be carried out by two Infantry Brigades, probably 101st. and 103rd.

4. The attack will be proceeded by Artillery Preparation for ½ hour and will be carried out under a creeping barrage at the rate of 100 metres in 3 minutes.

5. O.C. 152nd. Brigade RFA will move his Brigade less A battery to a position already pointed out to him.
O.C. 160th. Brigade RFA will move his Brigade less B battery to a position as far forward of his present position as is possible without coming under observation.
These batteries should be in position ready to open fire at daybreak 31st. inst.

6. A/152 and B/160 will fire in the first 15 minutes of the barrage and will then advance without further orders in close support of the Infantry, in the first instance to positions between the railway and the C.R.F. line, afterwards acting under the orders of G.Os.C. Infantry Brigades to whom Os.C. batteries should report.

7. As soon as the final barrage line is reached both Brigades will be prepared to move forward to positions indicated for the last attack between BOIS de MONTCEAU and Pt. 183. One section each of D/152 and D/160 joining A/152 and B/160 respectively and moving in close support under the orders of G.Os.C. Infantry Brigades.

8. ACKNOWLEDGE.

Captain,
Brigade Major.R.A.
34th. Divisional Artillery.

30th. July 1918.

Copies to 152nd. Bde. RFA.
160th. Bde. RFA.
34th. Div. "G".

"A" Form
MESSAGES AND SIGNALS.
Army Form C. 2121
(in pads of 100).
No. of Message..........

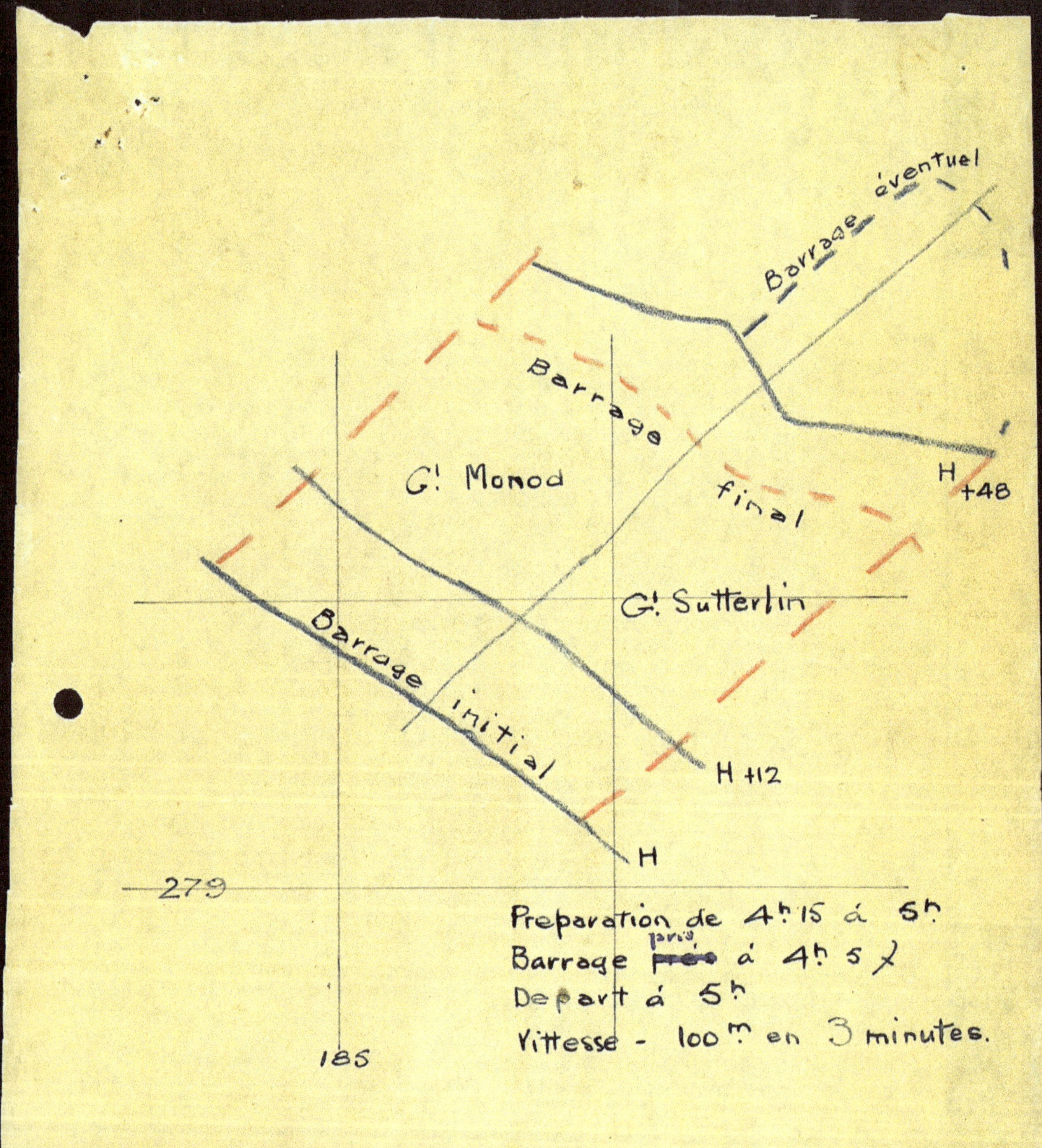
Barrage éventuel
Barrage final
Gl Monod
H +48
Gl Sutterlin
Barrage initial
H +12
H
279
185
Preparation de 4h 15 á 5h
Barrage pris á 4h 5
Depart á 5h
Vittesse - 100m en 3 minutes.

"A" Form.

MESSAGES AND SIGNALS.

Army Form C. 2121 (in pads of 100).

No of Message ....

Prefix .... Code .... m	Words	Charge	This message is on a/c of:	Recd. at .... m
Office of Origin and Service Instructions.	Sent		.... Service.	Date ....
	At .... m.			From ....
	To			
	By		(Signature of "Franking Officer.")	By ....

TO { C.R.A. — App XXXXII

Sender's Number.	Day of Month.	In reply to Number.	AAA
* G130	30th		

In	view	of	operation	to
be	undertaken	by	103rd	Brigade
tonight	vide	para	3	of
O.O.	240	AAA	will	you
please	arrange	as	follows	AAA
Heavy	Artillery	to	remain	on
BEUGNEUX	and	Hill	158	till
12.45	am	AAA	S.O.S.	Line
to	remain	where	it	is
till	1. am	AAA	at	that
hour	latter	should	be	moved
300	yards	E	of	village
and	remain	there	unless	G.O.C.
103rd	Brigade	tells	his	Group
Commander	that	the	enterprise	has
not	come	off	AAA	~~[illegible]~~
~~[illegible]~~	~~[illegible]~~	102nd	Brigade	is

From

Place

Time

The above may be forwarded as now corrected. (Z)

.... *Censor.* Signature of Addressor or person authorised to telegraph in his name.

* This line should be erased if not required.

100,000 Pads. W. 12093. M1217. McC. & Co., Ltd. 1/17. (E. 764). Forms C/2121/11.

Army Form C. 2121
(in pads of 100).

Form.

MESSAGES AND SIGNALS.

No. of Message ......

Prefix ...... Code ...... m	Words	Charge	This message is on a/c of:	Recd. at ...... m
Office of Origin and Service Instructions.	Sent		...... Service.	Date ......
	At ...... m.			From ......
	To			
	By		(Signature of "Franking Officer.")	By ......

TO

Sender's Number.	Day of Month.	In reply to Number.	AAA
*			

pushing	patrols	round	N.W	end
of	BAIGNEUX	at	1. am.	to
get	touch	with	103rd	Brigade
and	will	be	in	liaison
with	103rd	to	find	out
if	their	operation	has	been
successful	AAA	Latter	operation	will
demand	further	alteration	of	S.O.S.
barrage	AAA			

From 34 Div

Place

Time 10-10 pm

The above may be forwarded as now corrected. (Z)

Censor. Signature of Addressor or person authorised to telegraph in his name

J. Doyne [signature]

* This line should be erased if not required.

100,000 Pads. W. 12093. M1217. McC. & Co., Ltd. 1/17. (E. 764). Forms C/2121/11.

P.W.

SECRET

Copy No. 6

TO BE ACKNOWLEDGED BY WIRE.

34th DIVISION OPERATION ORDER No.240.

30th July 1918.

1. (a) Following movements will take place tonight -

(i) 2nd L.N.Lancs Regt. to 101st Brigade Area in relief of 1/4th Cheshire Regt.

(ii) On relief 1/4th Cheshire Regt. to 102nd Brigade Area in relief of 2/4th Somerset L.I.

(iii) On relief 2/4th Somerset L.I. to Divisional Reserve in BOIS DE LA BAILLETTE.

Movements to be completed by 1 a.m.

(i) Under orders of G.O.C. 101st Brigade, (ii) and (iii) arrangements to be made by G.Os.C. 101st and 102nd Bdes.

(b) Every endeavour will be made to relieve front line troops and to thin out in depth.

2. 101st and 102nd Brigades will, in conjunction, complete the establishment of a line of advance posts in or on the northern border of the woods north of the GRAND ROZOY-BEUGNEUX Road. G.O.C. 101st Brigade will ensure close liaison on this line with troops of 25th French Division on his left. G.O.C. 102nd Brigade will do the same with troops of the 103rd Brigade on his right.

3. G.O.C. 103rd Brigade will endeavour to establish a line of posts on the N.E. and N.W. borders of BEUGNEUX connecting this line with the 68th French Division on his right and 102nd Brigade on his left.

Supports for this line must be kept on the flanks of and clear of the village.

Hour of commencement and termination of this operation to be reported to this office so that the village can be kept under heavy artillery fire as late as possible.

Lt Col. Béranger knows

J.G. Dooner

Lieut-Colonel, G.S.,
34th Division.

Issued at 7.45 p.m.

Copy No.1 G.O.C.
2 101st Bde
3 102nd "
4 103rd ".
5 34 M.G.Bn.
6 C.R.A.
7 C.R.E.
8 2/4th Somerset L.I.
9 Signal Coy.
10 "Q".

Army Form C. 2121 (in pads of 100).
"A" Form
MESSAGES AND SIGNALS.
No. of Message........

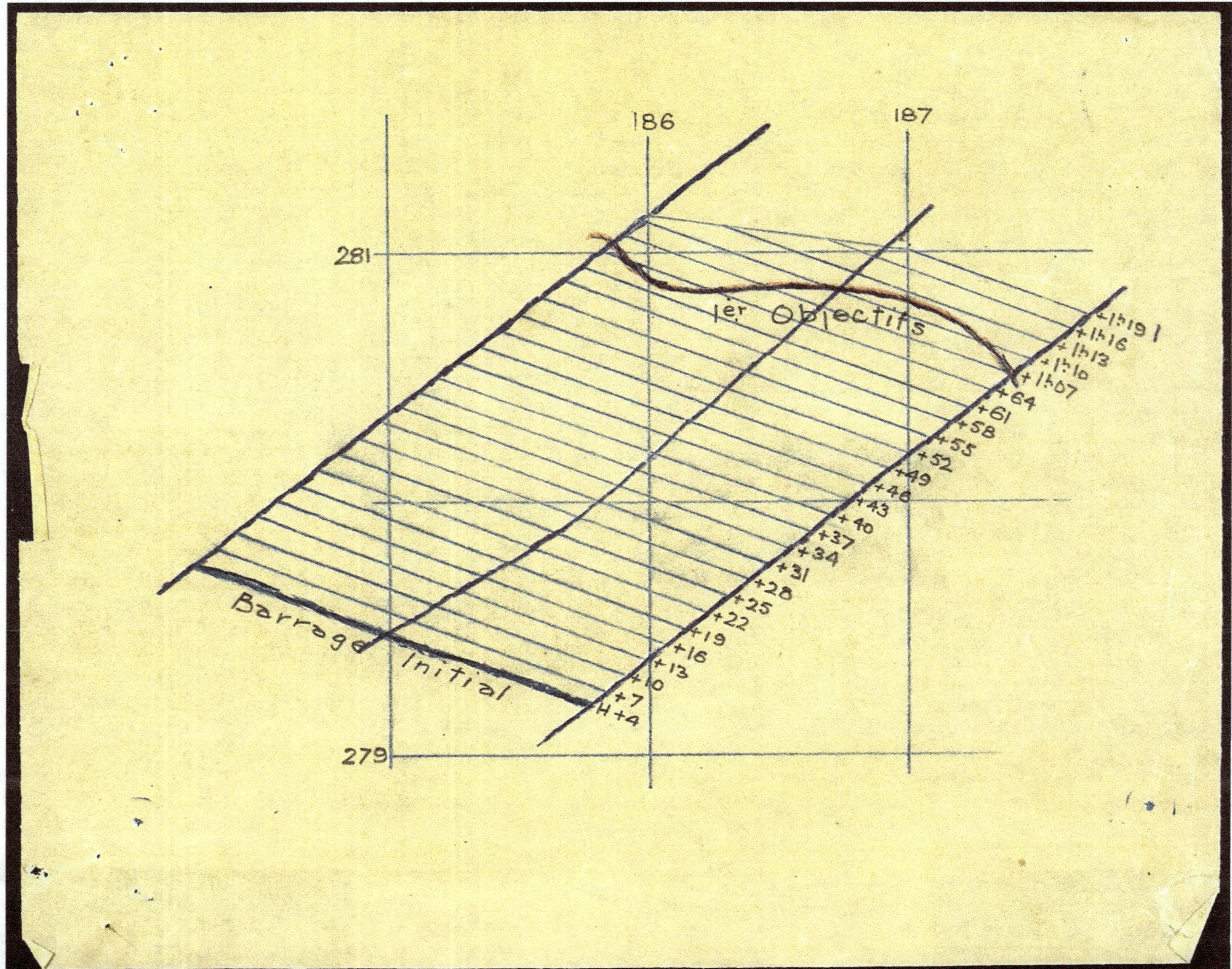
186
187
281
279
1er Objectifs
Barrage Initial
H+4
+7
+10
+13
+16
+19
+22
+25
+28
+31
+34
+37
+40
+43
+46
+49
+52
+55
+58
+61
+64
+1h07
+1h10
+1h13
+1h16
+1h19

SECRET. App XXXXIII Copy No. 6

34th. DIVISIONAL ARTILLERY OPERATION ORDER No. 11.

31st. July 1918.

1. The 34th. Division will attack at 4-45 a.m. in conjunction with the 25th. French Division on the left and XIth. Corps on right.
The attack will be supported by tanks.

2. Objectives.
Crest of ridge from GRAND ROZOY hill 205 hill 194 and northern slopes of this ridge.
As soon as this objective is reached the intention of the 30th. Corps is to exploit it in the direction of COURDOUX-LAUNOY.

3. 34th. Divnl. Boundaries.
Northern Boundary runs as follows - GRAND ROZOY exclusive - hill 1900 - 1800 yards N. of BEUGNEUX inclusive.
Southern Boundary - OULCHY LE CHATEAU - BEUGNEUX to hill 185 - hill 158 - South of BEUGNEUX - SERVENAY exclusive.

4. Jumping off Line.
BOIS de la TERRE a L'OR - point 40.02 - GRAND ROZOY BEUGNEUX Rd in BEUGNEUX - 2 houses on BEUGNEUX OULCHY le CHATEAU road. This line is subject to slight modification as the position of the Infantry may dictate.

5. Artillery Support.

152nd. Bde. RFA.	) Lt.Col. SAVILE
30nd. Regt d'Artillerie.	) Comdt SOTTERLIN.
160th. Bde. RFA.	) Lt.Col. WARBURTON.
5th. Regt. d'Artillerie.	) Lt.Col. MONOD.
V111/117) 155 cm Hows.	) Comdt. VIAL.
V111/118) " "	)

Corps Heavy Artillery.

6.(1) Employment of the Artillery.
Before "J" day.
(1) Harassing Fire by Corps H.A.
Field Artillery.
Ravines leading up to hill 205 and MONT JOUR.
(2) Mustard Gas Shelling by 75 mm of the BOIS de PLANTIS BOIS ST. JEAN, by 105 mm of the edges of BOIS de l'HERMITAGE.
(3) Registration of batteries on their principal targets.
Counter-Battery Work.
(4) Long Range ~~xxxxxx~~ Harassing fire on communications

(11) On "J" day.
The attack will be preceded by a Bombardment of ¾ hour.
This Artillery Preparation will begin at 4 a.m. and continue to 4-45 a.m. , the time of commencement of attack.
(a) Counter Battery neutralisation commencing at 4 a.m.
(b) Smoke barrage so as to blind hostile O.Ps. (Hills 197 - 194 180 Wood 1 hill 199 N.W. of SERVENAY.
(c) At 4-45 a.m. H.A. will turn on to COURDOUX and BOIS de BELIER and fire for 25 minutes afterwards remaining in readiness.

7........

7. **Attack.**
The Infantry Attack will take place at 4-45 a.m.

(a) It will be preceeded by a creeping barrage which will be put down at 4-44 a.m. and will creep in 50 metre lifts at the rate of 100 metres in 3 minutes.

Rates of fire – H minus 1 to H plus 8........ 4 r.p.g.p.m.
H plus 8 to H plus 28....... 2 – do –
H plus 28 to H plus 32....... 4 – do –
H plus 32 to H plus 46....... 2 – do –
H plus 46 to H plus 1-50.... ½ – do –

4.5" Hows. ½ 18-pdr rates until H plus 46 when they will fire at the same rate as the 18-pdrs.

(b) Two 18-pdr Batteries in the creeping barrage covering the whole of their respective Brigade zones.
One 18-pdr battery superimposed till H plus 18. Two sections per battery firing H.E., one section superimposed on the battery zone firing shrapnel 100 metres beyond the barrage line.
Howitzers will fire on points selected by the Group Comdrs. lifting 500 metres ahead of the Infantry.

8. **Artillery Preparation.**

As in para. 6 of French Artillery Instructions No. 8879. Group Commanders to arrange with affiliated French sub-groups Commanders.
H plus 1-20 to H plus 1-50 Protective barrage should take the form of short bursts of fire on the heads of ravines from which counter-attacks might be launched.

Harassing fire for tonight – same targets as for last night – double the expenditure.

9. **Advance of Batteries.**
vide my Warning Order No. 6 d/30-7-18.

10. **Liaison & O.P. Arrangements.**
As for the attack of 29th. inst.

11. H.Q.R.A. will be established at Fme GENEMENIL from 1 a.m. August 1st.

12. ACKNOWLEDGE.

Captain,
Brigade Major.R.A.
34th. Divisional Artillery.

Issued at 7 p.m.
31-7-18.

Copy No. 1 & 2. 152nd. Bde. RFA.
3 & 4. 160th. " "
5. 34th. Div. "G".

SECRET   G.134.

101st Infantry Brigade
102nd " "
103rd " "
C. R. A.
C. R. E.
2/4th Somerset L.I.

34th Bn. M.G. Corps
Signal Coy. R.E.
A.D.M.S.
A.P.M.
"Q"

App XXXXIV

Reference 34th DIVISION OPERATION ORDER No. 241 of to-day:

H (Zero) Hour will be 4.45 a.m. August 1st. Brigades to acknowledge.

Walter Major
for Lieut. Colonel, G.S.
34th Division.

31-7-18.

S E C R E T.   Copy No. 5

TO BE ACKNOWLEDGED BY WIRE.

34th DIVISION OPERATION ORDER No.241.

Reference Sheets   31st July, 1918.
OULCHY LE CHATEAU) 1:20,000.
FERE EN TARDENOIS)

1. As a result of the operations of the 29th July, the 30th French Corps now holds the line BOIS DE LA TERRE D'OR - Point 183 - thence along the Southern edge of the GRAND ROZOY - BEUGNEUX Road - cross roads Eastern end of GRAND ROZOY - about 100 yards South of GRAND ROZOY - BEUGNEUX Road to Western border of Wood South of that road. Thence to buildings 500 yards S.W. of BEUGNEUX thence along a line South of and parallel to the CRAMOISELLE - CRAMAILLE Road.

2. The operations of 29th July will be continued tomorrow by the 30th and 11th French Corps.

The 34th Division is the right Division of the 30th French Corps and has the 206th Regiment of the 68th French Division on its right and the 98th Regiment of the 25th French Division on its left.

The objective of the 68th French Division on the right of the 34th Division, is a line SERVENAY - N.W. corner of the BOIS d'ARCY and then in the direction of ARCY.

The objective of the 25th French Division on the left of the 34th Division is the line ORME du GRAND ROZOY - Point 203.

3. (a) The objective of the 34th Division will be the BROWN Line given on the map attached to Instructions No. 1 dated 28.7.1918. This Line shows approximately the Line which must be reached and the main line of resistance in case of counter-attack.

(b) The dividing lines between flank Divisions and the dividing line between the two attacking Brigades are shown on the attached tracing (already communicated to G.Os.C. Brigades).

The G.O.C. 103rd Brigade is authorised to cross the Southern Divisional boundary in order to turn the village of BEUGNEUX from the South if he wishes.

(c) The starting line for the leading waves of the infantry is shown in the attached tracing (already communicated to G.Os.C. Infantry Brigades).

The initial line of barrage will be 150 yards East of the starting line.

4. Distribution of troops for the operation is as follows :-

(a) 103rd Brigade plus 1 Coy 34th M.G.Bn. on the right.
101st Brigade plus 1 Coy 34th M.G.Bn. on the left.

(b) Divisional reserve.
(i) 102nd Brigade plus 2/4th Somerset L.I.
(ii) 207th, 208th and 209th Field Coys. R.E. and 34th M.G. Bn. (less 2 Coys).

(c) Available Artillery.
34th Divisional Artillery plus two Regiments of French Field Artillery and two French Groups of 6" Howitzers.
TOTAL. (108 Field Guns.
(32 Howitzers.

5. P.T.O.

5. The following preliminary movements will take place as soon as possible after nightfall today.

(a) The 102nd Brigade will be withdrawn from its present positions to an area West of the BOIS DE MONTCEAU to be selected by G.O.C. 102nd Brigade. The 101st and 103rd Brigades will simultaneously extend their inner flanks to the inter-Brigade boundary.

The advanced posts of the 102nd Brigade will not be withdrawn during this movement but will remain in position, covering the movement.

This movement must be completed before midnight 31st/1st August.

(b) During the above movement the 101st and 103rd Infantry Brigades will take up their fighting formations with the leading waves as close as possible to the starting line and in close liaison with flank Divisions. These positions must be taken up as early as possible (not later than midnight) and troops will dig themselves in to gain cover from possible hostile counter-preparation.

(c) The 2/4th Somerset L.I. will move to the position selected by G.O.C. 102nd Brigade in (a) under his orders. Movement to commence as early as possible after nightfall tonight.

(d) The three Field Coys.R.E. and 34th M. G. Bn. less two Coys. will be assembled in BOIS DE LA BAILLETTE ready to move by 4 am.

6. The action of the Artillery will be as follows :-

(a) H minus 45 to H, Heavy Artillery on BEUGNEUX and nautralization of enemy batteries.

(b) At H the Field Artillery will open on the initial barrage line remaining on that line until H plus 4.

(c) The barrage will then advance at the rate of 100 yards in three minutes without a pause until it has passed the objective (BROWN Line). It will remain beyond that line for 30 minutes when it will cease.

The role of the Artillery will then be to cover the consolidation of the position and support further advance.

(d) At H plus 15 minutes A/152 R.F.A. Brigade and B/160 R.F.A. Brigade will move to advanced positions already selected and come under the command of the G.Os.C. 103rd and 101st Infantry Brigades respectively. The Battery Commanders will report themselves to the G.Os.C. Infantry Brigades when the Batteries move.

7. The action of the Infantry will be as follows :-

(a) At H the leading waves of the Infantry will move up as close as possible to the initial barrage line and advance to the attack when the barrage lifts.

(b) The attack will follow the barrage as closely as possible throughout (with the exception noted in (c) below) until the BROWN Line is reached.

The village of BEUGNEUX and Hill 158 will not be

attacked ...

attacked frontally. G.O.C. 103rd Brigade will turn both by the South detailing special parties to mop up both Hill and village when the leading waves have passed them.

The G.O.C. 101st Brigade will direct his right flank well to the North of the village and will detail a special party to mop up the village from the North.

(c) When the objective has been reached the position will be consolidated under cover of Advanced Guards.

(d) Special parties previously detailed will also occupy the Copses immediately South of LE MONT JOUR (101st Brigade), the Copse West of Point 199 (101st Brigade) and the two Copses N.E. of Point 172 (103rd Brigade).

G.O.C. 102nd Brigade will also detail parties for all these Copses to be used if the leading Brigades are unable to deal with them.

(e) The Reserve Brigade and 2/4th Somerset L.I. will move under orders from Divisional Headquarters to the line of the GRAND ROZOY - BEUGNEUX Road. The Field Coys will remain in position

The 34th M.G. Bn. less two Coys. will move to positions about the BOIS DE MONTCEAU to cover and support the action of the Infantry.

The further action of the above units cannot be forecasted.

8. A detachment of Tanks operating with the Right of the 25th French Division will operate in a N.E. direction to deal with nests of Machine Guns which may be holding up the advance of the Infantry of the 34th Division.

9. Divisional Battle Straggler Posts will be established at BILLY SUR OURCQ and ST. REMY-BLANZY.

10. Prisoners' Cage will be established at EDROLLE FARM, 2,000 yards West of BILLY SUR OURCQ.

11. (a) Advanced Dressing Stations will be established in the neighbourhood of BILLY SUR OURCQ and OULCHY-la-VILLE

(b) The Main Dressing Station will be established in the neighbourhood of CHOUY.

(c) The Walking Wounded Collecting Post will be at BILLY SUR OURCQ.

12. The following roads are allotted to the Division for use during the operations :-

(a) <u>Horse Transport.</u>

Route DU PENDU[x] - Route LONGPONT[x] - CORCY - Route de la VALLEE DE NADON - FERME NADON - FONTAINE ALIX.

(b) <u>Motor Transport.</u>

(i) Following the circuit - VILLERS COTTERETS - CORCY - LONGPONT - Carrefour MONTGOBERT.

(ii) In common with 11th French Corps - Route CORCY[x] - MAUGREUX CHATEAU[x] - CHOUY - BILLY SUR OURCQ - FERME GEROMENIL.

([x] See VILLERS COTTERETS Sheet, 1:20,000).

Para. 13 P.T.O.

13. Positions of Headquarters will be notified later.

[signature]

for Lieut. Colonel, G.S.
34th Division.

Issued at 5 pm.

Copy No. 1 G.O.C.
2 101st Infantry Brigade. X
3 102nd " " X
4 103rd " " X
5 C.R.A. X
6 C.R.E. X
7 2/4th Somerset L.I.
8 34th Bn. M.G. Corps. X
9 Signal Coy.
10 A.D.M.S.
11 "Q". X
12 A.P.M.
13 30th French Corps. X
14 25th French Division. X
15 68th French Division. X
16 127th French Division.

X With Maps.

SECRET
****

G.S. 286/100.

TO BE ACKNOWLEDGED BY WIRE

34th DIVISION
SPECIAL INSTRUCTIONS No. 1

1\. The 127th French Division is being held in readiness to move through the 25th French Division and the 34th Division, as soon as these Divisions have reached their objectives.
It will operate in the direction of LAUNOY.

2\. The 127th French Division will be assembled in the BOIS DE LA BAILLETTE Area South of a line FERME GEROMENIL - Point 175, by 3.45 am to-morrow, 1st August, and its leading troops will be in the line of the SOISSONS - OULCHY Railway at 4.45 am.
The 207th, 208th and 209th Field Coys. R.E. will therefore remain in their present positions in readiness to advance when ordered.
The 34th Machine Gun Battalion, less 2 Coys., will move to covered position between the SOISSONS - OULCHY Railway and the BOIS DU MONTCEAU by 3.30 am, 1st August. This cancels para. 5 (d) of 34th Division Operation Order No. 241 dated 31-7-18.

3\. The 34th Division will cover the right of the advance of the 127th French Division by occupying and holding strongly the high ground about LE MONT JOUR and the spur S.E. of BUCY LE BRAS.
For this purpose the G.O.C. 102nd Brigade will detail two Battalions. Both these Battalions will follow the rear echelons of the attacking Brigades as closely as possible. When the leading lines of the two attacking Brigades halt on the objective, these two Battalions will pass through and move, one to the high ground immediately South of the BUCY LE BRAS FARM, and the other to the high ground about LE MONT JOUR.
The role of the Battalion on the right is to get into touch with and cover the flank of the 68th French Division which will be advancing on ARCY STE RESTITUE.
The rôle of the Battalion on the left is to get into and keep in touch with and cover the flank of the 127th French Division which will be advancing on LAUNOY. They must also keep touch on their own inner flanks so as to form a covering screen across the front of the 34th Division. These Battalions will establish themselves in the most favourable positions for carrying out those rôles but they will not advance beyond the places named.

Issued at 6.30 pm
31st July, 1918.

Lieut. Colonel, G.S.
34th Division.

Issued to -
101st Infantry Brigade
102nd " "
103rd " "
C. R. A.
C. R. E.
2/4th Somerset L.I.
34th Bn. M.G. Corps.
Signal Coy. R.E.
A.D.M.S.
"Q"
A.P.M.
XXX French Corps
25th French Division
68th French Division
127th French Division.

S E C R E T
***********   G.S.286/105

TO BE ACKNOWLEDGED BY WIRE.

34th DIVISION
SPECIAL INSTRUCTIONS No. 2.
****

1. The Divisional Commander wishes to impress upon Brigade and Battalion Commanders the absolute necessity of close liaison between Infantry and Artillery.

A counter-attack at any time during tomorrow's operations, especially on the final objective, is most probable. The weight of Artillery in support is such, that no counter-attack has any chance of success if the system of liaison between Infantry and Artillery is complete.

All Commanders must therefore maintain this liaison by all means in their power.

2. Finally / the Div.Commander has just been informed by the General Commanding the 10th French Army that the earliest possible information of the capture of the objective is of the greatest importance in view of the fact that the commencement of other operations depends on it. G.Os.C. 101st and 103rd Brigades and Artillery Groups will use every means in their power to get this information back as early as possible.

31-7-18.

for
Lieut-Colonel, G.S.,
34th Division.

Issued to 101 Inf.Bde.
102 "
103 "
C.R.A. 34 Div.

S E C R E T. G.S. 286/109.

TO BE ACKNOWLEDGED BY WIRE.

34th DIVISION.

SPECIAL INSTRUCTIONS No.3.

LIAISON WITH FRENCH DIVISIONS.

1. 103rd Infantry Brigade with 68th Division -

G.O.C. 103rd Brigade will detail a Liaison Detachment of 1 Officer (French speaking) ½ Section Infantry and 2 Signallers to meet a French Detachment of similar strength at Point 129 at midnight tonight.

This Detachment will proceed to the right flank of the support Coy of the Right Battalion and advance with it at such distance as will ensure the necessary liaison.

2. 101st Infantry Brigade with 25th French Division.

G.O.C. 101st Brigade will detail a Detachment, strength as in para. 1, to meet a French Liaison Section at cross-roads 136 South of GRAND ROZOY at 2 am. tomorrow.

The combined Detachment will advance abreast of the support Coy of the Left Battalion at such distance as to ensure liaison.

3. 102nd Infantry Brigade with 127th and 68th French Divs.

(a) Battalion moving on MONT LE JOUR with 127th French Division.

A Detachment, strength as in para. 1, will report itself to the Officer Commanding the Right Battalion of the Division (355th Regiment) on the line of OULCHY - SOISSONS Railway at 4.45 am. tomorrow. This Detachment will accompany the 355th Regiment throughout the operations.

(b) A special Detachment of Signallers under an Officer will accompany the support Coy of the Battalion proceeding to MONT LE JOUR for the purpose of keeping touch with the Detachment in (a).

(c) Battalion moving on BUCY LE BRAS and 68th French Div. A special Detachment of Signallers will be detailed to keep up Signalling communication with the Detachment mentioned in para. 1, from the time the latter advances beyond SERVENAY.

Issued at 7.30 pm.
31st July, 1918.

Lieut. Colonel, for G.S.
34th Division.

Issued to -

101st Infantry Brigade.
102nd Infantry Brigade.
103rd Infantry Brigade.
C.R.A.
11th French Corps.
30th French Corps.
25th French Division.
68th French Division.
127th French Division.

S E C R E T.

G.S. 286/201.

101st Infy Bde.	Signal Coy.
102nd Infy Bde.	A.D.M.S.
103rd Infy Bde.	"Q"
C.R.A.	A.P.M.
C.R.E.	30th French Corps.
2/4th Somerset L.I.	25th French Division.
34th Bn.M.G.Corps.	68th French Division.
	127th French Division.

Reference para. 13 of 34th Division Operation Order No. 241 dated 31.7.1918.

1. Advanced Divisional Headquarters will be established at the FERME GEROMENIL at 10 pm. tonight.
Advanced "Q" will remain at FERME d'EDROLLE.
Rear Divisional Headquarters, ("A", A.D.M.S., DADVS and French Mission,)will remain at LA LOGE FARM.

2. Brigade Headquarters will remain in their present Headquarters until the objective has been reached when they will move forward to their selected positions in the PARIS Line.
They will however move forward sooner if they find it impossible to control their Brigades from their present Headquarters.

3. As soon as they move forward an Advanced Divisional Report Centre will be established at Point 122 junction of the stream and the SOISSONS - OULCHY Railway.

31st July, 1918.

Lieut. Colonel, G.S.
34th Division.

"A" Form
MESSAGES AND SIGNALS.
Army Form C. 2121
(in pads of 100).
No. of Message.........

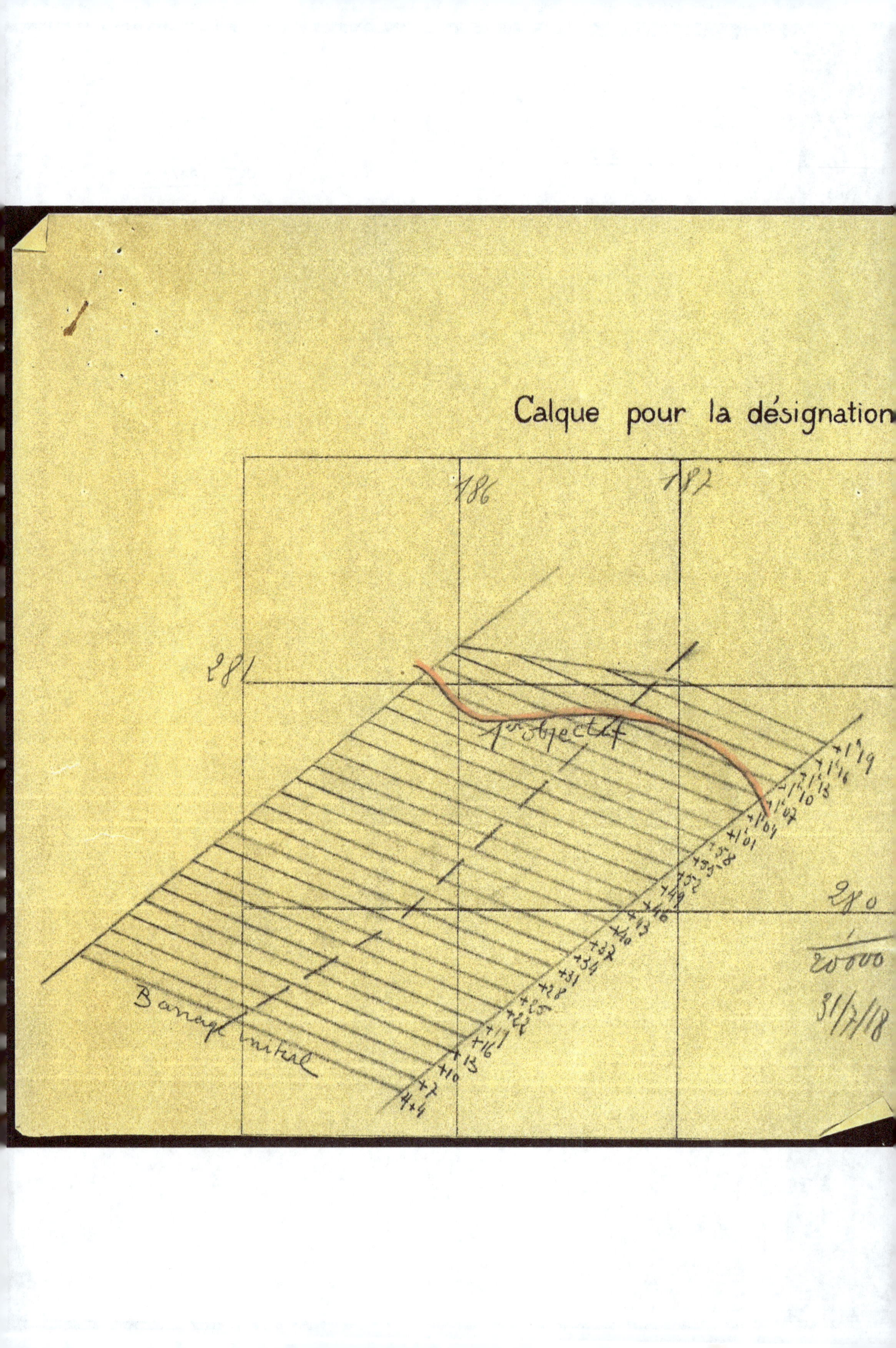

Calque pour la désignation

186 187

281

1er objectif

Barrage initial

280

1/20000

31/7/18

App XXXXV

A. D / 34

N° 5279

P.C.A.D. le 31 juillet 1918

PLAN d' EMPLOI DE l' ARTILLERIE

I.- Le 1er août , à H = Quatre heures 45 , la 34° D.I. W encadrée par la 25° D.I. à l' Ouest , par la 68° D.I. à l' Est attaquera la position Cote 205- Servenay.

Après l' arrivée des 2 D.I. sur le 1er objectif , la 127° D.I. se portera vers le Nord sur LAUNOY- COURDOUX.

La 25° D.I. est appuyée par les tanks Renault qui déboucheront au Nord du Grand Rozoy entre l' Orme et la Cote 205.

Ci-joint le Plan d' action de la 34° D.I. W.

Objectifs et limites de la D.I. W. et de ses 2 Brigades(calque ci-joint .)

II.- ORGANISATION DU COMMANDEMENT (sans changement)

Les nouveaux emplacements occupés dans la nuit du 31 au 1er août seront à 6.500 m. au plus de l'objectif .

III.- OBSERVATION -

O. T. Chaque Groupement a un Observatoire de renseignements, occupé en permanence par un Officier et envoyant ses renseignements à l' A.D. - Grpt. NORD en 16.85 - Grpt.Sud en 06-64 , A.L.C. en 97-86

O. A. Ballon 29 (Cap. BARADEZ) Point d'ascension : 58-95
Cantonnement : 46-79

Escadrille SAL 52 à Russy-Bémont .

IV.- LIAISONS :

a) Téléphoniques : (voir schéma)
b) T. S. F. : (voir tableau des indicatifs)
c) 1 Officier et 1 agent de liaison montés par Grpt. à l'AD

V.- Avant le jour J :

a) Réglage minutieux des batteries sur les barrages initiaux et finaux (A.C.) et leurs principaux objectifs (A.L.C.)
b) Harcèlement pendant la nuit (programme double des jours précédents .

VI.- PREPARATION (de 4 h à 4 h 45)

A.L.C. : 1 Groupe sur les Bois 1 , 3 , 4 , 7 , 9 , 10 , lisières Nord de 6 , chemin creux de 56-99 à 56-02, éléments de tranchée en 36-99.

1 Groupe sur Beugneux , mamelon 158 , Carrières 59-99, P.C. de Régiment en 74-05 .

Cadence : 1 c.p.p.m. , portée à 2 c.p.p.m. de H - 5 à H + 5.

A.C. : Groupement NORD : Concentrations sur les Bois 1 , 4. 5 , 6 , 7 , 9 , 10, croupe 189 à 192.

Groupement SUD : Concentrations sur Mamelon 158 , Beugneux (2 Bies) route 62-95 à 59-95.5 , ravin Nord de Beugneux (de cote 148 à Cote 192.)

Cadence : 1 c.p.p.m.

VII.- ACCOMPAGNEMENT PAR LES FEUX .

a) Barrage roulant et ratissage - Assis à H - 1' (4 h.44) sur ligne du calque à 200 m. en avant de l' Infanterie .

A H + 4' , le barrage se met en marche à vitesse de 100 m. en 3 minutes par bonds de 100 mètres .

Dans chaque sous groupement , la brigade britannique et 1 groupe en barrage roulant , 1 groupe en ratissage dans une zône entre 200 et 800 mètres au delà du barrage (dans chaque groupe 2 Bies en O.E. percutants , 1 Bie en O.B. fusants)

Les heures indiquées sur le calque sont celles auxquelles le barrage quitte la ligne correspondante .

b) ....

App XXXXVI

SECRET
****

G.S.286/105

TO BE ACKNOWLEDGED BY WIRE.

34th DIVISION
SPECIAL INSTRUCTIONS No. 2.
****

1. The Divisional Commander wishes to impress upon Brigade and Battalion Commanders the absolute necessity of close liaison between Infantry and Artillery.

A counter-attack at any time during tomorrow's operations, especially on the final objective, is most probable. The weight of Artillery in support is such, that no counter-attack has any chance of success if the system of liaison between Infantry and Artillery is complete.

All Commanders must therefore maintain this liaison by all means in their power.

2. Finally / the Div.Commander has just been informed by the General Commanding the 10th French Army that the earliest possible information of the capture of the objective is of the greatest importance in view of the fact that the commencement of other operations depends on it. G.Os.C. 101st and 103rd Brigades and Artillery Groups will use every means in their power to get this information back as early as possible.

[signature]
for
Lieut-Colonel, G.S.,
34th Division.

31-7-18.

Issued to 101 Inf.Bde.
102 "
103 "
C.R.A. 34 Div.

App XXXXVII

"A" Form
MESSAGES AND SIGNALS.

Army Form C. 2121
(in pads of 100.)

No. of Message..................

SECRET.

34th. Div. Arty. No. G/648.

34th. DIVISIONAL ARTILLERY INSTRUCTIONS.

During the present form of semi-mobile warfare Brigades when changing positions will send to this office, with as little delay as possible, the following information:-

Approximate co-ordinates of Hd.Qrs.
Batteries.
O.Ps.
Approximate switch of Batteries.
Mininum range at which 18-pdr batteries can clear the crest.

[signature]
Captain,
Brigade Major.R.A.
34th. Divisional Artillery.

31-7-18.

HQ RA 34 D
Vol 32

WAR DIARY

for

AUGUST 1918

H.Q.R.A. 34 DIVISION
152 BDE. R.F.A.
160. BDE. R.F.A.
34. D.A.C.
34. D.T.M.O

160 BDE. RFA

Army Form C. 2118.

Instructions regarding War Diaries and Intelligence Summaries are contained in F. S. Regs., Part II. and the Staff Manual respectively. Title pages will be prepared in manuscript.

WAR DIARY
or
INTELLIGENCE SUMMARY.
(Erase heading not required.)

H. Q. R. A., 34th Division.

Month of AUGUST 1918.

Page 1.

Place	Date	Hour	Summary of Events and Information	Remarks and references to Appendices
GEROMENIL FARM. (Sheet, OULCHY-Le CHATEAU)	Aug. 1.		Narrative of the 34th Divisional Artillery Operations during the period July 22nd to August 2nd 1918, vide.	App. I.
			An attack on the high ground N of GRAND ROZOY was launched at 4.45 a.m. Previous to the attack the objective had been steadily bombarded by Heavy Artillery. Field Artillery afforded the creeping barrage in support of the advance. At 6-5 a.m., British troops were reported 500 yards E. of BEUGNEUX, while an airman's report, timed 6-25 a.m., stated "Friendly troops 49.12." At 6-30 a.m. the C.R.A., 34th Division issued orders for the 152nd Brigade R.F.A., and the 160th Brigade R.F.A., to move forward by batteries to selected positions.	
			At 6-25 a.m. A/152 and B/160, batteries under the command of the G.O.C's Infantry Brigades, were reported to have advanced and to be in communication.	
		7 a.m.	Information was received that the 127th (French) Division had requested the R.A. 30th C.A. to advance batteries to positions from which they could fire on LAUNOY and the BOIS DE SIX SOUS.	
			At 7-15 a.m. both Infantry Brigades reported themselves on their objectives.	
		7-15 a.m.	Heavy Artillery was ordered to lift N of the line through LE MONT JOUR and BUCY LE BRAS FARM	
		7-45 a.m.	Headquarters 160th Brigade R.F.A. moved to the QUARRY 07.85.	
		7-50 a.m.	25th (French) Divisional Artillery reported that French troops were believed to have reached BOIS DU BELIER, and at 8-3 a.m. 152nd Brigade F.O.O. reported, French troops on the southern outskirts of SERVENAY.	

(A7092). Wt. W12839/M1293. 75 ,0.0. 1/17. D. D. & L., Ltd. Forms/C.2118 14.

Army Form C. 2118.

WAR DIARY
or
INTELLIGENCE SUMMARY.

Instructions regarding War Diaries and Intelligence Summaries are contained in F. S. Regs., Part II. and the Staff Manual respectively. Title pages will be prepared in manuscript.

Month of AUGUST 1918. *(Erase heading not required.)*

H. Q. R. A. 34th Division.

Place	Date	Hour	Summary of Events and Information	Remarks and references to Appendices
GEROMENIL FARM	Aug. 1.	10-35 a.m.	34th Division Situation Wire vide.	Appl III
(Sheet, OULCHY - LE CHATEAU.			At 11-30 a.m. the 152nd Brigade were located as follows Headquarters 38.85.) A/152 50.85.) Sheet, B/152 37.80.) OULCHY -LE-CHATEAU. C/152 37.80.) 1/20,000 D/152 for the time being remained in their old position at the foot of the BUTTE CHALMONT.	
			A forward ammunition dump was established in the BOIS DE LA BAILLETTE (17.78.)	
			Batteries were ordered to clear old positions and to get up 200 rounds per gun to the new positions, as soon as possible.	
		12-35 p.m.	Troublesome M.G. fire from the cross roads W of BUCY LE BRAS was dealt with by occasional bursts of fire by 18-pounders.	
			At 12-45 p.m. 152nd Brigade R.F.A. reported one section of D/152 to have advanced to position at 50.85.(Sheet, OULCHY LE CHATEAU), and the remainder of the battery to have been ordered up to this position.	
		1 p.m.	Batteries under the command of G.O.C's Infantry Brigades reverted to the control of Group Commanders for the purpose of S.O.S.	

(A7092). Wt. W12839/M1293. 75 ,0.0. 1/17. D. D. & L., Ltd. Forms/C.2118/14.

Army Form C. 2118.

Instructions regarding War Diaries and Intelligence Summaries are contained in F. S. Regs., Part II. and the Staff Manual respectively. Title pages will be prepared in manuscript.

WAR DIARY
or
INTELLIGENCE SUMMARY.

(Erase heading not required.)

Month of AUGUST 1918.

H. Q. R. A., 34th Division.

Page 3.

Place	Date	Hour	Summary of Events and Information	Remarks and references to Appendices
GEROMENIL FARM. (Sheet, OULCHY LE CHATEAU).	Aug. 1.	4-17 p.m.	To assist French troops in occupying the ravine 172, point 199 overlooking this, was engaged at a slow rate by 4.5" Howitzers.	
		8-55 p.m.	Batteries fired on S.O.S. in responce to signal.	
			34th Division Operation Order No.242. vide.	App. IV.
			Harassing night-fire Orders (French) vide.	App. V.
			34th Divisional Artillery Night firing Orders, vide.	App. VI.

(A7092). Wt. W12839/M1293. 75 ,0.0. 1/17. D. D. & L., Ltd. Forms/C.2118 14.

Instructions regarding War Diaries and Intelligence Summaries are contained in F. S. Regs., Part II. and the Staff Manual respectively. Title pages will be prepared in manuscript.

Army Form C. 2118.

WAR DIARY
or
INTELLIGENCE SUMMARY.

(Erase heading not required.)

Month of AUGUST 1918.

H. Q. R. A., 34th Division.

Place	Date	Hour	Summary of Events and Information	Remarks and references to Appendices
GEROMENIL FARM (OULCHY LE CHATEAU)	Aug. 2.	10 a.m	The enemy no longer being within our range, batteries were ordered to remain in positions of observation, and return to the ammunition dump all ammunition in excess of their echelons.	
			34th Division Situation Wires, vide.	App. VII
		4.35 p.m.	Orders received from 30th Corps (French) to suspend all movement to the rear, and for units to be reformed in their present stations, ready to march forward. ...	App. VIII
			At 6-15 p.m., the following moves were ordered:- (1) Batteries to withdraw to their Wagon Lines. (2) Wagon Lines to move to the Valley of RUE DE CHAUDAY. (3) D.A.C. to move to the BOIS DE LA BAILLETTE. (4) Brigades and D.A.C. to be prepared to move forward early tomorrow morning (3rd.)	App. IX

(A7092). Wt. W12839/M1293. 75 ,0.0. 1/17. D. D. & L., Ltd. Forms/C.2118 14.

Army Form C. 2118.

WAR DIARY
or
INTELLIGENCE SUMMARY.

(Erase heading not required.)

Instructions regarding War Diaries and Intelligence Summaries are contained in F. S. Regs., Part II. and the Staff Manual respectively. Title pages will be prepared in manuscript.

Month of AUGUST 1918.

H. Q. R. A., 34th Division.

Place	Date	Hour	Summary of Events and Information	Remarks and references to Appendices
GEROMENIL FARM (Sheet, OULCHY LE CHATEAU)	Aug. 3.		34th Divisional Artillery Operation Order No.12 vide.	App. X.
FARM D'EDROLLE. (Sheet, OULCHY LE CHATEAU)		Noon.	H.Q.R.A. moved to FME d'EDROLLE (Sheet, OULCHY le CHATEAU)	
	4.		March and Entraining Orders vide.	Apps. XI & XII.

A5834 Wt. W4973/M687 750,000 8/16 D. D. & L. Ltd. Forms/C.2118/13.

Army Form C. 2118.

WAR DIARY
or
INTELLIGENCE SUMMARY.

(Erase heading not required.)

Instructions regarding War Diaries and Intelligence Summaries are contained in F. S. Regs., Part II. and the Staff Manual respectively. Title pages will be prepared in manuscript.

Month of August 1918.

H. Q. R. A., 34th Division.

Place	Date	Hour	Summary of Events and Information	Remarks and references to Appendices
NANTEUIL (Sheet, SOISSONS 1/80,000)	Aug. 4.		H.Q.RA. moved to NANTEUIL. (Sheet, SOISSONS, 1/80,000)	
	5.		H.Q.R.A. entrained at LE PLESSIS (Sheet SOISSONS, 1/80,000), and detrained at 4 a.m. on August 7th at ESQUELBECQ (Sheet, 27 1/40,000)	
ESQUELBECQ (Sheet, 27, 1/40,000)	7	6 a.m.	Headquarters R.A. was established at ESQUELBECQ.	
	7		34th Divisional Artillery Location Statement vide.	App. XII.
COUTHOVE CHATEAU. (27/F.21.a.)	12		The 34th Divisional Artillery moved from the DROGLANDT Artillery Area to the HAANDEKOT Artillery Area, and H.Q.R.A. moved to COUTHOVE CHATEAU 27/F.21.a.	App. XIII & XIV.

A5834 Wt. W4973 M687 750,000 8/16 D. D. & L. Ltd. Forms/C.2118/13.

Army Form C. 2118.

Instructions regarding War Diaries and Intelligence Summaries are contained in F. S. Regs., Part II. and the Staff Manual respectively. Title pages will be prepared in manuscript.

WAR DIARY
or
INTELLIGENCE SUMMARY.
(Erase heading not required.)

Month of AUGUST 1918

H.Q.R.A., 34th Division.
Page 7.

Place	Date	Hour	Summary of Events and Information	Remarks and references to Appendices
COUTHOVE CHATEAU (27/F.21.a.)	Aug. 12.		One section per battery moved into action in positions covering the IInd Corps EAST POPERINGHE Line.	
			The responsibility for the defence of this line, was borne by the 30th (American) Division, supported by the 34th Divisional Artillery.	App. XV.
LA LOVIE CHATEAU (Sheet, 27 1/40,000)	22	noon.	H.Q.R.A. moved to LA LOVIE CHATEAU.	
			34th Divisional Artillery relieved the 49th Divisional Artillery in the line.	
			Forward Sections were relieved on the night 21/22 August, and Main Battery positions on the following night.	App. XVI.
	23		34th Divisional Artillery Location Statement vide.	App. XVII.
	29		The 34th Division (less Artillery) was relieved in the line by the 14th Division on the nights, August 28/29th, and the 29/30th, command passing to the G.O.C. 14th Division at 3 a.m. 29th. August.	
COUTHOVE CHATEAU (27/F.21.a.)			H.Q.R.A. joined the 14th Divisional Headquarters at COUTHOVE CHATEAU at 10 a.m. August 29th. ...	App. XVIII.

A5834 Wt. W4973/M687 750,000 8/16 D. D. & L. Ltd. Forms/C.2118/13.

Army Form C. 2118.

WAR DIARY
or
INTELLIGENCE SUMMARY.

(Erase heading not required.)

Instructions regarding War Diaries and Intelligence Summaries are contained in F. S. Regs., Part II. and the Staff Manual respectively. Title pages will be prepared in manuscript.

Month of AUGUST 1918.

H.Q.R.A., 34th Division.

Page 8.

Place	Date	Hour	Summary of Events and Information	Remarks and references to Appendices
COUTHOVE CHATEAU (27/F.21.a.)	29.		The S.A.A. Section 34th D.A.C. on relief by the S.A.A. Section, 14th D.A.C., was moved to K.21.d.9.8. Sheet 27. ...	App. XIX.
	31.		34th Divisional Artillery Location Statement vide.	App. XX

P.C. Walthall

Brigadier-General,

C.R.A., 34th Division.

App I

NARRATIVE OF 34th. DIVISIONAL ARTILLERY.

22nd. July to 2nd. August 1918.

Ref. Map OULCHY le CHATEAU,
1/20,000.

On July 23rd. the Artillery supporting the 34th. Division was organised under the command of Brig. Gen. E.C. WALTHALL, C.M.G. D.S.O. assisted by Colonel BERANGER of the 32nd. Regt d'Artillerie (38th. Divisional Artillery) and H.Q. established at CHAVIGNY FARM.

The Artillery was divided into two groups - the Northern which supported the 102nd. Infantry Brigade composed of the 152nd. Bde.RFA. and the 32nd. Regt d'Artillerie under Lt.Col. SAVILE, D.S.O. assisted by Commandant SATTERLIN - and the Southern which supported the 101st. Infantry Brigade composed of the 160th. Bde. RFA and the 41st. Regt. d'Artillerie under Lt. Col. WARBURTON, D.S.O. assisted by Lt. Col. THOUVENOT.

A "groupe" of Heavy Artillery (12 - 155 mm hows) was also allotted to the division.

On the night 22nd/23rd the 160th. Brigade came into action, battery positions West of the BOIS de MAULOY, and supported an attack by the 34th. Division on the front from BOIS de CURJENNE to HARTENNES et TAUX.

The main attack was delivered by the XXth. Corps on VILLEMONTOIRE and a subsidary operation by the XXXth. Corps was launched as soon as the main attack appeared to be successful.

The subsidary operation included an attack on the CRETE de GRAND ROZOY ridge as well as that of the 34th. Division. Neither of these secondary attacks achieved any definite result.

On the night of the 23rd/24th. the batteries of the 152nd. Brigade moved into positions near VIERZY.

On the 25th. the 32nd. Regt. d'Artillerie was transferred to the XXth. Corps necessitating a readjustment of the artillery barrage, one "groupe" of the 41st. Regt. being told off to cover the front of the Northern Group.

The 18-pdrs were substituted for the 75 mm in the close S.O.S. barrage and the 75 mm employed in a combing barrage on selected areas.

On the afternoon of the 27th. the 34th. Division was ordered on the 30th. to attack the ridge from Hill 203 to SERVENAY in conjunction with the XIth. Corps on the right and the 25th. Division on the left.

On the morning of the 28th. the XIth. Corps captured the BUTTE CHALMONT and so made it possible to fix the forming up line for the attack of the 34th. Division. This line ran from the G.H.P. trench at point 123 along the N.W. fork of the RU de CHAUDAY to the SOISSONS OULCHY le CHATEAU Railway.

The success of the operation on the BUTTE CHALMONT caused the attack of the 34th. Division to be antedated to the 29th.

On the night of 27th/28th. batteries were withdrawn from their positions and the Divisional Artillery concentrated in the BUISSON de HAUTWISON.

On the morning of the 28th. reconnaissances were carried out, and areas allotted to Brigades and Regiments at at a conference at FONTAINE ALIX FARM.

All batteries that could possibly do so sent forward single guns during the afternoon of the 28th. to register from their new positions.

On the night 28th/29th. batteries moved into their new Battle positions in the following areas:- 152nd. Bde. N.W. of OULCHY la VILLE, 160th. Bde. BOIS de MARTIN PRE, 32nd. Regt BOIS de SAVART, 224th. Regt FERME de FRONTENY.

H.Q. of the 160th. Brigade and the affiliated 5e Regt d'Artillerie (Lt.Col. MONOD) were established in GERCHENIL FARM the batteries of the 5e Regt being already in action in that neighbourhood. H.Q. of the 152nd. Brigade and 32nd. Regt were in the BOIS ST. HILAIRE and the division in FERME d'EDROLLE.

Three "groupes" of Heavy Artillery already in position under Commandant VIAL were allotted to the 34th. D.A. and used during the 28th in conjunction with the Heavy Artillery of the XXXe Corps in preparation of the G.M.P. line, BOIS de MONTCEAU and BEUGNEUX.

The attack was launched and barrage put down at 4-10 a.m. 29th.

The barrage commenced to creep at 4-14 a.m. at the rate of 100 metres in 4 minutes and stopped altogether at 6-35 a.m. on the protective barrage 300 metres beyond the 1st. objective.

The H.A. and 4.5" Hows. were employed in crash barrages not less than 500 metres beyond the Infantry.

On each Infantry Brigade front the creeping barrage consisted of two 18-pdr batteries and two 75 mm "groupes" firing H.E., one 18-pdr battery and one 75 mm "groupe" firing shrapnel 100 metres beyond the H.E. barrage line.

Reports were received at 7-15 a.m. to the effect that the Infantry had reached their 1st. objective, the valley of the stream from point 118 to point 128 about 1000 metres East of the G.M.P. line

At 8 a.m. a concentration of all available artillery was fired on BEUGNEUX and hill 158 to check hostile M.G. fire.

Heavy Infantry fighting took place about 9 a.m. in BEUGNEUX and in the Woods to the N.W. .

On the night of the 28th/29th. the enemy had a fresh Guards Ersatz Division in reserve between BEUGNEUX and COURDOUX which he made use of to counter-attack the BEUGNEUX Woods and GRAND ROZOY about mid-day on the 29th.

The bulk of the 34th. Division Infantry were back in the G.M.P. line by 3 p.m. with certain elements holding posts and short lengths of trench further to the East.

The 25th. Division were, after a severe hand to hand fight, driven off the BOIS de la TERRE a l'OR and into GRAND ROZOY.

During the night of the 29th/30th. heavy harassing fire was put down while the Infantry reorganised, pushed forward and consolidated on the line of their 1st. objective.

The 152nd. Brigade advanced in the night 18-pdrs to positions on the BETHUNE road North of OULCHY le CHATEAU and 4.5" Hows. to a Wood at D in RU de CHAUDAY.

The 160th. Brigade also advanced slightly to positions on the ridge N.W. of the BOIS de la BAILLETE.

The positions thus vacated were occupied by the 32e Regt and the 5e Regt.

Orders were issued to be in readiness to resume the attack on the morning of the 31st. subsequently postponed to August 1st.

On the 31st. the Infantry outpost line was further pushed forward to some sheds on the OULCHY le CHATEAU - BEUGNEUX road, thence to the B in BEUGNEUX , then along the BEUGNEUX - GRAND ROZOY road.

160th. Brigade H.Q. moved to a Quarry near the BOIS de MARTIN PRE.

Divisional H.Q. moved to GERCHENIL FARM.

The attack was launched at 4-45 a.m. after ½ hour preparation by all natures of artillery.

It was supported by numerous tanks on the left, and covered by a creeping barrage indentical in character to that of the 29th. less the 224° Regt in superimposition.

The objective was the crest of the same ridge forming the 2nd. objective on the 29th.

Two batteries, A/152 and B/160 each with a section of howitzers attached were taken out of the creeping barrage at 5 a.m. and advanced in close support of the Infantry to positions at point 158 and 500^x S.W. of the BOIS de MONTCEAU.

About 6 a.m. reports were received to the effect that the Infantry had substantially gained their objectives; so the 127° division held in reserve, was launched to exploit the success by passing through the left of the 34th. Division and pushing forward in the direction of COURDOUX and LAUNOY.

At 6-30 a.m. Brigades commenced moving forward by batteries, 160th. Brigade to join D/160 S.W. of the BOIS de MONTCEAU, B/152 and C/152 to the same area D/152 to the fork of stream due North of A/152. 152nd. H.Q. moved to the G.H.P. line at BOIS de MONTCEAU.

The 32° Regt moved to the vicinity of point 123 and the 5° Regt to the valley running S.W. from GRAND ROZOY.

At 10-30 a.m. the 68th. Division reported the capture of SERVENAY and the 25th. that of the BOIS de BELIER.

Al 11 a.m. aviators reported dense masses of the enemy forming up behind BOIS de HOUSSE and in the DROIZY ravine and advancing on BUCY le BRAS FARM and LAUNOY. This counter-attack was delivered by the 18th. Wurttemburg Division and was dealt with successfully by concentrations of all artillery firing at their maximum rates for 10 mins.

At 12-35 p.m. hostile M.G. fire being reported from BUCY le BRAS FARM, bursts of fire from all available guns were fired on it.

At 4-17 p.m. point 199 whence hostile M.Gs. were reported firing was treated to a concentration.

At 5-50 p.m. verbal orders were issued for an infantry attack covered by a creeping barrage starting on the line of a track running S.E. from point 199. The attack took place at 7 p.m. and gained its objective, the spur running N.N.E. from point 199.

An S.O.S. barrage was put down in response to signals at 8-55 p.m.

Heavy harassing fire was put down during the night of 1st/2nd. August on the MUZE valley and BOIS d'HOUSSE la BUTTE JEANNE.

Counter Preparations were fired at 4-10 a.m. and 4-30 a.m. on the 2nd.

At 9 a.m. the 127° Division were reported in LAUNOY, the 25° Divn to have cleared the BOIS de PLESSIER and the 68° the BOIS d'ARCY.

At 10 a.m. Brigades were ordered to remain in positions of observation, but in anticipation of withdrawal to clear all ammunition surplus to echelons.

At 4-35 p.m. orders were received from the XXX° Corps to suspend all movement to the rear and report when ready to move forward in pursuit.

The Infantry were ordered to concentrate in the BRUGNEUX area, Brigades R.F.A. in the RU de CHAUDAY, D.A.C. in the BOIS de BAILLETE, all/ready to move forward on the morning of the 3rd.

TO be

APP V

S E C R E T.

Copy ......

34th. DIVISIONAL ARTILLERY OPERATION ORDER No. 7/2.

1st. August 1918.

1. Harassing Fire tonight.
Field Guns 1000 rounds (200 Rds per Bde 18-pdrs 600 for 75's)
4.5" Howitzers 300 rounds (150 per battery)
On Valleys, tracks and Woods in Divisional Zone up to limit of range

152nd. Brigade 10 p.m. to 1 a.m.
160th. " 1 a.m. to 4 a.m.
32nd. Regt. 10 p.m. to 4 a.m. (1 group at a time)

2. Counter-Preparation
Two bursts of 4 mins each at 4-10 a.m. and 4-30 a.m.
Field Guns 2 rds p.g.p.m.
4.5 Hows. 1 rd. p.g.p.m.

Commencing 300 yards beyond S.O.S. lines and searching back 400 yards, particularly dense on the valleys on each flank of Divisional Zone.
4.5" Howitzers on BUZY-le-GRAS farm and BOIS du BAS - BEAUDET.

3. Orders for French Howitzers are issued separately.

4. Cs.C. Brigades will please arrange S.O.S. lines with G.Cs.C. 101st. and 103rd. Infantry Brigades respectively and communicate them to Commdt. SATERLIN (at 152nd.B.Hs.) whose Regiment now covers the whole divisional front.
Rate and duration as usual.

Captain,
Brigade Major.R.A.
34th. Divisional Artillery.

Issued at 7 p.m.

Copy No. 1. 152nd. Bde. RFA.
2. 160th. Bde. RFA.
3. 32nd. Regt d'Artillerie.
4. 34th. Divn. "G".
5. File.

App IX

S E C R E T. Copy No. 6

34th. DIVISIONAL ARTILLERY OPERATION ORDER No. 12.

3rd. August 1918.

1. Brigades and D.A.C. will move this afternoon to Woods in area between VICHEL and Fme d'EDROLLE and be prepared to march to their entraining stations tomorrow.

2. Route - OULCHY LA VILLE ROZET ST ALBIN.

3. Times of starting - 152nd. Brigade 1 p.m.
160th. Brigade 2 p.m.
D.A.C. 3 p.m.

4. Brigades and D.A.C. will send representative to Fme d'EDROLLE at 10-30 a.m. today to meet the S.C.R.A. who will allot them Wagon Lines.

5. R.A.H.Q. will reopen at FME. d'EDROLLE at 12 noon today.

6. Units will report location of their H.Q. to this Office as soon as possible, and will each detail a mounted orderly acquainted with this location to report at FME.d'EDROLLE by 6 p.m. tonight.

7. Brigades and D.A.C. please ACKNOWLEDGE.

Captain,
Brigade Major.R.A.
34th. Divisional Artillery.

Issued at 8-30 a.m.

Copy No. 1 - 152nd. Bde. RFA.
2. 160th. " "
3. D.A.C.
4. S.C.R.A.
5. 34th. Div. "G".
6. File. War Diary

App X

SECRET. Copy No. 19.

34th. DIVISIONAL ARTILLERY OPERATION ORDER No. 13.

Ref Maps SOISSONS & BEAUVAIS 1/100,000.

3rd. August 1918.

1. Brigades and D.A.C. will march at the following times on 4th. August:-
160th. Brigade RFA....... 8-0 a.m.
152 ~~D.A.C~~.................. 8-30 a.m.
DAC 152nd. Brigade RFA....... 9-0 a.m.

2. Starting Point.
Railway Crossing PRINGY, DAC ~~152nd. Bde.~~ to be clear of this point by 10 a.m.

3. Intervals.
200 yards between Brigades and D.A.C.
100 " " batteries and sections D.A.C.
25 " " every six vehicles.

4. Route.
NEUILLY ST FRONT DAMMARD MAREUIL sur OURCQ.

5. Halts. 10 minutes before each clock hour.

6. Watering.
The head of the column will halt for watering when it reaches the T Roads 1¼ miles W. of ST. QUENTIN. Units will pull off the road as far as possible and water in the Ru d'ALLANT.

7. Destination.
152nd. ST. MARTIN & COLLINANCES.
160th. ETAVIGNY.
D.A.C. BOULLARE.
R.A.H.Q. Transport MAREUIL.
No. 1 Coy. Train. road junction ST MARTIN & COLLINANCES.

8. No. 1 Cpy. Train will march independently under the orders of the O.C. and avoid blocking the units of the D.A.

9. R.A.H.Q. will close at Fme d'EDROLLE and reopen at NANTEUIL le HAUDOUIN at 6 p.m.

10. Brigades will send teams for guns at I.O.M. tomorrow and arrange for them to rejoin batteries at their destinations on the 4th. inst. All guns (not condemned) and carriages will be removed whether repaired or not.

11. Brigades, D.A.C. & No. 1 Coy. Train please ACKNOWLEDGE.

[signature]
Captain,
Brigade Major.R.A.
34th. Divisional Artillery.

10-45 p.m.
Copies: 1-5. 152nd. Bde. RFA.
6-10. 160th. " "
11-14. 34th. D.A.C.
15. No. 1 Coy. Train.
16. 34th. "G".
17. S.C.R.A.
18-19. War Diary.
20. File.

App XI

SECRET. Copy No. 22

34th. DIVISIONAL ARTILLERY OPERATION ORDER No. 14.

4th. ~~July~~ August 1918.

1. The 34th. Division will be withdrawn to the British Zone, moving by rail from the following Stations:- ORMOY VILLERS - NANTEUIL - LE PLESSIS BELLEVILLE - DAMMARTIN.

2. Detraining Stations AUVIN WAVRANS-HESDIN. The destinations of particular trains cannot yet be given.

3. Units will entrain as shown on Entraining Table attached.

4. The complement of the D.A.C. entraining with each battery will join the battery by 10 a.m. on the 5th. inst and remain under the orders of the Battery Commander till it reaches its destination.

5. Moves to Entraining Stations will take place independently by order of O.Cs. Brigades and O.C. D.A.C. will arrange times and routes for H.Q. D.A.C. and S.A.A. Section.

6. Officers for duty at Entraining Stations and arrangements on the journey vide Administrative Instructions attached.

7. Please ACKNOWLEDGE.

[signature]
Captain,
Brigade Major.R.A.
34th. Divisional Artillery.

Issued at 6.30pm
Copies: 1-5. 152nd.Bde.RFA.
6-10. 160th.Bde.RFA.
11-14. O.C. 34th. D.A.C.
15-17. D.T.M.O.
18. O i/c R.A. Sigs.
19. S.C.R.A.
20. No. 1 Coy. Train.
21-22. War Diary.
23. File.

P. T. O.

ENTRAINING TABLE.

Serial No.	Entraining Station.	Date	Time of departure.	Composition.	Remarks.
1.	ORMOY VILLERS	5th.	3 p.m.	1 Bty 152nd.Bde. 1 G.S. & 4 Ammunition Wagons of No. 1 Section D.A.C.	A/152.
2.	NANTEUIL	"	4 p.m.	1 Bty 152nd.Bde. with 1 G.S. & 4 Ammunition Wagons of No. 1 Section D.A.C.	B/152.
3.	LE PLESSIS BELLEVILLE	"	5 p.m.	1 Bty 160th.Bde. 1 G.S. & 4 Ammunition Wagons of No. 2 Section D.A.C	A/160.
4.	DAMMARTIN	"	6 p.m.	1 Bty 160th.Bde. 1 G.S. & 4 Ammunition Wagons of No. 2 Section D.A.C.	B/160.
5.	ORMOY VILLERS	"	7 p.m.	1 Bty 152nd.Bde. 1 G.S. & 4 Ammunition Wagons of No. 1 Section D.A.C.	C/152.
6.	NANTEUIL	"	8 p.m.	H.Q.152nd.Bde."X" T.M.B. No. 1 Section D.A.C. less 4 G.S. and 16 Ammunition Wagons.	
7.	LE PLESSIS BELLEVILLE	"	9 p.m.	1 Bty 160th.Bde.1 G.S. & 4 Ammunition Wagons No. 2 Section D.A.C.	C/160.
8.	DAMMARTIN	"	10 p.m.	H.Q.160th.Bde."Y" T.M.B. No. 2 Section D.A.C. less 4 G.S. and 16 Ammunition Wagons.	
9.	ORMOY VILLERS	"	11 p.m.	1 Bty 152nd. Bde. 1 G.S. & 4 Ammunition Wagons of No. 1 Section D.A.C.	D/152.
10.	NANTEUIL.	"	12 mdnt.	H.Q.R.A. H.Q.D.A.C. H.Q.No. 1 Coy.Train.	
11.	LE PLESSIS BELLEVILLE	6th.	1 a.m.	1 Bty 160th.Bde. 1 G.S. & 4 Ammunition Wagons of No. 2 Section D.A.C.	D/160.
12.	DAMMARTIN	"	2 a.m.	H.Q. & 1½ Subsections of S.A.A.Section.	
13.	DAMMARTIN	"	3 a.m.	1½ Subsections of S.A.A. Section.	

S E C R E T.

34th. DIVISIONAL ARTILLERY ADMINISTRATIVE INSTRUCTIONS
issued in conjunction with 34th. D.A. O.O. No. 14 today.

-.-

1. SUPPLIES.

Supplies for consumption 6th. will be drawn at Entraining Stations on 5th. and will consist of 24 hours Train Rations.

Supplies for consumption 7th. will also be drawn at Entraining Stations and loaded on Supply Wagons, which will entrain with units.

Supplies for consumption 8th. will be delivered in the new area.

2. ENTRAINMENT.

Each unit will find its own loading and unloading parties.

All units must be at Station at least 3 hours before hour of departure of train.

Entrainment should be completed ½ hour before hour of departure.

O.C. each unit will hand an entraining state to R.T.O. immediately on arrival at Station.

3. DISCIPLINE.

Divisional Commander directs strictest train discipline be enforced during journey.

4. Officers i/c Entraining Stations.

These Officers, who should have experience of entraining, will be found as follows:-

ORMOY VILLERS.............. by 152nd. Brigade RFA.
NANTEUIL.................. by D.T.M.O.
PLESSIS BELLEVILLE........ by 34th. D.A.C.
DAMMARTIN................. by 160th. Brigade RFA.

Each Officer should have a Timetable of the entrainment at his station.

These Officers represent R.A.H.Q. and will report any difficulties to R.A.H.Q. at NANTEUIL. Their duties are to keep in touch with R.T.O., reconnoitre station approaches, ramps and nearest watering place, etc. and give information to units on arrival. They are to be at their Station 4 hours before departure of first train and leave by last R.A. train from that station.

5. Advance Parties.

Advance parties of 1 Officer per Brigade, D.A.C. or Train Coy. with an N.C.O. per battery or section D.A.C. will proceed as follows:-

152nd. Bde. by first train from ORMOY VILLERS.
160th. Bde. " " " " PLESSIS. BELLEVILLE.
D.A.C. " " " " NANTEUIL.
No. 1 Coy. Train " " " DAMMARTIN.

A bicycle for each member of party must be taken and also 2 days rations. On arrival at Detraining Station Officers i/c Advance parties will report to 34th. Divisional Staff Officer for instructions as to billets, etc. and after reconnoitring, return to guide units to destination.

6. Miscellaneous.

Approximate duration of journey is 17 hours.

Haltes repas (about ½ hour) have been arranged at US-ACHIRES (4 hours after departure) and at NOYELLES (10 hours after departure).

[signature]
Captain,
Staff Captain,
34th. Divisional Artillery.

4th. July 1918.

Copy to 152nd. Bde. RFA. (5)
160th. Bde. RFA. (5)
No. 1 Coy Train (1)
O.C. D.A.C. (4)
D.T.M.O. (3)

App XII

34th Divisional Artillery Location Report.

Reference Sheet 27.

UNIT.	LOCATION.
R.A.Hd Qrs.	~~K.8.a.0.3.~~ C.7.b.7.2
H.Q. 152nd Bde.	K.1.a.8.4.
A/152.	J.6.a.1.7.
B/152.	D.29.d.5.2.
C/152.	D.29.c.0.9.
D/152.	J.4.b.6.7.
H.Q. 160th Bde.	~~K.2.c.1.6.~~ K.1.d.95.60
A/160.	J.6.c.6.0.
B/160.	J.11.b.6.4.
C/160.	J.11.a.5.9.
D/160.	J.5.c.3.7.
H.Q. D.A.C.,	E.26.c.2.5.
No.1.Sec.	E.27.d.8.8.
No.2.Sec.	E.27 .c.6.4.
S.A.A.Sec.	K.8.b.2.2.
No.1.Coy, 34 Div. Train and "X" & "Y" T.M.Btys.	(BORDEN CAMP.) K.3.d.8.5.

7th August 1918.

for Captain.
Staff Captain.
34th Divnl Artillery.

War Diary

App XIII

S E C R E T.

34th. DIVISIONAL ARTILLERY MARCHING ORDER NO. 6.

1. The Divisional Artillery will move to HAANDEKOT area on the 12th. inst.

2. Allotment of billets will be notified tomorrow ~~morning~~.

3. R.A.H.Q. will move to COUTHOVE CHATEAU and reopen there at 12 noon on the 12th. inst.

4. One section per battery will be in action in positions covering the EAST POPERINGHE or BLUE LINE by 10 p.m. on the 12th. inst.
Further instructions regarding positions and O.Ps. will be issued later.

Captain,
Brigade Major.R.A.
34th. Divisional Artillery.

10-8-18.
Copies: 152nd. Bde. RFA.
160th. Bde. RFA.
34th. D.A.C.
34th. Div. "Q".
IInd. Corps "Q".
R.A. Sigs.

App XIV

SECRET. **ADDENDUM to**

34th. DIVISIONAL ARTILLERY WARNING ORDER No. 6.

1. No restrictions as to time of starting or route.

2. One section per battery will be in action in positions covering the EAST POPERINGHE line by 10 p.m. 13th. August.

3. The following positions will be occupied:-

Positions for 152nd. Brigade RFA. ("A" Brigade)

Position No.	Map Ref.	Battery.
BL.21.	L.16.a.12.58.	A/152.
BL.22.	L.4.d.25.42.	B/152.
BL.23.	L.4.a.70.10.	C/152.
BL.24.	L.10.b.30.66.	D/152.

Positions for 160th. Brigade RFA. ("G" Brigade)

Position No.	Map Ref.	Battery.
BL.13.	A.10.b.82.66.	A/160.
BL.14.	A.18.d.00.8[illegible].	B/160.
BL.15.	A.19.c.89.85.	C/160.
BL.16.	F.24.a.37.50.	D/160.

4. Sufficient personnel will be left with each section to man the guns if required and to continue work on the positions.

5. A Map has already been issued to each Brigade showing positions for nine Brigades of F.A. for the defence of the EAST POPERINGHE line.
G.C. 152nd. Bde. RFA is responsible for the maintenance and improvement of positions for A, B, C, D & E Brigades, G.C. 160th. Bde. for F, G, H & I Brigades.

6. 200 rounds of ammunition will be dumped in the positions occupied.

7. A list of O.Ps. is appended. Brigade Commanders will allot them to batteries and notify this office of their distribution.

8. The responsibility for the defence of the EAST POPERINGHE line now rests with the 30th. American Division supported by the 34th. Divisional Artillery.

9. Brigade Commanders will get into touch with the Brigadiers of the sectors they cover, arrange S.O.S. lines in consultation with them and notify this office of the result.

10. Brigades and D.A.C. please ACKNOWLEDGE.

Captain,
Brigade Major.R.A.
34th. Divisional Artillery.

11th. August 1918.

Copies: 152nd. Bde. RFA.
160th. Bde. RFA.
34th. D.A.C.
D.T.M.O.
34th. Div. "G".
R.A. IInd. Corps.
30th. American Division.

OBSERVATION POSTS.

No.	Name.	Location.	Description of work required.	Allotted No.
1.	[illegible]	A.21.c.12.61.	Two trees.	
2.	[illegible]	A.26.d.35.56.	Two trees.	
3.	[illegible]	[illegible].55.47.	Concrete in house.	
4.	[illegible]	[illegible]	Concrete in house.	
5.	[illegible]	[illegible]	Concrete pillbox in corner of hedge.	
6.	[illegible]	[illegible]	Concrete pillbox behind hedge.	
7.	[illegible]	C.1.b.1.8.	Tower O.P. in Chateau.	
8.	[illegible]	C.3 .c.30.10.	Tower in [illegible] Shed.	
9.	[illegible]	C.8.a.13 .17.	Accommodation in Bde H.Q. in cellars.	
10.	[illegible]	C.14.b.38.77.	Concrete in house.	
11.	[illegible]	C.15.[illegible]	Fresh line trench O.P.	
12.	[illegible]	C.16.a.[illegible]	Concrete tunnel on top of pill box.	
13.	[illegible]	[illegible]	Chimney in Brewery to be made accessible, and accommodation in cellars of Bde H.Q.	

SECRET.
& PRESSING.

34th. Div. Arty. No. 1205/A.

Ref. sheet 27.

1... Reference 34th. Div. Arty. Warning Order No.6., 34th. Divisional Artillery and Train Coy. will move to wagon lines on Monday 12th. inst. as follows:-

152nd. F.A. Bde.

H.Q.	E.10.c.3.5.
A/152.	E.10.c.3.5.
B/152.	E.16.c.8.6.
C/152.	E.16.a.9.4.
D/152.	E.21.b.8.8.

160th. F.A. Bde.

H.Q.	E.11.c.0.7.
A/160.	E.10.d.5.8.
B/160.	E.10.b.4.8.
C/160.	E.11.a.6.8.
D/160.	E.17.b.0.9.

34th. D.A.C.

H.Q.	E.17.b.9.7.
No.1.Sect.	E.17.b.8.6.
" 2 "	E.12.c.2.5.
S.A.A. "	E.16.d.2.7.

Trench Mortar Batteries E.10.a.6.4.

No.1.Coy. Divl. Train. E.23.c.4.2.

2... No restrictions as to time of starting or route.

3... O.C. 34th. D.A.C. will place 4 G.S. wagons at the disposal of the D.T.M.O. for transport purposes. They will report to D.T.M.O. not later than 9 a.m. 12th. inst.

4... Headquarters 34th. Divisional Artillery will close at [illegible] at 10 a.m. and open at GOU HOVE [illegible] at 12 noon. 16. inst [illegible].

[signature]

Captain,
Staff Captain,
34th. Divisional Artillery.

11th. August 1918.

Copies to:- 152nd. F.A. Bde.
160th. F.A. Bde.
34th. D.A.C.
D.T.M.O.
No.1.Coy. Divnl Train.

34th. Division "G".
" " "Q".
A.D.M.S.
A.D.V.S.
O.C. 34th. Divnl Train.

34th DIV.
G. S. O. 1
G. S. O. 2
G. S. O. 3
I. O.

App XV

S E C R E T.

34th.Div.Arty. o. 0/403.

Reference 34th. D.A. Warning Order No. 7.

1. Para. 2. Forward Sections will relieve on the night of 21st/22nd. Main battery positions on the night 22nd/23rd.

2. Trench Mortars on the night of 21st/22nd.

3. Brigades will move from HAANDEKOT area to their new Wagon Lines on the 21st. No restrictions as to time or route.

4. D.A.C. on the 22nd.

5. R.A.H.Q. will move to LA LOVIE at 12 noon on 22nd.

R.W. Forrestal

Captain,
for Brigade Major.R.A.
34th. Divisional Artillery.

16th. August 1918.

Copies to all recipients of 34th. D.A. W.O. No. 7.

SECRET.

34th. DIVISIONAL ARTILLERY WARNING ORDER No. 7.

1...... The 34th. Divisional Artillery will relieve the 49th. Divisional Artillery in the line.

2...... Probable dates - Forward Sections on the night 22/23dr. Main positi ons night 23/24th.
All Trench Mortars night 22/23rd.

3...... The D.A.C. will move into their new area to a time to be notified later.

4...... Locations in new area appended.

5...... A Defence Scheme will be issued shortly.

6...... Brigades, D.A.C. & D.T.M.O. to ACKNOWLEDGE.

Captain,
Brigade Major.R.A.
34th. Divisional Artillery.

15th. August 1918.

Copies: 152nd. Bde. RFA. (5)
160th. Bde. RFA. (5)
D.A.C. (3)
D.T.M.O. (3)
34th. Div. "G". (1)
49th.Div.Arty. (1)
30th. (American) Divn. (1)
War Diary (2)
File. (1)

SECRET.

34th. DIVISIONAL ARTILLERY LOCATION STATEMENT.

Ref: Sheets 27 & 28 1/40,000. 15th. August 1918.

Headquarters 34th. Divisional Artillery. LOVIE CHATEAU 27/F.16.d.4.5.

Unit.	Location.	No. of Guns.	Wagon Lines.
WARBURTON's Bde. (160th) Lt. Col. W.A. WARBURTON, D.S.O.			
H.Q. H.Q.	H.5.a.00.85.		A.22.b.8.6.
A/160.	H.5.d.90.10.	2 guns	F.30.a.7.8.
	I.7.a.5.8.	2 "	
	H.6.d.98.15.	2 "	
B/160.	B.29.c.45.40.	4 "	A.14.c.0.6.
	B.3 0.d.95.15.	2 "	
C/160.	B.29.d.4.1.	4 "	A.14.a.5.3.
	I.2.c.68.15.(On Rly)	1 gun	
	H.6.b.6.4.	1 "	
D/160.	B.30.a.5.0.	4 Hows.	F.24.a.8.5.
	I.7.a.6.9.	2 "	
SAVILE's Bde. (152nd) Lt. Col. L.W. SAVILE, D.S.O.			
H.Q.	MACHINE GUN FARM (H.5.c.90.90)		A.28.a.2.7.
A/152.	I.1.a.50.60.	2 Guns	A.22.a.10.60.
	H.5.b.3.2.	4 "	
B/152.	H.6.d.50.40.	2 "	A.3.a.50.20.
	B.29.c.00.80.	4 "	
C/152.	I.1.c.40.50.	2 G"	F.18.c.40.80.
	H.5.a.55.45.	4 "	
D/152.	I.1.b.48.39.	2 Hows.	A.21.a.8.8.
	I.1.b.38.72.	2 "	
	H.11.b.90.35.	2 "	

D.T.M.O. 34th. Division. A.27.c.70.90.
H.Q.X/34 T.M.Bty. A.27.c.70.90.
H.Q.Y/34.T.M.Bty. I.14.a.70.60.

6" Newton Trench Mortars.

1 at I.14.a.35.59.
1 at I.14.a.58.50.
1 at I.8.d.05.47.
1 at I.8.d.15.55.
1 at I.9.c.65.03.
1 atI.9.c.65.05.
1 at I.3.d.35.40.
1 at I.4.a.40.30.
2 at H.11.b.80.15.
2 at H.11.b.85.45.

34th. D.A.C. Colonel C.N. SIMPSON, D.S.O.

Headquarters. A.25.b.1.8.
No. 1 Section. F.24.a.9.5.
No. 2 Section. A.19.d.1.9.
S.A.A. Section. A.19.b.08.28.

[signature]

Captain,
Brigade Major.R.A.
34th. Divisional Artillery.

Copies to recipients of 34th. D.A. Warning Order No. 7.

SECRET. Copy No. 25.

34th. DIVISIONAL ARTILLERY OPERATION ORDER NO. 15.

17th. August 1918.

In continuation of 34th. D.A. Warning Order No. 7 and this office No. 0/403.

1. Times of relief - No movement is to take place East of VLAMERTINGHE before 8 p.m.

2. Completion of relief will be reported by telephone to H.Q.R.A. at La LOVIE Chateau on each night. Code Word "BUGGINS".

3. D.A.C. will move into their new lines by noon 22nd. August and will take over dumps and the responsibility for the supply of ammunition as soon after noon as possible.

4. Liaison with Infantry will be taken over by 6 p.m. on the 22nd. O.Ps. at the same time.

5. Reference para. 3 of 0/403.
Owing to limited accommodation, only one section per battery will move from HOUTKERQUE area to their new Wagon Lines on the 21st. inst, the remainder on the 22nd. inst.

6. Receipts will be given, and copies forwarded to this office, for the following :-

- Planchettes
- Aeroplane Photos.
- Target map and programme for harassing fire.
- Trench Stores.
- Defence Schemes.
- Panoramas.
- Position Calls.
- Ammunition.
- S.O.S. Signals.

7. D.A. units to ACKNOWLEDGE.

Captain,
Brigade Major.R.A.
34th. Divisional Artillery.

Issued at 6 pm

Copies: 1-5. 152nd . Bde. RFA.
6-10. 160th. Bde. RFA.
11-14. 34th. D.A.C.
15-17. D.T.M.O.
18. B.C.R.A.
19. 34th. Div. "G".
20. R.A. IInd. Corps.
21. R.A. 49th. Div.
22. 30th. (American) Divn.
23. C.A.D.I. 12th. Belgian Divn.
24-25. War Diary.
26. File.

War Diary

App XVI

S E C R E T.

34th. DIVISIONAL ARTILLERY LOCATION STATEMENT.

Ref Sheets 27 & 28 1/40,000. 23rd. August 1918.

Unit		Location.	Wagon Lines.
R.A., 34th. Division.		LOVIE CHATEAU.	
160th. Brigade RFA.	H.Q.	H.5.a.00.85.	A.22.b.8.6.
A/160.	4 guns	H.5.d.90.10.	F.30.a.7.8.
	2 "	I.7.a.5.8.	
B/160.	4 "	B.29.c.45.40.	A.14.c.0.6.
	2 "	B.30.d.95.15.	
C/160.	5 "	B.29.d.4.1.	A.14.a.5.3.
	1 gun	I.2.c.68.15.	(On Rly)
D/160.	4. Hows.	B.30.a.5.0.	F.24.a.8.5.
	2 "	I.7.a.6.9.	
152nd. Brigade RFA.	H.Q.	MACHINE GUN FARM (H.5.c.90.90)	A.28.a.2.7.
A/152.	4 guns	H.5.b.3.2.	A.22.a.10.60.
	2 "	I.1.a.50.60.	
B/152.	4 "	B.29.c.00.80.	A.3.a.50.20.
	2 "	H.6.d.50.40.	
C/152.	4 "	H.5.a.55.45.	F.18.c.40.80.
	2 "	I.1.c.40.50.	
D/152.	2 Hows.	I.1.b.48.39.	A.21.a.8.8.
	2 "	I.1.b.38.72.	
	2 "	H.11.b.90.35.	
D.T.M.O. 34th. Divn.		A.27.c.2.6.	
H.Q. X/34 T.M. Bty.		A.27.c.70.90.	
H.Q. Y/34 T.M. Bty.		I.14.a.70.60.	

6" Newton Trench Mortars.

1 at I.14.a.35.59.	1 at I.8.d.15.55.	1 at I.4.a.40.30.
1 at I.14.a.58.50.	1 at I.9.c.65.03.	2 at H.11.b.80.15.
1 at I.8.d.05.47.	1 at I.9.c.65.05.	2 at H.11.b.85.45.
	1 at I.3.d.35.40.	

34th. Div. Amn. Col.	H.Q.		A.25.b.1.9.
No. 1 Section.			F.24.a.9.5.
No. 2 Section.			A.19.d.1.9.
S.A.A. Section.			A.19.b.08.28.
34th. A.R.P.		A.23.a.8.3.	

[signature]

Captain,
Brigade Major.R.A.
34th. Divisional Artillery.

S E C R E T. 34th.Div.Arty.No. O/409.

App XVIII

1. The 34th. Division (less Artillery) will be relieved by the 14th. Division by 3 a.m. 29th. Aug.

2. H.Q.R.A. 34th. Division will move to COUTHOVE CHATEAU probably on the 29th. inst.

3. The 41st. Infantry Brigade will relieve the 103rd. Infantry Brigade.

(Sd) G. O. Smyth.

Captain,
Brigade Major.R.A.
26-8-18. 34th. Divisional Artillery.

Copies to: 152nd. Bde. RFA.
160th. " "
34th. D.A.C.
D.T.M.O.
War Diary.
File.

"A" Form
MESSAGES AND SIGNALS.

Army Form C. 2121 (in pads of 100).

No of Message ....

APP XIX

Prefix.......... Code..........m.	Words	Charge.	This message is on a/c of:	Recd. at..........m.
Office of Origin and Service Instructions.	Sent		..........Service	Date..........
Copy	At..........m.			From..........
	To..........			
	By..........		(Signature of "Franking Officer.")	By..........

TO 34 D A C

Sender's Number.	Day of Month.	In reply to Number.	AAA
* S 25	28		

S.A.A. Section will now move tomorrow 29th inst.

From 34 Div Arty
Place
Time

The above may be forwarded as now corrected. (Z) (Sd) H. Smith

Censor. Signature of Addressor or person authorised to telegraph in his name.

* This line should be erased if not required.

(18065.) Wt. W12952/M1294. 187,500 Pads. 1/17 McC. & Co., Ltd. (E. 818.)

Army Form C. 2121
(in pads of 100).

"A" Form

MESSAGES AND SIGNALS.

No of Message ....

Prefix .... Code .... m.	Words	Charge.	This message is on a/c of:	Recd. at .... m.
Office of Origin and Service Instructions.	Sent		.... Service	Date ....
Copy	At .... m.			From ....
	To			
	By		(Signature of "Franking Officer.")	By ....

TO 34 D A C

Sender's Number.	Day of Month.	In reply to Number.	AAA
* S 23	28		

S.A.A. Sectn will move to 27/R.21 c 9.5 by road on the 30th inst by most direct route AAA Details of relief by S.A.A. Sectn 14th Div will be arranged between Section Commanders

From 34 Div Art

Place

Time

The above may be forwarded as now corrected. (Z)

Censor. Sd. G. F. Surry Lt

Signature of Addressor or person authorised to telegraph in his name.

* This line should be erased if not required.

RWH

(18065.) Wt. W12952/M1294. 187,500 Pads. 1/17 McC. & Co., Ltd. (E. 818.)

App XI

S E C R E T.

34th. DIVISIONAL ARTILLERY LOCATION STATEMENT No. 2.

Ref: Sheets 27 & 28 1:40,000. 31st August 1918.

Unit.		Location.	Wagon Lines.
R.A.H.Q. 34th. Divn.		COUTHOVE CHATEAU.	
Right Bde.RFA. (152) H.Q.		MACHINE GUN FARM (H.5.c.90.90)	A.28.a.2.7.
A/152.	4 guns	H.5.b.3.2.	A.22.a.10.60.
	2 "	I.1.a.50.60.	
B/152.	4 "	B.29.c.00.80.	A.3.a.50.20.
	2 "	H.6.d.50.40.	
C/152.	4 "	H.5.a.55.45.	F.18.c.40.80.
	2 "	I.1.c.40.50.	
D/152.	2 Hows.	I.1.b.48.39.	A.21.a.8.8.
	2 "	I.1.b.38.72.	
	2 "	H.11.b.90.35.	
Left Bde.RFA. (160) H.Q.		H.5.a.00.85.	A.13.d.0.1.
A/160.	4 guns	H.5.d.90.10.	F.30.a.7.8.
	2 "	H.6.d.98.15.	
B/160.	4 "	B.29.c.45.40.	F.18.c.7.5.
	2 "	B.30.d.95.15.	
C/160.	5 "	B.29.d.4.1.	A.19.b.08.28.
	1 gun	I.2.c.68.15.	
D/160.	4 Hows.	B.30.a.5.0.	A.19.b.1.9.
	2 "	I.7.a.6.9.	

D.T.M.O. 34th. Divn. A.27.c.2.6.
H.Q. X/34 T.M.Bty. A.27.c.70.90.
H.Q. Y/34 T.M. Bty. I.14.a.70.60.

6" Newton Trench Mortars.

(1) I.4.a.5.5.	(5) I.9.c.65.10.	(9) I.14.a.40.60.
(2) I.4.a.45.10.	(6)	(10) H.11.b.7.2.
(3) I.3.d.4.4.	(7) I.8.d.05.45.	(11) H.11.b.7.4.
(4) I.3.d.3.6.	(8) I.8.d.10.60.	(12) At Workshops.

34th. Div. Amm. Col. H.Q.	A.25.b.1.9.
No. 1 Section.	F.24.a.9.5.
No. 2 Section.	A.19.d.1.9.
S.A.A. Section.	A.19.b.08.28.

34th. A.R.P. A.23.a.8.3.

[signature]

Captain,
Brigade Major.R.A.
34th. Divisional Artillery.

GS 1/31

Copy No. 19...

SECRET.

34th. DIVISIONAL ARTILLERY OPERATION ORDER NO. 15.

17th. August 1918.

In continuation of 34th. D.A. Warning Order No. 7 and this office No. O/403.

1. Times of relief - No movement is to take place East of VLAMERTINGHE before 8 p.m.

2. Completion of relief will be reported by telephone to H.Q.R.A. at La LOVIE Chateau on each night. Code Word "BUGGINS".

3. D.A.C. will move into their new lines by noon 22nd. August and will take over dumps and the responsibility for the supply of ammunition as soon after noon as possible.

4. Liaison with Infantry will be taken over by 6 p.m. on the 22nd. O.Ps. at the same time.

5. Reference para. 3 of O/403.
Owing to limited accommodation, only one section per battery will move from HERZEELE area to their new Wagon Lines on the 21st. inst, the remainder on the 22nd. inst.

6. Receipts will be given, and copies forwarded to this office, for the following :-

- Planchettes
- Aeroplane Photos.
- Target map and programme for harassing fire.
- Trench Stores.
- Defence Schemes.
- Panoramas.
- Position Calls.
- Ammunition.
- S.O.S. Signals.

7. D.A. units to ACKNOWLEDGE.

[signature]

Captain,
Brigade Major.R.A.
34th. Divisional Artillery.

Issued at 6 pm

Copies: 1-5. 152nd . Bde. RFA.
6-10. 160th. Bde. RFA.
11-14. 34th. D.A.C.
15-17. D.T.M.O.
18. S.C.R.A.
19. 34th. Div. "G".
20. R.A. IInd. Corps.
21. R.A. 49th. Div.
22. 30th. (American) Divn.
23. C.R.D.I. 12th. Belgian Divn.
24-25. War Diary.
26. File.

OULCHY-LE-CHATEAU
HARTENNES OULCHY
(SOISSONS)
Echelle 1:20.000
Groupe des Canevas de Tir
Secret N°
Chaudun
Buzancy
Ambrief
Chacrise
Villemontoire
Vierzy
Droizy
Hartennes et Taux
Parcy-Tigny
Villers-Hélon
Louâtre
Blanzy
St Rémy-Blanzy
Plessier-Huleu
Grand-Rozoy
Beugneux
Bois de Hartennes
Bois du Plessier
Bois de St Jean
Bois de Plantis
Coutremain

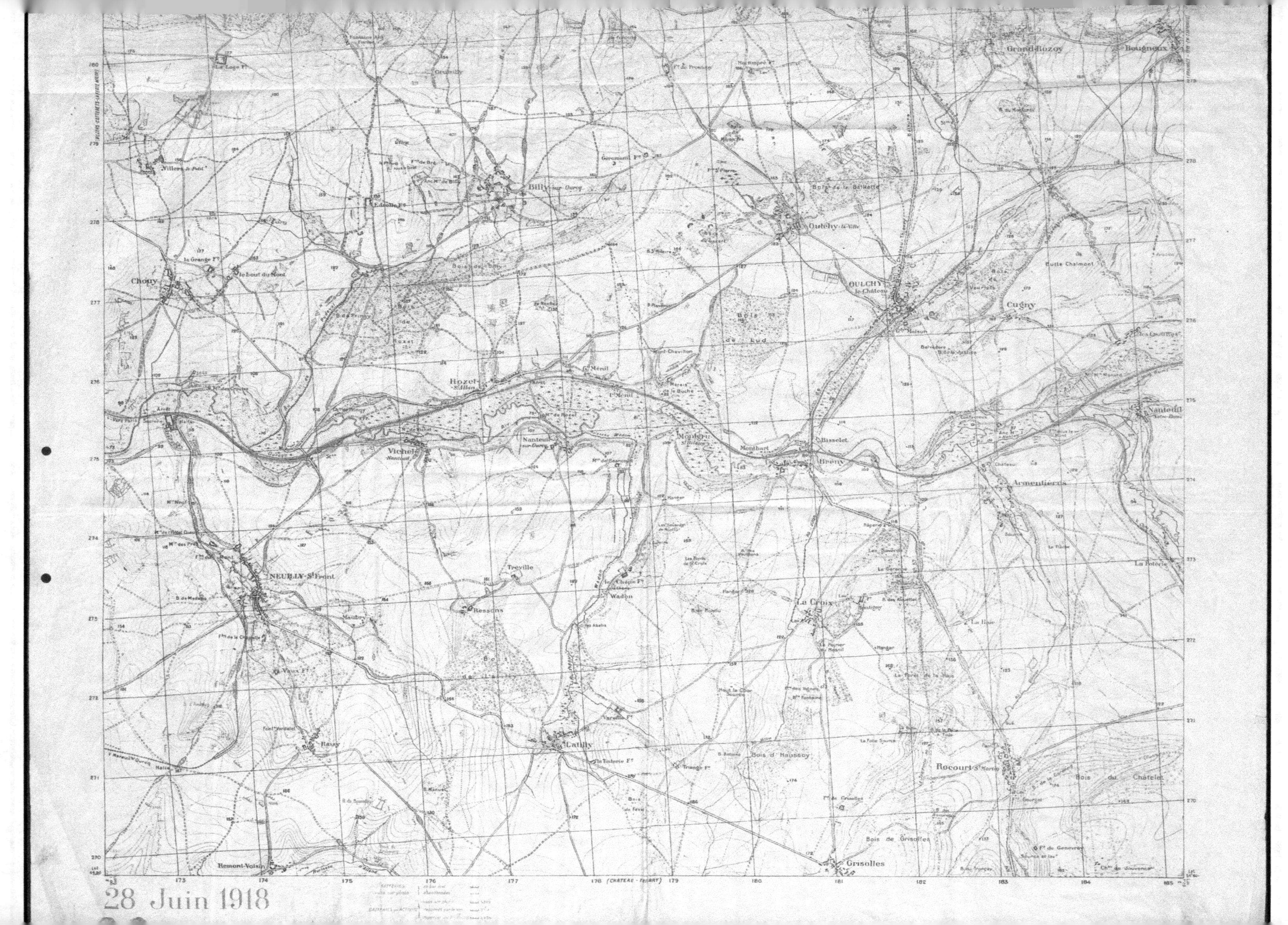

Grand-Rozoy
Bougneux
Billy-sur-Ourcq
Oulchy-la-Ville
OULCHY le-Château
Cugny
Chouy
Villers-le-Petit
Rozet-St-Albin
Vichel-Nanteuil
Nanteuil-sur-Ourcq
Montgru-St-Hilaire
Bisselet
Breny
Armentières
Nanteuil-Notre-Dame
NEUILLY-St-Front
Treville
Ressons
Wadon
La Croix
La Poterie
Latilly
Rassy
Remont-Voisin
Rocourt-St-Martin
Bois du Châtelet
Bois de Grisolles
Grisolles
Bois d'Haussoy
Bois de Lud
Butte Chalmont
Bois de la Baillette
28 Juin 1918

Vol 33

WAR DIARY

FOR

SEPTEMBER 1918.

H.Q.R.A. 34 DIVISION

~~152ND~~ BRIGADE R.F.A.

~~160TH~~ BRIGADE R.F.A.

~~34TH~~ D.A.C.

~~34TH~~ TRENCH MORTARS

Army Form C. 2118.

Instructions regarding War Diaries and Intelligence Summaries are contained in F. S. Regs., Part II. and the Staff Manual respectively. Title pages will be prepared in manuscript.

WAR DIARY
or
INTELLIGENCE SUMMARY.

(Erase heading not required.)

Month of September, 1918.

H.Q.R.A., 34th. Division.

Page 1.

Place	Date	Hour	Summary of Events and Information	Remarks and references to Appendices
	Sept.			
COUTHOVE CHATEAU. (27/F.21.a)	1		On the night 31st./1st., the 160th. Brigade, R.F.A., were withdrawn to their Wagon Lines, the 152nd. Brigade, R.F.A., covering the 14th. Divisional front.	App I
			S.O.S. lines and arrangements for liaison and manning of O.P.'s, vide	App II
			During 1st. September, the 160th. Brigade, R.F.A., moved to Wagon Lines of the 24th. Brigade R.F.A., (6th. Division) and relieved the same Brigade in the line covering the 27th. (American) Division, the following night	App III
	2		The 152nd. Brigade, R.F.A., hav ing been relieved in the line covering the 14th. Division by the 35th. Divisional Artillery, marched to temporary wagon-lines adjacent to the wagon-lines of the 2nd. Brigade, R.F.A., (6th. Division) during the day of the 2nd., and relieved the 2nd. Brigade R.F.A. in the line covering the 27th. (American) Division the following night. ...	App IV
	2		The 34th. D.A.C. relieved the 6th. D.A.C., and became responsible for the supply of ammunition from 12 noon, 2nd. September.	AppIV
	2		34th. Divisional Trench Mortars occupied the Camp at 27/L.2.d.6.6, vacated by the 6th. Divisional Trench Mortars.	App VI
DOUGLAS CAMP, (27/L.14.a.2.0)	3		H.Q.R.A. moved from COUTHOVE CHATEAU, 27/F.21.a, on the 2nd. September, spent the night at	

A5834 Wt. W4973/M687 750,000 8/16 D. D. & L. Ltd. Forms/C.2118/13.

Army Form C. 2118.

Instructions regarding War Diaries and Intelligence Summaries are contained in F. S. Regs., Part II. and the Staff Manual respectively. Title pages will be prepared in manuscript.

WAR DIARY
or
INTELLIGENCE SUMMARY.
(Erase heading not required.)

H.Q.R.A., 34th. Division.

Month of September, 1918.

Page 2.

Place	Date	Hour	Summary of Events and Information	Remarks and references to Appendices
DOUGLAS CAMP, 27/L.14.a.2.0.	Sept			
	3		the 34th. Division Rear H.Qrs., 27/K.24.c.2.2, and joined the 27th. (American) Division at DOUGLAS CAMP (27/L.14.a.2.0) the next day.	
			At 10 a.m., the C.R.A., 34th. Division, assumed the responsibility of covering the 27th. (American) Division in the line South of YPRES.	App IV
	3		34th. Divisional Artillery Location Statement, vide	App V
	3		The 27th. (American) Division was relieved in the line by the 41st. (British) Division, and the C.R.A. 34th. Division assumed the responsibility of covering the 41st. Division.	
	4		At 5.30 a.m., the 41st. Division, in conjunction with the 34th. Division on their right, attacked the outskirts of the WYTSCHAETE Ridge.	
			A creeping barrage was afforded by 18-pounders, while 6" and 4.5" Howitzers assisted with fire on selected points	App VI
	5		Moves of the 160th. Brigade, R.F.A. Wagon-Lines, and the 34th. D.A.C.	App VII
			34th. Divisional Artillery Location Statements vide	App VIII
	8		The relief of the 41st. Divisional Artillery covering the 34th. Division in the WYTSCHAETE Sector by the 34th. Divisional Artillery, was completed.	

A5834 Wt. W4973 M687 750,000 8/16 D. D. & L. Ltd. Forms/C.2118/13.

Army Form C. 2118.

Instructions regarding War Diaries and Intelligence Summaries are contained in F. S. Regs., Part II. and the Staff Manual respectively. Title pages will be prepared in manuscript.

WAR DIARY
or
INTELLIGENCE SUMMARY.
(Erase heading not required.)

Month of September 1918

H.Q.R.A, 34th. Division.

Page 3

Place	Date	Hour	Summary of Events and Information	Remarks and references to Appendices
DOUGLAS CAMP, 27/L.14.a.2.0.	8		The relief was carried out in three nights, two batteries being relieved each night. ...	App IX
27/K.24.c.2.3.	8		H.Q.R.A. moved from DOUGLAS CAMP and joined 34th. Division Head-quarters at 27/K.24.c.2.3, the C.R.A., 34th. Division, assuming the responsibility of covering the 34th. Division at 10 am.	App IX
do.	10		34th. Divisional Artillery Location Statement	App X
			Amendment to do. do. do.	App XI
27/L.36.c.5.5.				
	16		34th. Divisional Artillery Location Statement	App XII
do.	21		do. do. do. do.	App XIII
do.	26		34th. Divisional Artillery Instructions No. 1	App XIV
			do. do. do. do. ,, 2	App XV
			do. do. do. do. ,, 3	App XVI
			34th. Divisional Artillery Operation Order No. 22, ...	App XVII
	27		do. do. do. do. No. 23, ...	App XVIII
	28		At 5.30 a.m., [struck through] the left flank of the 34th. Division co-operating with the 14th. Division, under cover	

A5834 Wt. W4973 M687 750,000 8/16 D. D. & L. Ltd. Forms/C.2118/13.

Instructions regarding War Diaries and Intelligence Summaries are contained in F. S. Regs., Part II. and the Staff Manual respectively. Title pages will be prepared in manuscript.

WAR DIARY
or
INTELLIGENCE SUMMARY.
(Erase heading not required.)

Army Form C. 2118.

H.Q.R.A., 34th. Division.

Month of September 1918

Page ~~5~~ 4

Place	Date	Hour	Summary of Events and Information	Remarks and references to Appendices
27/L.36.c. 5.5.	28		of a creeping barrage, attacked and captured the high ground about ST. ELOI.	
			On the remainder of the Divisional Front, careful watch was maintained for any signs of withdrawal.	
			Commencing at 5.30 a.m., a smoke barrage was put down on the WYTSCHAETE HILL, while batteries not engaged in this or the creeping barrage on the ST. ELOI front, fired, simulating a creeping barrage on targets shewn on MAP "A" of Appendix XVII, and lifting to keep pace with an imaginary rolling barrage at the rate of 100 yards in 3 minutes.	
			Situation, 7.45 a.m. AAA "Line runs WARSAW CRATER (inclusive) E. edge of PETIT BOIS - spur N.18.d.central - Northern BRICKSTACK - CREONAERT Chapel - N. edge of BOIS QUARANTE - PICCADILLY FARM (inclusive) AAA Total prisoners to date 1 officer, 58 O.R. AAA Enemy attempted to retake SPANBROEKMOLEN crater at 4 a.m., but was held up 100 yards from the crater AAA ."	App XIX
do.	28		8.25 a.m., 34th. Divisional Intelligence Wire	App XX
			9.10 a.m., 35th. Division Situation Report, ...	App XXI
			10.55 a.m., 41st. Division Situation report, ...	App XXIII
			Situation Report, timed 11.50 a.m. AAA Line runs Road N.30.c.8.2 - SPANBROEKMOLEN PECKHAM	

A5834 Wt. W4973/M687 750,000 8/16 D. D. & L. Ltd. Forms/C.2118/13.

Army Form C. 2118.

WAR DIARY
or
INTELLIGENCE SUMMARY.
(Erase heading not required.)

Instructions regarding War Diaries and Intelligence Summaries are contained in F. S. Regs., Part II. and the Staff Manual respectively. Title pages will be prepared in manuscript.

Month of September 1918.

H.Q.R.A, 34th. Division.

Page 6

Place	Date	Hour	Summary of Events and Information	Remarks and references to Appendices
27/L.36.c 5.5	28		and WARSAW Craters inclusive - old trenches N.24.d.2.5 - spur N.18.d.central - just West of UNNAMED WOOD - W. edge of GRAND BOIS - CREONAERT Chapel - 200 yards E. of PICADILLY FARM.	
			Parties of enemy seen retiring over crest in O.19.b abd O.14.c.	App XXII
			Situation at 12.30 p.m., vide	App XXIV
			Situation at 1.30 p.m., vide	App XXV
			Situation Report, vide	App XXVI
			Information from prisoners of the 5th. Battery, 97th. Field Artillery Regiment ...	App XXVII
			Contact Patrol report, timed 6 p.m., ...	App XVIII
			Situation at 8.30 p.m., vide	App XXIX
	29		WYTSCHAETE WOOD was occupied at 6.45 a.m.	App XXX
	30		Situation on the BELGIAN front	App XXXI

P.C. Walthall

Brigadier-General,

C.R.A., 34th. Division.

A5834 Wt. W4973/M687 750,000 8/16 D. D. & L. Ltd. Forms/C.2118/13.

WD APP I

SECRET.

34th. DIVISIONAL ARTILLERY OPERATION ORDER No. [illegible]

1. 160th. Brigade RFA will be withdrawn to its Wagon Lines tonight (31st/1st.

2. It will not be relieved. 152nd. Brigade RFA will cover the whole of the Divisional Front.

3. On the night of the 1st/2nd. 152nd. Brigade RFA will be relieved by a Brigade of the 36th. Divisional Artillery and will go back to its Wagon Lines.

4. A and B batteries 152nd. Brigade may be required to send forward tonight a section each to take the place of Forward Sections of A/160 and B/160 at H.6.d.98.15 and B.30.a.95.15.

5. Trench Mortars will be relieved on the night of the 1st/2nd. by Trench Mortars of the 14th. Division. The necessary reconnaissances should be carried out at once.

6. Brigades and D.T.M.O. ACKNOWLEDGE.

Captain,
Brigade Major R.A.
34th. Divisional Artillery.

31-8-18.

Copies to: 152nd. Bde. RFA.
160th. Bde. RFA.
D.T.M.O.
14th. Div. "G".
R.A. 11th. Corps.

S E C R E T. App II File Copy No. 3 W.D.

34th. DIVISIONAL ARTILLERY OPERATION ORDER No. 18.

31st August 1918.

1. S.O.S. Barrage for the period subsequent to the withdrawal of the 160th. Brigade RFA until relief by 35th. Divisional Artillery is complete.

152nd. Brigade RFA.

One 18-pdr Battery C.29.c.6.0 to I.5.a.3.4.
" " " I.10.d.5.6 to I.10.d.0.5.
" " " I.16.d.2.6 to I.16.d.0.2.

One How. "K" track I.5.c.3.6.
" " "P" " I.5.c.0.1.
I.16.b.4.4.
I.22.a.9.6.
Two Hows. I.22.c.95.10 - I.22.c.05.70.

2. Liaison and O.P.

An Officer from 152nd. Brigade RFA will proceed at once to SAPPER O.P., I.3.c.95.00. to relieve the Officer of the 160th. Brigade RFA acting as F.O.O. and Liaison Officer with the Left Battalion Left Brigade.

The Belgian Liaison Officer will move from the 160th. Bde. H.Q. to 152nd. Bde. H.Q.

3. The time at which the 160th. Brigade ceases to be responsible for the defence of its sector will be notified by the telephone message "DINNER AT ...."

C. S. Smyth

Captain,
Brigade Major.R.A.
Issued at 4 p.m. 34th. Divisional Artillery.

Copy No. 1 to 152nd. Bde. RFA.
2 160th. " "
3. File.

WD App III

S E C R E T. Copy No. 7...

34th. DIVISIONAL ARTILLERY OPERATION ORDER NO. 17.

Ref: Sheets 27 N.E.)
28 S.E.)

31st August 1918

1. The 160th. Brigade RFA will move on Sept 1st to Wagon Lines of 24th. Brigade RFA, 6th. Divnl. Arty.

2. No restrictions as to route in the IInd. Corps area except that the rear of the column must be clear of the X Roads at L.11.a.4.6. by 11 a.m.

3. The 160th. Brigade RFA will relieve the 24th. Brigade RFA of the 6th. Divisional Artillery in the line on night 1st/2nd.
A/160 will relieve 110 Battery RFA.
B/160 - do - 111 " "
C/160 - do - 112 " "
D/160 - do - 43 " "

4. Details of relief will be arranged by Os.C. Brigades.

5. Locations of Main Wagon Lines of the 6th. D.A. are as under -
H.Q. 24th. Bde. L.16.d.50.50.
110th. Bty. L.16.c.40.40.
111th. " L.17.c.20.60.
112th. " L.16.d.50.60.
43rd. " L.16.d.80.80.

6. Guides from batteries of 24th. Brigade will be at Group Headquarters, G.18.b.10.30 at 11 a.m. to meet such representatives of batteries as O.C. 160th. Brigade may detail.

7. ACKNOWLEDGE, 160 Brigade by WIRE.

G. O. [signature]
Captain,
Brigade Major R.A.
34th. Divisional Artillery.

Issued at 10-15 p.m.

Copy No. 1. 152nd. Bde. RFA.
2. 160th. " "
3. 34th. D.A.C.
4. H.Q.R.A.
5. File.

File

Identification Trace for use with Artillery Maps.

1 Battery
LEFT GROUP

1 Battery
LEFT GROUP

RIGHT
GROUP

INITIAL BARRAGE
2nd OBJECTIVE
FINAL PROTECTIVE
BARRAGE

NOTE.—(1). These traces are intended to facilitate the communication of information as to the position of targets, which have been located on a squared map.

(2). The squares on this trace are 1,000 yards in length on the 1:20,000 scale, and 2,000 yards in length on the 1:40,000 scale.

(3). The squares on the trace are fitted to the squares of the map showing the targets, which are then drawn on the trace. Sufficient letters and numbers must also be added to enable the recipient to place the trace in the correct position on his own map. A little detail may also be traced, but this is not essential. The name and scale of the map to which the trace refers must be always given. The trace can be used for either the 1:20,000 or 1:40,000 scale.

S.S.G.S. 4029

Tracing taken from Sheet ....

of the 1: .... map of ....

Signature .... Date ....

Identification Trace for use with Artillery Maps.

N O

12

8

18

14

6" hows 1st targets

6" hows 2nd targets

6" hows targets after Z + 57. bursts of fire at intervals ~~[illegible]~~

4.5" hows Right Group Z to Z + 15

4.5" hows Right Group Z + 15 to Z + 57

NOTE.—(1). These traces are intended to facilitate the communication of information as to the position of targets, which have been located on a squared map.

(2). The squares on this trace are 1,000 yards in length on the 1/20,000 scale, and 2,000 yards in length on the 1/40,000 scale.

(3). The squares on the trace are fitted to the squares of the map showing the targets, which are then drawn on the trace. Sufficient letters and numbers must also be added to enable the recipient to place the trace in the correct position on his own map. A little detail may also be traced, but this is not essential. The name and scale of the map to which the trace refers must be always given. The trace can be used for either the 1/20,000 or 1/40,000 scale.

G.S.G.S. 3023

Tracing taken from Sheet ....

of the 1: .... map of ....

Signature .... Date ....

App IV

SECRET. Copy No. 28..

34th. DIVISIONAL ARTILLERY OPERATION ORDER NO. 18.

Ref: Sheets 28 N.W.
27 N.E.

1st. September 1918.

1. The 34th. D.A. will relieve the 6th. D.A. covering the 27th. (American) Divisi on in the line as follows.

2. On the night of Sept 1st/2nd 160th. Bde. RFA will relieve the 24th. Bde. RFA marching to their Wagon Lines, locations of which are as follows:-

H.Q. 24th. Bde.	L.16.d.50.50.
110th. Bty.	L.16.c.40.40.
111th. "	L.17.c.20.80.
112th. "	L.16.d.50.80.
43rd. "	L.16.d.50.80.

3. On 2nd. September the 34th. D.A.C. will march from their present lines at 8 a.m. in relief of the 6th. D.A.C. located as under -

H.Q. D.A.C.	K.23.d.40.40.
No. 1 Section.	K.23.a.central.
No. 2 Section.	K.23.d.40.50.

They will be responsible for the supply of ammunition in the new area from 12 noon the 2nd. inst.

4. On Sept. 2nd. the 152nd. Bde. RFA will march from their present lines at 9 a.m. to temporary Wagon Lines located as under-

A/152.	L.14.c.5.2.
B/152.	L.20.a.4.2.
C/152.	L.15.b.9.2.
D/152.	L.11.c.3.3.

On the night of Sept 2nd/3rd the 152nd. Bde. RFA will relieve the 2nd. Bde. RFA. in the line.

Guides will meet the O.C. Brigade and such representatives of batteries as he may detail at Left Group H.Q. H.8.c.65.10.

5. Details of relief will be arranged between Os.C. Brigades.

6. On Sept. 3rd. 152nd. Bde. RFA will move into permanent Wagon Lines located as under, as soon as they are vacated by the 2nd. Bde. RFA.

H.Q.	L.20.a.0.3.
21st. Bty.	K.18.d.3.5.
42nd. "	L.19.c.8.9.
53rd. "	L.14.d.2.0.
87th. "	L.22.a.5.7. (Hows).

7. 34th. Div. Trench Mortars will proceed on the morning of the 2nd. to L.2.d.60.60 and take over the camp there from the D.T.M.O. 6th. Division.

8. No. 1 Coy. 34th. Div. Train will march on the 2nd. to K.17.b.8.5. in relief of No. 1 Coy. 6th. Div. Train. No restrictions as to time or route.

9. R.A.H.Q. 34th. Div. will close at COUTHOVE CHATEAU at 10 a.m. on the 2nd. and reopen at 34th. Div. Rear H.Q. K.24.c.2.2. at 12 noon close again at 10 a.m. on the 3rd. reopening at the same hour at DOUGLAS CAMP L.14.a.2.0.

10. D.A. Units please ACKNOWLEDGE.

[signature]
Captain,
Brigade Major.R.A., 34th. Division.

Issued at 2 p.m.

P.T.O.

Distribution:

Copies 1-5. 152nd. Bde. RFA.
6-10. 160th. Bde. RFA.
11-13. 34th. D.A.C.
14-16. D.T.M.O.
17. No. 1 Coy. 34th. Train.
18. 14th. Div. "G".
19. 34th. " "
20. 27th. (American) Div.
21. 66th. D.A.
22. 6th. D.A.
23. R.A. IInd. Corps.
24. H.A. " "
25. R.A. XIXth. Corps.
26. O i/c R.A. Sigs.
27. S.C.R.A.
28-29. War Diary.
30. File.

App V

S E C R E T.

34th. DIVISIONAL ARTILLERY LOCATION STATEMENT NO. 3.

Ref. Sheets 27 & 28, 1/40,000.

Unit.	Location.	Wagon Lines.
R.A.H.Q. 34th. Div.	DOUGLAS CAMP (L.14.a.2.0)	L.13.d.9.9.
Right Group (160) H.Q.	H.32.a.5.0.	~~L.16.d.5.5.~~
A/160.	N.3.c.1.7.	~~L.16.c.4.4.~~
B/160.	N.3.a.4.2.	~~L.17.c.2.8.~~
C/160.	H.32.d.1.0.	~~L.16.d.5.8.~~
D/160.	N.3.b.2.7.	~~L.16.d.5.8.~~
83rd. Battery.	N.3.b.6.1.	(Attd)
Left Group. (152) H.Q.	Walker Farm H.27.b.6.7.	G.17.a.2.8.
A/152.	H.33.b.8.9.	K.18.d.3.5.
B/152.	H.28.c.50.25.	L.19.c.8.9.
C/152.	H.28.d.30.65.	L.14.d.2.0.
D/152.	H.28.c.50715.	L.22.a.5.7.
84th. Battery.	H.28.d.75.85.	(Attd)
34th. D.A.C., H.Q.		~~K.23.d.4.4.~~
No. 1 Section.		~~K.23.a.central.~~
No. 2 Section.		~~K.23.d.4.5.~~
34th. A.R.P.		L.17.a.99.50.
No. 1 Coy. 34th. Train.		~~K.17.b.8.5.~~
34th. T.M.Bs.		L.2.d.6.6.

Captain,
Brigade Major.R.A.
34th. Divisional Artillery.

3rd. September 1918.

Copies: 152nd. Bde. (6)
160th. " (6)
34th. D.A.C.(3)
D.T.M.O. (3)
S.C.R.A.
No. 1 Coy. Train.
34th. A.R.P.
11th. Army Bde.RFA.

R.A. XIXth. Corps.
H.A. " "
41st. Div. "G".
" " "Q".
34th. Div. "G".
" " "Q".

S E C R E T. File W.D. App VI

34th. DIVISIONAL ARTILLERY WARNING ORDER No. 9.

Ref: Sheet 28 S.E.

1. The advance will be resumed tomorrow morning 4th. Sept. to the 2nd. objective - KRUISSTRAAT Cab. - PROGRES - E edge of PETIT BOIS - Cross Roads O.13.c.4.7 - O.7.a.25.20 - thence N. along road to cross roads O.1.a.15.35.

Should resistance be slight the advance will be continued to the line MESSINES - ST. ELOI road, which when taken will be consolidated and outposts pushed out in front of it.

2. The advance will be carried out by 122nd. Infantry Bde. on Right and 124th Infantry Brigade on Left.

Dividing line between Brigades - N.11.d.central - O.7.c.0.7 O.8.a.7.2.

3. Groups will be prepared to put a Creeping H.E. barrage down on Right Infy. Bde. front as far as the 2nd. objective, 4.5" Hows. will fire on selected localities.

4. After the objective is reached, any further advance will be covered by Groups working under the orders of G.Os.C. Infantry Brigades to which they are affiliated.

5. Groups will tell off one 18-pdr battery each to follow in close support of the Infantry if necessary after the 2nd. objective is reached.

6. Zero Hour probably 5-30 a.m.

7. Brigades ACKNOWLEDGE BY WIRE.

Captain,
Brigade Major.R.A.
34th. Divisional Artillery.

3rd. September 1918.

Copies: 152nd. Bde. RFA.
160th. " "
4th. Bde. RGA.
41st. Div. "G".
66th. D.A.
41st. D.A.
File. ✓

SECRET.

Copy No. 22.

34th. DIVISIONAL ARTILLERY OPERATION ORDER NO. 19.

Ref: Map 28 S.W.2 1/10,000.
WYTSCHAETE.

3rd. September 1918.

Reference 34th. D.A. Warning Order No. 9.
Zero Hour is 5-30 a.m.

1. The Creeping Barrage, as per attached tracing will be put down by Right Group and two 18-pdr batteries of the Left Group.
   The Barrage will remain on the Initial Barrage Line till Zero plus 15 minutes and then commence to roll at the rate of 100 yards in 3 minutes till it forms up on the Protective Barrage Line reached by the last gun at Z plus 42 minutes.
   Fire will cease at Z plus 57 minutes.

2. Howitzer tasks as per attached tracing.

3. Rates of fire - (18-pdrs and 4.5" Hows.)

Z to Z plus 5 mins............	Intense.
Z plus 5 mins to Z plus 15 mins.	Normal.
Z plus 15 " " Z " 20 "	Intense.
Z " 20 " " Z " 42 "	Normal.
Z " 42 " " Z " 57 "	Slow.

4. Ammunition.
   18-pdrs Z to Z plus 42 mins A.X. (106 Fuze where available)
   Z plus 42 to Z plus 57. 50% A.X.)
   50% A.)
   4.5" Hows. B.X.

5. Tasks for 60-pdrs, Rates of fire and lifts for Heavy Artillery will be detailed by O.C. 4th. Brigade R.G.A.
   After Z plus 57 mins he will fire bursts at intervals.

6. Left Group (less two 18-pdrs batteries) will act under the orders of G.O.C. Left Infantry Brigade from Zero Hour.

7. At Z plus 57 mins Both Groups will act as detailed in 34th. D.A. Warning Order No. 9 paras. 4 and 5.

8. Brigades and H.A. Bde. ACKNOWLEDGE BY WIRE.

[signature]
Captain,
Brigade Major.R.A.
34th. Divisional Artillery.

Issued at 11 p.m.

Copies: 1-4. 152nd. Bde.
5-10. 160th. "
11-16. 4th. Bde. RGA.
17. 41st. Div. "G".
18. 66th. D.A.
19. 41st. D.A.
20-21. War Diary.
22. File.

GS 218

S E C R E T.

34th DIVISIONAL ARTILLERY INSTRUCTIONS No.1.

The Divisional Front is to be held by one Infantry Brigade with one Infantry Brigade in support, and the third Infantry Brigade in a Rear Training Area.

Liaison Arrangements.

(1) A senior Artillery Liaison Officer detailed by O.C. Left Group will live at 101st Infantry Brigade H.Q. at PETIT KEMMEL, and will be in communication with both Groups, and conversant with their dispositions.

(2) The Right and Left Groups will find a junior Liaison Officer with the Right and Left Battalions in the line.

(3) This will come into force at 6 p.m. on September 9th.

(4) Brigades please ACKNOWLEDGE.

Captain,
Brigade Major R.A.
34th Divisional Artillery.

8th September 1918.

Copies to:-

152nd F.A. Brigade.
160th F.A. Brigade.
34th Division "G".
Officer i/c, R.A. Signals.

G.S. 214/1

SECRET. Copy No.

34th. DIVISIONAL ARTILLERY OPERATION ORDER No. 22.

Ref. Sheet: 28 N.W. 1/20,000. 8th. September, 1918.

(1) D/152 will commence moving its present position at N.27.c.50.10, as soon as O.C., 152nd. F.A. Brigade may direct, to the position vacated by D/11 at N.14.b.70.65.

(2) The move will be carried out by moving one section the first night, and the remainder of the Battery the second night.

(3) The ammunition left at N.27.c.50.10. will be taken over by D/160.

(4) This office will be notified of the commencement and completion of relief.

(5) Brigades ACKNOWLEDGE.

Captain,
Brigade Major R.A.
34th Divisional Artillery.

8-9-18.

Copies to:
152nd Brigade.
160th Brigade.
34th Division "G".

App VII

34th. Div. Arty. No.1441/A.

O.C. 152nd Brigade R.F.A.
O.C. 160th Brigade R.F.A.
O.C. 34th. D.A.C.
O.C. No.1. Coy. 34th Divn. Train.
Officer i/c, 34th A.R.P.
Area Commandant, HATTEKOT Area.
" " BUSSEBOOM Area.

1..... The following moves of wagon lines (already ordered) will take place to-morrow, 5th Sept.

H.Q. 160 Bde. W.L.	to	G.22.b.70.70.	Sheet 28
A Bty. " W.L.	to	G.22.a.5.4.	
B " " W.L.	to	G.22. ?	
C " " W.L.	to	G.22.a.2.4.	
D " " W.L.	to	G.22.c.8.7.	

H.Q. D.A.C.	to	present H.Q.160 Bde.W.L. L.16.d.5.5.
No.1. Sec.	to	" A/160 Bde.W.L. L.16.c.4.4.
No.2. "	to	" C/160 Bde.W.L. L.16.d.5.8.

No.1.Coy.34th. Divn. Train, to present B/160 Bde.W.L. L.17.c.2.8.

D/160's W.L. L.16.d.5.8. is also placed at the disposal of O.C. 34th. D.A.C. 160th Brigad e R.F.A. will be clear of present W.L. by 3 p.m. 5th. September.

2..... 3 4th. A.R.P. will move from HOPOUTRE A.R.P. to CORDOVA A.R.P. (G.24.d.4.4.Sheet 28).
Ammunition will be supplied from HOPOUTRE Dump until 5 p.m. 5th September and from CORDOVA A.R.P. after that hour.

3..... Refilling point, 5th September, ABEELE - POPERINGHE Road 27/L.17.c.4.7., 2 p.m.

R.W. Howe [signature]
Captain,
Staff Captain,
34th. Divisional Artillery.

4th September 1918.

App VIII

S E C R E T.

34th. DIVISIONAL ARTILLERY LOCATION STATEMENT No. 4.

Ref: Sheets 27 & 28 1/40,000.

Unit.	Location.	Wagon Lines.
R.A.H.Q. 34th. Div.	DOUGLAS CAMP (L.14.a.2.0)	L.13.d.9.9.
Right Group (160) H.Q.	H.32.a.5.0.	G.22.b.7.7.
A/160 6 guns	N.3.c.1.7.	G.22.a.5.4.
B/160 6 "	N.3.a.4.2.	G.22.
C/160. 6 "	H.32.d.1.0.	G.22.a.2.4.
D/160. 6 Hows.	N.3.b.2.7.	G.22.c.8.7.
83rd. Battery.	N.3.b.6.1.	G.25.b.5.3.
Left Gro up.(152) H.Q.	H.27.b.6.7.	H.8.c.65.10.
Rear Bde H.Q.	H.8.c.65.10.	
A/152. 6 guns	H.33.b.8.9.	G.16.b.4.9.
B/152. 6 "	H.29.c.45.15.	G.10.c.7.2.
C/152. 4 "	H.28.d.30.65.	G.16.d.45.80.
2 "	H.28.a.4.6.	(ELGIN FARM)
D/152. 6 Hows.	H.28.c.50.15.	G.11.a.2.2.
84th. Battery.	H.29.a.0.7.	(QUERY FARM)
34th. D.A.C.,H.Q.		L.16.d.5.5.
No. 1 Secti on.		L.14.c.4.4.
No. 2 Section.		L.16.d.5.8.
34th. T.M.Bs.		L.2.d.6.6.
34th. A.R.P.		CORDOVA (G.24.d.4.4.
No. 1 Coy. Train.		L.17.c.2.8.

J Thompson Lt.
for Captain,
Brigade Major.R.A.
34th. Divisional Artillery.

5th. Sep tember 1918.

Copies: 152nd. Bde . (6)
160th. Bde. (6)
D.A.C. (3)
D.T.M.O. (3)
S.C.R.A.
No. 1 Coy. Train.
34th. A.R.P.
11th. Army Bde.RFA.
R.A. XIXth. Corps.
H.Q. " "
C.B.S.O. " "
41st. Div. "G".
" " "Q"
34th. Div. "G".
" " "Q"

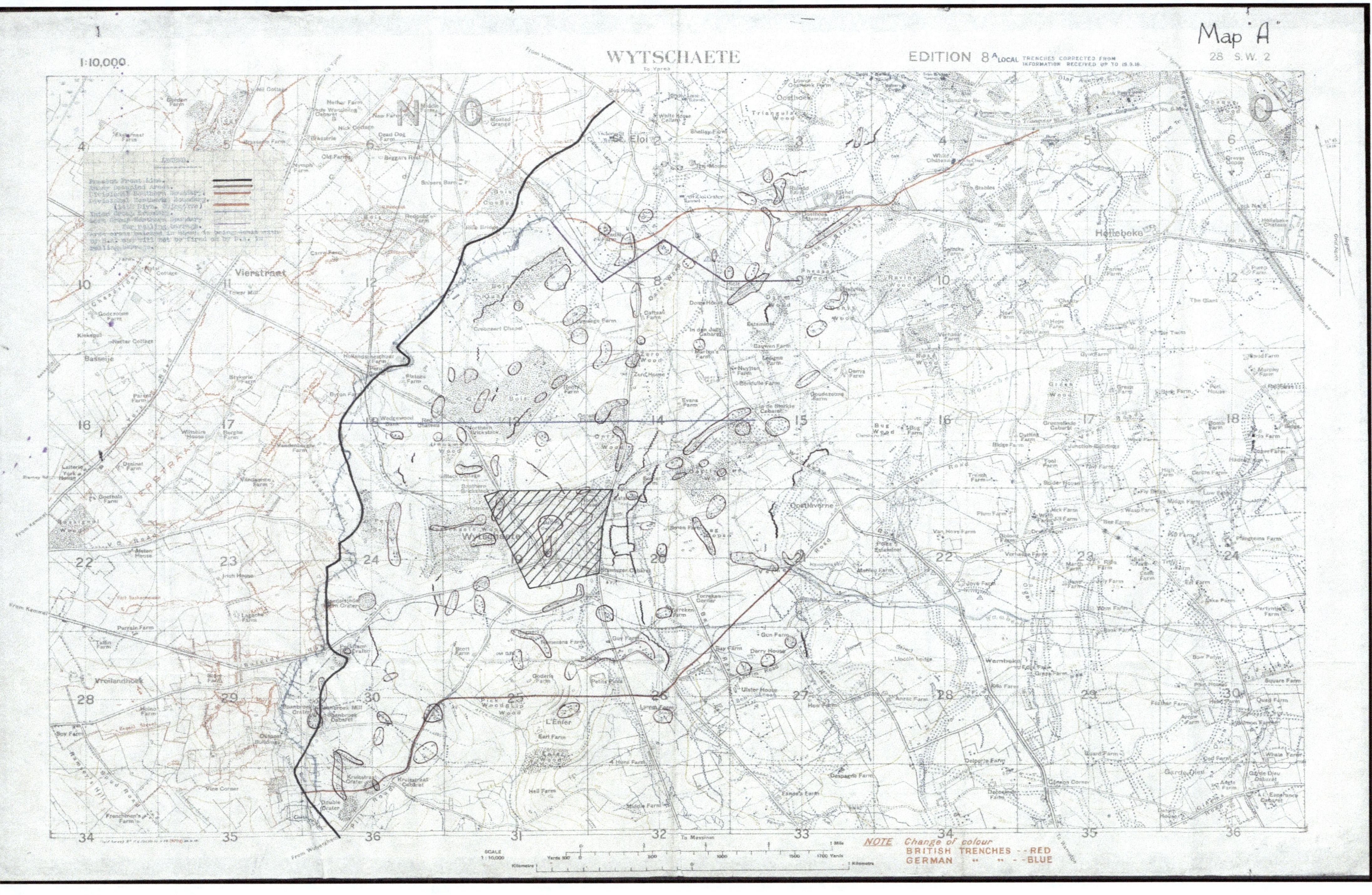

Map 'A'
1:10,000
WYTSCHAETE
EDITION 8A LOCAL TRENCHES CORRECTED FROM INFORMATION RECEIVED UP TO 15.9.16.
28 S.W. 2
NOTE Change of colour
BRITISH TRENCHES - - RED
GERMAN " " - -BLUE
Vierstraat
St. Eloi
Hollebeke
Oosttaverne
Wytschaete
L'Enfer
Vroilandhoek

S E C R E T.

34th. DIVISIONAL ARTILLERY LOCATION STATEMENT NO. 5.

Ref: Sheets 27 & 28 1/40,000.

Unit	Location	Wagon Lines.
R.A.H.Q. 34th. Div.	DOUGLAS CAMP (L.14.a.2.0.)	L.13.d.9.9.
Right Group (160) H.Q.	H.32.a.5.0.	G.22.b.7.7.
A/160. 6 guns	N.3.c.1.7	G.22.a.5.4.
B/160. 6 "	N.3.a.4.2.	G.28.b.5.4.
C/160. 6 "	H.32.d.1.0.	G.22.d.2.4.
D/160. 6 Hows.	N.3.b.2.7.	G.22.c.[illegible]
83rd. Battery.	N.3.b.6.1.	G.25.b.5.3.
Left Group (152) H.Q.		H.8.c.65.10.
Bde.H.Q.	H.8.c.65.10.	
A/152. 6 guns	H.33.b.8.9. ∅	G.16.b.4.9.
B/152. 6 "	H.29.c.45.15.	G.10.c.7.2.
C/152. 4 "	H.28.d.30.65.	G.16.d.45.80.
2 "	H.28.a.4.6.	(ELGIN FARM)
D/152. 6 Hows.	H.28.c.50.15.	G.11.a. 7.7.
84th. Battery.	H.29.a.0.7.	(QUERY FARM)
34th. D.A.C. H.Q.		L.16.d.5.5.
No. 1 Section.		L.16.c.4.4.
No. 2 Section.		L.16.d.5.8.
34th. T.M.Bs.		L.2.d.6.6.
34th. A.R.P.		CORDOVA. (G.24.d.4.4).
No. 1 Coy. Train.		L.17.c.2.8.

Captain,
Brigade Major.R.A.
34th. Divisional Artillery.

5th. September 1918.

Copies: 152nd.Bde. (6)
160th. " (6)
D.A.C. (3)
D.T.M.O. (3)
S.C.R.A.
No. 1 Coy. Train.
34th. A.R.P.
11th. Army Bde. RFA.
R.A. XIXth. Corps.
H.A. " "
C.B.S.O." "
41st. Div. "G".
" " "Q"
34th. Div. "G"
" " "Q"
41st. D.A.
66th. D.A.

∅ Positions for two guns each have been selected at H.29.a.3.5 and 3.7. and H.23.c.2.4.

W.D. Ap. IX

S E C R E T. Copy No. 9.

34th. DIVISIONAL ARTILLERY OPERATION ORDER NO. [illegible].

Ref: Sheet 28, 1/40,000. 8th. September 1918.

1. The 34th. Divisional Artillery and 41st. Divisional Artillery will relieve each other commencing tonight 8/9th. Sept.

2. During this afternoon A & B/160 will change over Wagon Lines with A & B/187 and A/152 with A/190. After dark A & B/160 and A/152 will withdraw from action and proceed to the gun positions similarly vacated by A & B/187 and A/190 and get into touch as quickly as possible.

3. Representatives of these 3 batteries will proceed forthwith to the new gun positions to take over before dark and await the arrival of their batteries.

4. All camouflage in situ, ammunition, maps, telephone lines, etc. will be handed over and receipts exchanged.

5. Routes. Right Group - HALLEBAST - LA CLYTTE - [illegible] [illegible] - [illegible]
(A/152 using road from [illegible] central through [illegible] and [illegible].)

Left Group - HALLEBAST - LA CLYTTE.

6. Map Locations -

	Guns.	Wagon Lines.
A/187	[illegible]	[illegible]
B/187	[illegible]	[illegible]
A/190	[illegible]	[illegible]

7. Orders for remainder of relief will be issued later.

8. Completion of relief each night to be reported to this office by Code Word "[illegible]".

9. Groups ACKNOWLEDGE BY WIRE.

C. L. Walthall
Brig. Gen.
for Captain,
Brigade Major.R.A.
34th. Divisional Artillery.

Issued at 11-40 a.m.

Copies:1. 152nd. Bde.
2. 160th. Bde.
3. 41st. Div. "G".
4. 34th. Div. "G".
5. 41st. D.A.
6. R.A. XIXth. Corps.

S E C R E T. Copy No. 25

34th. DIVISIONAL ARTILLERY OPERATION ORDER No. 21.

5th. September 1918.

In continuation of O.O. No. 20.

1. The relief will be continued on the nights 6/7th and 7/8th September; the same procedure being followed.

2. On the night 6/7th. B/160 will relieve B/187 and B/152 will relieve B/190.
On the night 7/8th. C/160 will relieve C/187 and C & D/152 will relieve C & D/190.

3. Routes as given in O.O. 20 para. 5.

4. Map Locations as per 41st. D.A. Location Statement, copy attached.

5. Commands of Groups will pass at 10 a.m. on 8th. Sept. Exact details to be arranged between Groups concerned but the Adjutants of Brigades and Signalling Officer should change over on afternoon of 7th. Sept.

6. 34th. Div. Arty. H.Qrs. will close at DOUGLAS CAMP at 10 a.m. 8th. Sept. reopening at the same hour at EL TEB.

7. 34th. D.A.C. will relieve 41st. D.A.C. on the morning of 8th. Sept. No restrictions as to routes.
34th. D.A.C. will take over responsibility of Ammunition Supply to 34th. D.A. at 12 noon 8th. Sept. , handing over CORDOVA Dump to 41st. D.A.C. at the same hour.

8. 34th. Divnl. T.M. Batteries will move to 27/L.29.d.80.20. in relief of 41st. Divnl. T.M. Batteries on the morning of 8th. Sept. handing over the present Camp to 41st. D.T.M.O.

9. No. 1 Coy. 34th. Div. Train will move in relief of 41st. No. 1 Cpy. 41st. Div. Train. Further orders will be issued for this move.

10. D.A. Units to ACKNOWLEDGE BY WIRE.

Captain,
Brigade Major.R.A.
34th. Divisional Artillery.

Copies:
1-5. 152nd. Bde.
6-11. 160th. Bde.
12-15. D.A.C.
16. D.T.M.O.
17. No. 1 Cpy. Train.
18. R.A. XlXth. Corps.
19. 41st. Div. "G".
20. 34th. Div. "G".
21. 41st. D.A.
22. 66th. D.A.
23. S.C.R.A.
24-25. War Diary.
26. File.

App I

SECRET.

34th. DIVISIONAL ARTILLERY.

LOCATION STATEMENT.

Ref: Sheets 27 & 28 1/40,000. 2 p.m., 10th. Septr., 1918.

		Position in Action.	Wagon Lines.
Head-quarters, 34th. Divisional Artillery,		27/K.24.c.2.3.	
H.-Q. 152nd. Bde., R.F.A.,		FROWSTY HOUSE, M.6.c.3.4	M.5.d.2.8
A Battery, 152nd. Bde.,	4 guns,	N.14.a.7.6	M.5.d.3.8
	2 ,,	N.14.b.90.25	
B ,, ,,	6 guns,	N.13.b.9.0	M.3.b.40.90
C ,, ,,	4 ,,	N.14.a.3.4	G.33.d.80.50
	2 ,,	N.14.b.75.20	
D ,, ,,	6 hows,	N.14.b.8.6	M.4.a.3.2
H.-Q. 160th. Bde., R.F.A.,		SCHERPENBERG, M.17.b.8.7	M.3.d.90.90
A Battery, 160th. Bde.,	6 guns,	T.3.c.20.95	M.3.d.90.90.
B ,, ,,	6 ,,	N.32.d.10.50	G.32.d.60.20
C ,, ,,	4 guns,	N.32.b.80.90	M.3.c.60.70.
	2 ,,	N.27.c.30.50	
D ,, ,,	4 hows,	N.32.b.50.20	M.9.b.20.90.
	2 ,,	N.26.d.40.20	

34th. DIVISIONAL AMMUNITION COLUMN.

Head-quarters, ...G.33.c.80.40
No. 1 Section, ...G.33.c.80.80
No. 2 ,, ...G.33.a.50.50
No. 3 (S.A.A.) Secti on, ...K.18.d.30.40

34th. A.R.P., G29.d.20.80, (ROBSON DUMP).

Headquarters, D.T.M.O., ...L.29.b.50.20
1 6" Newton T.M. at N.19.d.9.8
1 ,, ,, ... N.29.a.27.40
1 3" T.M. at N.23.b.27.22
1 ,, ... N.23.b.21.35

No. 1 Coy., 34th. Divisional Train, ...R.5.a.6.2

[signature]
Captain,
Brigade-Major, R.A.,
34th. Divisional Artillery.

Distribution:-
152nd. Bde., RFA,
160th. Bde., RFA,
34th. D.A.C.,
34th. D.T.M.O.,
No. 1 Coy. 34th.Div.Train,
34th. Divnl. Gas Officer,
S.C.R.A., 34th. Divn.,
Signals, 34th. D.A.,
R.A. XIX Corps,
C.B.O., XIX Corps,
H.A., XIX Corps,
34th. Divn., "G",
41st. D.A.,
30th. D.A.,
No. 10 Squadron, R.A.F.,
39th. Kite Balloon Section.
War Diary & File.

App XI

34th DIVISIONAL ARTILLERY.

LOCATION STATEMENT.

Amendment No.1.

Ref: Sheets 27 & 28 1/40,000. 13th September 1918.

		Position in Action.
H.Q., 160th Bde. R.F.A.		SCHERPENBERG M.17.b.8.7.
"A" Battery, 160th Bde.	4 guns.	T.3.c.18.70.
	2 ,,	N.34.d.0.6. (TEA FARM)
"B" ,, ,,	4 ,,	N.32.d.10.50.
	2 ,,	N.21.c.5.6.
"C" ,, ,,	4 ,,	N.32.b.80.90.
	2 ,,	N.27.c.60.20.
"D" ,, ,,	4 Hows.	N.20.c.8.9.
	2 ,,	N.26.d.50.15.

34th DIVISIONAL AMMUNITION COLUMN.

Head-quarters. ... ... G.32.a.3.6.

Captain,
Brigade Major R.A.,
34th Divisional Artillery.

Copies to:- All recipients of 34th Divl. Arty. Location Statement.

S E C R E T.

App XII

34th DIVISIONAL ARTILLERY.

LOCATION STATEMENT. (Forecast).

Ref: Sheets 27 & 28 1/40,000. 16th. Septr. 1918.

		Position in Action.	Wagon Lines.
Headquarters, 34th Divisional Artillery, 27/L.36.c.5.5.			
H.Q., 152nd Bde., R.F.A.		FROWSTY HOUSE M.6.c.3.4.	M.6.a.2.9.
"A" Bty. 152nd Bde.	4 guns	N.14.a.7.6.	M.4.b.5.1.
,,	2 ,,	N.14.b.90.25.	
"B" ,, ,,	6 ,,	N.13.b.9.6.	M.3.b.5.8.
"C" ,, ,,	4 ,,	N.14.a.3.4.	G.33.d.6.6.
,,	2 ,,	N.14.b.75.20.	
"D" ,, ,,	6 Hows	N.14.b.8.6.	M.11.c.3.5.
H.Q. 160th. Bde., R.F.A.		Scherpenberg M.17.b.80.60.	G.32.d.4.9.
"A" Bty. 160th Bde.	4 guns	N.13.d.6.2.	G.31.b.38.89.
,,	2 ,,	N.20.b.4.9.	
"B" ,, ,,	4 ,,	N.19.b.25.95.	G.32.d.2.3.
,,	2 ,,	N.21.c.35.60.	
"C" ,, ,,	4 ,,	N.19.a.80.82.	M.3.c.7.7.
,,	2 ,,	N.27.c.60.20.	
"D" ,, ,,	4 Hows	N.20.c.8.9.	G.32.c.1.4.
,, ,,	2 ,,	N.26.d.50.15.	

34th DIVISIONAL AMMUNITION COLUMN.

Headquarters.	L.35.d.0.1.
No.1.Section.	G.33.c.8.8.
No.2.Section.	G.33.a.5.5.
S.A.A. Section.	27/K.18.d.3.4.

D.T.M.O. X & Y/34 T.M. Batteries. L.29.d.9.2.

3 4th A. R. P., G.29.d.20.80. (ROBSON DUMP).

No.1.Coy. 34th Divisional Train. R.5.a.6.2.

C Thompson. Lt.

for. Captain,
Brigade Major R.A.
34th Divisional Artillery.

Distribution.:-

152nd Bde.,R.F.A.	Signals 34th D.A.
160th Bde.,R.F.A.	34th Division "G".
34th D.A.C.	34th D.G.O.
34th D.T.M.O.	30th D.A.
No.1.Coy.34th Divnl. Train.	41st D.A.
S.C.R.A. 34th Divn.	R.A. XIX Corps.
No.10.Squadron R.A.F.	H.A. XIX Corps.
39th K.B.S.	C.B.S.O. XIX Corps.
War Diary & File.	

App XIII

34th DIVISIONAL ARTILLERY.

LOCATION STATEMENT

Amendment No.2.

Ref:Sheets 27 & 28 1/40,000

		Position in Action.
Headquarters, 152nd Bde. R.F.A.		H.32.b.50.90.
"A" Bty. 152nd Bde. R.F.A.	6 guns.	N.4.d.30.95.
"B" ,, ,,	6 ,,	N.4.b.40.20.
"C" ,, ,,	6 ,,	N.4.c.80.70.
"D" ,, ,,	6 Hows.	N.4.d.25.30.

Headquarters, 160th Bde. R.F.A.		SCHERPENBERG M.17.b.80.60.
"A" Bty. 160th Bde. R.F.A.	6 Guns.	N.20.b.4.9.
"B" ,, ,,	6 ,,	N.15.b.40.80.
"C" ,, ,,	6 ,,	N.27.c.60.20.
"D" ,, ,,	6 Hows.	N.14.b.8.6.

D.T.M.O. X & Y/34 T.M. Batteries. 28/B.1.a.3.3.

[signature]

Captain,
Brigade Major R.A.
34th Divisional Artillery.

21st September 1918.

App XIV

SECRET.

34th. DIVISIONAL ARTILLERY INSTRUCTIONS No.1.

Reference 34th. Div.Arty. INSTRUCTIONS No. 1, para. 12,-

(1) The day " J " is
The hour " H " is
(2) ACKNOWLEDGE by wire.

Captain,
Brigade-Major, R.A.,
34th. Divisional Artillery.

27-9-18.

To:-

152nd. F.A. Bde.,
160th. F.A. Bde.,
34th. D.A.C.

S E C R E T.

34th DIVISIONAL ARTILLERY INSTRUCTIONS No.1.

Amendment No.1.

Para.4. (a) For H hour, read H - 5.

(b) For H, read H - 5.
For H+3, read H.
For H+72, read H+67.

Para.5. For H throughout read H - 5
For H+72 read H+67.

C Thompson Lt.
for Captain,
Brigade Major R.A.,
34th Divisional Artillery.

27th September 1918.

Copies to: All recipients of 34th Div. Arty. Ins.No.1.

S E C R E T.

34th DIVISIONAL ARTILLERY INSTRUCTIONS No.1.

1. Reference 34th Division G.S. Instructions No.7 (not issued to Artillery Brigades), the following instructions are issued for the Divisional Artillery for their action on J day, commencing at H hour.

2. The boundaries of the Division, Inter-Brigade boundaries, and objective lines, in case of advance, are shown on map attached (issued to Artillery Brigades only).

3. Careful watch must be maintained by Artillery F.O.Os for any signs of withdrawal after H hour on J day.

4. (a) Certain batteries according to the wind, but not more than 2 18-pdr and 2 4.5"How. batteries, will fire a smoke barrage on WYTSCHAETE Hill commencing at H hour; this barrage will be maintained till orders are received from higher authority to cease fire. Detailed orders have been issued to those concerned.

(b) The remainder of the Divisional Artillery will fire as follows:- At H open on S.O.S. lines, at H + 3' start lifting at the average rate of 100 yards in 3', searching and sweeping in their respective zones so as to bring to bear on all localities, fire O.Ps etc., at H hour + 72, cease firing.

This barrage will be modified on the left of the Divisional front and will probably continue till about H + 130' to coordinate with the barrage of the Division on our left. Detailed instructions as to this barrage will be issued later.

5. Heavy Artillery.

(a) H onwards, intense Counter-Battery Work.

(b) H to H + 72, all batteries not engaged on C.B. work. Creeping barrage on localities etc., in advance of the Divisional Artillery barrage between S.O.S. safety limits and grid line N and S between O.4. & O.5.

(c) After H + 72', bombard selected points as asked for by Divisions.

(d) 4 6" Howitzers firing bursts of gas shell into O.19. from H onwards, particularly O.Ps and the HOSPICE.

6. On the conclusion of these tasks the Right and Left Artillery Groups will come under the orders of the G.Os.C. Right and Left Infantry Brigades respectively. Arrangements are being made for the closest liaison to be maintained between Artillery and Infantry.

7. (a) If the advance is made by day the artillery will cover it by keeping known centres of resistance under fire as long as possible.

(b) By night the artillery will stand to, ready to cover each patrol, but will only open fire at the request of the Infantry Brigade concerned. A certain amount of 18-pdr Incendiary shell will be issued to batteries for use as a guide to patrols by night.

(c) Batteries must be pushed forward during each advance as necessary to cover each line as it is reached but not more than 1/3 of each group of Divisional Artillery must be out of action at the same time. Instructions as to routes, H.Qs, suitable battery areas etc., have been issued verbally to Group Commanders.

8. GF calls will be answered by Divisional Artillery Brigades in their own zones. LL calls will be answered by all guns and howitzers that can bear. Batteries firing the smoke barrage will not answer GF and LL calls.

9. During the advance every possible means will be employed to maintain touch and send back information. In addition to F.O.O. parties provided with telephones and visual signalling equipment, mounted patrols will be used, and two officers parties provided with Aldis lamps will be sent out for the special task of communicating with No.25 balloon, who will pass on any messages received direct to Artille ry Group Commanders, repeating to this office.

10. Instructions as regards Signal arrangements in case of advance have been issued to those concerned.

11. Instructions as regards Administrative arrangements have been issued to those concerned by S.C.R.A.

12. H hour and J day and arrangements for synchronization of watches will be notified later.

13. Divisional Artillery/please ACKNOWLEDGE.
units.

Captain,
Brigade Major R.A.,
34th Divisional Artillery.

25th September 1918.

Copies to:-

152nd Bde. R.F.A.
160th Bde. R.F.A.
34th Division "G".
101st Infy. Bde.
102nd ,, ,,
103rd ,, ,,
30th Divl. Arty.
41st ,, ,,
R.A., X Corps.
H.A., X Corps.
39th K.B.S.

App XV

S E C R E T.

34th DIVISIONAL ARTILLERY INSTRUCTIONS No.2.

Arrangements are being made by the Infantry Brigades for patrols to signal the fact that they have reached the second (GREEN) line, using the following Signal Rifle Grenades:-

(a) By day, RED Smoke.
(b) By night, WHITE over WHITE, over WHITE.

Patrols will signal when they are held up by the enemy by using a BLUE Smoke Rifle Grenade Signal.

This signal will also be used once by each patrol when it starts from our present front line.

The positions from which these signals will be sent up, should be known to D.A., O.Ps.

[signature]

Captain,
Brigade Major R.A.,
34th Divisional Artillery.

26th September 1918.

Copies to:- All recipients of 34th Div. Arty. Ins. No.1.

App XVI

S E C R E T.

34th DIVISIONAL ARTILLERY INSTRUCTIONS No.3.

Watches will be synchronised by a Divisional Staff Officer on J - 1 day as follows:-

160th Brigade R.F.A., at Bde. H.Q. LITTLE KEMMEL at 5-30 pm.

152nd Brigade R.F.A., at Advanced Bde. H.Q. N.10.b.3.7. at 7 pm.

Captain,
Brigade Major R.A.,
34th Divisional Artillery.

26th September 1918.

Copies to: All recipients of 34th Div. Arty. Ins.No.1.

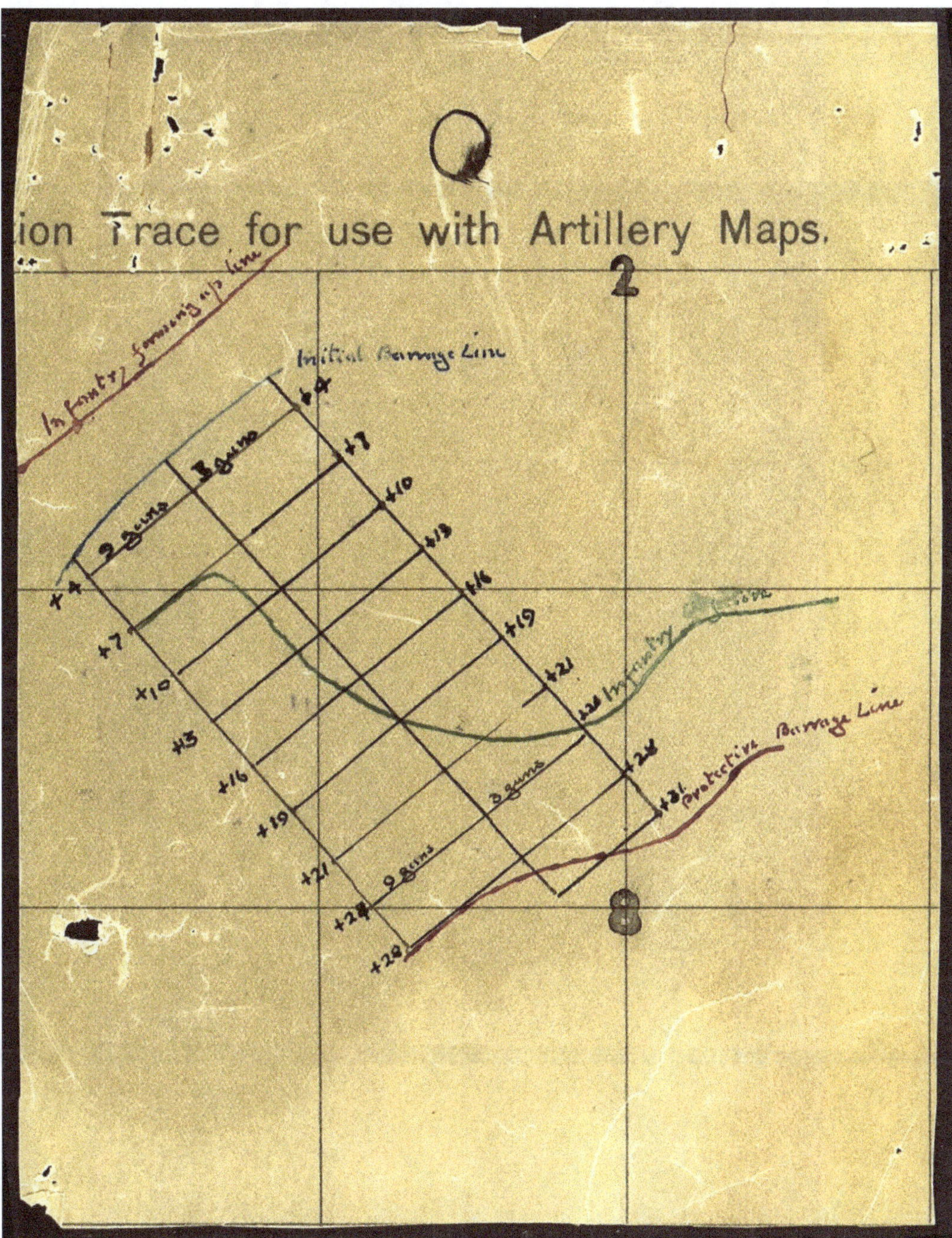
ion Trace for use with Artillery Maps.
2
8
Initial Barrage Line
Protective Barrage Line
9 guns
Infantry

App XVII
11

SECRET.   Copy No......

ADDENDUM No.1. to 34th DIV. ARTY. O.O. No.22.

Batteries while engaged in tasks detailed in above order, will NOT answer GF or LL Calls.

Captain,
Brigade Major R.A.,
34th Divisional Artillery.

26th September 1918.

Copies to:- All recipients of above order.

Secret.

Copy No. 10

34th DIVISIONAL ARTY. OPERATION ORDER No.22. TABLE "A".

AMENDMENT No.1.

Time.

For H to H+4, read H - 5 to H.

For H+4 to H+31, read H to H+27.

For H+31 to H+45, read H+27 to H+41.

Captain,
Brigade Major R.A.,
34th Divisional Artillery.

27th September 1918.

Copies to: All recipients of 34th Div. Arty. O.O.No.22.

S E C R E T Copy No. 10.

34th DIVISIONAL ARTILLERY OPERATION ORDER No.22.

1. Reference 34th Divisional Artillery Instructions No.1. At H hour on J day two batteries (A & B) of the 152nd Brigade R.F.A. will put down a creeping barrage as per attached tracing, 3 guns firing on the Northern Lane, and 9 guns firing on the Southern Lane until H + 45.

2. From H + 45 to H + 96 batteries will fire bursts at irregular intervals, searching up and down their lanes from the Protective Barrage line to a distance of 500 yards beyond it.

3. From H + 96 to H + 109 the left battery will fire on EIKHOF FARM (0.3.d.4.2.) and from H + 109 to H + 129 lift on to the DAMM STRASSE in 0.9.c. From H + 96 to H + 129 the right battery will fire on the DAMM STRASSE in 0.9.a. & c.

4. Procedure, rates of fire, and ammunition as in Table "A" attached.

5. Please ACKNOWLEDGE.

Captain,
Brigade Major R.A.
34th Divisional Artillery.

26th September 1918.

Copies to:-

No.	
1-2	152nd Brigade R.F.A.
3	160th Brigade R.F.A.
4	34th Division "G".
5	14th Divl. Arty.
6	30th Divl. Arty.
7	R.A., X Corps.
8	R.A., XIX Corps.
9	H.A., X Corps.
10-11	War Diary.
12-14	Spare.

TABLE "A".

Time.	Procedure.	Ammunition	Rate of fire.
H – 5 to H ~~H to H + 4.~~	Barrage comes down on opening line.	AX	Rapid.
H to H + 27 ~~H + 4 to H + 31.~~	Creep forward to PROTECTIVE BARRAGE Lifting 100 yards every 3 minutes.	AX.	Normal.
H + 27 to H + 41 ~~H + 31 to H + 45~~	Remain stationary on PROTECTIVE BARRAGE.	AX	Normal.
H + 45 to H + 96.	Bursts of fi re searching up to 500 yards beyond line of PROTECTIVE BARRAGE.	A 75% AX 25%	(Normal) (Average rate)
H + 96 to H + 129.	Bursts of fire on targets detailed.	A 50% AX 50%	(Normal) (Average rate)
H + 129.	Stop firing.		

App XVIII

SECRET.

Copy No. 10

34th DIVISIONAL ARTILLERY OPERATION ORDER No.23.

Amendment No.1.

H is the hour the Infantry advance and the barrage makes its first lift.

All guns and howitzers ordered to open fire at H will now open fire at H - 5 minutes, ceasing fire at H+ 67 instead of H+ 72.

Captain,
Brigade Major R.A.,
34th Divisional Artillery.

27th September 1918.

Copies to: All recipients of 34th Div. Arty. O.O. No.23.

S E C R E T.   Copy No.10.....

34th DIVISIONAL ARTILLERY OPERATION ORDER No.23.

Ref: Maps "A". "B"."C".

1. Reference 34th Divisional Artillery Instructions No.1. para.4 (b).
Batteries not engaged in firing smoke barrages or other tasks, will fire simulating a creeping barrage as follows. At H, open on first target in their own lanes lifting on to the subsequent targets to keep pace with an imaginary rolling barrage commencing on the S.O.S. lines and creeping at the rate of 100 yards in 3 minutes until H+72.

2. Map "A" (issued to Brigades and Batteries only) shows in BROWN, the areas to be engaged and the boundaries of the Groups. Group Commanders will sub-divide their areas into battery areas according to the number of batteries available.

3. The area cross hatched in black on Map "A" is being dealt with by H.A. and smoke, and will not be engaged by the Right Group.

4. Map "B" (issued to Brigades and Batteries only) shows the lifts of the imaginary rolling barrage, and is for guidance only. Map "C" (issued to Brigades only) shows the barrage lifts on the right flank and is for information only.

5. Rates of Fire.

H	to H+3.	Intense.
H+3	to H+20.	Rapid.
H+20	to H+69.	Normal.
H+69	to H+72.	Intense.

6. Ammunition.

50%	A	30% on graze.
50%	AX	106 Fuze.
100%	BX	106 Fuze.

7. D.A. Units please acknowledge.

Captain,
Brigade Major R.A.
34th Divisional Artillery.

26th September 1918.

Copies to:

1-2	152nd Brigade R.F.A.
3	160th Brigade R.F.A.
4	34th Division "G".
5	14th Divl. Arty.
6	30th Divl. Arty.
7	R.A., X Corps.
8	R.A., XIX Corps.
9	H.A. X Corps.
10-11	War Diary.
12-14	Spare.

App XIX

101 Bde	10 Corps
102 Bde	14 Div
103 Bde	30 Div
C.R.A.	65 Bde R.G.A.
C.R.E.	53 SQn R.A.F.

G. 177 28th

Situation 7-45 am AAA Line runs WARSAW Crater(inclus) - E.edge PETIT BOIS - Spur N.18.d. central - Northern BRICKSTACK - CROONAERT Chapel - N.edge BOIS QUARANTE - PICCADILLY FARM (inclus) AAA Total prisoners to date 1 Officer 58 O.R. AAA Enemy attempted to retake SPANBROEKMOLEN CRATER 4 am but was held up 100 yards from Crater AAA Added Corps reptd Flank Divs & Div Units

FROM 34th Division.

7-50 am.

for Lieut Colonel G.S.

Army Form C. 2123.
(In books of 100.)

"C" Form.

MESSAGES AND SIGNALS.

No. of Message

Prefix .... Code .... Words	Received.	Sent, or sent out.	Office Stamp.
£ s. d.	From	At .... m.	[illegible] IX 18
Charges to Collect	By	To	
Service Instructions.		By	APPX

Handed in at .... Office .... m. Received .... m.

TO CRA.

*Sender's Number.	Day of Month	In reply to Number.	AAA
	24		

Prisoner of 20th BAV RIR captured
in N24 [illegible] is
west of Ridge and is to be held
aaa [illegible] position of 20th BAV
RIR [illegible]
[illegible] company
forward [illegible]
about 500 [illegible] back [illegible]
[illegible] old [illegible]
east of ridge [illegible]
[illegible] WERVICQ aaa
attack [illegible]
Corps aaa 5th BAV RIR
[illegible] TOURCOING [illegible] days
ago [illegible]
[illegible] 10 Coys [illegible]
[illegible] CRA

FROM [illegible]
TIME & PLACE

*This line should be erased if not required.

[illegible]

101 Bde	C.R.A.	65 Bde R.G.A.
102 Bde	C.R.E.	53 Squadron R.A.F.
103. Bde		

APPX XI

G 178 28

---

35 Div report 8 am aaa Captured Hill 60 and CANADA Tunnel I.30.a. aaa 100 prisoners

FROM: 34th Div

9.60

Lieut. Colonel, G.S.

101 Bde	C.R.E.	41 Div	2/4 Som L.I.
102 Bde	10 Corps	10 Corps HA	Sig. Coy.
103 Bde	14 Div	53 Sqn R.A.F.	"Q"
C.R.A.	30 Div	34 Bn M.G.Corps	A.D.M.S.

App XXII

G.186. 28.

Situation 11-50 am AAA Line runs Road N.30.c.8.2 - SPANBROEKMOLEN PECKHAM and WARSAW Craters inclus - old trenches N.24.d.2.5 - Spur N.18.d.cen - Just W. UNNAMED WOOD - W. edge of GRAND BOIS - CREONAERT CHAPEL - 200 yds E. of PICCADILLY FARM XXXXXXXXXXX XXXXXXXXXX Parties of enemy seen retiring over crest in O.19.b. and 14.c. AAA 84 prisoners in cage 100 reported captured AAA Addsd Cols W.X. & Y plus 53 Sqn 41 Div & 10 Corps HA.

FROM 34th Div.

J Harter Major
for Lieut Col GS

101 Bde.   C.R.A.
102 "   14 Div
103 "   41 "

G.182   28

41st Div start from line Hill 60 to I.30.b.1.7. at 1.15 pm. and move S.E. with right on Canal AAA Objective line P.13 cent - P.8.d.cent. which they expect to reach at 4.30 pm. AAA They will drop on Canal Bank AAA Inform all patrols of this AAA The movement will probably begin to affect enemy on front of 103 Bde about 3 pm and in front of 101 Bde after that hour AAA Every endeavour must be made to report positionsof our patrols so that 41 Div may be informed AAA Addsd 101 & 103 Bdes Reptd 102 Bde. C.R.A. & 14 & 41 Divs

FROM:- 34 Div   Lieut-Colonel, G.S.

TIME:- 10.55 a.m

URGENT OPERATIONS PRIORITY to x
remainder PRIORITY

x101 Bde	C.R.E.	x14 Div.	2/4 Som.L.I.
102 "	x10 Corps	10 Corps H.A.	Sig.Coy.
x103 "	x14 Div.	53 Sqn R.A.F.	"Q"
C.R.A.	x30 "	34 Bn.M.G.C.	A.D.M.S.

G.187 28

Situation AAA Arty.Reconn.Offr. reports WYTSCHAETE clear of enemy except for nest in old O.Ps. O.19.b.5.6. AAA Our troops seen at O.19.d.3.9. O.13.c.9.3. and also well beyond RENTY FARM Road AAA Hostile M.G. seen firing on our people from old O.P. AAA Enemy seen running South from Cross Roads at O.19.d.4.9.

FROM:- 34 Div.

for Lieut-Colonel, G.S.

TIME:- 12.30 p.m.

PRIORITY.

101 Bde	C.R.E.	10 Corps H.A.	Sig Coy
102 Bde	10 Corps	53 Squadron RAF	"Q"
103 Bde	14 Div	34 Bn MG Corps	A.D.M.S.
C.R.A.	30 Div	2/4 Som L.I.	41 Div

G 192 28th

Situation at 1.30 pm as follows aaa Our troops Right Bde in touch with 30 Div at N.30.c.8.1 established on line just East of SPANBROEKMOLEN PECKHAM and WARSAW Craters and Eastern edge of PETIT BOIS with patrols in WYTSCHAETE Wood who are being fired at by M.Gs from high ground N and S of WYTSCHAETE aaa A strong patrol has been sent to push through WYTSCHAETE Wood starting at 1.30 pm aaa Right Bn one Coy on BLUE Line Northern brickstacks to S. of GRAND BOIS one Coy clear of Eastern edge of GD BOIS moving on ZERO HOUSE right Coy patrols now pushing forward to ONREAT Wood aaa Left Bn 3 Coys on BLUE Line with right at ZERO HOUSE aaa Left Bn ordered to advance in conjunction with 42nd Bde on line DOME HOUSE - ZERO HOUSE

FROM:- 34th Div

(Sgd) B.C. BATTYE,
Lieut. Colonel, G.S.

APP XXVI

PRIORITY

101 Bde 102 Bde 34 Bn MG Corps
103 Bde C.R.A.

14 Div 41 Div
~~30 Div~~ ~~10~~ Corps

G 202 28th

35th Div has taken ZANDVOORDE aaa 41st Div has passed bend of Canal in O.6.a. moving East of Canal on HOUTHEM aaa 15th Corps has reached line U.8.central U.9.d.0.0. U.16.c.0.0. U.22. c.20 and is advancing ~~on~~ [illegible] aaa The 34 Div will continue the advance to the BROWN Line and endeavour to reach that line before dark aaa One Bn 102 Bde is placed at disposal of each of 101 & 103 Bdes aaa These Bns will move as soon as possible to localities selected by 101 and 103 Bdes aaa Reserve Coy 34 Bn M.G.Corps now at FROUSTY HOUSE is placed at disposal of 101 Bde aaa Left of 103 Bde will operate against ONRAET Wood to enable 101 Bde to turn WYTSCHAETE ridge from North aaa Heavy Artillery is now engaging O.Ps in O.19.b. and O.25.a.

aaa Addsd 3 Bdes C.R.A. M.G.Bn

reptd 10 Corps 14 41 & 30 Divs

FROM:- 34th Div

Lieut. Colonel, G.S.

across the DOUVE in U10 #1

Army Form C. 2123
(In books of 100.)

"C" Form.

MESSAGES AND SIGNALS.

No. of Message............

Prefix........ Code .... Words........

£ s. d

Charges to Collect

Service Instructions

Received

From ....

By............

Sent, or sent out.

At..........m.

To ....

By............

Office Stamp

Handed in at........................Office........m. Received........m.

TO

*Sender's Number	Day of Month	In reply to Number	AAA

FROM

TIME & PLACE

*This line should be erased if not required.

(7750.) W528/M1970 100,000 Pads. 5/17 C. & R. Ltd. (E. 1213.)

"A" Form

Army Form C. 2121
(In pads of 100)

MESSAGES AND SIGNALS.

No. of Message...............

Prefix............ Code.............m	Words.	Charge.	This message is on a/c of:	Recd. at..........m.
Office of Origin and Service Instructions	Sent		.... Service.	Date.............
	At...............m.			From ....
	To.................			
	By.................		(Signature of "Franking Officer.")	By ....

APP XXVIII

TO	14 Div	101 Bde		
	50 "	102 "	C.R.A.	
		103 "		

Sender's Number.	Day of Month.	In reply to Number.	AAA
G.204	28		

Contact plane report 6 pm AAA Hostile rifle and M.G. fire from DAMM STRASSE O.9.a.6.1 O.16.b. and along Ridge between MESSINES and WYTSCHAETE about O.26.cent AAA DOME HOUSE apparently unoccupied AAA Flares seen in WYTSCHAETE WOOD O.19.a.4.2. and 4.6. ZERO WOOD and O.8.b.8.5. AAA Added Nos. 1 to 4, 7 & 8

From	
Place	34 Div
Time	

The above may be forwarded as now corrected. (Z)

Censor. Signature of Addressor or person authorised to telegraph in his name.

* This line should be erased if not required.

(6719) Wt. W3011/F911 2,125,000 Ibis. 2/16 C. & Co. (2824)

PRIORITY

101 Bde.	C.R.A.	14 Div.	10 Corps H.A.
102 "	C.R.E.	30 "	53 Sqn R.A.F.
103 "	10 Corps	41 "	

G.210 28

Situation about 8.30 p.m. AAA Right Bn. Right Bde. advancing with little opposition through SCOTT FARM O.25.a. on WHITEHALL O.19.d. AAA Left Bn. Right Bde. in touch with Left Bde. E.of ONRAET FARM AAA Left Bn. Left Bde. on line MARTINS FARM - DOME HOUSE - O.8.b.7.0. advancing AAA Total prisoners 133

FROM:- 34 Div. Lieut-Colonel. G.S.
TIME:- 10 p.m.

App XX

101 Bde	C.R.E.	41 Div	2/4 Som L.I.
102 Bde	10 Corps	65 Bde RGA	Signal Coy
103 Bde	30 Div	53 Squadron RAF	"Q"
C.R.A.	14 Div	34 Bn MG Corps	A.D.M.S.

G 232 29th

WYTSCHAETE Wood occupied 6.45 am by WAZU aaa Addsd Lists "W" "X" and "Y"

FROM:- 34 Div

(Sgd) J. HARTER, Major
for Lieut. Colonel, G.S.

101 Bde	C.R.A.	2/4 Som L.I.	"G" Rear
102 Bde	C.R.E.	A.D.M.S.	Signal Coy
103 Bde	34 Bn MG Corps	"Q" Rear	Div Recep: Camp

G 257 30th

App X23

Brit: Mission Belg Army report 9.45 pm 29th aaa Belgians have captured STADENBERG aaa Report received that Cavalry patrols are on roads 2 km West of ROULERS aaa Belgians have captured 5000 prisoners and 100 guns aaa 3rd Army have captured TILLOY and RUMILLY N and S of CAMBRAI respectively aaa 8000 prisoners 28th and 29th aaa 4th Army have captured GOUY East of LE CATELET

FROM:- 34th Divn
TIME:- 10.30 am

V Hackerbuzapp
for Lieut. Colonel, G.S.

Bdes DAC
DTMO. 30/9/18

Vol 34

WAR DIARY

HQRA 34th DIVISION

~~152nd BRIGADE RFA~~

~~160th BRIGADE R.F.A.~~

~~34th DAC~~

~~34 DTMO~~

OCTOBER 1918

Instructions regarding War Diaries and Intelligence Summaries are contained in F. S. Regs., Part II. and the Staff Manual respectively. Title pages will be prepared in manuscript.

Army Form C. 2118.

WAR DIARY
or
INTELLIGENCE SUMMARY.
(Erase heading not required.)

H.Q.R.A., 34th. Division,
Page 1.

Month of October, 1918

Vol

Place	Date	Hour	Summary of Events and Information	Remarks and references to Appendices
	Oct.			
Sheet 28, O.6.a.4.7	2		H.Q.R.A. moved to 28/O.6.a.4.7. 152nd. Brigade and 160th. Brigade remained in positions of readiness near KORTEWILDE and KRUISEECKE. Reconnaisances were carried out for the purpose of covering the 34th. Division, should they be ordered to take the line of the WERVICQ-MENIN railway Batteries came into action during the afternoon. LOCATIONS:- 152nd. Bde., H.Qrs., P.3.d.4.4 A/152, P.5.c.5.9 B/152, P.11.c.1.6 C/152, P.10.d.9.4 D/152, P.5.a.8.0 160th. Bde., H.Qrs., J.35.a.4.2. A/160, 5 guns, P.5.b.3.9 1 ,, J.36.d.3.5 B/160, 5 guns, J.35.b.7.5 1 ,, P.5.b.8.1 C/160, 5 guns, J.35.a.4.3 1 ,, J.35.d.9.2 D/160, 5 hows, J.35.d.4.5 1 ,, P.6.d.6.6	App I
	2		34th. Divisional Artillery Location Statement,	App II
	7	7	34th. Divisional Artillery Order No. 1,	App III
			34th. Divisional Artillery Instructions No. 1,	App IV
			34th. Divisional Artillery Operation Order No. 31,	App V
	8		34th. Divisional Artillery Location Statement,	App VI
	11		34th. Divisional Artillery Operation Instructions No. 1,	App VII

Army Form C. 2118.

Instructions regarding War Diaries and Intelligence Summaries are contained in F. S. Regs., Part II. and the Staff Manual respectively. Title pages will be prepared in manuscript.

WAR DIARY
or
INTELLIGENCE SUMMARY.
(Erase heading not required.)

H.Q.R.A., 34th. Division.
Page 2.

Month of October, 1918

Place	Date	Hour	Summary of Events and Information	Remarks and references to Appendices
Sheet 28, O.6.a.4.7	Oct.			
	11		34th. Divisional Artillery Operation Order No. 32,	App VIII
			34th. Divisional Artillery Operation Order No. 32, Addendum No. 1,	App IX
	12		34th. Divisional Artillery Operation Instructions No. 2,	App X
			34th. D ivisional Artillery Operation Order No. 33,	App XI
			34th. Divisional Artillery Operation Order No. 34,	App XII
			34th. Divisional Artillery Operation Order No. 35,	App XIII
			34th. Divisional Artillery Operation Instructions No. 3,	App XIV
			34th. Division Operation Order,	App XV
			34th. Division Operation Instructions No. 1,	App XVI
			34th. Division Operation Instructions No. 2,	App XVII
	14		34th. Divisional Artillery Operation XXXXXXXXXXX Order No. 36,	App XVIII
			The advance of the Second Army was resumed at 05.35. The advance of the 34th. Division was covered by an 18-pdr. creeping barrage, creeping forward at the rate of 100 yards in two minutes, field howitzers and heavy artillery moving ahead of the 18-pdr. barrage and engaging all targets within their zones.	
			The village of GHELUWE was specially treated with smoke shell and thermite.	
			For the attack, the 102nd. Infantry Brigade was on the right and the 103rd. Infantry Brigade on the left, the division being supported by the 152nd. Brigade, R.F.A., on the right, 160th. Bde. in the centre, the 96th. (ARmy) F.A. Bde. on the left, and a considerable amount of Heavy Artillery.	

Army Form C. 2118.

WAR DIARY
or
INTELLIGENCE SUMMARY. H.Q.R.A., 34th. Division.

(Erase heading not required.)

Instructions regarding War Diaries and Intelligence Summaries are contained in F. S. Regs., Part II. and the Staff Manual respectively. Title pages will be prepared in manuscript.

Month of October, 1918

Place	Date	Hour	Summary of Events and Information	Remarks and references to Appendices
Sheet 28, O.6.a.4.7	Oct. 14		At 09.45, the attack was reported successful. The line ran:- COUCOU (incl.) - FLAME FARM QUERY FARM - Q.12.d.9.1 - Dump, R.7.c.3.3 - JOB FARM - , with the 103rd. Infy. Bde. on their second objective. GHELUWE was reported cleared.	App XX
			Situation reports timed 19.30, 22.35, 23.30, vide	App XIX
			34th. Division Operation Order No. 277,	App XXI
			34th. Division Operation Order No. 278,	App XXII
	15		34th. Division Operation Order No. 279,	App XXIII
	16		The 101st. Infy. Bde. relieved the 124th. Infy. Bde. of the 41st. Division on the front from the railway line in R.2.b to cross roads L.35.d.2.3 during the night 15th./16th. October. The front was covered by the 41st. Divisional Artillery until 06.00, October 16th., when the 34th. Divisional Artillery became responsible for the artillery defence. The 102nd. Infy. Bde. was relieved in the line by the 90th. Infy. Bde. of the 30th. Division during the night 16th./17th. October. The 3 0th. Divisional Artillery took over the artillery defence of the line at 06.00, 16th. October.	
	15		34th. Division Operation order No. 280,	App XXIV
			102nd. Infy. Bde. reported, "Patrols have reached MONGREL Bridge, R.19.a.3.5, Locks R.13.d.5.7 and R.14.c.7.0, MARATHON Bridge and BRULEE FARM. All these bridges are destroyed. MONGREL Bridge is passable by single men. Enemy are in ROOMY Wood, R.13.d."	App XXV
	16		At 09.45, our troops held the North bank of the River LYS. Hostile machine guns and trench mortars in HALLUIN were dealt with by the Divnl Artillery. Our operations were confined to establishing an outpost line South of the LYS with bridge-heads at available crossings.	App XXVI

(A7092). Wt. W12839/M1293 75,0.0. 1/17. D. D. & L., Ltd. Forms/C.2118/..

Army Form C. 2118.

WAR DIARY
or
INTELLIGENCE SUMMARY.

(Erase heading not required.)

Instructions regarding War Diaries and Intelligence Summaries are contained in F. S. Regs., Part II. and the Staff Manual respectively. Title pages will be prepared in manuscript.

H.Q.R.A., 34th. Division.

Month of October, 1918

Place	Date	Hour	Summary of Events and Information	Remarks and references to Appendices
Sheet 29, Q.6.a.4.7	Oct. 17		After relief by the 3 0th. Division, the 102nd. Infy. Bde. and the 96th. A.F.A. Bde. formed the divisional reserve in readiness to move at one hour's notice. The O.C., 96th. (Army) F.A. Bde. at K.26.c.4.3, maintained close liaison with the G.O.C., 102nd. Infy. Bde. at JOHNSTON'S FARM, K.36.a.	
	16		The 152nd. Bde. R.F.A. and the 160th. Bde. R.F.A. were placed at the disposal of the G.O's.C. 101st. and 102nd. Infy. Bdes. respectively, sections of batteries being used to push forward with infantry batallions.	App XXVII
			Situation Reports, vide	App XXVIII
ARTOISHOEK, 28/K.30	17		H.Q.R.A. closed at 28/Q.6.a.at 12 o'clock, and re-opened at the same time at ARTOISHOEK (K.30.central, Sheet 28). At 11.50, our troops were reported in LAUWE and to have crossed the river at RUDDY FARM. LAUWE was evacuated by the enemy at 06.30. At 19.00, the general line ran:- S. of RECKHEM, M.2.6.a, KNOCKE (incl.), M.16.c.O.7. AELBEKE was occupied by the enemy. A pontoon bridge fit for artillery was constructed at R.17.d.5.8.	App XXIX
	18		The 101st. Infy. Bde. took over the whole divisional front during the night October 17/18. The 152nd. Bde. R.F.A. and 160th. Bde. R.F.A. afforded the artillery support, the O.C. 152nd. Bde. acting as liaison Officer for both Brigades.	App XXX
	19		During the night 17th./18th., the line remained firm, but on the night 18th./19th. October and the morning of the 19th., the enemy withdrew under pressure to the approximate line of L BELLEGHEM and the high ground about the TOURNAI Road in 29/T.5 and 29/T.11	
		8 a.m.	An advanced H.Q.R.A., was established for the morning's operations at KRUISHOEK 28/R.5.a, the head-quarters being later moved to LAUWE 29/M.14.c.3.3. The 152nd. Bde., 160th. Bde. and the 96th. Bde. A.F.A. crossed the LYS by pontoon bridges the 160th. and 96th. Bdes. occupying positions of readiness S.E. of LAUWE. The 152nd. Bde., co-operating with the 101st. Infy. Bde., moved to the vicinity of ST. ANNE with one battery in action in close support of the infantry advance.	

(A7092). Wt. W12839/M1293. 75,0.0. 1/17. D. D. & L., Ltd. Forms/C.2118/14.

Instructions regarding War Diaries and Intelligence Summaries are contained in F. S. Regs., Part II. and the Staff Manual respectively. Title pages will be prepared in manuscript.

Army Form C. 2118.

WAR DIARY
or
INTELLIGENCE SUMMARY.
(Erase heading not required.)

Month of October, 1918.

H.Q.R.A., 34th. Division.
Page 5.

Place	Date	Hour	Summary of Events and Information	Remarks and references to Appendices
Sheet 28, O.6.a.4.7	Oct. 19		96th. (Army) F.A. Bde. moved to AELBEKE area during the afternoon. The situation at noon was as follows:- "Queen's" on the line ROLLEGHEM - ROLLEGHEMHOEK. ROLLEGHEM is clear of the enemy. BELLEGHEM is still held by the enemy." M.G.s in BELLEGHEM and a section of 77 cm. guns were effectively engaged by A/152.	App XXXI
	20		The 30th. Division passed through the 101st. Infy. Bde. and took over the 34th. Division front at noon. The 34th. Division became the Xth. Corps reserve division.	App XXXII
BELLEGHEM	23		H.Q.R.A. moved to BELLEGHEM 29/N.27. On the night 23rd./24th. October, the 102nd. Bde. Group (including the 96th. (Army) F.A. Bde. relieved the Right Brigade (124th. Bde.) of the 41st. Division, and the artillery covering them on the front V.18.a to O.22.c. 96th. (Army) F.A. Bde. occupied positions in U.9.a and established Brigade H.Q. at V.3.a.5.1.	App XXXIII App XXXIV
	24		152nd. Bde. R.F.A. and 160th. Bde. R.F.A. came into action to cover the 101st. Infy. Bde. 34th. D.A.C. moved to area N.W. of ROLLEGHEM (29/N.31). Location of 96th. (Army) F.A. Bde., vide Situation at 08.00, vide 34th. Divisional Artillery Operation Order No. 37, 34th. Division Operation Instruction No. 1, 34th. Division Operation Order No. 289,	App. XXXV App XXXVI App XXXVII App XXXVIII App XXXIX App XL
	25		The attack was resumed at 09.00 by the IInd. Corps, XIXth. Corps and the 34th. Division, with the object of gaining the line of the ESCAULT. The objective of the 34th. Division was the river between BOSSUYT (U,24.b) and AUTRYVE (V.9.c) both inclusive. the attack being carried out by the 102nd. Infy. Bde., 96th. (Army) F.A. Bde., 152nd. Bde. and the 160th. Bde. R.F.A. The main attack from the north about O.22.central, was directeddown the E. bank of the COURTRAI - BOSSUYT canal, with a subsiduary attack across the canal by the most suitable points about the locks 3, 4 and 5. The main attack from the North was covered by an 18-pdr. creeping barrage put down by the 41st. Divisional Artillery and thickened on the 34th. Division front by two batteries of the 34th. Divisional Artillery. MOEN was specially dealt with. Two 4.5 how. batteries fired	

(A7092). Wt. W12839/M1293. 75,0.0. 1/17. D. D. & L., Ltd. Forms/C.2118/14.

Army Form C. 2118.

WAR DIARY
or
INTELLIGENCE SUMMARY.

(Erase heading not required.)

Instructions regarding War Diaries and Intelligence Summaries are contained in F. S. Regs., Part II. and the Staff Manual respectively. Title pages will be prepared in manuscript.

H.Q.R.A., 34th. Division.

Month of October, 1918

Page 6.

Place	Date	Hour	Summary of Events and Information	Remarks and references to Appendices
BELLEGHEM	Oct. 25		alternate bursts of H.E. and smoke-shell on it during the advance, and the fire of two 18-pdr. batteries was directed on the village for 15 minutes previous to the mopping-up. 4.5. how fire of H.E. and smoke was lifted to OKKERDRIESCH and houses in V.8.b and V.1.a. For the subsiduary attack, 34th. Division batteries afforded a smoke and H.E. barrage on the MOEN-BOSSUYT road, with thick smoke east of Locks 3, 4 and 5, to cover the crossing of the COURTRAI-BOSSUYT canal. After 81 minutes, batteries lifted on MARAILLESTRAAT, HEESTERSTRAAT and houses north of AUTRYVE . Hostile fire during the morning's advance was practically nil. Later increased shelling was experienced about MOEN and the COURTRAI-BOSSUYT canal. Night fire was directed on BOSSUYT Chateau, U.18.d and the outskirts of AUTRYVE. Various M.G.s were engaged by the field artillery during the advance. Situation at 10.45, vide 102nd. Infy. Bde. report, timed 18.20, "All objectives gained, including AUTRYVE aaa Casualties light, probably under 100 aaa 51 prisoners captured."	App XLI
	26		The 34th. Division was relieved in the line by the 30th. Division during the night October 26th./27th., and moved by brigade groups (vide App. XLII) into IInd. Corps area, to take over the front held by the 36th. Division. The 160th. Bde., R.F.A., moved under orders of the G.O.C., 101st. Infy. Bde. to the OYGHEM area on the morning of October 26th. The 96th. (Army) F.A. Bde. remained in action, and came under the orders of the 30th. Divn. During the afternoon, the 152nd. Bde. moved under the orders of the G.O.C., 103rd. Infy. Bde to the AELBEKE area, and proceeded the next day to the area of the IInd. Corps.	App XLIII
LAUWE	27		H.Q.R.A. moved to LAUWE.	
BEVEREN	28		H.Q.R.A. moved to BEVEREN (29/C.25), C.R.A. 34th. Division assumed the responsibility of covering the 101st. Infy. Bde. in the line at 11.00. 34th. Divisional Artillery Location Statement, 34th. Divisional Artillery Operation Order No. 39,	App XLIV App XLV App XLVI

(A7092). Wt. W12839/M1293. 75,0.0. 1/17. D. D. & L., Ltd. Forms/C.2118/14.

Army Form C. 2118.

WAR DIARY
or
INTELLIGENCE SUMMARY.
(Erase heading not required.)

H.Q.R.A., 34th. Division.

Instructions regarding War Diaries and Intelligence Summaries are contained in F. S. Regs., Part II. and the Staff Manual respectively. Title pages will be prepared in manuscript. Month of October, 1918

Page 7.

Place	Date	Hour	Summary of Events and Information	Remarks and references to Appendices
BEVEREN Sheet 29, C.25	Oct. 29		34th. Divisional Artillery Operation Order No. 40,	App XLVII
			34th. Divisional Artillery Location Statement (Battle Positions),	App XLIX
	30		34th. Divisional Artillery Operation Order No. 42,	App L
	31		In conjunction with the 41st. (French) Division, on the left, and the 30th. (British) Divn. on the right, the 34th. Division resumed the attack at 05.25. The attack was carried out by the 103rd. Infy. Bde., supported by the 152nd. Bde. R.F.A., and the 51st. Bde. R.F.A., grouped under the 152nd. Bde., on the right, and the 160th. Bde. and the 113th. (Army) F.A. Bde., grouped under the 160th. Bde., on the left. A creeping barrage was put down 200 yards in front of the forming-up line, and creeping at the rate of 100 yards every 3 minutes, until the protective barrage line 300 yards beyond the final objective was reached. One gun per 18-pdr. battery fired smoke shell in the barrage, while 4.5 hows. fired smoke shell with a proportion of H.E. on selected localities.	
	31		At 10.15 am., the 103rd. Infy. Bde. was reported on the final objective, At 15.45, our line was reported:- "K.31.b.8.0 - K.31.b.7.3 - thence along railway to J.30.d.9.1 - J.30.b.9.0 to about J.30.b.3.7 - J.23.d.7.1. French line:- WINTERKAN (incl.) - about J.23.b.9.9 - thence along road to STEENBRUGGE." "Pockets of enemy in KRUISWEG and about J.24.d.6.0 now being cleared." During the night our patrols occupied BOSCHKANT (K.26.a.), and found it clear of the enemy; also HILL 74 in K.26.d.	

Lieut.-Colonel,
C.R.A., 34th. Division.

(A7092). Wt. W12839/M1293. 75 ,o o. 1/17. D. D. & L., Ltd. Forms/C.2118/14.

APP I

SECRET.

34th DIVISIONAL ARTILLERY OPERATION ORDER No.95.

Reference extracts from 34th Division O.O. No.272.

1. The 9th Division has broken through the [illegible] switch at LEDEGHEM and ROLLEGHEM CAPPELLE.

2. It is proposed to make an attack with the II and XIX Corps from this line in a S.E. direction to gain the line of the LYS from WERVICQ to COURTRAI.

3. The 41st Division and the 35th Division will attack to-morrow from their present line along the GHELUWE - WERVICQ Road and endeavour to establish themselves on the line of the WERVICQ - MENIN Railway.

4. Should they be successful they will be relieved on the whole of this front by the 102nd Bde, covered by the 152nd Bde. R.F.A. on the right, and the 160th Bde. R.F.A. on the left.

5. If the 34th Division has to attack in order to gain the line of the WERVICQ - MENIN Railway it will do so with the 102nd Bde., supported by the 152nd Bde. R.F.A. on the right, and the 103rd Bde. supported by the 160th Bde. R.F.A. on the left. Dividing line as laid down in 34th Division O.O. No.272.

6. Brigades will carry out reconnaissances for these purposes as early as possible to-morrow morning. 160th Bde will move into a position of readiness near [illegible], and 152nd Bde remain in readiness in their present wagon lines. 34th D.A.C. will remain in their present wagon lines and supply ammunition to battery wagon lines.

7. O.C. 152nd Bde. R.F.A. will get into touch with G.O.C. 102nd Infantry Bde.; 160th Bde R.F.A. will get into touch with G.O.Cs 102nd and 103rd Infantry Bdes.

8. 157th Brigade R.F.A. are at [illegible], with batteries in action W of TENBRIELEN - ZANDVOORDE Road. Positions taken up by batteries of the 34th D.A. should be East of TENBRIELEN - ZANDVOORDE Road.

Captain,
Brigade Major R.A.,
1st October 1918. 34th Divisional Artillery.

Copies to: 152nd Bde. R.F.A.
160th Bde. R.F.A.
34th D.A.C.

SECRET.

Ref: Map Sheet 28,
1/40,000.

34th. DIVISIONAL ARTILLERY OPERATION ORDER No. 24.

(1) The Divisional Artillery will move to-morrow, 1st. October, to the KORTEWILDE area.

(2) The 152nd. Brigade RFA, and H.Q., D.A.C. and Nos. 1 and 2 Sections, will move by the NORTHERN ROUTE; 152 Bde. via HALLABAST, DICKEBUSCH, CAFE BELGE, VOORMEZEELE, ST. ELOI, HOLLEBEKE, ECLUSE No. 5; D.A.C., H.Q., and Nos. 1 and 2 Sections, LA CLYTTE, and thence as for 152 Bde. No. 1 Coy. Train as for D.A.C.

(3) The 160th. Brigade, R.F.A., will move by the SOUTHERN ROUTE, WYTSCHAETE, OOSTAVERNE, road junction O.17.c.6055, O.23.b.05.50, P.13.c.05.43, P.19.b.05.35, P.20.a.10.00.

(4) Starting Points:-
152nd. Bde., RFA, ST. ELOI, 4 p.m.
D.A.C., ST.ELOI, to follow 152nd. Bde.,
No. 1 Coy. TRAIN, ST. ELOI, to follow D.A.C.,
160th. Bde., RFA, OOSTAVERNE, 4 p.m.

(5) Billeting parties from D.A. Units and No. 1 Coy. Train, will meet the S.C.R.A. at WYTSCHAETE cross roads (O.19.b.3.0.) at 10 a.m. on 1st. October.

(6) R.A.H.Q. will close at LITTLE KEMMEL at 10 a.m., and will re-open at 12 noon at L.30.c.central.

(7) D.A.C. will collect and take with them Lt. CROOKES and party from DIMITRI DUMP, and also Lt. LOMAS and party from LA POLKA DUMP.

(8) D.T.M.O. and Medium T.M. Batteries will accompany D.A.C.

(9) Artillery Units and No. 1 Coy. Train to acknowledge.

[signature]

Captain,
Brigade-Major, R.A.,
34th. Divisional Artillery.

30th. September, 1918.

Distribution:-
152 Bde., RFA,
160 Bde., RFA,
34th. D.A.C.,
D.T.M.O.,
34th. Divn., "G",
S.C.R.A.,
No. 1 Coy. Train,
10th. Corps, R.A.

x Does not . . . 8AA
Sect.

SECRET.

EXTRACT FROM 34th DIVISION O.O.272.

102nd Bde. will move to a position of readiness near AMERIKA Q.7.a. by 8 am to-morrow.

103rd Bde. to a position of readiness immediately E of road in P.6.c.& d. by 9 am to-morrow.

102nd Bde. will be prepared to take over front from 35th and 41st Divisions from CHELUWE - MENIN Road exclusive to WERVICQ exclusive.

Under certain circumstances 102nd and 103rd Bdes will both take over this front.

If so 102nd Bde will be on right and 103rd Bde. on left dividing line N.W. & S.E. line through Q.9.central, Q.16.central, Q.23.central.

102nd Bde. will also be prepared to support troops in front during day but will not move without orders.

Divisional Artillery will be prepared to take up positions covering the line of WERVICQ - MENIN Railway between above points as early as possible to-morrow morning.

Captain,
Brigade Major R.A.,
34th Divisional Artillery.

1st October 1918.

By Special D.R.

D.A.C.
S.A.A.Section

B.M.30 1

The S.A.A.Section will accompany the D.A.C. into the Arty.Area around KORTEWILDE marching in rear of Nos.1 and 2 Sections, D.A.C. AAA

O.C. D.A.C. will be responsible for issuing orders to S.A.A. Section as to starting point and route and time of starting AAA

The S.A.A. Section is located at N.5.b. AA

Acknowledge

FROM:- G.O.C. R.A.

TIME:- 11.55 a.m.

BM RA

App II

SECRET.

LOCATION STATEMENT.

34th. DIVISIONAL ARTILLERY.

Reference MAP,
Sheet 28,
1/40,000.

H.Qrs., 34th. Div.Arty., O.6.a.4.7.

H.Qrs., 152nd. Bde., R.F.A., P.3.d.4.4.
A/152, - P.5.c.5.9.
B/152, - P.11.c.1.6.
C/152, - P.10.d.9.4.
D/152, - P.5.a.8.0.

H.Qrs., 160th. Bde., R.F.A., J.35.a.4.2.
A/160, - 5 guns, P.5.b.3.9.
1 gun, J.36.d.3.5.
B/160, - 5 guns, J.35.b.7.5.
1 gun, P.5.b.8.1.
C/160, - 5 guns, J.35.a.4.3.
1 gun, J.35.d.9.2.
D/160, - 5 hows, J.35.d.4.5.
1 how., P.6.d.6.6.

4th. October, 1918.
Issued at 11.00.

Captain,
Brigade-Major, R.A.
34th. Divisional Artillery.

Distribution:-

152 Bde.,	34th. Div. "G",
160 Bde.,	30th. D.A.,
34 D.A.C.,	41st. D.A.,
D.T.M.O.,	X Corps R.A.,
S.C.R.A.,	X Corps H.A.

S E C R E T.

34th DIVISIONAL ARTILLERY ORDER No.1.

1. 102nd Infantry Bde. will be relieved by 101st Infantry Bde. on night 7/8th October.

2. Relief to be completed by 00.00, at which hour G.O.C. 101st Infantry Bde. will take over command of the whole Divisional Front.

3. Hd.Qrs 101st Infantry Bde. will be at DE VOORSTRAAT Cabaret.

4. O.C. 152nd Brigade R.F.A. will act as liaison with 101st Infantry Bde, it will not be necessary for a liaison officer to live at 101st Infantry Bde. Hd.Qrs.

5. Battalion liaison officers will be found as follows:-

152nd Bde. Right Battalion H.Q. at Q.1.c.9.3.

160th Bde. Left Battalion H.Q. at K.31.c.8.7.

6. D.A. units to ACKNOWLEDGE.

Captain,
Brigade Major R.A.,
34th Divisional Artillery.

7th October 1918.

Copies to:-

152nd Brigade R.F.A.
160th Brigade R.F.A.
34th Division "G".
101st Infantry Bde. (For information).
War Diary.
File.

App IV

SECRET.

34th DIVISIONAL ARTILLERY INSTRUCTIONS No.1.

The following number of rounds per gun will be dumped at battery positions for expenditure on day of attack.

18 pdr. 400 rounds per gun.

4.5" How. 300 ,, ,, how.

In both cases this is exclusive of either gas or smoke shell.

Captain,
Brigade Major R.A.,
34th Divisional Artillery.

7th October 1918.

Copies to:- 152nd Bde. R.F.A.
160th Bde. R.F.A.
90th Bde. R.F.A.
34th Division "G".
R.A., XIX Corps.

34th Division "G"

Ref: "Extracts from 34th Division O.O. No. 274.

Para. 1. line. 4. For Q. 4. a. 9. 0.

Read Q. 4. c. 9. 0.

BS

[illegible]

Lieut RA
for Brigade Major
34th Divisional Artillery.

5th October 1918

G.334

S E C R E T.

EXTRACT FROM 34TH DIVISION OPERATION ORDER No.274.

1. The Division will take up the front from KLIJTHOEK [illegible] exclusive, to road junction [illegible].34.c.9.1., on night 5/6th inst. This front will be held by two Brigades - 102nd Bde. on the right and 101st Bde. on the left. The Inter-Brigade boundary will be C.4.a.9.0.

Told RA JH.

2. 152nd Brigade R.F.A. will support the 102nd Infy.Bde. on the right.

   160th Brigade R.F.A. will support the 101st Infy.Bde. on the left.

3. H.Q. of both Infantry Brigades will be at [illegible] for the present. The liaison officer at present found by 160th Bde. will act as liaison to both Infantry Brigades. The necessary battalion liaison officers will be found by both Brigades.

4. The artillery defence of this front will pass to the D.A. on completion of reliefs by infantry Brigades.

Captain,
Brigade Major, R.A.,
34th Divisional Artillery.

5th October 1918.

Copies to:-

152nd Brigade R.F.A.
160th Brigade R.F.A.
34th Division "G".
Xth Corps R.A.

SECRET.

34th. DIVISIONAL ARTILLERY OPERATION ORDER No. 30.

Ref: Map
Sh. 28.SE
1/20,000

(1) The whole of the Divisional Front will be taken over to-night by the 102nd. Infantry Brigade, which will move its H.Qrs. back to DE VORSTRAAT Cabt.

(2) Liaison with the Infantry Brigade will continue for the present to be found by the 160th. Bde., RFA.

(3) The Inter-Artillery Brigade Boundary will run as follows:-
Q.8.a.8.0 - Q.8.c.1.3 - along track to Q.14.b.8.5 - thence grid S.E.

(4) New S.O.S. Lines will be reported to this Office as soon as decided upon.

(5) D.A. Units please ACKNOWLEDGE.

Captain,
Brigade-Major, R.A.,
34th. Divisional Artillery.

4th. October. 1916.

To:- 152nd. Bde. RFA,
160th. Bde. RFA,
34th. Divn. G,
Xth. Corps R.A.

O.C. 2/4th Somerset L.I. (Pioneers)

Please detail one half company, in addition to the two half companies already at the disposal of G.Os.C. 102nd and 103rd Infantry Brigades, to be at the disposal of G.O.C., 101st Infantry Brigade when that Brigade goes into the line to-night.

The Officer commanding the half company detailed will report at the 101st Brigade Hd.Qrs as soon as possible after the receipt of this order, and will ascertain personally from the G.O.C. or one of his Staff Officers, what work he wishes the half company to carry out.

L. 31 b. 0. 7

H Dobson

H.Q. R.E.
15/10/1918.

Lieut-Colonel,
C.R.E. 34th Division.

101st Infantry Brigade (for information)
34th Division "G" (" ")

(861)

Time:- 18.00 hrs

O.C. 207th Field Co. R.E.

Please detail 1 section to be at the disposal of G.O.C. 101st Infantry Brigade when this Brigade goes into the line. The officer commanding the section detailed will report as soon as possible at the Brigade Hd.Qrs. and ascertain personally what work his section will be required to do.

Acknowledge by telephone.

Bde H.Q will be at L.31.b.0.7

H Dobson
Lieut-Colonel,
C.R.E. 34th Division.

H.Q. R.E.
15/10/1918.

101st Infy Bde (for information)
34th Division "G". (for information)

Time:- 18.00 hrs

(860)

App V

S E C R E T.

34th DIVISIONAL ARTILLERY OPERATION ORDER No.31.

1. The Divisional Boundaries now run as under:-

Right Boundary. F.13.c.0.4. F.17. central F.18.c.4.8. F.18.b.3.4.
L.8.c.8.2. .15.b.0.6. .17.c.3.2. F.13.c.3.2.

Left Boundary. F.1.a.0.4. F.3.a.6.3. F.5. central .8.a.3.0.
K.33.c.0.0. L.31.d.0.0. R.6.d.4.1. F.11.c.0.5.

2. The Inter-Artillery Group Boundary will be an E & W grid line through QUARANTINE FARM (F.10.a.) inclusive to the Southern Group.

Captain,
Brigade Major R.A.,
34th Divisional Artillery.

7th October 1918.

Copies to:-
152nd Brigade R.F.A.
160th Brigade R.F.A.
34th Division "G".

S E C R E T.

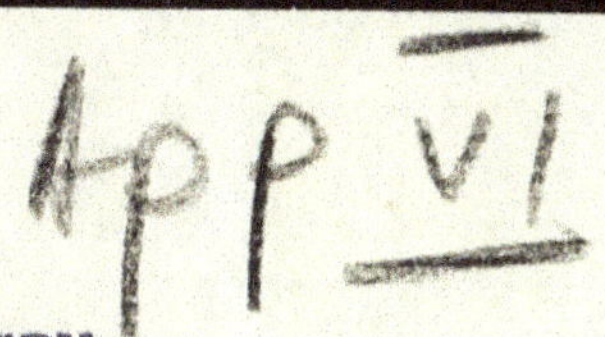

34th DIVISIONAL ARTILLERY.

LOCATION STATEMENT No.1.

Reference Map: 28/1/40,000.

Headquarters 34th Divnl. Artillery. O.6.a.4.7.

		Position in action	Wagon Lines.
H.Q. 152nd Bde. R.F.A.		P.3.d.4.3.	O.5.c.6.4.
A/152nd Bde. R.F.A.	4 guns.	P.5.a.5.4.	P.2.c.4.8.
" " "	2 "	P.5.a.3.5.	
B/152nd " "	4 "	P.11.c.1.6.	J.32.c.1.9.
" " "	2 "	J.35.d.05.50.	
C/152nd " "	4 "	P.4.c.9.2.	J.32.c.4.6.
" " "	2 "	P.5.d.5.9.	
D/152nd " "	4 Hows.	P.5.a.8.0.	J.31.a.9.9.
" " "	2 "	J.35.c.5.2.	
H.Q. 160th Bde. R.F.A.		J.35.a.4.2.	H.28.d.4.4.
A/160th Bde. R.F.A.	5 guns.	P.5.b.3.9.	H.29.c.4.2.
" " "	1 "	J.36.d.3.5.	
B/160th " "	5 "	P.5.a.50.75.	H.29.c.4.2.
" " "	1 "	P.5.b.72.65.	
C/160th " "	2 "	J.35.b.73.40.	H.33.c.2.9.
" " "	4 "	P.6.d.70.48.	
D/160th " "	2 Hows.	J.35.d.4.5.	H.33.a.4.2.
" " "	4 "	P.6.d.6.6.	

Captain,
Brigade Major R.A.
34th Divisional Artillery,

Issued at 22.00
8th October 1918.

Copies to:- 152nd Bde. R.F.A.
160th Bde. R.F.A.
96th Bde. A.F.A.
34th D.A.C.
D.T.M.O.
S.C.R.A.
34th Division "G".
30th Div. Arty.
41st Div. Arty.
C.B.S.O. X Corps.
H.A. X Corps.
R.A. X Corps.

S E C R E T.

34th DIVISIONAL ARTILLERY.

LOCATION STATEMENT No.2. (O.Ps)

Reference Map: Sheet 28, 1/40,000

A/152nd Brigade R.F.A.		O.P.	P.5.d.0.7.
B/152nd	" "	O.P.	P.5.b.5.0.
C/152nd	" "	O.P.	P.5.d.7.7.
D/152nd	" "	O.P.	P.5.b.5.0.

IDLE O.P. Q.7.a.57.70.
DISSOLUTE O.P. P.5.d.45.98.

Issued at 22.00
8th October 1918.

Captain,
Brigade Major R.A.,
34th Divisional Artillery.

Copies to:-

152nd Brigade R.F.A.
160th Brigade R.F.A.
96th Brigade A.F.A.
D.T.M.O.
34th Division "G".
30th Div. Arty.
41st Div. Arty.
C.B.S.O. X Corps.
H.A. X Corps.
R.A. X Corps.

App VII

SECRET.

Ref.Maps 1/20,000)28 NE.
)28 SE.

34th DIVISIONAL ARTILLERY.

OPERATION INSTRUCTIONS No.1.

1. The advance of the Second Army will be resumed on "J" day, (not earlier than 14th October).

The objective lines, Inter-Divisional and Brigade Boundaries and Infantry Starting Line are shown on attached . Map."A".

The advance will be divided into three phases:-

1st Phase to BLACK line.
2nd ,, ,, BLUE and portions of BROWN line.
3rd ,, ,, Final objective, BROWN line.

2. The attack will be carried out by 102nd Bde. on the right and 103rd Bde. on the left.

3. ARTILLERY PLAN. The Division will be supported by 152nd Brigade R.F.A. on the right, 160th Brigade R.F.A. in the centre, and 96th Army F.A. Brigade on the left, and a considerable amount of Heavy Artillery.

1st Phase. The advance will commence at H hour, at H - 2 the 18-pdr. batteries will put down a barrage on a line 300 yds in front of the Infantry Starting line and will commence to creep at H+ 2, moving forward at the rate of 100 yds in 2' until it reaches a protective barrage line 200 yds East of the BLACK line.

2nd Phase. At H+45' the barrage will again commence to creep at the same pace, moving forward until it reaches a line 250 yds E of the BLUE line where it will remain for 17 minutes.

The batteries of the Right (152) Brigade will not creep as far as this line but will stop on the final protective barrage line as they reach it.

During the 1st and 2nd phases the Field and Heavy Howitzers will fire a Jumping Barrage, moving from target to target (given on Target Map already issued) 300 yds and 500 yds respectively ahead of the 18-pdr creeping barrage. During the first pause fire being concentrated on such portions of the support and front lines and intervening wire of the TERHAND line, as safety conditions permit.

During the second pause targets being engaged 300 yds and 500 yds respectively East of the 18-pdr protective barrage, the Heavy Artillery paying particular attention to the exits from MENIN.

GHELUWE will be specially treated with smoke and thermite from H - 2 to H+ 28, but D/160 must be prepared in case of certain directions of wind, to fire smoke shell into the Eastern half of the village from H - 2 to H+ 28. Special instructions will be issued as to this.

3rd Phase. At H+ 90 the advance will be continued to the final objective, covered by Heavy Artillery and such Field batteries as are still within range, firing bursts of fire East of certain lines which will be laid down.

All fire will cease at an hour to be notified later except observed fire or fire ordered from this office, and the Infantry will push out patrols at least as far as the line of the MENIN-WERVICQ railway, one patrol being specially detailed to seize the Knoll at R.3.c.0.0. to cover the flank of the 41st Division whose objective is R.3.central.

4. During the 3rd phase Field batteries will be prepared to move forward so as to be able to cover the line of the WERVICQ-MENIN - LEDEGHEM railway and as far East of it as possible. Positions should be reconnoitred as far as possible beforehand; 160th Brigade S of Menin Road suggested Q.2.b. will move first and on arrival in forward positions will passto the command of G.O.C. Left (103) Infantry Bde; 96th Army Brigade next to positions N of MENIN Road and West of GHELUWE; 152nd Brigade finally will move forward such batteries as are necessary to fulfil conditions laid down above. Orders for the commencement of this forward move will be given from this office.

5. Each Brigade will provide a F.O.O party under an officer equipped with telephone and visual signalling equipment.

160th Brigade in addition will provide an officer and 2 men with Aldis lamp to communicate with No.25 Balloon under instructions issued previously.

152nd Brigade will be responsible for liaison with Right (102) Infantry Bde. at SHEET Farm Q.1.d.9.3. and 160th Brigade with Left (103) Infantry Bde. at K.31.d.1.3.

6. Barrage tables and detailed instructions will be issued later.

7. ACKNOWLEDGE. (D.A. units only)

[signature]

Captain,
Brigade Major R.A.,
34th Divisional Artillery.

11th October 1918.

Copies to:-

96th Army Brigade. %
152nd Brigade R.F.A. %
160th Brigade R.F.A. %
34th D.A.C.
34th Division "G".
X Corps R.A. +
X Corps H.A. +
30th Divl. Arty.
41st Divl. Arty.
87th Bde. R.G.A.
101st Infantry Bde.
102nd ,, ,,
103rd ,, ,,

% Map "A" issued.
+ Map "A" issued with 34th Divn. Operation Ins.No.1.

App VIII

SECRET.

34th DIVISIONAL ARTILLERY OPERATION ORDER No.32.

October 11th 1918.

Reference 34th D.A. Operations Instructions No.1.

1. (a) On the night J - 3/J - 2 the 103rd Infantry Bde. will relieve the 101st Infantry Bde. on that portion of the front from Left Divisional boundary to the Pillbox at Q.10.a.22.70. exclusive, but its H.Qrs will remain at BASSEVILLE Cabaret until it moves to Advanced H.Q. at K.31.d.1.3.

(b) On the night J - 2/J - 1,

(i) The 102nd Infantry Bde. will relieve the 101st Infantry Bde. from the above Pillbox inclusive to Q.9.c.0.5., with H.Qrs at Q.1.d.9.3.

(ii) The 101st Infantry Bde. will be relieved on the remainder of its present front from Q.9.c.0.5. to the present Right Divisional boundary by the 30th Division.

(c) On completion, the Divisional and Inter-Brigade Boundaries will be as shown on Map "A" and the 152nd Brigade and 160th Brigade will cover the fronts of the right and left Infantry Bdes respectively and be responsible for the necessary liaison.

3. On the night J - 1/J, the 102nd and 103rd Infantry Bdes will straighten the line of their inner flanks so that the front line of posts runs from Q.10.a.0.3. to Q.4.c.00.95.

4. D.A. units ACKNOWLEDGE.

[signature]

Captain,
Brigade Major R.A.,
34th Divisional Artillery.

Copies to:- All recipients of 34th Div. Arty. Operations Instructions No.1.

App IX

SECRET.

34th DIVISIONAL ARTILLERY OPERATION ORDER No.32.

ADDENDUM No.1.

:-:-:-:-:-:-:

1. The relief of the portion of the 101st Infantry Bde. front from the present Southern Divisional boundary to Q.9.c.0.5. by the 90th Infantry Bde. will take place on the night October 11/12th instead of J - 2/J - 1 night as described in para.1.b. of 34th Divisional Artillery Operation Order No.32. The responsibility for the Artillery defence of this front will pass from the 34th Divisional Artillery to the 30th Divisional Artillery at 07.00 on October 12th.

2. The 103rd Infantry Bde. will relieve the 101st Infantry Bde. on that portion of the front from the Left Divisional boundary to the pillbox at Q.10.a.22.70.(excl.) on night October 11/12th.

The responsibility for the Artillery support of the 101st Infantry Bde. will be assumed by the 152nd Brigade R.F.A. and the 103rd Infantry Bde. by the 160th Brigade R.F.A. at 07.00 on October 12th.

3. The 102nd Infantry Bde. will relieve the 101st Infantry Bde. on the front from Q.10.a.22.70. to Q.9.c.0.5. on night October 12/13th.

4. D.A. units please ACKNOWLEDGE.

[signature]

Captain,
Brigade Major R.A.,
34th Divisional Artillery,

11th October 1918.

Copies to: All recipients of 34th D.A.,O.O.No.32.

App X

SECRET.

Reference Map: 1/20,000
Sheet 28 NE & SE.

34th DIVISIONAL ARTILLERY OPERATION INSTRUCTIONS No.2.

1. The order of battle for the attack is:-

Right Bde. 102nd. H.Q. Q.1.d.9.3.
Right Battn. 1/7th Cheshires H.Qrs Q.9.a.1.1.
Left ,, 1/4th ,, ,, Q.9.b.1.7.

Left Bde. 103rd. H.Qrs K.31.c.9.5.
Right Battn. Scottish Rifles H.Qrs Q.3.d.9.2.
Left ,, K.O.S.B. ,, Q.3.b.8.4.

2. F.O.Os should take every opportunity to get into touch with the battalions covered by their Brigades and in event of a forward move keep their Brigades informed as to where Battn. Hd.Qrs are.

3. If ground permits, it is a distinct advantage for F.O.Os to establish their O.Ps in close proximity to Battn. Hd.Qrs, in which case they should always inform the Battn. Hd.Qrs concerned as to where the O.P. is.

4. D.A. units please ACKNOWLEDGE.

[signature]

Captain,
Brigade Major R.A.,
34th Divisional Artillery.

12th October 1918.

Copies to: All recipients of 34th D.A., O.O. No. 35.

App XI

SECRET.

Reference Map: 1/20,000
Sheet 28 NE.
,, ,, SE.

34th DIVISIONAL ARTILLERY OPERATION ORDER No.33.

1. Reference 34th D.A. Operation Ins.No.1.
"J" Day will be October 14th, this is not to be communicated to the troops till the last possible moment.

2. The following batteries, if not already in their battle positions will move into those positions on the night 12/13th October, ready to take part in a gas bombardment on the evening of the 13th;- B/152, C/152, and C/160.
The remainder will occupy their battle positions ready to open fire by daybreak on October 14th.

3. Advanced wagon lines comprising gun limbers and F.B. wagons ready to move forward, will be established by Brigades within reach of their battle positions by H 90 on J day (152nd Bde in their present wagon lines).

Captain,
Brigade Major R.A.,
34th Divisional Artillery.

12th October 1918.

Copies to: All recipients of 34th D.A. Operation Ins.No.1.

SECRET.

App XII

34th DIVISIONAL ARTILLERY OPERATION ORDER No.34.

1. A Gas Bombardment with "BB"(Mustard Gas) shell will be carried out on October 13th, zero hour 19.00.

2. The following batteries of the D.A. will be employed:- B/152, C/152, c/160.

3. The detail of targets and allotment of ammunition is as follows;

B/152.

1.	Cross Roads COUCOU Village Q.17.d.8.6.	150	rounds.
2.	SCOUT FARM Q.23.b.3.4.	150	,,
3.	Houses Q.18.d.10.32.	200	,,
4.	SLUMBER FARM Q.22.d.9.8.	150	,,
5.	Houses Q.22.a.8.2.	100	,,
6.	Houses Q.24.a.1.7.	150	,,

C/152.

1.	RATHO Junction R.13.c.8.8.	150	rounds.
2.	Depot R.13.a.2.1.	200	,,
3.	RASCALS RETREAT R.13.c.6.1.	200	,,
4.	Cross Roads R.13.b.70.35.	100	,,
5.	MONGREL BRIDGE R.19.a.[illegible].6.	100	,,

C/160.

1.	Cross Roads R.13.b.3.6.	200	,,
2.	House R.13.a.7.8.	150.	,,
3.	MENIN Station yard R.7.d.3.0.	300	,,
4.	Cross Roads R.7.d.8.1.	200	,,

4. Targets may be engaged in any order, and it is left to the discretion of Brigade Commanders whether targets will be engaged by batteries in turn or two or more targets engaged simultaneously.

5. RATES OF FIRE.

Each target will be engaged by 2 minutes gun fire, followed by a slow rate of fire not exceeding 2 r.p.g.p.m. The full allotment of ammunition must be fired at each target.

6. Attention is drawn to the contents of S.S.217,. The attention of all ranks should be drawn to para.10, Precautions in handling BB Shell.

7. In the event of batteries not being in possession of this publication the shell ranges similarly to H.E. with 106 fuze.

8. The necessary amount of ammunition, viz:, B/152 900 rounds, C/152 750 rounds, and C/160 850 rounds, will arrive at the D.A.C. on the morning of October 12th., and must be got up to battle positions on the night of 12/13th. Staff Captain R.A., will issue the necessary instructions.

9. D.A. units please ACKNOWLEDGE.

[signature]

Captain,
Brigade Major R.A.,
34th Divisional Artillery.

12th October 1918.

Copies to: All recipients of 34th D.A. Operation Ins.No.1.

SECRET.

34th DIVISIONAL ARTILLERY OPERATION ORDER No.34.

1. A Gas Bombardment with "BB"(Mustard Gas) shell will be carried out on October 13th, zero hour 19.00.

2. The following batteries of the D.A. will be employed:- B/152, C/152, C/160.

3. The detail of targets and allotment of ammunition is as follows:

B/152.

1. Cross Roads COUCOU Village Q.17.d.8.6. 150 rounds.
2. SCOUT FARM Q.23.b.3.4. 150 "
3. Houses Q.18.d.10.35. 200 "
4. STIRRUP FARM Q.22.d.9.8. 150 "
5. Houses Q.[illegible] 100 "
6. Houses Q.24.a.1.7. 100 "

C/152.

1. RAILW Junction R.13.c.8.8. 150 rounds.
2. Dump R.13.[illegible] 200 "
3. RASCALS RETREAT R.13.c.6.4. 200 "
4. Cross Roads R.13.b.70.35. 100 "
5. [illegible] BRIDGE R.19.a.[illegible].6. 100 "

C/160.

1. Cross Roads R.13.b.3.6. 200 "
2. House R.13.a.7.8. 150. "
3. MENIN Station yard R.7.d.5.0. 300 "
4. Cross Roads R.7.d.8.1. 200 "

4. Targets may be engaged in any order, and it is left to the discretion of Brigade Commanders whether targets will be engaged by batteries in turn or two or more targets engaged simultaneously.

5. RATES OF FIRE.

Each target will be engaged by 3 minutes gas fire, followed by a slow rate of fire not exceeding 2 r.p.g.p.m. The full allotment of ammunition must be fired at each target.

6. Attention is drawn to the contents of S.S.417. The attention of all ranks should be drawn to para.10, Precautions in handling BB Shell.

7. In the event of batteries not being in possession of this publication the shell ranges similarly to H.E. with 106 fuze.

8. The necessary amount of ammunition, viz. B/152 900 rounds, C/152 750 rounds, and C/160 850 rounds, will arrive at the D.A.C. on the morning of October 12th., and must be got up to battle positions on the night of 12/13th. Staff Captain R.A., will issue the necessary instructions.

9. D.A. units please ACKNOWLEDGE.

Captain,
Brigade Major R.A.,
34th Divisional Artillery.

12th October 1918.

Copies to: All recipients of 34th D.A. Operation Ins.No.1.

SECRET.

Reference Maps, 1/20,000
Sheets 28 NE & SE.

App XIII

34th DIVISIONAL ARTILLERY OPERATION ORDER No.35.

1. Reference 34th Divisional Artillery Operation Instructions No.1. and Map "A".
The Objective Lines, Divisional Boundaries, and Infantry Starting Line will be modified in accordance with the attached X Corps Barrage Map.

2. The initial lift on the Xth Corps Barrage Map will be omitted on the 34th Divisional Front.
The barrage will come down at H - 3 on the second line shown on the Barrage map, lift off at H 2, and thence forward roll in accordance with the timing shown.

3. One battery in each Brigade will be superimposed on the whole Brigade Front, and will be available to answer GF and LL calls during the pauses. These calls will not be answered while the Infantry are actually advancing.

4. The line of the Railway marked in BLUE is the line of the Final Protective Barrage. Batteries will halt on this line when they arrive on it and continue firing until H 115, at which hour Brigades will conform to the lines shown on the Barrage Map except in the cases of (a) Counter Attack (b) Observed Fire (c) Orders from this office, but in all these cases fire must be kept strictly within the Divisional Boundaries as shown in Map "A".

5. RATES OF FIRE AND AMMUNITION.

	18-pdrs.	4.5 Hows.
H - 3 to H 4	Intense AX	Intense.
H 4 to H 28	Rapid AX	Rapid.
H 28 to H 40	Slow 50% A. 50% AX	Slow.
H 40 to H 47	Rapid AX	Rapid.
H 47 to H 73	Normal AX	Normal.
H 73 to H 83	Slow A where range permits.	Slow.
H 83 to H 115	Bursts of fire AX Average rate normal.	Bursts of Fire. Average Rate Normal.

6. SYNCHRONISATION
(a) An officer from 152nd Bde. R.F.A. will be at VORSTSTRAAT Cabaret at 16.30 on October 13th to synchronise with an Officer of the Divisional Staff.
(b) Officers from the 96th Bde. R.F.A. and 160th Bde. R.F.A. will attend at 160th Bde. H.Q. P.36.a.1.6. at 15.00 on October 13th to synchronise with an officer of 34th D.A.

7. D.A. units please ACKNOWLEDGE.

[signature]
Captain,
Brigade Major R.A.,
34th Divisional Artillery.

12th October 1918.

Copies to:

96th Bde.R.F.A. %	R.A. Signals.	53rd Squadron R.A.F.
152nd Bde.R.F.A.%	34th Div. "G".	No.25 Balloon.
160th Bde.R.F.A.%	87th Bde.R.G.A.	101st Infantry Bde.
34th D.A.C.	X Corps R.A.	102nd ,, ,,
D.T.M.O.	X Corps H.A.	103rd ,, ,,
S.C.R.A.	41st Div. Arty.	
R.O.R.A.	30th Div. Arty.	

% Receives 5 copies of Barrage Map.

App XIV

SECRET.

34th DIVISIONAL ARTILLERY OPERATION INSTRUCTIONS No.3.

1. The following Smoke Rifle Grenade Signals will be used.

BLUE SMOKE	-	WE ARE HERE.
RED SMOKE	-	WE ARE HELD UP.

2. The RED Smoke signal will not be used unless Artillery support is required.

3. Whenever the RED Smoke signal has been used a BLUE Smoke signal will be sent up immediately the resistance has been overcome.

[signature]
Captain,
Brigade Major R.A.,
34th Divisional Artillery.

12th October 1918.

Copies to: All recipients of 34th D.A., O.O. No.35.

App XV

SECRET.

G.S.583

101st Inf.Bde.
102nd " "
103rd " "
C.R.A.
C.R.E.
2/4th Somerset L.I.
34th Bn. M.G.Corps
Signal Coy. R.E.
"Q" Advanced
A.D.M.S.
O.C., "P" Coy. No.4 Spec.Coy. R.E.
O.C., "C" Coy. X Corps Cyclist Bn.
87th Brigade R.G.A.

---

1. Reference 34th Division Operations Order No.276, para 12, Z hour will be 0535 on October 14th.

2. Acknowledge by wire.

[signature] Major
for Lieut-Colonel, G.S.,
34th Division.

13-10-18.

App XVI

SECRET

34th DIVISION.

Copy No. 9

OPERATION INSTRUCTIONS No.1.

1. The advance of the Second Army will be resumed on "J" day (not earlier than 14th October).
The objective lines, Inter-Divisional and Brigade Boundaries and Infantry starting line are shown on the attached map."A".
The 34th Division will attack with the 30th Division on its right and the 41st Division on its left.

The advance will be divided into three phases :-

1st Phase to the BLACK LINE
2nd Phase to the BLUE Line.
3rd Phase to final objective, BROWN Line.

PLAN OF ATTACK.

A ARTILLERY.

2. 1st Phase.

(a) The Infantry advance will commence at H hour. At H-2 3 minutes the Field Artillery will put down a barrage on a line 300 yards in front of the starting line and will lift off that line at H plus 2 minutes. During the 4 5 minutes from H-2 minutes to H plus 2 minutes the leading troops of the Infantry will get as close as possible up to the barrage.

(b) The barrage will move forward at the rate of 100 yards in two minutes by lifts of 100 yards until it reaches a line 200 yards East of the BLACK Line at H plus 28 minutes when it will halt for 15 17 minutes.

(c) During this phase the Field Howitzers and Heavy Artillery will move ahead of the 18 pr barrage engaging all targets within their zones, resting at the end of the phase on a line 500 yards East of the BLACK Line, and continuing to engage targets East of that line.

3. 2nd Phase.

(a) At the end of the 15 minute pause (H plus 43 45 minutes) the creeping 18 pr barrage will move forward at the same rate as before until it reaches a line 250 yards East of the BLUE Line at H plus 173 minutes,* where it will remain for 15 minutes.

(b) The Field Howitzers and H.A. Barrage will move forward ahead of the 18 pr barrage as described in para.2 (c) until it reaches a line 500 yards East of the BLACK BLUE Line, when it will engage all targets East of that line.

4. 3rd Phase.

(a) At the end of the 15 minute pause East of the 2nd Objective (BLUE Line) a proportion of the Field Artillery will form a protective barrage covering the southern part of the objective which should be reached by Right Inf.Bde.and a portion of the Left Bde. during the 2nd Phase.

* See Footnote at end.

A proportion of the Heavy Artillery will engage targets East of the Field Artillery protective barrage line, paying particular attention to the exits from MENIN, within their zones.

(b) At the end of the 15 min. pause (H plus "90" mins) the remainder of the Field and Heavy Artillery will cover the advance of the Left Brigade to its final objective by engaging all targets in their respective zones. No fire will be brought West of the N. and S. grid line between R.1 and 2. and 7. and 8. after H plus "c" mins. At H plus "d" mins. the Field Artillery will form a protective barrage 250 yards beyond the final objective in their zone, and the Heavy Artillery will engage targets East of the protective barrage line, paying special attention to the exits from MENIN.

(c) At H plus "e" mins. the Field Artillery will cease fire and one Brigade Field Artillery will come under the orders of G.O.C. Left, 103rd, Brigade.

B. INFANTRY

5. (a) The Infantry Brigades detailed for the attack - 102nd on the Right, 103rd on the Left - will be in their assembly positions, leading troops on the starting line (see map) by H-2 hours.

(b) At this hour Battalions must be disposed in depth in their fighting formations, distance between echelons while in assembly positions to be reduced as much as possible.

(c) The attack will be carried out in three phases and it is left to the discretion of Brigades as to whether they pass troops through leading line (leapfrog) or not.

6. (a) As far as can be ascertained the defence of the area to be attacked consists of fortified farms and pill-boxes, and these conditions probably exist in the trench system of the TERHAND SWITCH. For this reason the Infantry should advance in small groups (vide I.G.Training Leaflet No.4) and not in successive lines. As far as possible one or more platoons or sections should be detailed for each known pill-box or fortified farm. (Those which are being engaged by Artillery are shown on the map).

(b) As, however, the advance will be carried out under a creeping barrage, it is essential that the leading troops should push straight on as close as possible to the barrage leaving the defensive posts to be cleared by the supporting echelons. The free use of smoke rifle grenades by the leading groups to mask the defensive posts will facilitate their advance.

(c) Throughout the advance the closest liaison possible must be kept by specially detailed parties in all echelons between the flanks of Brigades and with Flank Divisions. This does not mean that the advance is to be stopped because troops on flanks are held up. The principle of pushing on where resistance is least instead of reinforcing held-up troops must invariably be observed.

7. <u>1st Phase.</u>

(a) (i) The leading groups of the Infantry will close up to the initial barrage line and advance as close as possible under it, to the 1st objective, where they will halt for 15 minutes, H plus 28 mins. to H plus 43 mins.

(ii) During this pause troops must be reorganised into their proper formations. Troops detailed to clear defensive posts must rejoin their formations as soon as their task is completed.

(b) (i) No troops will advance under the barrage through GHELUWE Village, but the G.O.C. 103rd Brigade will detail special troops to deal with the Village as described below.

The Village will be smoked and engaged with Thermite shell from H-2 mins. till H plus 28 mins., by Special Coy. R.E.

(ii) The leading troops will pass North and South of the Village, none being within 100 yards of the line on the map marking the limits of the Village.

To do this troops of the 103rd Brigade moving south of the Village will move in the 102nd Brigade area where necessary. As they clear it the inner flanks of troops moving North and South of the Village will incline inwards and get in touch on the MENIN Road East of the Village.

(iii) Troops specially detailed to deal with the Village should advance with the 2nd or 3rd Echelon and clear the Village from North and South. This should be done thoroughly and as rapidly as possible and troops employed will rejoin their unit on completion of their task.

8. <u>2nd Phase.</u>

(a) The advance will be resumed at H plus 43 mins., the leading troops having previously closed up to the protective line, and will be continued to the 2nd Objective (BLUE Line) as before.

(b) On the front of the 102nd Brigade and on the right of the 103rd Brigade (i.e. from the Farm at Q.12.d.95.80 inclusive southwards to the MENIN Road) the 2nd Objective is also the final objective. The barrage in front of this portion of the line will remain 250 yards beyond it and troops as they arrive on the line will at once reorganise and consolidate the tactical points on the line. These should be selected beforehand if possible by Brigade and Battalion Commanders.

(c) On the remainder of the front of the 103rd Brigade troops on reaching the 2nd Objective will reorganise and prepare for the advance to the final objective.

9. <u>3rd Phase.</u>

(a) Troops which have already reached their objective, vide para. 8(b) will continue consolidation and reorganisation.

(b) The remainder will continue the advance at H plus "c" mins. pivoting on the right about the Farm mentioned in para. 8(b), to the final objective (BROWN Line). On arrival on this line the tactical points will be consolidated and troops re-organised. It should be pointed out to the troops engaged in this advance that there will be no continuous barrage line in front of them, but see para.4 (b).

10. Exploitation of Success.

The protective barrage will lift off the whole of of the whole line at H plus "e" mins. Strong patrols m be pushed out well to the front, at least to the line WE MENIN Rly and the Western exits of MENIN.

One patrol will be specially detailed to sieze the k about R.3.c.0.0. to cover the flank of the 41st Division, objective is the high ground about R.3.central.

11. In addition to the consolidation of the final objecti (BROWN Line), the line shown on the map in YELLOW is also consolidated as a support line of strong posts. This is taken in hand as early as possible. Specially detailed pa should be told off for this work.

12. The Reserve (101st) Brigade will remain in its area in state of constant readiness to move from H plus 60 mins. onw

The G.O.C. 101st Brigade will detail officers to keep h touch with the progress of the action.

The most probable use will be to relieve troops of the attacking Brigades during the night J/J plus 1 or J plus 1 J plus 2.

NOTE. - THE EXACT TIMINGS OF THE ABOVE LIFTS ARE LIABLE TO CH AND WILL THEREFORE BE NOTIFIED WHEN FINALLY SETTLED B STATING THE VALUE TO BE ALLOTTED TO THE SMALL LETTERS QUOTED.

R.C. Battye
Lieut-Colonel, G.S.,
34th Division.

Issued by D.R.
at 6 a.m. Oct.10th 1918.

DISTRIBUTION:-

Copies Nos.1 & 2 File.
3 & 4 War Diary.
5 G.O.C.
6 *101st Inf.Bde
7 *102nd " "
8 *103rd " "
9 *C.R.A.
10 C.R.E.
11 2/4th Somerset L.I.
12 *34th Bn.M.G.Corps
13 Signal Coy. R.E.
14 "Q" Adv
15 A.D.M.S.
16 O.C. "P" Section, No.4 Special Coy. R.E) To be
17 O.C. "C" Coy., X Corps Cyclist Battn.) handed over personally
18 X Corps H.A
19 53rd Squadron, R.A.F.
20 41st Division.
21 30th Division.
22-23 X Corps
24 87th Brigade, R.G.A.

* By Special D.R.

34th DIVISION

MAP "A" +TRACE A1

To accompany Operation Instructions
No. 1 dated 10.10.1918.

Infantry
Starting Line

Left Div. and
Corps boundary

Right Div. boundary.

1st Objective.

2nd "

Final "

Yellow Defensive
Line.

Limits of GHELUWE
Village.

TARGETS

URGENT OPERATIONS PRIORITY to * PRIORITY TO REMAINDER

*101 Bde
*102 "
*103 "
*30 Div
C.R.A.
34 Bn. M.G.C.
10 Corps
35 Div

App XXXII

G.28 19

O.O.284 AAA 30 Div will take over Divl.front and pass through 101 Bde at 0730 tomorrow AAA 101 Bde Group will then assemble in ROLLEGHEMKNOK Area (M.20.cent) AAA 102 Bde Group will reconnoitre approaches to BELLEGHEM Area and be prepared to move thence at one hour's notice any time after 0730 tomorrow AAA 103 Bde Group will be prepared to move at one hour's notice any time after 1000 tomorrow AAA "C" Coy 10 Corps Cyclists will come under orders of 30 Div from midnight tonight AAA Instructions will be communicated to G.O.C.101 Bde direct who will pass them on to "C" Coy AAA Acknowledge AAA Addsd Bdes C.R.A. M.G.Bn 10 Corps 30 & 35 Divs

FROM:- 34 Div
TIME:- 2245

Lieut-Colonel, G.S.

URGENT OPERATIONS PRIORITY TO 102 Bde

App XXXIII

101 Bde	C.R.A.	M.G.Bn.	Sig.Coy.	
102 "	C.R.E.	A.D.M.S.	10 Corps	41 Div
103 "	Som.L.I.	"Q"	30 Div	

G.108 22

Addendum No.1 to O.O. 285 AAA Adv.Div.H.Q. will close at LAUWE and open at BELLEGHEM at 1700 AAA H.Q.102 Bde will be opened in vicinity of square N.36.d. by 1200 AAA Area to which 102 Bde Group moves tomorrow morning will include square U.1. AAA Addsd 102 Bde. to ack /reptd all recipients of O.O.285

Lieut-Colonel, G.S.

FROM:- 34 Div
TIME:- 2245

CRA

App XXXIV

U.O.P. to 102nd Bde
PRIORITY to 10 Corps, 30 & 41 Divs, C.R.A.C.R.E., M.G.Bn
and 2/4 Som L.I.

101 Bde	C.R.E.	"Q"	41 Div
102 Bde	34 Bn M.G.Corps	Signal Coy	
103 Bde	2/4 Som L.I.	10 Corps	
C.R.A.	A.D.M.S.	30 Div	

G 103 22nd

O.O. 285 aaa With a/ view to relieving the Right (124th Bde) of the 41 Div tomorrow night Oct 23rd/24th on front U.18.a. to O.22.c. the 102nd Bde Group will move tomorrow morning to area N.36. and O.31. Move to be complete by 1200 aaa H.Q. 124th Bde N.29.c.3.7. aaa Adv Div H.Q. will move to BELLEGHEM tomorrow afternoon a aa Exact time and place will be notified later aaa Addsd 102 Bde to ackne reptd Cols W X and Y less 9

FROM:- 34th Div
TIME:- 1915

Lieut. Colonel, G.S.

"A" Form

Army Form C. 2121
(In pads of 100.)

MESSAGES AND SIGNALS.

No. of Message..............

Prefix.............. Code..............m | Words. | Charge.

Office of Origin and Service Instructions

Sent

At..................m.

To..................

By..................

This message is on a/c of:

.... *Service.*

(Signature of "Franking Officer.")

Recd. at..........m.

Date..........

From..........

By..........

APP XXXV

TO O.C. 152nd Bde RFA

Sender's Number.	Day of Month.	In reply to Number.	AAA
* BM 59	23		

152nd Bde will come into action tomorrow 23rd/24th night in the area U30 prepared to cover the line of the SCHELDT from BOSSUYT to AUTRYVE. Route BELLEGHEM LE CHAT CABT T5D32 N36d 53 O31c81. To be clear of T5b by 12.00.

96 Bde in action in U2a HQ at U8a [illegible]. DAC is moving tomorrow to N31 area. Line at present runs U12c U5d O34d O27a O22c O23a O17d.

[illegible signature]

From BM RA 34th Div.

Place N33d 59

Time 19.00

The above may be forwarded as now corrected. (Z)

....

Censor.

Signature of Addressor or person authorised to telegraph in his name.

* This line should be erased if not required.

(4715) Wt. W3253/P311 1,113,336 Shts. 2/18 C. & Co. (2634)

"A" Form

Army Form C. 2121 (In pads of 100.)

MESSAGES AND SIGNALS.

No. of Message..............

Prefix.............. Code..............m | Words. | Charge. | This message is on a/c of: .... Service. | Recd. at..........m.

Office of Origin and Service Instructions

Sent At..............m. To.............. By..............

(Signature of "Franking Officer.")

Date..............

From..............

By..............

TO OC BAC 96th Army Brigade RFA.

Sender's Number.	Day of Month.	In reply to Number.	AAA
* BM 58	23	APP XXXVI	

Locations	of 96 th	Bde	as under
HQ	8 U 3 a 5 1		
407 Bty	U 9 a 3 0		
408 Bty	U 9 a 9 9		
409 Bty	U 9 a 3 3		
410 Bty	U 9 a 0 7		
407 Bty	U 3 a 20.05 (detached section)		

Mounted training should be sent out as early as possible tomorrow morning to reconnoitre the routes to the above positions

From	BM	96th	DA
Place	N 33 b 5 0		
Time	18 00		

The above may be forwarded as now corrected. (Z)

....

Censor. Signature of Addressor or person authorised to telegraph in his name.

* This line should be erased if not required.

(4715) Wt. W3253/P511 1,113,336 Shts. 2/18 C. & Co. (2634)

SECRET OPERATIONS PRIORITY to -

PRIORITY to remainder

*10 Corps
*30 Div
*21 Div
102 Bde
103 "
C.R.A.

G.a.10 [illegible] 19

App XXXI

Situation at noon AAA Queens on line [illegible] [illegible] AAA [illegible] clear of enemy AAA In touch with 30 Div AAA [illegible] still in enemy's hands with M.Gs. and a section of 77 AAA Situation being dealt with AAA Added Corps & Flank Divs Reptd 102, 103 Bdes & C.R.A.

FROM:- 34 Div
TIME:- 1200

Lieut-Colonel, G.S.

S.135. 17/10/18.

App XXX

SECRET

TO BE ACKNOWLEDGED BY WIRE.

Copy No. 9

34th DIVISION OPERATION ORDER No.282.

Reference Map 1/40,000.Sheets 28 - 29. 17-10-1918.

1. 101st Inf.Bde. will relieve the 103rd Inf.Bde. and take over the whole Divl.front tonight, October 17/18th under arrangements to be made direct between B.G.Cs.

2. 103rd Inf.Bde. on relief will assemble in the area R.3, 4, 9, and 10, with H.Q. at RUMANIAN FARM (R.1.d.5.3.) and be in support ready to move at one hour's notice.

3. The two M.G.Coys. now in front will be attached to the 101st Inf.Bde The third Coy. now on wheels at 101st and 103rd Bde H.Q. will assemble on wheels in L.35.b. and be attached to the Support Bde.

4. The Divl.front will continue to be covered by 152nd and 160th F.A.Bdes. C.R.A. is arranging for O.C., 152nd F.A.Bde. to act as liaison officer with 101st Inf.Bde. for both F.A.Bdes.

5. (i) C.R.E. will attach 1 Field Coy. and 1 Coy. Pioneers to the 101st Inf.Bde. in place of the 2 R.E.Sections and 2 half Coys. now attached to Bdes in the line.

(ii) The C.R.E. will arrange for a Horse Transport Bridge to be constructed across the LYS near RUDDY FARM (R.17.b) as soon as possible and for the repair of craters on all main roads leading to the front.

[signature]

Lieut-Colonel, G.S.,
34th Division.

Issued by D.R. at 1820.

DISTRIBUTION:-

Copies Nos.		Copies Nos.	
1 & 2	File	11	2/4th Somerset L.I.
3 & 4	War Diary	12	*34th Bn.M.G.Corps
5	G.O.C.	13	Signal Coy.
6	*101st Inf.Bde.	14	A.D.M.S.
7	*102nd " "	15	"Q" Adv.
8	*103rd " "	16-17	*X Corps
9	C.R.A.	18	*30th Div
10	*C.R.E.	19	*35th Div.

Wired Priority:- 1730.

Paras.1 & 2 - X Corps, 30 & 35 Divs.
" 1 & 3 - 34th Bn.M.G.Corps
" 1 & 5 - C.R.E.

* Special D.R.

MESSAGES AND SIGNALS. 82 No. of Message..........

Prefix..........Code..........m.	Words	Charge.	This message is on a/c of:	Recd. at......m.
Office of Origin and Service Instructions	Sent		..........Service.	Date..........
~~Urgent~~	At ....m.			From ....
~~Operations~~	To ~~[illegible]~~			
~~Priority (Cld)~~	By		(Signature of "Franking Officer")	By..........

TO ~~10 Corps~~ ~~30 Div~~ ~~35 "~~ ~~103 Bde~~ CRA App XXIX

Sender's Number.	Day of Month.	In reply to Number.	AAA
G 1002	17		

Left Bde report our troops in LAUWE we have crossed the river at RUDDY FARM & patrol ~~at~~ in R.14.a.5.a AAA Coy HQ established at ROYAL FARM (R.17.b) AAA Civilian now at Bde HQ who crossed on raft at RUDDY FARM say enemy evacuated LAUWE at 0630 AAA RECKHAM reported clear but patrols not yet in at AAA Added [illegible] flank div 103 Bde CRA

From 34 Div
Place
Time 1150

The above may be forwarded as now corrected. (Z)

Censor. Signature of Addressor or person authorised to telegraph in his name

* This line should be erased if not required.

Order No. 1625 Wt. W3253/ P 511 27/2 H. & K., Ltd. (E. 2634)

"A" Form

Army Form C. 2121
(In pads of 100.)

MESSAGES AND SIGNALS.

No. of Message..........

Prefix..........Code..........m. | Words. | Charge.

Office of Origin and Service Instructions

Sent
At..........m.
To..........
By..........

This message is on a/c of:
..........Service.
....
(Signature of "Franking Officer.")

Recd. at..........m.
Date..........
From..........
By..........

TO 101 Bde. C.R.A.
102 "
103 "

Sender's Number.	Day of Month.	In reply to Number.	AAA
* G.711	16		

Report times 1000 states British troops reached M.4.a.5.0. - M.4.b.5.2. AAA Held up by M.G. fire from MARCUE and COURTRAI Right Bank of LYS also by M.G. fire from trench W. of M.10.b. M.11.a. M.5.d. AAA Two Coys. advancing from G.35.central AAA Our guns dealing with MARCUE and COURTRAI AAA Addsd 3 Bdes. C.R.A.

From 34 Div
Place
Time 1200

The above may be forwarded as now corrected. (Z)

....
Censor.

Signature of Addressee or person authorised to telegraph in his name. W. Hart [signature]

* This line should be erased if not required.

(7981) Wt. W.92/M1647 150,000 Pads 5/17 D. D. & L. E1187

101 Bde   103 Bde   34 Bn MGC
102 Bde   C.R.A.   2/4 Som L.I.

G 712   16th

Contact patrol reports 0715 column of troops and transport on road X.22.c. and d. going East aaa Enemy troops seen in LE BLANC FOUR RONCQ RECKEM aaa No movement in LINSELLES aaa LINSELLES Switch apparently empty aaa Our troops seen Q.33.a.5.5. going South aaa Patrol in W.3.b.3.3. going towards PAUL BUCQ at 0750 aaa Small party W.6.b.3.3. going South aaa M.G. fire from R.31.a.3.4. aaa Visibility poor

FROM:- 34th Div
TIME:- 1235

Lieut. Colonel, G.S.

"A" Form

Army Form C. 2121
(In pads of 100)

MESSAGES AND SIGNALS.

No. of Message..............

Prefix..........Code..........m. Words. Charge.

Office of Origin and Service Instructions

Sent

At..........m.

To..........

By..........

This message is on a/c of:

..........Service.

(Signature of "Franking Officer.")

Recd. at..........m.

Date..........

From..........

By..........

TO { 101, 102 & 103 Bdes C.R.A.

Sender's Number.	Day of Month.	In reply to Number.	AAA
* G.714	18		

Sectionsof Fld.Arty Battys will be placed at disposal of Infy.Bde.Cmdrs. to push forward with Inf.Battns. if desired AAA Addsd 3 Bdes. reptd C.R.A.

From

Place 34 Div

Time 1245

The above may be forwarded as now corrected. (Z)

Censor.

Signature of Addressor or person authorised to telegraph in his name.

* This line should be erased if not required.

(7081) Wt. W.92/M1647 130,000 Pads 5/17 D. D. & L. E1187

101 Bde 103 Bde M.G.Bn
102 Bde C.R.A.

G 716 16th

---

30 Div report aeroplane reports our troops on high ground W.6 and R.31 at 0700 aaa Since then no further ~~xxxx~~ report received

FROM:- 34th Div

TIME:- 1340

W. Scott Capt.

Lieut. Colonel, G.S.

Priority to 10 Corps

10 Corps	101 Bde	C.R.A.
35 Div	102 Bde	
30 Div	103 Bde	

G 725 16th

Line reported as the line of the LYS within Div boundary except R.15.c. and R.19.a. where posts have been established along right bank of river aaa In touch with 35 Div on left on the Eastern outskirts of WEVELGHEM aaa Exact points to be notified later

FROM:- 34th Div
TIME:- 1950

Lieut. Colonel, G.S.

URGENT OPERATIONS PRIORITY to * REMAINDER PRIORITY

*101 Bde 10 Corps
*103 "
C.R.A. 30 Div
C.R.E.

G.754 16

Addendum No.1 to O.O.281 AAA 30 Div will move eastward tomorrow pivoting on its left on the LYS about R.15. central AAA Troops of 103 Bde between MARATHON BRIDGE and R.16.c.8.0. should be withdrawn to reserve after left of 30 Div have passed East of that point AAA 101 Bde will endeavour to establish a bridgehead at LAUWE if it can be done without serious fighting a smoke screen should be put down on southern bank on both sides of selected point of passing of LYS AAA ack AAA Added 101 & 103 Bdes. reptd C.R.A. C.R.E. 10 Corps and 30 Div

S.134. 16/10/18.

FROM:- 34 Div
TIME:- 2155

Lieut-Colonel, G.S.

App. XXVIII

101 Bde	C.R.A	M.G.Bn.	A.D.M.S.
102 "	C.R.E.	"Q" Adv.	Sig.Coy.
103 "	Som.L.I.	"Q" Rear	Reception Camp.

G.707 16

Situation report AAA Bridgehead established S. of LYS near WERVICQ SUD AAA Enemy reported holding PAHU, BUCQ and BOUSBECQUE in strength AAA After heavy fighting yesterday during their advance 7000 yds troops pushed forward again last night to the banks of River LYS north of COURTRAI AAA One Division has established itself between HEULE and COURTRAI AAA CUERNE has been captured and also HEKTE after severe fighting AAA A bombing plane was caught in our searchlights and brought down by a direct hit from A.A. gun

G. Levy(?) Lt
for Lieut-Colonel, G.S.,
34th Division.

FROM:- 34 Div
TIME:- 1130

S.133. 16/10/18

App XXVII

SECRET.

TO BE ACKNOWLEDGED BY WIRE.

Copy No. 9

34th DIVISION OPERATION ORDER No.281.

Reference Sheets 28 & 29 1/40,000.

16-10-1918.

1 The enemy is still on the right bank of the LYS on the Divl. front.

2. Until further orders operations will be confined to establishing an out-post line south of the LYS, if this can be done without serious fighting, and to keeping touch with the enemy by means of patrols

3. (a) The outpost line to be secured is :-

REOKEM (inclusive to 30th Div) - HOOGPOORT (M.20.c) - KNOCK (M.21.b) - KLARENTHOEK (M.17.b).

(b) Patrols should be pushed out to the general line :-

CROISE (R.36.a) - PRESHOEK (M.26.a) - high ground in M.24.b.

(c) The main line of resistance is to be established along the left bank of the LYS with bridgeheads at all available crossings.

4. After relief by the 30th Div. today the 102nd Brigade and 96th Army Field Artv.Bde. will form the Divisional Reserve in readiness to move at an hour's notice. G.O.C. 102nd Brigade and O.C. 96th A.F.A. Bde. will maintain close liaison with one another (Inf.Bde H.Q.- K.36.a. - JOHNSTON'S FARM, - 96th A.F.A.Bde.H.Q. K.26.c.4.3)

5. 152nd R.F.A.Bde and 160th R.F.A.Bde. are placed at the disposal of G.Os.C. 101st and 103rd Brigades respectively.

6. The C.R.E. will arrange to place half the available bridging equipment at the disposal of G.Os.C. 101st and 103rd Brigades respectively. This equipment will be kept ready to move forward at short notice in localities to be selected by G.Os.C. 101st and 103rd Inf.Bdes.

7. Adv.Divl.H.Q. will close at O.6.a. at 1200 tomorrow, and reopen at the same time at ARTOISHOEK (K.30.c.central).

8 The Inter-Bde Boundary ordered in Addendum No.1 to O.O.279 will be continued to PRESHOEK (inclusive to 101st Inf.Bde.).

for Walter [illegible]
Lieut-Colonel, G.S.,
34th Division.

Issued by D.R. at 1815

DISTRIBUTION:-

Nos 1 & 2	File				
3 & 4	War Diary	12	*34 Bn.M.G.C.	20	Camp Commandant
5	G.O.C.	13	Sig.Coy.R.E.	21	"Q" Rear
6	*101st Bde	14	"Q" Adv.	22-23	*X Corps
7	*102nd "	15	A.D.M.S.	24	*30th Division
8	*103rd "	16	D.A.P.M.	25	*35th "
9	*C.R.A	17	Div.Train	26	41st "
10	*C.R.E.	18	S.S.O.	27	53rd Squadron R.A.F.
11	2/4 Som.L.I.	19	D.A.D.O.S.	28	87th Bde.R.G.A
29	6th Bde.R.G.A.	30	"C" Coy., X Corps Cyc.Bn		

* By Special D.R..

Urgent Operations Priority.

10 Corps   41 Div
30 Div   C.R.A.

G 672   15th

---

102 Bde report patrols have reached MONGREL Bridge R.19.a.3.5 LOCKS R.13.d.5.7 and R.14.c.7.0 MARATHON Bridge [illegible] and BRULEE Farm aaa All above bridges reported destroyed aaa MONGREL Bridge passable by single men aaa Enemy reported in ROOMY Wood R.13.d aaa 103 Bde report explosions continually occurring in MENIN believed to be mines aaa Crater 35 ft diameter on Road at R.2.c.5.4 aaa 2 Pontoons on opposite bank of LYS at MARATHON Bridge aaa HALLUIN in flames being set on fire at 0800 aaa Our troops fired on at R.20.a.6.9 aaa Two field guns observed firing N.W. from approx R.20.b.8.2 aaa No infantry seen

App XXV

FROM:- 34th Div
TIME:- 1330

Lieut. Colonel, G.S.

101 Bde   C.R.A.   2/4 Som L.I.   "Q" Adv
102 Bde   C.R.E.   A.D.M.S.   "Q" Rear
103 Bde   34 Bn MGC   Signal Coy

App XXVI

G 705   16th

Situation reported 0945 aaa Enemy has reoccupied HALLUIN and has M.Gs & T.Ms there aaa Our troops are on N bank of river except 1 Coy 103 Bde which is dug in South of MARATHON Bridge across bend of river aaa Our Arty are dealing with HALLUIN aaa WEVELGHEM reported clear of enemy at 0630

FROM:- 34th Div
TIME:- 1030

W. Stott Capt.
Lieut. Colonel, G.S.

S.132 15/10/18

APP XXIV

SECRET.

Copy No. 9

34th DIVISION OPERATION ORDER No.280.

October 15th 1918.

1. 102nd and 103rd Inf.Bdes. will send patrols across the LYS immediately to ascertain if the enemy has evacuated HALLUIN, and to send back word immediately if this is the case. If HALLUIN is found to be evacuated these patrols will at once be reinforced and a line of advanced posts established from LE MALPLAQUET Q.30.b. to Southern edge of HALLUIN in R.28.c. around the S.E. face of HALLUIN Town to the WEAVING MILL in R.27.a. thence along the line of stream to the LYS in R.22.a., thus forming a large bridgehead to cover the reconstruction of bridges South of MENIN.

2. The Inter-Brigade Boundary for the purpose of this operation will be :-

MARATHON Bridge (incl.to103rd Bde) - S. bank of LYS to R.20.b.0.7. - thence along N.E. face of HALLUIN Town to the WEAVING MILL and Bridge at R.27.a.7.2.

3. No general advance across the LYS is to be made without orders from Div.Hd.Qrs.

4. Acknowledge by wire.

Issued by wire at 1930.

Lieut-Colonel, G.S.,
34th Division.

DISTRIBUTION:-
Copies Nos.1 & 2 File
3 & 4 War Diary
5 G.O.C.
6 x 101st Inf.Bde.
7 =102nd " "
8 =103rd " "
9 C.R.A.
10 *34th Bn.M.G.Corps
11 *10 Corps
12 *30 Division
13 *41 Division.
14 x C.R.E.

URGENT OPERATIONS PRIORITY to =

PRIORITY to *

App XXIII

S.181. 15/10/18

SECRET

TO BE ACKNOWLEDGED BY WIRE

Copy No. 9

34th DIVISION OPERATION ORDER No.279.

Reference Map, Sheet 28 N.E. 1/20,000. — 15th October 1918.

1. (i) The 102nd Inf.Bde. will be relieved by the 90th Inf.Bde. of the 30th Div. (H.Q. till 1400 16th inst P.14.b.4.3) on night October 16/17th on the front from the present Right Div.Boundary to MARATHON Bridge (excl).

   (ii) All details to be arranged direct between Bde.Commanders concerned. Transfer of command to ~~21st~~ 90th Inf.Bde. and 30th Division on completion of Infantry relief.

   (iii) On completion of relief, 102nd Inf.Bde. will move to the area in K.35 and K.36., with H Q. at JOHNSTON'S FARM (K.36.a).
   All moves by half platoons at 100 yards interval by the most direct route.

2. (i) "A" Coy.34th Bn.M.G.Corps at present in position on the 102nd Inf.Bde. front will be relieved by a Coy. of the 30th Bn. M.G.Corps. Arrangements to be made direct between Os.C. M.G.Bns. concerned.

   (ii) "A" Coy., 34th Bn. M.G.Corps on relief will relieve "B" Coy. covering the 103rd Brigade front, which will be withdrawn to Divisional Reserve. All 3 M.G.Coys. in the line will then revert to the command of the O.C., 34th Bn.M.G.Corps.

3. The section of Field Coy.R.E. and half Coy Pioneers, at present attached to 102nd Bde., will be withdrawn and rejoin their units. Another Section of Field Coy.R.E. and half Coy. Pioneers will be attached to 101st Bde. to assist in the consolidation of the front and the opening up and repair of communications.

4. C.R.A. 34th Division is arranging direct with C.R.A. 30th Division for the relief of the Field Arty.Group covering the 102nd Brigade front by 0600 on October 18th in accordance with para.2 of Addendum No.2 to O.O.278.

5. Instructions regarding the move of No.3 Coy., 34th Divisional Train, the establishment of a new Refilling Point for the 102nd Brigade and the destination of first line transport will be notified separately by 34th Division "Q" Advanced.

6. On completion of this relief and of the relief described in O.O.278, the Divisional front will extend from MARATHON Bridge (incl) to Cross Roads at L.35.d.2.3.
   The Right Div.Boundary will run from MARATHON Bridge to stream at R.14.b.8.7., thence stream round N.& E. sides of MENIN up to the BRIDGE OF ASSES R.7.c.(incl to 34 Div) - JOB FARM (incl to 30 Div).
   The Left Div Boundary will run from L.35.d.2.3 - L.25.c.6.0., to K.29.central.
   Administrative Boundaries in rear will be notified later.

7. Adv.Div.H.Q. will remain as at present pending further orders.

Issued by D.R. at 1845.

Lieut-Colonel, G.S.
34th Division.

[illegible] on P.T.O.

DISTRIBUTION.

Copies Nos. 1 & 2 File.
3 & 4 War Diary.
5 G.O.C.
x 6 101st Infantry Brigade.
x 7 102nd Infantry Brigade.
x 8 103rd Infantry Brigade.
x 9 C.R.A.
x 10 C.R.E.
x 11 2/4th Somerset L.I. (Pioneers).
x 12 34th Bn. M.G. Corps.
13 Signal Coy. R.E.
14 "Q".
15 A.D.M.S.
16 D.A.P.M.
17 34th Div. Train.
x 18)
x 19) Xth Corps.
x 20 30th Division.
x 21 41st Division.
22 Xth Corps R.A.
23 53rd Squadron R.A.F.
24 'C' Coy. Xth Corps Cyclist Bn

Paras 1 - 3 and part of 4 Wired Priority to - 102nd Bde., 34th Bn. M.G.Corps & C.R.E., and 30th Division.

x By Special D.R.

SECRET.

TO BE ACKNOWLEDGED BY WIRE.

Copy No. 9

ADDENDUM No. 2 to 34th DIVISION OPERATION ORDER No. 278.

15th October, 1918.

1. In para. 6 for "1 M.G.Coy only" read "2 M.G. Coys".

2. Reference para. 5, the 41st Divisional Artillery will be covering the new front from R.2.d.4.7 Eastwards until 0600 on the 16th October at which hour the 34th Divisional Artillery will cover the new front.

The 30th Divisional Artillery are taking over the responsibility for covering that portion of the existing Divisional front from R.7.c.central to the Right Divisional boundary from 0600 on the 16th inst.

3. The 102nd Infantry Brigade will probably be relieved by the 21st Infantry Brigade of the 30th Division on the night 16/17th Oct.

[signature]

Lieut. Colonel, G.S.
34th Division.

Issued by D.R. at 1215

DISTRIBUTION. -

As per O.O. No. 278 minus Nos 11,16,17 and 22 to 25.
Wired Priority to 101 & 102 Bdes, M.G.Bn & C.R.A. at 1130
By Special D.R. to 103 Bde. Signal Coy., "Q" Adv,
A.D.M.S., 30th & 41st Divs & X Corps.

Addendum No.1 to O.O.278 sent to 101 & 102 Bdes only.

Urgent Operations Priority

101 Bde   C.R.A.
102 Bde
M.G.Bn

G 667   15th

Add No.2 to 34 Div O.O. 278 aaa In para. 6 for 1 M.G. Coy only read 2 M.G.Coys aaa Ref para. 5 aaa The 41 Div Arty will be covering the new front from R.2.d.4.7 Eastwards untill 0600 on the 16th Oct at which hour the 34th Div Arty will cover the new front aaa The 30th Div Arty are taking over the responsibility for covering that portion of the existing Div front from R.7.c.central to the Right Div boundary from 0600 on the 16th inst aaa The 102nd Bde will probably be relieved by the 21st Bde of the 30 Div on the night 16/17th Oct aaa ACKNOWLEDGE aaa Added 101 & 102 Bdes M.G.Bn & C.R.A.

S.130 15/10/18

FROM:- 34th Div

TIME:- 1130   Lieut. Colonel, G.S.

RO.3 14/10/18

App XXII

S E C R E T.

TO BE ACKNOWLEDGED BY WIRE.

Copy No. 9

34th DIVISION OPERATION ORDER No.278.

Reference Map 1/20,000 Sheet 28 N.E.

October 14th 1918.

1. The 101st Inf.Bde. will relieve the 124th Inf.Bde. of the 41st Division (H.Q.- L 31.b.0.7) on the night October 15/16th, on that portion of its present front from railway line in R.2.b. to the cross roads in L 35.d.2.3.

2. The 101st Inf.Bde.(less 2/4th R.W.Surrey Regt) will move at dawn tomorrow morning to the area K.35 and K.36 by the most direct route, establishing Bde.H.Q. at JOHNSTON'S FARM (K.36.a).

The 2/4th R.W.Surrey Regt. will rejoin the Brigade on relief by a Battalion of 30th Division some time tomorrow.

3. All details of relief to be arranged direct between Brigade Commanders.

Transfer of command to 101st Inf.Bde. and 34th Division on completion of relief.

4. On completion of relief the H.Q. of the 101st Inf.Bde. will be established at L.31.b.0.7.

5. The C.R.A. 34th Division will make the necessary adjustments of Artillery in consultation with the C.R.A. 41st Division so as to cover the new front with the Field Artillery at present at the disposal of the Division.

6. The O.C., 34th Bn. M.G.Corps will arrange for the relief of the two M.G.Coys. at present in position on the 124th Inf.Bde. front, using one M.G.Coy. only for the purpose.

All details will be arranged direct between the Machine Gun Battalion Commanders concerned.

7. Instructions for the move of No.2 Coy. 34th Div.Train and for the establishment of a new Brigade Refilling Point and destination of 1st Line Transport will be notified by 34th Division Adv."Q".

J Harris Major

for Lieut-Colonel, G.S.,
34th Division.

Issued by D.R. at 2045.

DISTRIBUTION:-

Copies Nos.		Nos.		Nos.	
1 & 2	File	10	C.R.E.	17	*Div.Train
3 & 4	War Diary	11	2/4 Som.L.I.	18-19	X Corps
5	G.O.C.	12	*34 Bn.M.G.C.	20	30 Division
6	*101 Bde.	13	Signal Coy.	21	*41 "
7	102 "	14	*"Q" Adv.	22	X Corps H.A.
8	103 "	15	A.D.M.S.	23	87th Bde. RGA
9	*C.R.A.	16	D.A.P.M.	24	53rd Sqn. RAF.
				25	"C" Coy., X Corps Cyc.Bn.

* By Special D.R.

Paras.1 & 6 telephoned to 101st Bde. & M.G.Bn. at 2000.

E. R.E. & PIONEERS.

10. The C.R.E. will arrange to place 1 Section of a Field Coy R.E., and half a Pioneer Coy at the disposal of each of the attacking Brigades to assist in the consolidation of :-

(a) The final objective.
(b) The YELLOW Line of Defence referred to in para. 11 of Operation Instructions No. 1.

11. The remainder of the R.E. and Pioneers of the Division will concentrate on the repair, maintenance and screening of the HOLLEBEKE - ZANDVOORDE - KRUISHECKE - ROSSIGNOL Cabaret (K.31.a) Road.

F. ROYAL AIR FORCE.

12. A contact patrol of 53rd Squadron R.A.F. will fly over the line at specified times.
This plane will be marked by two black rectangular flaps attached to or projecting from the lower plane on each side of the fuselage, and a trailing streamer on the rudder.

13. It is of the greatest importance that advance troops should be warned to show this plane their positions whenever called for. Red flares will be used and discs flashed.

14. Two Artillery Machines and a counter-attack patrol will be out from dawn onwards.

15. The Squadron will be prepared to drop ammunition if asked for by Battalions with a "V" panel.
So far as this Division is concerned the most suitable place would be :-

(i) The old landing ground in R.1.c. on the Left Brigade front.

(ii) Vicinity of QUANDARY Farm (Q.17.b.1.9) on the Right Brigade front.

16. The Squadron will also be prepared to drop pigeons if asked for by Battalions. The signal for this purpose will be four panels placed in a rectangle.

10th Oct. 1918.

Issued by D.R. at 2 p.m.

Lieut. Colonel, G.S.
34th Division.

DISTRIBUTION.

Copies Nos			
1 & 2	File.	15	A.D.M.S.
3 & 4	War Diary	16	* O.C."F" Sec. No.4 Special Coy. R.E.
5	G.O.C.	17	* O.C."C" Coy. X Corps Cyclist Bn.
6	101st Inf.Bde.	18	X Corps H.A.
7	102nd Inf.Bde.	19	53rd Squadron R.A.F.
8	103rd Inf.Bde.	20	41st Division.
9	C.R.A.	21	30th Division.
10	C.R.E.	22)	X Corps.
11	2/4th Som.L.I.	23)	
12	34 Bn M.G.C.	24	87th Bde. R.G.A.
13	Signal Coy R.E.		
14	"Q" Adv.		

* To be handed over personally.

S E C R E T.

App XVIII

34th DIVISIONAL ARTILLERY OPERATION ORDER No.36.

Reference 34th D.A. Operation Instructions No.1.

"H" hour will be ....05:35.......... 14th October.

G. F. Smyth

Captain,
Brigade Major R.A.,
34th Divisional Artillery.

13th October 1918.

Copies to: 152nd Bde. R.F.A. (5)
96th Bde. R.F.A. (5)
160th Bde. R.F.A. (5)
34th D.A.C. (1)

URGENT OPERATIONS PRIORITY TO *

101 Bde	*X Corps	34 Bn. M.G.C.	A.D.M.S.
102 "	*30 Div	2/4 Som.L.I.	
103 "	*41 Div	Sig.Coy.	
C.R.A.	87 Bde RGA	"Q" Rear	
C.R.E.	53 Sqn. RAF	"Q" Adv.	

APPX IX

G.624 24

Situation as reported by 0945 AAA Right Bde Right Battn. line runs COUCOU (incl) FLAMP FARM - QUERY FARM - Q.12.d.9.1.- Dump R.7.c.3.3.- JOB FARM AAA Left Bde. report 0920 two coys. Argylls went through on second objective and prisoners taken by them already coming in AAA . . . . AAA GHELUWE cleared of enemy AAA H.Q. 103 Bde moving to Q.4.c.0.8. Added Cols.W, X & Y & 53 Sqn RAF

FROM:- 34 Div
TIME:- 1000

[signature]
Lieut-Colonel, G.S.

App XX

URGENT OPERATIONS PRIORITY to *

*X Corps	101 Bde	C.R.A.	M.G.Bn	"Q" Adv
*30 Div	102 "	C.R.E.	Sig.Coy.	"Q" Rear
*41 Div	103 "	2/4 Som.L.I.	A.D.M.S.	Reception Camp.

G.649 14

Situation AAA Line Right Bde - Q.17.c.2.2.- in touch with DARU Q.17.c.4.4. - Q.17.c.8.8.- Q.17.b.0.0.- Q.17.b.9.1.- Q.18.a.3.3. (FLAME FARM) - GROUP FARMS AAA QUERY FARM reported occupied by enemy AAA Steps are being taken to occupy it AAA Line Left Bde - Q.12.d.7.2. - JOB FARM - R.7.a.1.9.- UNIFORM FARM - VAN AKKERS FARM AAA LEVY ordered to gain RUMANIAN FARM 1700 and ROUNDABOUT AAA Total prisoners 628 including 26 Offrs and 43 wounded AAA Added Cols.W, X & Y minus No.9

Stanley Maw

for Lieut-Colonel, G.S.

FROM:- 34 Div
TIME:- 1930

App XXI

SECRET.

TO BE ACKNOWLEDGED BY WIRE.

34th DIVISION OPERATION ORDER No.277.

Copy No. 9

October 14th 1918.

1. (a) The 102nd and 103rd Inf.Bdes. will tonight consolidate the positions won today in depth, forming a main line of resistance on the final objective, and a support line on the YELLOW Line.
An outpost system will be established covering the final objective.

(b) Patrols must be pushed well out to the front to keep touch with the enemy and advanced posts established to secure the Western exits of MENIN.
If MENIN is found to have been evacuated by the enemy, patrols will be pushed through to seize the river crossings South of the town between RASCAL'S RETREAT and MARATHON BRIDGE inclusive.

(c) Liaison posts will be established on the inner flanks of Brigades and with Divisions on the outer flanks.

(d) The G.O.C. 103rd Brigade will form a strong flank connecting his left with the right of the 41st Division on the ROUNDABOUT.

2. (a) The two Coys. 101st Bde. now at disposal of the G.O.C. 103rd Bde. will remain in their present position under his orders. The remaining Coys. and H.Q. of this same Battn. will move as soon as possible to a position of readiness in Q.1.d., and come under the orders of G.O.C. 102nd Brigade. An Officer of these Coys. to report himself to G.O.C. 102nd Brigade at his H.Q. (Q.9.a.10.10).

(b) The above troops of the 101st Brigade are not to be used to relieve the line or for patrols but are otherwise at the disposal of G.Os.C. 102nd and 103rd Brigades respectively.

(c) The remainder of the 101st Brigade will remain in their present position ready to move at an hour's notice.

3. G.Os.C. 102nd and 103rd Brigades will arrange their S.O.S. barrage lines with their supporting R.A.Group Commanders.
The remaining group R.F.A. will thicken the barrage under the orders of the C.R.A , who will also issue orders with regard to harassing fire to all three Brigades.

4. (a) G.Os.C. 102nd and 103rd Brigades will dispose the fire of the M.G.Coys. under their orders to thicken the Artillery barrage.

(b) The O.C. 34th Bn. M.G.Corps will lay down S.O.S. lines for the 2 Coys. now in the YELLOW Line.

Issued by D.R. at 1845.

Lieut-Colonel, G.S.,
34th Division.

P.T.O. for
Distribution.

DISTRIBUTION:-

Copies Nos. 1 & 2 File
3 & 4 War Diary
5 G.O.C.
6 *101st Inf.Bde.
7 *102nd " "
8 *103rd " "
9 *C.R.A.
10 C.R.E.
11 *34th Bn.M.G.Corps.
12 Signal Coy. R.E.
13 "Q" Advanced
14 "Q" Rear
15)
16)*X Corps
17 30th Division
18 41st Division
19 X Corps H.A.
20 87th Brigade R.G.A.

Para.1 telephoned to 102nd & 103rd Bdes., 1830
" 1 wired priority to 30th & 41st Divisions at 1830

Para.2 (b) wired priority to 101st Bde
102nd "

* By Special D.R.

G.S.624

S E C R E T.

34th DIVISIONAL ARTILLERY OPERATION ORDER No. 36.

Reference Maps. Sheets 28 SE & 29 SW.

1. 30th Division are advancing to the line STERHOEK - AELBEKE - M.23.d.8.8. 34th Division will continue this line to M.18.a.9.9. keeping clear of MARCKE. XIX Corps are endeavouring to secure MARCKE to-night.

2. 160th Bde. R.F.A. will commence to move across the R.LYS using the road via RIPE FARM R.16.a. and the pontoon bridge at R.16.d.9.3. coming into action in the area R.24.d. and M.19.c.&d., but keeping clear of LAUWE, covering the line M.23.d.8.8. to LES 3 ROIS Cabt. M.18.c.8.2.

3. 152nd Brigade R.F.A. will move forthwith to positions N of the R. LYS in M.7.d.& 8.c. to cover the line M.18.c.8.2. to M.18.a.9.9. Positions should be reconnoitred in M.15. to move to when MARCKE is in our hands; route via pontoon bridge at RUDDY Farm R.17.b.2.2., but batteries will not cross the river without orders from this office.

4. 6th R.G.A. Brigade will conform, but not to cross the R. LYS without orders from this office.

5. D.A. units please ACKNOWLEDGE.

Captain,
Brigade Major R.A.,
34th Divisional Artillery.

18th October 1918.

Copies to:-

96th (Army) Bde. RFA.
152nd Bde. RFA.
160th Bde. RFA.
34th D.A.C.
D.T.M.O.
S.C.R.A.
R.O.R.A.
No.1.Coy. Train.
6th Bde. RGA.
101st Infy.Bde.
102nd " "
103rd " "
34th Division "G".
30th Div. Arty.
41st Div. Arty.
Xth Corps R.A.
Xth Corps H.A.
XIXth Corps R.A.
53rd Squadron RAF.
25 Balloon Section.

App XVII

SECRET.

34th DIVISION.

Copy No. 9

OPERATION INSTRUCTIONS No. 2.

PLAN OF ATTACK (Continued)

C. MACHINE GUNS.

1. Three Machine Gun Companies of the 34th Bn. M. G. Corps will put down a barrage on areas "A", "B" and "C" shown on the attached Map "B" at H-2 minutes.
This barrage will cease firing at the following times :-

Area "A" - H plus 5 minutes.
" "B" - H plus 3 "
" "C" (GHELUWE Village) - H plus 15 minutes.

2. The fourth M.G. Company of this Battalion will be on pack in an assembly area to be arranged by O.C. 34th Bn. M.G. Corps with G.O.C. Right Brigade by H-2 hours, after which hour it will be attached to the Right Brigade in order to move forward and take up positions to cover the front of this Brigade after reaching its final objective.

3. Of the three M.G. Companies in the initial barrage one Company will be pulled out as soon as it ceases firing and be attached to the Left Brigade to move forward and take up positions to cover its front after reaching its final objective, special attention being paid to the exits from MENIN.

4. Of the two Companies attached to Brigades to cover the final objective, not more than one section of each Company must be attached to Battalions. The remainder must be kept intact for S.O.S. purposes.

5. The remaining two Companies in the initial barrage after ceasing fire will move forward and take up positions for the defence of the YELLOW Defence Line shown on Map "A", under the orders of the O.C. 34th Bn. M. G. Corps.

D. SPECIAL BRIGADE R.E.

6. "B" Section No. 4 Special Coy R.E. has been placed at the disposal of the Division for the purpose of smoking GHELUWE Village.

7. It will take up positions for two groups of approximately 3 mortars each at about Q.3.b.8.4 and Q.3.d.95.20., where they will be provided by the Infantry Brigade with accommodation for 6 men in each group under cover for fuze setting.

8. The mortars have a range of 900 yards and will fire smoke on the North, West and South faces of GHELUWE Village from H-2 minutes to about H plus 8 minutes, and Thermite from about H plus 8 minutes to H plus 28 minutes, and then cease fire.
The exact time of changing from smoke to thermite depends upon the strength and direction of the wind, and will be settled by the O.C. on the spot at the time.

9. If the wind is anywhere E. of S.S.W. and N.N.W., both inclusive, C.R.A. will arrange for Field Howitzers to assist in smoking the Eastern edge of the Village.

E. ...

Secret.

41st

Knoll referred to 112 p. 10. O.I. No 1.

30 Div

Gheluwe Landing Ground

Menin Aerodrome

MENIN

Halluin N.E. Aerodrome

HALLUIN

Halluin E. Aerodrome

Coucou Aerodrome

Reckem

Wijnberg

GHELUWE

WERVICQ

BLACK

Q R

Deleted

3 4 5 6 1 2

-Secrer-

9 10 11 12 7

15 16 17 18 13

Trace A1. to accompany MAP A.

Showing Targets referred to in Para 6 of Operation Instructions Nº1 of 10.10.18.

To Superimpose | Sheet 28. S.E.

Scale 1/20,000

NOTE.—(1). These traces are intended to facilitate the communication of information as to the position of targets, which have been located on a squared map.

(2). The squares on this trace are 500 yards in length on the 1/10,000 scale, 1,000 yards in length on the 1/20,000 scale, and 2,000 yards in length on the 1/40,000 scale.

(3). The squares on the trace are fitted to the squares of the map showing the targets, which are then drawn on the trace. Sufficient letters and numbers must also be added to enable the recipient to place the trace in the correct position on his own map. A little detail may also be traced, but this is not essential. The name and scale of the map to which the trace refers must be always given. The trace can be used for the 1/10,000, 1/20,000, or 1/40,000 scale.

G.S.G.S. 3023.

Tracing taken from Sheet..............................

of the 1:.................. *map of*..............................

Signature.............................. *Date*..................

-Secret-

MAP 'B' To accompany
Operation Instructions No 2.
d/ 10-10-18

36

J K

K

P Q

Q

6

Danger Zone
up to H+15

C
Cease fire at H+15

Danger Zone
up to H+8-

B.
Cease fire at H+8

Ref. SHEET 28 S.E.
1/20.000.

A.
Cease fire at H+8

NOTE.—(1). These traces are intended to facilitate the communication of information as to the position of targets, which have been located on a squared map.

(2). The squares on this trace are 500 yards in length on the 1/10,000 scale, 1,000 yards in length on the 1/20,000 scale, and 2,000 yards in length on the 1/40,000 scale.

(3). The squares on the trace are fitted to the squares of the map showing the targets, which are then drawn on the trace. Sufficient letters and numbers must also be added to enable the recipient to place the trace in the correct position on his own map. A little detail may also be traced, but this is not essential. The name and scale of the map to which the trace refers must be always given. The trace can be used for the 1/10,000, 1/20,000, or 1/40,000 scale.

G.S.G.S. 3023.

Tracing taken from Sheet..................................

of the 1:..................*map of*..................................

Signature..................................*Date*..................

59

App XXXVII

10 Corps   101 Bde   C.R.E.
41 Div   103 "   A.D.M.S.
30 "   C.R.A.   "Q" Rear

G.137   24

Situation 0800 AAA our line runs U.18.d.3.9.- U.12.c.3.5.- U.11.b.0.8.- U.6.central along road to O.28.a.7.0. AAA Advanced Posts at U.6.d.5.3.- U.18.c.7.5. - U.18.d.8.6. AAA 2 Coys. dug in 300 yds due West of tunnel in O.22. AAA Added all concerned

FROM:- 34 Div
TIME:- 10 35

Lieut-Colonel, G.S.

SECRET.

Ref: Map,
Sh. 29, 1/20,000

APP XXVIII

34th. DIVISIONAL ARTILLERY OPERATION ORDER No. 37.

1. The 34th. Division will attack in conjunction with the 41st. Division at an hour "H" on the day "J" to be notified later.
BOUNDARY. Between 34th. Division and 41st. Division.
KNOKKE - HOSKE road, thence a straight line to V.9.a.0.0.

2. Action of the Artillery. (a) 18-pdrs. will put down a standing barrage to cover the crossing of the COURTRAI-BOSSUYT canal at Lock No. 5 and Lock No. 3. For details vide Para. 3.
(b) 4.5" Hows. will put down a smoke screen to cover the crossing and the envelopement of MOEN from the East, vide Para. 4.

3. From H - 4 to H + 62. 18-pdrs of the 152nd. Bde. will barrage along the road from V.13.b.3.1 to V.7.a.5.0.
18-pdrs. of the 96th. Bde. A.F.A., will barrage along the road from V.7.a.5.0 to U.6.d.2.8.
From H + 62 to H + T (T equals time to be notified later).
18-pdrs of the 152nd. Bde., houses in V.7.d and V.8.c.
18-pdrs of the 96th. Bde., houses in V.7.b and V.8.a.

4. From H - 4 to H + 77. D/149 will fire smoke into the portion of MOEN Village South of the road running from U.6.a.0.5 to U.6.b.2.5.
D/160 will fire smoke into that portion of MOEN Village North of the road running from U.6.a to U.6.b.2.5.
Neither of these batteries will fire East of a line running through U.6.b.central and U.6.d.central.
From H + 62 to H + 92, D/160 will smoke Farm at P.31.d.8.2 with one howitzer.

From H - 4 to H + 62, D/152 will fire smoke as under:-
3 hows., distributed along road from V.7.c.9.0 to V.7.c.7.6.
3 Hows., distributed along road from V.7.a.0.6 to U.6.d.7.0.

From H + 62 until 41st. Division's creeping barrage comes on this line, D/152 will engage houses in the neighborhood of V.8.d.2.9 with H.E.

From H + 79 until 41st. Division's creep ing barrage arrives on this line, D/149 will engage houses in V.8.b; D/160 will engage farms at V.1.a.9.2 and V.2.c.4.2 with H.E.

---

5. Rates of Fire. 4.5" Hows. firing smoke, one salvo per battery every three minutes.
18-pdrs. H - 4 to H - 2, intense.
H - 2 to H, rapid.
H to H + 62, slow.
H + 62 to H + 66, intense.
H + 66 to STOP, slow.

4.5" Hows. firing H.E., H + 62 to H + 66, intense.
H + 66 to STOP, slow.

[signature]
Captain, R.A.,
Brigade-Major, R.A.
34th. Divisional Artillery.

24th. October, 1918.

Distribution:-
96th. Bde., A.F.A.,
152nd. Bde., R.F.A.,
160th. Bde., R.F.A.,
34th. D.A.C.,
S.C.R.A.,
34th. Divn., "G",
41st. D.A.,
X Corps, R.A.,
X Corps, H.A.

SECRET.

34th. DIVISIONAL ARTILLERY OPERATION ORDER No. 37;

ADDENDUM No. 1.

" J " Day will be October 25th

" H " Hour will be 09.04

Captain, R.A.
Brigade-Major,
34th. Divisional Artillery.

24th. October, 1918

S E C R E T

34th. DIVISIONAL ARTILLERY OPERATION ORDER No. 37;

ADDENDUM No. 2.

Reference Paras. 4 and 5 of O.O. No. 37:-

D/149 and D/160, in addition to firing one salvo of Smoke every three minutes into MOEN Village from H to H + 77, will also fire one salvo of H.E. every three minutes.

Captain, R.A.,
Brigade Major,
34th. Divisional Artillery.

24th. October, 1918.

S E C R E T.

34th DIVISIONAL ARTILLERY OPERATION ORDER No.37.

ADDENDUM No.3.

1. Two 18-pdr batteries of the 160th Brigade R.F.A. will put down a creeping barrage 200 yards beyond the Infantry Starting Line at H - 4 minutes and will commence to creep at H hour at the rate of 100 yards every two minutes dwelling for 5 minutes every 500 yards for the first 1,500 yards after which it will not halt till the PAUSE line is reached at H+79 (vide attached barrage tracing 2 copies forwarded to the 160th Brigade only).

2. The Infantry Starting Line of the 34th and 41st Divisions is the line 0.22. central 0.23.a.7.6. 0.23.a.85570. 0.23.a.95.95. 0.17.d.6.6. 0.18.c.35.80.

3. The boundaries of the barrage put down by the 160th Brigade will be

   Eastern A straight line from 0.22.b.500. to P.31.c.0.0.

   Western Along Canal from 0.22. central to 0.35.d.6.0.

4. On reaching the PAUSE Line at H+79 the 160th Brigade 18-pdr. batteries will lift on to MOEN Village and remain on it till H+96 when they will cease firing.

5. RATES OF FIRE.

H - 4 to H.	Intense.
H to H+10	Rapid.
H+10 to H+79	Slow.
H+79 to H+96	Normal.

6. D.A. units please ACKNOWLEDGE.

[signature]

Captain,
Brigade Major R.A.,
34th Divisional Artillery.

24th October 1918.

Copies to:- All recipients of 34th D.A. O.O. No.37.

SECRET.

AMENDMENT No. 2 to

34th. DIVISIONAL ARTILLERY OPERATION ORDER No. 37.

1. Para. 3, line 5, T = H + 140 mins.

2. Para. 4, line 7, delete "Farm at P.31.d.8.2." substitute V.1.a.8.2.

do. line 11, delete "Until 41st. Division's creeping barrage comes down," and substituto until H + 140 mins.

do. line 13, delete "41st. Division's creeping barrage," and substitute, "Until H + 140 mins.

3. Para. 5, line 7, for STOP substitute H + 140 mins.

do. line 9, do. do. do.

Captain, R.A.,
Brigade-Major,
34th. Divisional Artillery.

24th. October, 1918.

S E C R E T.

34th. DIVISIONAL ARTILLERY OPERATION ORDER No. 37.

AMENDMENT No. 1.

1. For H + 62 read H + 81 in -

   Para. 3, line 1,   Para. 5, line 3,
   ,, 5,   ,, 6,
   Para. 4, line 7,   ,, 8.
   ,, 8,
   ,, 11.

---

2. For H + 77, read H + 96 in para. 4, line 1 and line 13.

---

3. For H + 92 read H + 111 in para. 6, line 7.

---

4. For H + 66 read H + 85 in para. 8, lines 6, 7, 8 and 9.

Captain. R.A.,
Brigade-Major,
34th. Divisional Artillery.

24th. October, 1918.

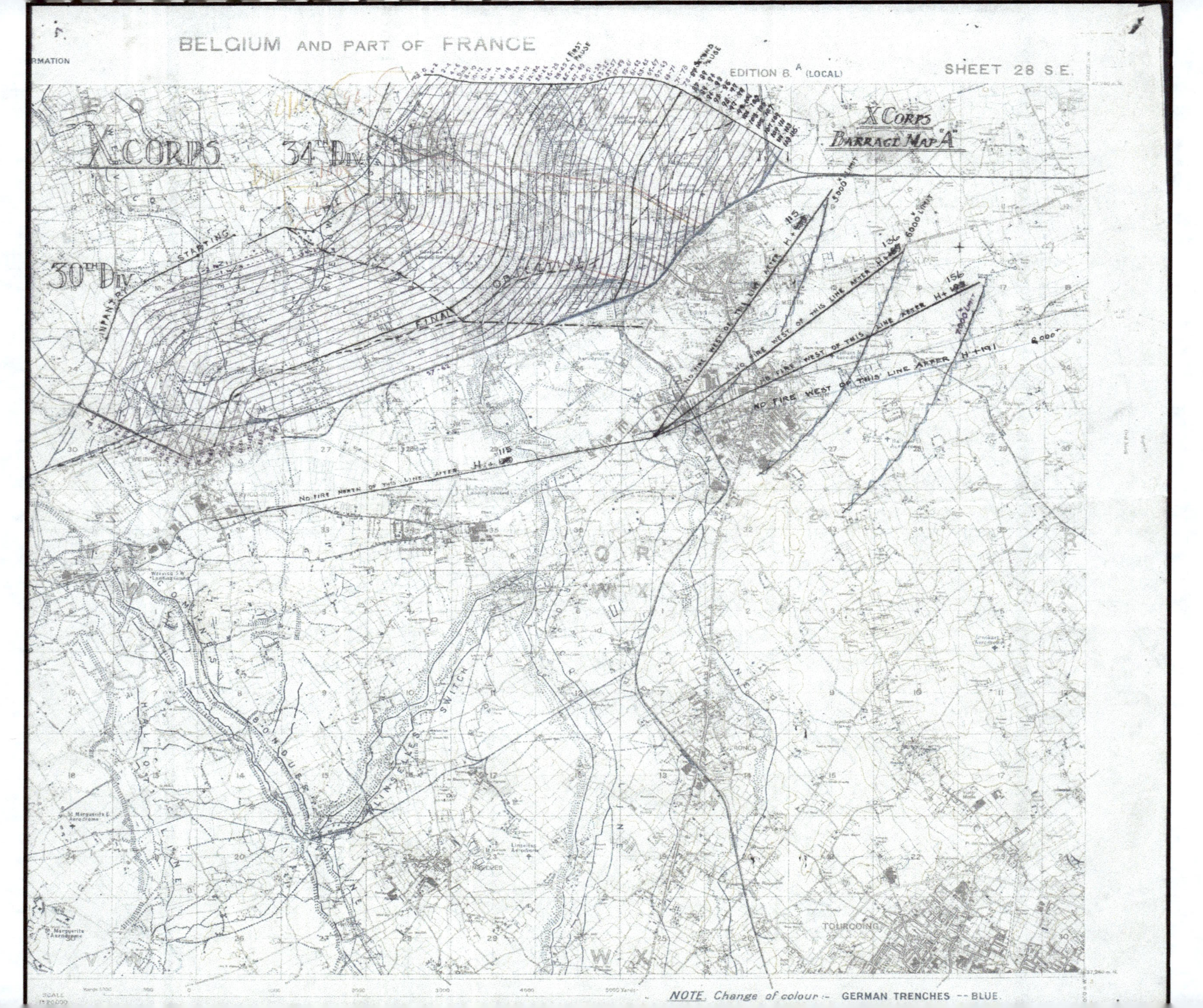
BELGIUM AND PART OF FRANCE
EDITION 8.A (LOCAL)
SHEET 28 S.E.
X CORPS
BARRAGE MAP "A"
X CORPS
34TH DIV.
30TH DIV.
INFANTRY STARTING
FINAL
NO FIRE NORTH OF THIS LINE AFTER H+115
NO FIRE WEST OF THIS LINE AFTER H+115
NO FIRE WEST OF THIS LINE AFTER H+136
NO FIRE WEST OF THIS LINE AFTER H+156
NO FIRE WEST OF THIS LINE AFTER H+191
5000 LIMIT
6000 LIMIT
COMINES
BONDUES
TOURCOING
SWITCH
NOTE. Change of colour :- GERMAN TRENCHES -- BLUE.

34th DIVISION. App XXXIX **SECRET.**

OPERATION INSTRUCTIONS No.1. Copy No. 9

"A" - MAIN ATTACK. 24-10-1918.

1. The left Divisional Boundary will be the KNOKKE - KEIBERG - HOSKE Road (exclusive) - V.1.central - V.9.a.0.0.

2. The 102nd Inf.Bde. will relieve troops of the 123rd Inf.Bde. (41st Div) on that portion of the front between O.22.central and the KNOKKE - KEIBERG - HOSKE Road exclusive as soon as possible after dusk this evening under arrangements to be made direct between B.Gs.C. concerned.

3. The Infantry starting line of the 34th and 41st Divisions is the line - O.22.central - O.23.a.7.6.- O.23.a.85.70.- O.23.a.95.95.- O.17.d.6.6.- O.18.c.35.80.

4. The attack will be made under a creeping barrage which will come down 200 yards beyond the above starting line at H - 4 mins.
The barrage will start creeping forward at H hour until it reaches the pause line - O.36.c.0.0.- P.31.c.0.0.- P.31.central - P.14.central at H plus 81 mins, pausing en route for an extra 5 mins every 500x. up to 1550x.

5. At H plus 83 mins. the barrage between O.36.c.0.0. and P.31.c.0.0. will cease and that on the remainder of the pause line at H plus 96 mins

6. The village of MOEN will be smoked by Field Howitzers from H - 4 mins. to H plus 96 mins, during which time the leading troops of the 102nd Inf.Bde. will pass between the village and the left Divisional Boundary and join hands with the other Battalion of the 102nd Inf.Bde. crossing Canal S. of MOEN.
At H plus mins the rear echelons of the attacking battalions will enter MOEN 96 from the N.E. and mop it up.

7. The creeping barrage for this attack is being put down by the 41st Divisional Artillery. The C.R.A. 34th Division will, however, arrange for 2 Batteries to thicken and extend the barrage in a S.W. direction so as to include the western bank of the Canal as far as O.35.d.8.0.

8. One and a half M.G.Coys will cover the main attack with a long range barrage as far as MOEN Village (exclusive) from positions in vicinity of South of HOOGSTRAATJE. This barrage must conform to the timings of the creeping barrage and cease fire entirely at H plus 81 mins.

"B" - SUBSIDIARY ATTACK.

1. One Battalion of the 102nd Inf.Bde. will cross the COURTRAI-BOSSUYT Canal at the most suitable points among the Locks 3, 4, and 5 under cover of smoke and Field Artillery barrage to be done by 34th Divisional Artillery on the MOEN-BOSSUYT Road at H-4 mins. and continued until H plus 81 mins. This barrage will be thickened so as to form a smoke screen round Locks 3, 4, and 5 so as to cover bridging operations.

2. As soon as the barrage lifts troops who have crossed the Canal at the above points will take a general line covering the crossings and will connect on the left with troops who have passed round the eastern face of MOEN.

P.T.O.

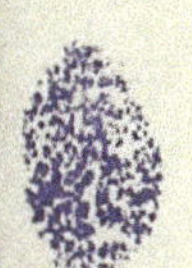

3. One M.G.Coy. will cover the subsidiary attack by putting down a long range barrage on the line of the railway cutting in V.1.c., Farm at V.1.a.8.2., and road through V.7.central from positions about BAVENGHEMKNOK. This barrage will cease fire at H plus 81 mins.

Half of a M.G.Coy. will be attached to 102nd Inf.Bde.

"C" CONTINUATION OF MAIN ATTACK.

1. The Infantry of the 41st Division are pausing on the above mentioned pause line (vide para."A" 4) until H plus 3 hours 21 mins.

2. At H plus 3 hours 19 mins (i.e. 2 mins. before the end of the pause) a barrage will come down on the pause line from P.31.c.0.0. northwards only and start to creep forward at H plus 3 hours 21 mins at the rate of 100 yds. in 2 mins. on the 41st Divl.Front only, until it reaches the line of the ESCAUT.

3. Troops of 102nd Inf.Bde. having joined hands in V.1.c. will pause on the general line - Eastern face of MOEN - V.1.central and MOEN - BOSSUYT Road facing East. At the end of the pause H plus 3 hours 21 mins the advance will be continued in a S.E. direction, the left flank being brought up so as to gain touch with the right of the 41st Division. The right flank will move along the BOSSUYT Canal.

4. During the pause the following villages will be kept under fire which will lift off them at times which will synchronise with the lifts of the barrage on the 41st Divl.Front:-

MARAILLESTRAAT, HEESTERTSTRAAT, AUTRYVE.

The Village of BOSSUYT, East of the Canal, will not be fired on unless called for by G.O.C. 102nd Inf.Bde.

5. Heavy Artillery will bombard the line of the L'ESPINOIS - ESCANAFFLES Road from H plus 81 mins.onwards.

ACKNOWLEDGE by wire.

Lieut-Colonel, G.S.,
34th Division.

Issued by Special D.R. at 1930.

DISTRIBUTION:-

Copies Nos.		Copies Nos.	
1 & 2	File	12	34th Bn.M.G.Corps
3 & 4	War Diary	13	Signal Coy.R.E.
5	G.O.C.	14	"Q"
6	101st Inf.Bde	15	A.D.M.S.
7	102nd " "	16-17	X Corps
8	103rd " "	18	30th Division
9	C.R.A.	19	41st Division
10	C.R.E.	20	X Corps H.A.
11	2/4th Somerset L.I.	21	53rd Squadron, R.A.F.
		22	35th Division.

S140
24/10/18

S E C R E T.
APP XXXX

TO BE ACKNOWLEDGED BY WIRE.

Copy No. 9

34th DIVISION OPERATION ORDER No. 289.

24th October, 1918.

Ref: Sheet 29, 1/40,000.

1. (a) The IInd and XIXth Corps and 34th Division will attack the enemy tomorrow with the object of gaining the line of the ESCAUT.

(b) The objective of the 34th Division is the River between BOSSUYT (U.24.b.) to AUTRYVE (V.9.c), both inclusive.

(c) The 41st Division will attack on the left of the 34th Division. On the right, the 30th Division will maintain their present positions on the ESCAUT, left at BOSSUYT, exclusive.

2. (a) The attack of the 34th Division will be carried out by the 102nd Infantry Brigade, 96th A.F.A. Brigade, 152nd and 160th F.A. Brigades, and 34th Bn. M.G. Corps (less 1 Comp any).

(b) Remainder of 103rd Brigade Group will be in support about BELLEGHEM BOSCH (T.5.a.); remainder of 101st Brigade in reserve about ROLIEGHEMKNOK.

3. (a) The attack will be carried out in accordance with the attached Instructions, the main attack being made from the North in conjunction with the 41st Division, a subsidiary attack being made from S.W. to N.E., South of MOEN, with the object of securing the crossing over the BOSSUYT Canal and thence hampering the retreat of the enemy East of the Canal.

(b) The main attack will be made under a creeping barrage at the rate of 100 yards in two minutes.

The subsidiary attack will commence under a smoke screen and will be covered by a standing barrage on the line of the MOEN - BOSSUYT Road.

Machine Guns will co-operate in both attacks.

The three Artillery Brigades and 34th Bn. M.G. Corps will be under Divisional control.

4. The Advanced Dressing Station is established in BELLEGHEM (N.27.c.8.3).

Main Dressing Station at M.29.d.3.4 in AELBEKE.

Car Collecting Post at T.5.b.2.6.

5. P.O.W. Cage will be in BELLEGHEM. P.O.W. should be conducted to the Church in BELLEGHEM where the Traffic Control will direct them to the Cage.

6. A Contact Patrol aeroplane will fly over the line at 1000, 1130 and 1300 hours and flares and discs flashed in reply to calls from the plane.

7. Advanced Divisional Headquarters will remain at BELLEGHEM.

8. "Z" Hour will be ~~0900~~ hours October 25th.
0904.

J. Hasler Major
for Lieut. Colonel, G.
34th Division.

Issued by Special D.R. at ~~1830~~ 1930

~~DISTR~~ Distribution P.T.O.

D I S T R I B U T I O N.

Copy Nos. 1 & 2	File.
3 & 4	War Diary.
5	G.O.C.
6	101st Infantry Brigade.
7	102nd Infantry Brigade.
8	103rd Infantry Brigade.
9	C. R.A.
10	C.R.E.
11	2/4th Somerset L.I.
12	34th Bn. M.G.Corps.
13	Signal Coy. R.E.
14	"Q".
15	A.D.M.S.
16) 17)	Xth Corps.
18	30th Division.
19	41st Division.
20	Xth Corps H.A.
21	53rd Squadron R.A.F.
22	35th Division.

PRESENT LINE OF POSTS BEING WITHDRAWN

BLUE LINE 1ST OBJECTIVE
RED LINE PAUSE LINE

190
119
11
187
18
23
24
29
30
31
33
35
6
O
P
U
V
Moen
Canal
STOP

-4 to H
H to +2
2-4
4-6
6-8
8-10
10-17
17-19
19-21
21-23
23-25
25-32
32-34
34-36
36-38
38-40
40-47
47-49
49-51
51-53
53-55
55-57
57-59
59-61
61-63
63-65
65-67
67-69
69-71
71-73
73-75
75-77
77-79

81-91
199-201
201-203
203-205
205-207
207-209
209-211
211-213
213-215
215-217
217-219

Pause Line 57-91

211-213
213-215
215-217
217-219 = 12.43

1457 9.0.Da

146

ARMY YCD 25.X.18 R TELEGRAPHS

App XXXXI

~~102 Bde~~ C.R.A.

G 175 25th

Contact patrol over line from 0945 to 1045 report 1030 our troops seen at O.30.d.5.2 - U.6.a.1.9 to O.36.c.7.0 in O.36.a. and O.35.b. and d. - U.12.c.5.8 to U.12.b.2.6 aaa Hostile M.G. fire from P.25.c. and V.7.a. aaa Enemy infantry retiring along road P.31.b to P.32.b.2.8 aaa Visib bad

FROM:- 34 Div
TIME:- 1445

Lieut. Colonel, G.S.

SECRET.

TO BE ACKNOWLEDGED BY WIRE.

App XXXXII
Copy No.

ADDENDUM No. 1 TO 34th DIVISION OPERATION ORDER No. 290.

26th October, 1918.

The Brigade Groups referred to in para. 1 will be constituted as follows for the purpose of this move -

(i) 101st Brigade Group.

101st Infantry Brigade.
160th Brigade R.F.A.
209th Field Coy. R.E.
"D" Coy. 34th Bn. M. G. Corps.
"A" Coy. 2/4th Somerset L.I. (Pioneers).
Detachment 104th Field Ambulance.
No. 2 Coy. 34th Divisional Train.

(ii) 102nd Brigade Group.

102nd Infantry Brigade.
208th Field Coy. R.E.
"B" Coy. 34th Bn. M. G. Corps.
"C" Coy. 2/4th Somerset L.I. (Pioneers).
Detachment 103rd Fie-ld Ambulance.
No. 3 Coy. Divisional Train.

(iii) 103rd Brigade Group.

103rd Infantry Brigade.
152nd Brigade R.F.A.
207th Field Coy. R.E.
"C" Coy. 34th Bn. M. G. Corps.
"B" Coy. 2/4th Somerset L.I. (Pioneers).
Detachment 102nd Field Ambulance.
No. 4 Coy. 34th Divisional Train.

Pod. Datye.

Lieut. Colonel, G.S.
34th Division.

Issued by D.R. at 1145.

DISTRIBUTION.

Copy Nos.	1 & 2	File.
	3 & 4	War Diary.
	5	G.O.C.
	6	101st Inf.Bde.
x	7	102nd Inf.Bde.
x	8	103rd Inf.Bde.
	9	C.R.A.
	10	C.R.E.
	11	2/4th Som.L.I.
	12	34th Bn.M.G.Corps.
	13	Signal Coy.
	14	"Q" Adv.
x	15	"Q" Rear.
x	16	A.D.M.S.
x	17	D.A.P.M.
x	18	Div.Train.
x	19	S.S.O.
x	20	D.A.D.O.S.
x	21	Camp Commandant.
	22	36th Division.
	23 & 24	Xth Corps.
	25 & 26	IInd Corps.

x By Special D.R.

Ro.

SECRET

Reference Map,
Sheet 29, 1/40,000.

App XXXXIIII

34th. DIVISIONAL ARTILLERY OPERATION ORDER No. 38.

1. The 34th. Division will be relieved on its present front by the 30th. Division, on the night of October 26th./27th., and will move by Brigade Groups into the IInd. Corps Area, and take over the front at present held by the 36th. Division.

2. The 102nd. Infantry Brigade will be relieved by the 21st. Infantry Brigade of the 30th. Division on the night of October 26th./27th.

3. The 96th. (Army) F.A. Brigade will remain in action in its present positions, and will come under the orders of the 30th. Division on completion of Infantry relief.

4. The 152nd. F.A. Brigade will move under the orders of the G.O.C. 103rd. Infantry Brigade to the AELBEKE area during the afternoon of October 26th.

5. The 160th. F.A. Brigade will move under the orders of the G.O.C. 101st. Infantry Brigade to the OYGHEM area on the morning of the 26th. October.

6. 34th. D.A. Units please ACKNOWLEDGE.

[signature]
Captain, R.A.,
Brigade-Major,
34th. Divisional Artillery.

26th. October, 1918.

Distribution:-
96th. Bde.,
152nd. Bde.,
160th. Bde.,
34th. D.A.C.
S.C.R.A.,
No.1 Coy. Train,
101 Infantry Bde.,
102 Infantry Bde.,
103 Infantry Bde.,
34th. Divn. "G",
30th. D.A.,
41st. D.A.,
Xth. Corps, R.A.,
Xth. Corps, H.A.,
File.

SECRET.

TO BE ACKNOWLEDGED BY WIRE. Copy No. 9

ADDENDUM No. 2 to 34th DIVISION OPERATION ORDER No.290.

Ref: Map 1/40,000,
Sheet 29.

27th October, 1918.

1. The moves shown in Table "A" attached will take place on October 28th.

2. 2nd and 3rd Echelons of Divisional Headquarters, Headquarters and No. 1 Coy. 34th Divisional Train, will move to DESSELGHEM Area on October 29th, via the route shown in Table "A", for Serial No. 3, under instructions to be issued later.

3. Field Ambulances will move to the new area in relief of Field Ambulances of the 36th Division under arrangements to be made between A.Ds.M.S. concerned.

4. Advanced Divisional Headquarters will close at LAUWE and open in the DESSELGHEM Area at 1100 October 28th at a place to be notified later.

Lieut. Colonel, G.S.
34th Division.

Issued by D.R. at 0915

DISTRIBUTION.

Copies Nos.	
1 & 2	File.
3 & 4	War Diary.
5	G.O.C.
6	101st Infantry Brigade.
7	102nd Infantry Brigade.
8	103rd Infantry Brigade.
9	C.R.A.
10	C.R.E.
11	2/4th Somerset L.I. (Pioneers).
12	34th Bn. M. G. Corps.
13	Signal Coy. R.E.
14	"Q"
15	A.D.M.S.
16	D.A.P.M.
17	Div. Train.
18	S.S.O.
19	D.A.D.O.S.
20	Camp Commandant.
21	D.G.O.
22	D.A.D.V.S.
23	44th Mob. Vet. Sec.
24	34th M.T. Coy.
25 & 26	Xth Corps.
27 & 28	IInd Corps.
29	36th Division.

SECRET.

TABLE "A".

Serial No.	Unit	From	To.	Route		Times during which column will pass COURTRAI Rly Stn.	
Col.No	1	2	3	4		5	
						Head	Tail
1.	Adv.Div.H.Q.	- Instructions will be issued separately -					
2	102 Bde.Group	STE.ANNE	DESSELGHEM Area - Exact locations will be notified later	POTTLEBERG or WALLE	Thence COURTRAI Rly.Stn. - LOCK No.9 (H.27.d) - STACEGHEM - HARLEBEKE.	-	0945
3.	34th Bn.M.G.C. less 3 Coys.	BELLEGHEM		KNOCK-WALLE		0945	0955
4.	D.A.C. and X & Y T.M.Btys	N.28.d.		" "		0955	1015
5.	S.A.A.Section D.A.C.	N.25.d.8.1.		" "		1015	1020

App XXXXV

SECRET

Reference Map:
Sheet 29, 1/40,000.

34th. DIVISIONAL ARTILLERY LOCATION STATEMENT No. 5 (Forecast).

H.Q., 34th. Divisional Artillery, I.3.a.5.9.

H.Q., 152nd. Brigade, R.F.A., I.12.d.9.9.
- A/152, ... I.12.c.5.4
- B/152, ... I.17.b.9.9
- C/152 ... I.18.c.0.8
- D/152, ... J.7.d.7.9.

H.Q. 160th. Brigade, R.F.A., J.19.a.7.3.
- A/160, ... J.25.b.4.6
- B/160, ... J.19.b.2.4
- C/160, ... J.19.c.8.1.
- D/160, ... J.19.a.8.9.

H.Q., 34th. D.A.C., ... C.25.b.9.7.
- No. 1 Section, I.2.a.0.5
- No. 2 Section, C.26.b.7.5

34th. A.R.P., ... C.26.central.

[signature]

Captain, R.A.,
Brigade-Major,
34th. Divisional Artillery.

26th. October, 1918.

Distribution:-

152 Bde. RFA,	103 Infy. Bde.,
160 Bde., RFA,	34th. Div. "G",
35th. D.A.C.,	No. 1 Coy Train,
D.T.M.O.	S.C.R.A.,
101 Infy. Bde.,	R.A., IInd. Corps,
102 Infy. Bde.,	H.A., IInd. Corps.

General Staff
34th Division

RECORD OF VERBAL MESSAGES

By - Telephone
Interview

FROM 103 Bde TO G

Date 26/10/18 Time 16/30

Brigadier would like to pass Courtrai Station between 1030 and 1330 and halt between Courtrai and Desselghem not entering Desselghem before 1700

Signed ....

Reference Map:
Sheet 29, 1/40,000

SECRET

APP XXXXVI

34th. DIVISIONAL ARTILLERY OPERATION ORDER No. 39.

1. The 152nd. Bde., R.F.A., will relieve the 173rd. Bde., R.F.A., to-morrow, October 27th. Orders as to times and routes will be issued by the 103rd. Brigade Group.

Locations of the 173rd. Brigade are as under:-

H.Qrs.,	I.12.d.9.9.
A Battery,	I.12.c.5.4.
B Battery,	I.17.b.9.9.
C Battery,	I.18.c.0.8.
D Battery,	J.7.d.7.9.

2. Command will pass on completion of relief.

3. O.C., 152nd. Brigade, will get into touch with C.R.A., 36th. Divn. head-quarters at I.3.a.5.9., as early as possible.

4. 34th. D.A., H.Qrs. will close at BELLEGHEM at 10 a.m. on the morning of October 27th., open at LAUWE at 12 noon; close at 10 a.m. on October 28th., and open at I.3.a.5.0 at 11 o'clock.

5. 34th. D.A.C. will remain in its present positions till the morning of October 28th, when it will move to area vacated by the 36th. D.A.C. Times of marching and route to be followed will be notified later.

Locations of 36th. D.A.C.:-

H.Qrs.,	C.26.b.9.7
No. 1 Section,	I.2.a.0.5
No. 2 Section,	C.26.b.7.5
A.R.P., ...	C.26.central.

An Officer will be sent over to-morrow, October 27th., to take over 36th. Divisional A.R.P.

6. 34th. D.A. please ACKNOWLEDGE by wire.

Captain, R.A.,
Brigade-Major,
34th. Divisional Artillery.

26th. October, 1918.

Distribution:-
152nd. Bde., R.F.A., } By special
103rd. Infantry Bde. } D.R.
34th. Divn., "G",
No. 1 Coy. Train,
160th. Bde. R.F.A.,
34th. D.A.C.

30th. D.A.,
41st. D.A.,
36th. D.A.,
Xth. Corps, R.A.,
IInd. Corps, R.A.

a/438

App XXXXVII

SECRET.

34th. DIVISIONAL ARTILLERY OPERATION ORDER NO. 41.

Batteries will move into their battle positions by the evening of Oct.30th ready to fire on the morning of October 31st.

All echelons will be kept full and 300 rounds per gun and howitzer dumped at battle positions.

Included in these dumps will be 200 rounds per battery A Smoke, and 250 rounds per battery B Smoke.

Captain,
Brigade Major R.A.,
34th Divisional Artillery.

29th October 1918.

Distribution.

51st Brigade R.F.A.
118th Brigade R.F.A.
152nd Brigade R.F.A.
160th Brigade R.F.A.
C.C.R.A.

APP XXXXVIII

SECRET.

Ref.Map:- Sheet 29, 1/40,000.

34th DIVISIONAL ARTILLERY INSTRUCTION No.1.

ATTACK.

1. The 34th Division will attack at an hour H on a day J to be notified later, in conjunction with the 164th French Division on the left and the 31st Division on the right.

The 34th Division will be the left Division of the II Corps.

The attack will be carried out by the 103rd Infantry Bde on a two battalion front with one battalion in reserve the 101st Infantry Bde. will be in support and the 102nd Infantry Bde. in reserve.

BOUNDARIES.

2. The Northern Divisional Boundary runs K.32.a.8.0., K.26.c.2.0., K.25. central, J.24.d.0.0., J.24.c.0.6., J.23.a.0.4., J.21.a.2.7., I.18.c.0.0., thence following present boundary.

The Southern Divisional Boundary runs K.32.a.3.0., J.34.c.4.0., thence following present boundary.

FORMING UP LINE.

3. The infantry will form up for the attack on the following line, J.16.d.7.1., J.22.b.3.5., J.22.d.6.5., J.28.b.8.6., J.29.a.0.0. J.29.c.3.7., J.35.a.2.2., J.34.d.2.6., P.4.b.9.6.

OBJECTIVE.

4. The final objective for the 34th Division will be the following line, K.25.a.1.5., K.25.c.0.8., J.30.c.7.1., J.36.c.5.0.

FIELD ARTILLERY.

5. The attack will be supported by the 152nd Brigade R.F.A., and the 51st Brigade R.F.A. grouped under the 152nd Brigade on the right; the 160th Brigade R.F.A. and the 113th (Army) Brigade R.F.A. grouped under the 160th Brigade on the left.

BARRAGE.

6. The attack will be covered by a creeping barrage of 18-pdrs. The barrage will come down 200 yards beyond the forming up line, creep at the rate of 100 yards every 3 minutes until the protective barrage line 300 yards beyond the final objective is reached. The barrage will pause for 15 minutes on this line and then stop. One gun per 18-pdr. battery will give smoke barrage. 4.5" Howitzers will be used to fire smoke and a proportion of H.E. at selected localities. Heavy Artillery will bombard selected localities (farms and strong points) maintaining a distance of 600 yards beyond the creeping barrage.

CLOSE SUPPORT.

7. Os.C. 152nd and 160th Brigades will each detail a section of 18-pdrs for the close support of the infantry which will not be required to take part in the creeping barrage. Each section will be accompanied by two selected officers.

Officer Commanding Sections will not be under the orders of any particular Infantry Commander; but will make every effort to keep in close touch with the situation, deal promptly with hostile forward guns and machine guns which have escaped the barrage and are checking the advance of the infantry. These sections will revert to the control of their respective Battery Commanders at dark on J day, or earlier should the situation permit.

PATROLS.

8. Os.C. 51st and 113th Brigades will detail officers patrols accompanied by sufficient signallers runners etc., to push forward in close touch with the Infantry and send back information of the progress of the attack to their respective Brigades by any means available.

LIAISON.

9. No artillery Liaison Officers will be found with Infantry battalions. 152nd Brigade R.F.A. will maintain close touch with 103rd Infantry Bde.

10. On completion of its task in the barrage 152nd Brigade R.F.A. will come under the command of G.O.C. 103rd Infantry Bde.

11. Artillery units please ACKNOWLEDGE.

Captain,
Brigade Major R.A.,
34th Divisional Artillery.

29th October 1918.

Issued at:- 21.00

Distribution.

51st Brigade R.F.A.
113th Brigade R.F.A.
152nd Brigade R.F.A.
160th Brigade R.F.A.
34th D.A.C.
S.C.R.A.
101st Infantry Bde.
102nd ,, ,,
103rd ,, ,,
34th Division "G".
34th M.G. Battalion.
A6D. 164th French Division.
31st Div. Arty.
II Corps R.A.
II Corps H.A.

App XXXXIX

SECRET

Reference Map,
Sheet 29, 1/40,000

34th. DIVISIONAL ARTILLERY LOCATION STATEMENT No. 3.

(Battle Positions)

Headquarters, 34th. Divisional Artillery, ... C.25.central.

H.Qrs., 51st. Brigade, R.F.A., ... I.35.d.5.9.
A/51, ... J.31.d.20.15
B/51, ... J.31.c.90.30.
C/51, ... P.1.a.1.8.
D/51, ... P.1.b.40.50.

H.Qrs., 113th. (Army) Brigade, R.F.A., ... J.25.a.10.50.
A/113, ... J.25.b.50.35.
B/113, ... J.25.b.00.50.
D/113, ... J.25.b.95.00.

H.Qrs. 152nd. Brigade, R.F.A. ... ... I.30.a.8.8.
A/152, ... J.31.b.3.1.
B/152, ... J.31.a.9.2.
C/152, ... J.31.b.7.3.
D/152, ... J.31.b.6.7.

H.Qrs., 160th. Brigade, R.F.A., ... J.19.a.8.2.
A/160, ... J.25.b.4.7.
B/160, ... J.26.a.1.1.
C/160, ... J.19.c.7.0.
D/160, ... J.25.b.70.85.

G. D. [signature]
Captain, R.A.,
Brigade-Major,
34th. Divisional Artillery.

29th. October, 1918.

Distribution:-

51st. Bde.,	101 Infy. Bde.,
113th. Bde.,	102 do.
152nd. Bde.,	103 do.
160th. Bde.,	31st. D.A.,
34th. D.A.C.,	A.D. 164 (French) Divn.,
S.C.R.A.,	IInd. Corps, R.A.,
34th. Divn. "G",	IInd. Corps, H.A.

G.S. 680
27th Oct
19.00

SECRET

Reference Map:
Sheet 29, 1/40,000.

34th. DIVISIONAL ARTILLERY OPERATION ORDER No. 40.

1. The 34th. D.A.C. and X and Y Trench Mortar Batteries will move to-morrow, October 28th. from their present area to positions vacated by the 36th. D.A.C.

Locations as under:-

H.Qrs., D.A.C., C.25.b.9.7.
No. 1 Section, I.2.a.0.5.
No. 2 Section, C.26.b.7.5.
S.A.A. Section, Exact location will be notified later.

X and Y T.M. Batteries. Accommodation will be arranged by O.C., 34th. D.A.C., in his area.

2. ROUTE WALLE - COURTRAI Railway Station - Lock No. 9 (H.27.d) - STACEGHEM - HARLEBEKE.

3. Times, during which columns will pass COURTRAI Railway Station:-

	Head of Column.	Tail.
34th. D.A.C., & T.M. Batteries,	09.55	10.15
S.A.A. Section, ...	10.15	10.30

4. D.A.C. to ACKNOWLEDGE.

[signature]
Captain, R.A.,
for Brigade Major,
34th. Divisional Artillery.

27th. October, 1918.

Distribution:-

152nd. Bde., RFA,
160th. Bde., RFA,
34th. D.A.C.,
D.T.M.O.,
101 Infy. Bde.,
102 Infy. Bde.,
103rd. Infy. Bde.,
34th. Divn., "G",
No. 1 Coy., Train,
S.C.R.A.,
R.A., IInd. Corps,
H.A., IInd. Corps.

34TH DIV.
G.S.O. 1
G.S.O. 2
G.S.O. 3
I.O.

S E C R E T. Ref.Map:- Sheet 29, 1/40,000.

34th DIVISIONAL ARTILLERY OPERATION ORDER No.42.

Reference 34th D.A. Instruction No.1. Map "A"(Barrage Map), Map "B" (4.5 How.tasks), Map "C" (Heavy Artillery tasks).

1. **ATTACK.**

(a) The 41st French Division will be on the left of the 34th Division and not the 164th as stated in 34th D.A. Ins.No.1.

(b) The attack of the 103rd Infantry Bde. will be supported by two companies of Light French Tanks.

(c) The movement of the tanks when crossing their forming up line will be covered by machine gun and artillery fire for which orders will be issued later.

2. **OBJECTIVE.**

(a) The objective laid down in para.4. 34th D.A. Ins.No.1. is the FIRST OBJECTIVE. There will be a pause of two hours on this objective.

(b) The advance will then be resumed by the 31st British Division on the right and the 41st French Division on the left under a creeping barrage.

(c) The 103rd Infantry Bde. will resume its advance to its final objective which runs from K.25.a.1.5. to K.32.a.7.4. without a barrage but covered by the 152nd Brigade R.F.A. and by the remainder of the Divisional Artillery as necessary.

3. **BARRAGE.**

(a) The 18-pdr. creeping barrage will come down on the initial BARRAGE LINE shown on Map "A" at H and move forward in accordance with the timings shown on Map "A" till it reaches the PROTECTIVE BARRAGE LINE. With the exception of the 160th [*+ 113 Bde*] Brigades R.F.A., Each gun on reaching its Protective Barrage Line will fire for 15 minutes then stop. Guns of the 160th and 113th Brigades will continue to fire on their Protective Barrage till H 96 irrespective of the time they arrive on the Protective Barrage Line.

(b) The 4.5 Howitzers will engage the targets in their Brigade Zones as shown on Map "B" lifting off them in accordance with the creeping barrage timings shown in Map "A" and maintaining a distance of 100 yards beyond the creeping barrage.

(c) The Heavy Artillery will engage the targets shown on Map "C" lifting off them in accordance with the barrage timings shown on Map "A" and maintaining a distance of 500 yards beyond the creeping barrage.

4. **RATES OF FIRE.**

18-pdrs. and 4.5 Hows.	H to H+3	Intense
	H+3 to H+12	Rapid
	H+12 to h+24	Normal
	H+24 to H+30	Rapid
	H+30 to H+51	Normal
	H+51 to H+69	Rapid
	H+69 to H+96	Slow

5. AMMUNITION.

18-pdrs H to H + 24 50% A. 50% A.X.
H + 24 to H + 96 100% A.X.

106 Fuze will be employed as far as possible.

One gun per 18-pdr battery will fire smoke throughout the barrage.

4.5" Hows. will fire 50% B.X. 50% B smoke throughout the barrage.

6. SYNCHRONISATION.

Watches will be synchronised by Divisional Staff Officer at 103rd Infantry Bde. H.Q. (I.24.d.2.2.) at 17.00 on October 30th. Representatives from 51st, 113th, 152nd, and 160th Brigades will attend.

7. Divisional Artillery units please ACKNOWLEDGE.

Captain,
Brigade Major R.A.,
34th Divisional Artillery.

30th October 1918.

Distribution.

51st Brigade R.F.A.
113th (Army) Brigade R.F.A.
152nd Brigade R.F.A.
160th Brigade R.F.A.
34th D.A.C.
S.C.R.A.
101st Infantry Bde.
102nd Infantry Bde.
103rd Infantry Bde.
34th Division "G".
34th M.G. Battalion.
A.D. 41st French Divn.
31st D.A.
II Corps R.A.
II Corps H.A.

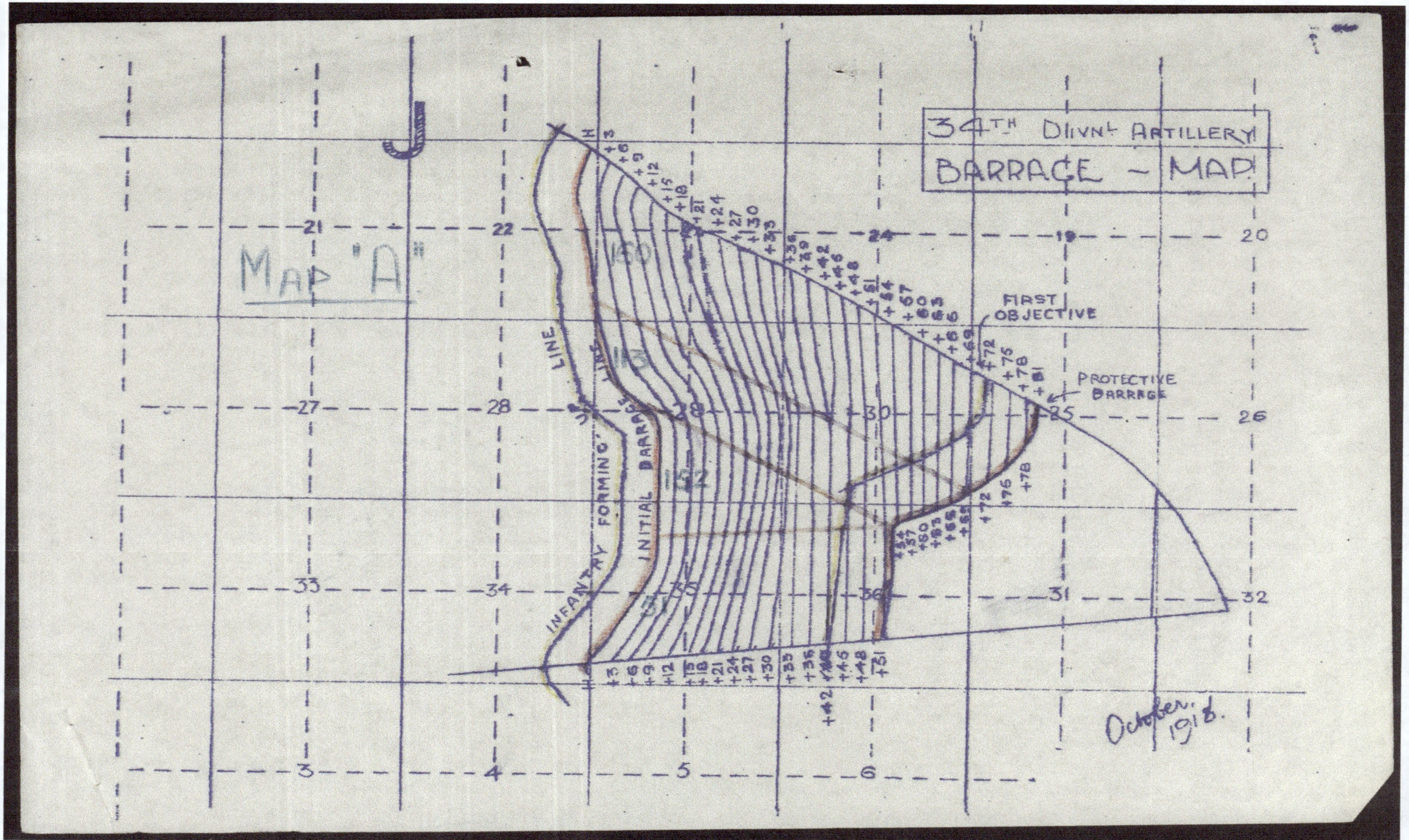

34TH DIVNL ARTILLERY

BARRAGE – MAP

MAP "A"

FIRST OBJECTIVE

PROTECTIVE BARRAGE

INITIAL BARRAGE LINE

INFANTRY FORMING LINE

October. 1918.

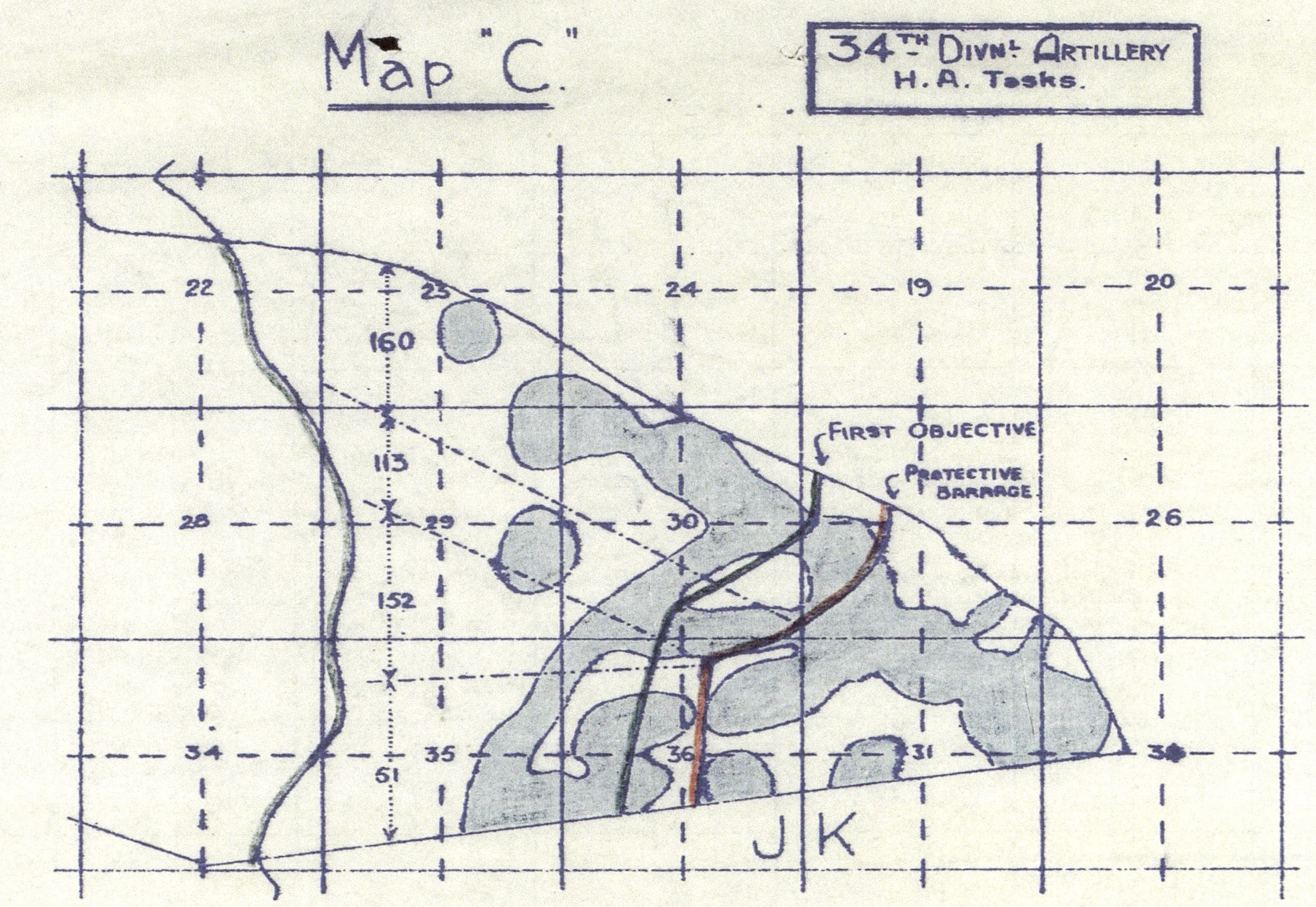
Map "C."
34TH DIVNL ARTILLERY
H. A. Tasks.
FIRST OBJECTIVE
PROTECTIVE BARRAGE
22
23
24
19
20
28
29
30
26
34
35
36
31
160
113
152
51
J
K

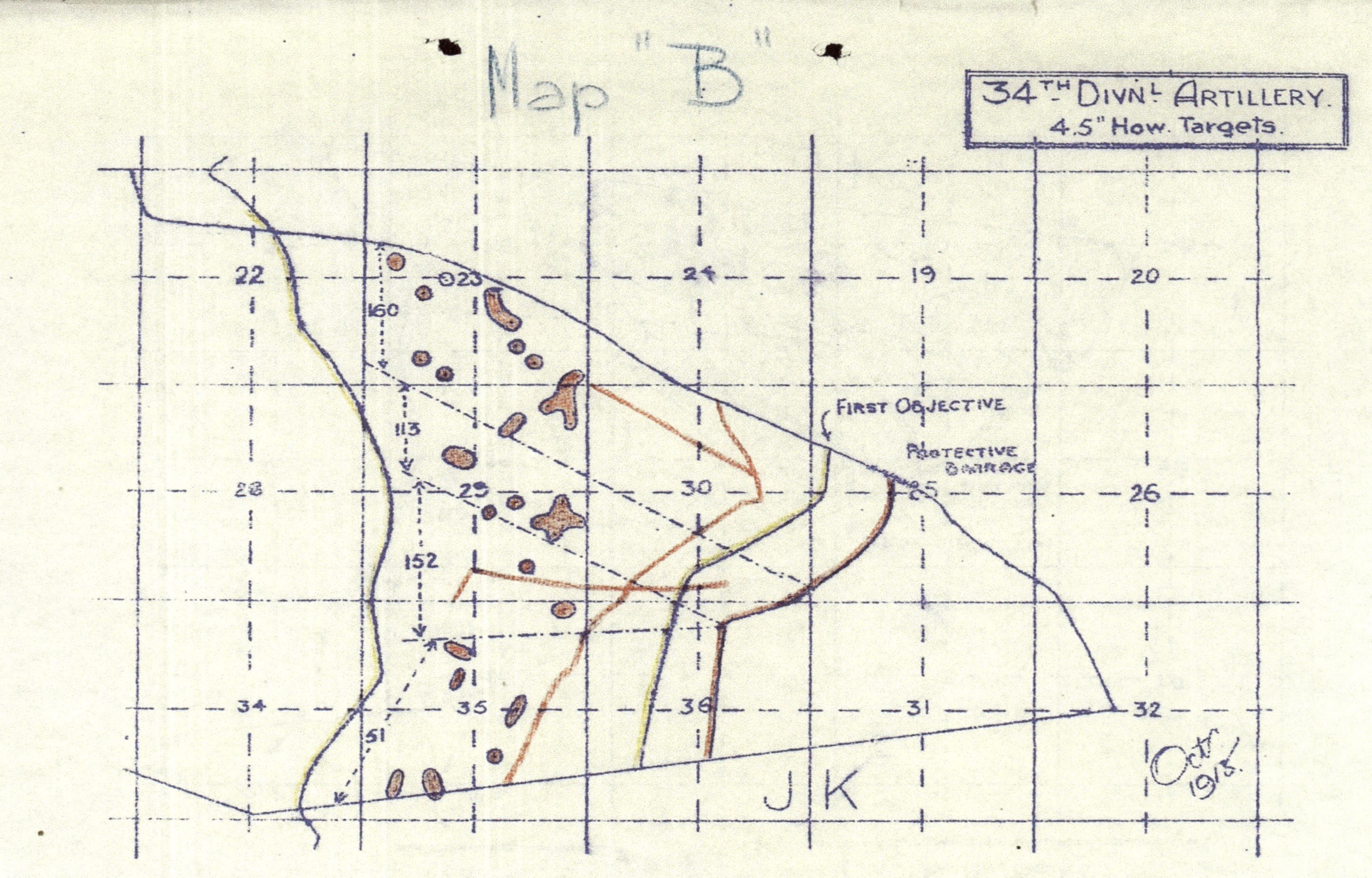

Map "B"
34TH DIVNL ARTILLERY.
4.5" How. Targets.
FIRST OBJECTIVE
PROTECTIVE BARRAGE
22
23
24
19
20
28
25
30
26
34
35
36
31
32
160
113
152
51
J K
Octr 1918.

Army Form C. 2118.

Instructions regarding War Diaries and Intelligence Summaries are contained in F. S. Regs., Part II. and the Staff Manual respectively. Title pages will be prepared in manuscript.

WAR DIARY
or
INTELLIGENCE SUMMARY.
(Erase heading not required.)

Month of NOVEMBER, 1918.

H.Q.R.A., 34th. Division.
Page 1.

Place	Date	Hour	Summary of Events and Information	Remarks and references to Appendices
BEVEREN, Sheet 29, C.25.cent.	Nov. 1		During the night the enemy withdrew beyond the SCHELDT, our patrols advanced, and by night had reached the line of the river.	
			The 160th. Bde., R.F.A., moved up in support of this advance, and came into action North of ANSEGHEM.	
	2		The 34th. Division having been squeezed out by the Divisions North and South, batteries in action withdrew to their wagon-lines.	
MOORSEELE, Sheet 28,	3		34th. Divisional Artillery moved to the MOORSEELE area.	
			34th. Divisional Operation Order No. 298.	App I
			34th. Division Location Statement, ...	App II
			Letter of congratulation from Brig.General E.C.W.WALTHALL, C.M.G., D.S.O., R.A., Commanding 103rd. Infantry Brigade	App III
			34th. Divisional Artillery Narrative of Operations since 26th. October, 1918,	App IV
	7		The 34th. Divisional Artillery (less H.Q.R.A., and No. 3 Section, D.A.C.), moved to wagon lines in 35th. Division area, coming under command of 35th. Divisional Artillery, in order to assist in creeping barrage on 11th. inst.	
			34th. Divisional Artillery Order No. 1, ...	App V
	10	20.00	Information was received that the enemy had accepted the ALLIED armistice Terms.	
	11		In accordance with terms of Armistice, hostilities ceased at 11 a.m.	
	12		34th. Divisional Artillery returned to Wagon-Lines vacated by them on 7th. November.	

D. D. & L., London, E.C.
(A10266) Wt W5300/P713 750,000 2/18 Sch. 52 Forms/C2118/16.

Army Form C. 2118.

WAR DIARY
or
INTELLIGENCE SUMMARY.
(Erase heading not required.)

Instructions regarding War Diaries and Intelligence Summaries are contained in F. S. Regs., Part II. and the Staff Manual respectively. Title pages will be prepared in manuscript.

Month of November, 1918.

H.Q.R.A., 34th. Division.
Page 2.

Place	Date	Hour	Summary of Events and Information	Remarks and references to Appendices
MOORSEELE	Nov. 12		34th. Divisional Artillery Operation Order No. 44, ...	App VI
	15		34th. Division having been selected to form part of Army of Occupation in RHINE LANDS, 34th. Divisional Artillery commenced its march to concentration area, and moved to COYGHEM-ST.GENOIS area.	
			34th. Divisional Artillery Operation Order No. 45. ...	App VII
Wattripont Sheet 29, W.29.c.4.9			H.Q.R.A. moved to WATTRIPONT.	
	16		34th. Divisional Artillery moved to ARC AINIERES - FRASNES (concentration) area.	
			34th. Divisional Artillery Operation Order No. 46.	App VIII
			34th Divisional Artillery Thanksgiving Service.	
			One Section was withdrawn from each Battery in order to reduce establishment to 4 gun Batteries as per 34th Div. Arty. No.1817/A dated 15-11-18.	App VIIIa.

D. D. & L., London, E.C.
(A10266) Wt W5300/P713 750,000 2/18 Sch. 52 Forms/C2118/16.

Instructions regarding War Diaries and Intelligence Summaries are contained in F. S. Regs., Part II. and the Staff Manual respectively. Title pages will be prepared in manuscript.

Army Form C. 2118.

WAR DIARY
or
INTELLIGENCE SUMMARY.
(Erase heading not required.)

H.Q.R.A., 34th Division.

Month of November 1918. Page. 3.

Place	Date	Hour	Summary of Events and Information	Remarks and references to Appendices
LESSINES	Nov. 16		113th Army Brigade R.F.A. attached to 34th Division.	App.IX.
			The 34th Divisional Artillery and 113th Army Brigade marched to LAHAMAIDE - OEUDEGHIEM area.	
			H.Q.R.A. moved to LESSINES.	App. X.
	17		34th Divml.Arty. Operation Order No.47 " " " " " No.48 " " " Location Statement	App.XI App.XII
			Owing to difficulty of supply, 34th Division remained at LESSINES, 34th Div.Arty. No.G.784	App.XIII
			The 34th Division being transferred from the Second to Fourth Army and from the II to X Corps, remained at LESSINES.	

Brigadier-General, R.A.,

C.R.A., 34th Division.

D. D. & L., London, E.C.
(A10266) Wt W5300/P713 750,000 2/18 Sch, 52 Forms/C2118/16.

App I

COPY.

101 Bde.	C.R.A.	Som.L.I.	"Q"Adv.	Camp Commandant.
102 "	C.R.E.	Sig.Coy.	"Q" Rear.	
103 "	M.G.Bn.	A.D.M.S.	Divnl.Train.	

G.404. 2. AAA

Warning OrderAAA 34 Div will move tomorrow Nov 3 to the area formed by the triangle COURTRAI - River LYS to MENIN - KEZELBERG with MOORSEELS included AAA To be clear of present areas by 14.00 AAA Probable locations Div.H.Q. and 102 Bde MOORSEELE 101 Bde WEVELGHEM 103 Bde BISSEGHEM and NEDERBEEK Artillery KAPPELHOEK Area M.G.Bn. KLJKUITHOEK and Pioneer Bn. WIJNBERG AAA Addsd List A plus Nos. 11 & 12.

SD. B. BATTYE,

Lieut-Colonel G.S.

From 34 Div.
Time:- 1700

SECRET.

TO BE ACKNOWLEDGED BY WIRE.

Copy No. 9

34th DIVISION OPERATION ORDER No.298.

Reference Map 1/40,000
Sheets 28 and 29.

2nd November, 1918.

1. The 34th Division will move tomorrow November 3rd to area formed by triangle - COURTRAI (excl) - River LYS to MENIN (incl) - KEZELBERG - MOORSEELE (incl) - SCHOON-WATER (incl) - Road to Railway crossing ¾ mile S.E. of HEULE, in accordance with attached March Table "A".

2. (a) Routes and composition of Brigade Groups in accordance with attached Appendix I.

(b) Intervals between Companies and equivalent Units to be as large as possible consistent with time restrictions in Table "A". All movements East of VICHTE to be by Platoons at large intervals.

3. The 102nd Field Ambulance (less detachment) will remain in charge of Divisional Rest Station at LEDEGHEM.

4. The 208th Field Coy. R.E., and "C" Company 2/4th Somerset Light Infantry (Pioneers) will remain in their present billets and continue work on Bridge North of BEVEREN.

5. Instructions for move of 104th Machine Gun Battalion and Nos. 1 and 4 M.M.G. Batteries will be issued later to those immediately concerned.

6. On arrival in new area the 2/4th Somerset Light Infantry (less "C" Company) will be concentrated in billets adjacent to its Headquarters under arrangements to be made direct between O.C. Pioneer Battalion and Brigade Group Commanders concerned. Concentration will be completed by noon November 4th.

7. Advanced Divisional Headquarters will close at BEVEREN at 1000 and reopen with 2nd and 3rd Echelons at MOORSEELE at the same hour.

B D Batty e

Lieut. Colonel, G.S.
34th Division.

Issued by Special D.R. at 2130.

DISTRIBUTION.

No.s 1 & 2	File.
3 & 4	War Diary.
5	G.O.C.
6	101st Inf.Bde.
7	102nd Inf. Bde.
8	103rd Inf. Bde.
9	C.R.A.
10	C.R.E.
11	2/4th Somerset L.I.
12	34th Bn.M.G.Corps.
13	Signal Coy.
14	"Q".
15	A.D.M.S.
16	D.A.P.M.
17	Div. Train.
18	S.S.O.
19	D.A.D.O.S.
20	Camp Commandant.
21 - 22	IInd Corps.
23	9th British Division.
24	31st British Division.
25	41st French Division.

(For Appendix I P.T.O.)

SECRET

APPENDIX "I"

To accompany 34th Division Operation Order No. 298

1 .... ROUTES

Route 'A' ..... Bridge H.11.b.4.4. - Road Junction H.11.b.1.9. - LAYHOEK. - Bridge H.15.c.9.8. - WATERMOLEN - G.24.c.7.5. - G.20.d.8.2.

Route 'B' ..... Road Junction H.12.a.6.9. - COURTRAI - Bridge H.25.d.3.4. - BISSEGHEM.

Route 'C' ..... Route 'A' to Road Junction H.20.b.4.8. - Cross-roads H.25.b.0.3, thence route "B".

2 .... COMPOSITION OF BRIGADES

101st Brigade Group	101st Brigade 207th Field Coy. R.E. 'A' Coy., 2/4th Somerset L.I. (Pioneers) No. 2 Coy. Div. Train. 104th Field Ambulance
102nd Brigade Group	102nd Brigade No. 3 Coy. Div. Train. Det., 102nd Field Ambulance
103rd Brigade Group	103rd Brigade 209th Field Coy. R.E. 'B' Coy., 2/4th Somerset L.I. (Pioneers) No. 4 Coy., Div. Train. 103rd Field Ambulance

SECRET

TABLE "A".

Serial No.	Date.	Unit.	From.	To.	Route	Remarks.
Col.No.	1.	2.	3	4	5	6
1.	Nov. 3	102 Bde.Group	HARLEBEKE	MOORSEELE	A	To be clear of LYS by 0900
2.	"	Hd.Qrs.& No.1 Coy.Div.Train	"	SCHOON-WATER	A	To cross LYS between 0900 and 0910.
3.	"	Hd.Qrs. 2/4th. Som.L.I.	DEERLYCK	WIJNBERG	C	To cross LYS between 0910 and 0915
4.	"	2nd & 3rd Echelons D.H.Q	HARLEBEKE	MOORSEELE	A	To start at 0920 and follow item 3.
5.	"	Div.Arty.(incl. S.A.A.Sec. D.A.C) less 152 F.A.Bde.	VICHTE Area	KAPPELHOEK and KLOEFHOEK	B	To pass Road junction H.12.a.6.9 between 0930 and 1045
6.	"	34 Bn.M.G.Corps	VICHTE	KLJKUITHOEK	B	To pass Road Junction H.12.a.6.9. between 1045 and 1115
7.	"	152 F.A.Bde.	VICHTE	KAPPELHOEK Area	As per Item 9	Head to enter STACEGHEM at 1130. Not to pass H.27.a.2.1. till tail of M.G.Bn. is clear.
8.	"	101 Bde.Group.	DEERLYCK	WEVELGHEM	C	To pass Road Junction H.12.a.6.9.between 1145 and 1315. Not to pass Road Junction H.25.b.1.2. until tail of 152 F.A.Bde is clear.
9.	"	103 Bde.Group	STERHOEK Area	BISSEGHEM	VICHTE - I.29.d.- I.34.a.- I.20.d.- STACEGHEM - Lock 9 - H.27.a.2.1. - thence Route B.	Not to enter STACEGHEM before 1330 and not to pass H.25.b.1.2. till tail of 101 Bde.Group is clear

- To accompany 34th Division Operation Order No.298.-

App II

34th. Divnl.Arty. No.O/443.

34th. DIVISIONAL ARTILLERY LOCATION STATEMENT.

H.Qrs., 34th. Divnl.Artillery, MOORSEELE, 28/L.23.b.0.8.

H.Qrs., 152nd. Bde., R.F.A.,		28/R.4.b.8.0
A/152,	...	R.3.b.3.6
B/152,	...	R.4.a.6.5
C/152,	...	R.3.d.3.6
D/152,	...	R.3.b.8.3
H.Qrs., 160th. Bde., R.F.A.,		28/L.30.a.0.3
A/160,	...	L/36.a.9.9
B/160,	...	L/30.a.8.5
C/160,	...	L/30.a.9.0.
D/160,	...	29/G.26.c.6.4
H.Qrs., 34th. D.A.C.,		29/M.1.b.35.90.
No. 1 Section,	...	G.31.d.5.2
No. 2 Section,	...	M.1.b.3.7
S.A.A. Section,	...	G.31.d.3.4
34th. D.T.M.O.,	...	28/L.36.c.5.3

[illegible] Major, R.A.
Brigade-Major,
34th. Divisional Artillery.

5th. November, 1918.

App III

COPY.

Head-quarters,
103rd. Infantry Brigade.

2nd. November, 1918.

My dear Warburton,

Would you kindly convey to your batteries our thanks and appreciation for the very excellent support afforded to us on 31st. October?

I hear nothing but praise of the barrage, and, in fact, all the artillery work. I walked over the ground yesterday, and full confirmation of the accuracy and deadliness of the barrage is easily visible.

The French Tank Commander was also delighted with the covering fire provided for his assembly, which he stated to be entirely adequate.

A roving section of 18-pounders (C/160) also did very good work.

Yours very sincerely,

(Signed) P. C. WALTHALL,
Brigadier-General,
Comndg. 103rd. Infy. Brigade.

44 IV

34th. Divnl.Arty. No.G/445.

34th. DIVISIONAL ARTILLERY NARRATIVE OF OPERATIONS

since 26th. October, 1918.

On the morning of the 26th. October, the 160th. Brigade, R.F.A., moved under orders of G.O.C., 101st. Infantry Brigade, relieving a brigade of the 36th. Divisional Artillery in action in positions 29/J.19 and 25, from these positions covering the 101st. Infantry Brigade who moved into the line that evening.

The 152nd. Brigade, R.F.A., moved on the 26th. under orders of G.O.C. 103rd. Infantry Brigade to the AELBEKE area, and proceeded the following day to the IInd. Corps area, relieving the remaining brigade of the 36th. Divisional Artillery in positions in 29/I.12 and 18, and from there covered the 101st. Infantry Brigade in the line.

On 27th. October, R.A.H.Q. moved to LAUWE and the following day to BEVEREN, assuming the resp onsibility for covering the 101st. Inf. Bde. at 11.00 on 28th.

On 29th. October, battle positions were reconnoitred and occupied, -
152nd. Bde. in 29/J.31 and
160th. Bde. in 29/J.25.
200 rounds per gun being dumped at the positions.

Harassing fire was carried out during the night of the 30th., and early morning of the 31st. to cover the advance of tanks.

On 31st. October, at 05.25, the 34th. Divisional Artillery, re-inforced by the 51st. and 113th. Brigades R.F.A., supported the attack of the 34th. Division, 18-pdrs. firing a creep ing barrage with sufficient smoke to deny observation to the enemy, 4.5 hows. firing smoke and H.E. on selected points and areas. Two sections were detached and sent forward with roving co mmissions in close support of the Infantry, and these proved most useful in dealing with machine guns and detached enemy field guns. By 10.15, reports received showed our Infantry to have reached their final objective, and brigades moved forward:-
152nd. Bde. to 29/J.34, and
160th. Bde. to 29/J.27.

Little or no firing was done from these positions as the situation did not demand it, and no targets presented themselves.

On the morning of the 1st. November, a further advance of our Infantry was reported, and the 160th. Bde. moved forward to positions in 29/K.19 to cover our Infantry should they remain in the line. The 152 d. Bde. reconnoitred positions in K.25, but did not occupy them.

On the afternoon of the 1st., batteries were ordered to assemble at their wagon-lines, and on November 3rd., the Divisional Artillery marched by COURTRAI to billets in the WEVELGHEM area.

Major, R.A.,
Brigade-Major,
34th. Divisional Artillery.

5th. November, 1918.

0/446

SECRET.

REFERENCE Map Sheet 29
1/40,000

AH IV

34th. Divisional Artillery Order No. 1

1. The 34th. Divisional Artillery will move to-morrow 7th. inst. to wagon lines in the 35th. Divisional area.

2. Areas for wagon lines are allotted as follows;-
   152 Bde. R.F.A. & No.1 Section D.A.C. squares I.27, 33,&
   160 Bde. R.F.A. & No.2 Section D.A.C. squares I. 28, 21, 22.
   No. 1 Coy. Div. Train Any of the above squares

   Places outside the 35th. Divisional area within the squares allotted are not available.

3. The tail of the column of the 152nd Brigade will be clear of WEVELGHEM Church L.8.a. by 10.00.
   The tail of the column of 160th Brigade will be clear of the same point by 11.00

4. On arrival in this area Brigades of the 34th D.A. will come under the orders of the 35th D.A. and will report their locations to H.Q. 35th D.A. SWEVEGHEM (O.1.d.) as early as possible.

5. Nos. 1 & 2 Sections D.A.C. are placed under the command of Os.C. 152nd Brigade and 160th Brigade respectively from the receipt of this order.

6. D.A. units please acknowledge.

[signature]
Captain,
Brigade Major R.A.
34th Divisional Artillery.

6th November 1918.

Distribution.
152nd Brigade R.F.A.
160th Brigade R.F.A.
34th D.A.C.
34th Div. "G".
35th D.A.
II Corps R.A.
XIX Corps R.A.
No.1 Coy. Div. Train.

34th Div. Arty. No. G. 768.

34th. D.A.C.

Nos. 1 & 2 Sections 34th D.A.C. are placed under the orders of Os. C. 152 & 160 Bdes. R.F.A. forthwith.

Captain, R.A.
Brigade Major,
34th. Divisional Artillery.

6-11-18.

S E C R E T　　　　　　　　　　　　　　　　　　0/448.

34th. DIVISIONAL ARTILLERY LOCATION STATEMENT.

H.Qrs., 34th. Divisional Artillery,　　　MOORSEELE, 28/L.23.b.0.8.

H.Qrs., 160th. Bde., R.F.A.,　　...　　...　　29/I.28.d.c　. 1.
A/160,　　I.28.d.3.5.
B/160,　　I.28.c.0.3.
C/160,　　I.22.d.2.1.
D/160,　　I.28.a.8.7.

H.Qrs., 152nd. Bde., R.F.A.,　　...　　...　　29/I.27.c.9.6.
A/152,　　I.33.d.7.9.
B/152,　　I.33.a.8.6.
C/152,　　I.33.c.9.[illegible].
D/152,　　I.27.a.5.3.

H.Qrs., 34th. Divisional Ammunition Column,　　29/M.1.b.35.90.
No. 1 Section,　　29/I.27.d.5.0.
No. 2　,,　　I.27.a.8.7.
S.A.A.　,,　　29/G.31.d.3.4.

34th. Divisonal Trench Mortar Officer,　　...　　29/L.36.c.5.3.

35th. Divisi onal A.R.P.,　　...　　...　　29/O.4.c.6.8.

[signature]

Brigade-Major, R.A.,
34th. Divisional Artillery.

9th. November, 1918.

App VI

SECRET

Reference Maps,
Sheets 28 & 29,
1:40,000.

34th. DIVISIONAL ARTILLERY OPERATION ORDER No. 44.

1. The Divisional Artillery will march to-morrow, 12th. November, to the MOORSEELE area.

2. 152nd. and 160th. Bdes. R.F.A., will proceed to their former billets in R.3 and 4, and L.30.
   34th. D.A.C. to the HERTHOEK area, L.28.central.

3. ROUTE. ST. LOUIS cross-roads, I.32.b, STEENBRUGGE, STACEGHEM, LOCK No. 9, COURTRAI, BISSEGHEM, WEVELGHEM.

4. STARTING POINT. Cross-roads, I.32.b.

5. Units will be clear of the starting-point by the following times:-

   160th. Bde., ... 10.00
   152nd. Bde., ... 11.00
   34th. D.A.C., ... 12.00

6. No. 1 Coy., Divisional Train, will move in rear of the D.A.C.

7. D.A. Units please ACKNOWLEDGE.

Captain, R.A.,
Brigade-Major,
34th. Divisional Artillery.

11th. November, 1918.
Issued at 19.45.

Distribution:-

152nd. Bde., R.F.A.,
160th. Bde., R.F.A., } By Special D.R.
34th. D.A.C.,
No. 1 Coy. Train,

S.C.R.A.,
34th. Divn., "G",
IInd. Corps, R.A.

S E C R E T.

34th DIVISION.

LOCATION REPORT No.26.

Reference Map Sheets 28 & 29 1/40,000 — 6 a.m. 9th Nov.1918.

1.	34th Div.H.Q.	MOORSEELE
2.	101st Inf.Bde.H.Q.	29/M.7.b.6.6.
3	2/4th R.W.Surrey Regt.	29/M.10.a.1.9.
4.	4th R.Sussex Regt.	28/R.17.b.1.6.
5.	2nd L.N.Lan Regt	29/M.8.a.4.5.
6.	101st L.T.M.Bty.	29/M.7.b.8.9.
7.	102nd Inf.Bde.H.Q.	28/L.23.d.4.9.
8.	1/4th Cheshire Regt.	28/L.23.a.7.2.
9.	1/7th " "	28/L.23.a.2.5.
10.	1/1st Hereford Regt.	28/L.23.b.5.8.
11.	102nd L.T.M.Bty.	28/L.23.b.2.2.
12.	103rd Inf.Bde.H.Q.	28/R.26.b.1.7.
13.	5th K.O.Sco.Bord.	28/R.26.b.9.9.
14.	8th Scottish Rifles.	28/R.26.a.7.6.
15.	5th Arg.& Suth'd Highrs.	HALLUIN, 90, Rue de Procession.
16.	103rd L.T.M.Bty.	" 27 "
17.	C.R.A.	MOORSEELE
18.	152nd Brigade R.F.A.	29/I.27.c.9.6.
19.	160th "	29/I.28.d.c
20.	D.T.M.O.	28/L.36.c.5.3.
21.	X/34th T.M.Bty. R.F.A.	"
22.	Y/34th "	"
23.	34th Div.Amm.Col.	29/M.1.b.35.90.
24.	C.R.E.	MOORSEELE
25.	207th Field Coy.R.E.	WEVELGHEM (Brewery) 29/M.8.a.3.8.
26.	208th " "	29/B.18.d.8.1.
27.	209th " "	28/R.26.c.7.4.
28.	2/4th Somerset L.I.	28/L.36.c.9.6.
29	34th Bn.M.G.Corps.	28/R.5.c.8.6.
30.	34th Div.Sig.Coy.	MOORSEELE
31.	A.D.M.S.	"
32.	102nd Field Ambulance	" Convent.
33.	103rd " "	MENIN, Billet 32 La Grande Place.
34.	104th " "	WEVELGHEM convent.
35.	34th Divl.Train H.Q.	28/L.23.b.2.5.
36.	No.1 Coy.	29/I.16.central
37.	No.2 "	29/M.2.d.4.3.
38.	No.3 "	28/L.17.a.1.7.
39.	No.4 "	28/R.20.c.central.
40.	44th Mob.Vet.Sec.	28/L.23.c.5.6.
41.	D.A.D.O.S.	28/L.23.a.5.6.
42.	D.A.D.V.S.	MOORSEELE
43.	D.A.P.M	"
44.	D.G.O.	"
45.	34th M.T.Coy.	29/H.2.d.6.6.
46.	231st Employment Coy.	MOORSEELE
47.	Railhead	BEYTHEM
48.	Reception Camp.	MENIN 62 & 64 Rue de Lille.

for Lieut-Colonel, G.S.,
34th Division.

App VII

SECRET.

Reference Maps,
Sheets 28 & 29, 1:40,000.

34th. DIVISIONAL ARTILLERY OPERATION ORDER No. 45.

1. The 34th. Divisional Artillery will move on 15th. November 1918, to the area - COYGHEM - SAINT-GENOIS.

2. ROUTE. WEVELGHEM - LAUWE - AELBEKE - ROLLEGHEM - RUDDERVOORDE.

3. STARTING POINT. KLOEFHOEK cross-roads, 28/G.31.d.3.0.

4. TIME. Head of the column will pass the starting-point at the following times:-

152nd. Bde., R.F.A.,	08.30
160th. Bde., R.F.A.,	09.30
34th. D.A.C., ...	10.30

5. X and Y Trench Mortar Batteries, and No. 1 Coy., Divisional Train will march in rear of 34th. D.A.C.

6. D.A. Units please ACKNOWLEDGE.

[signature] Lt. for
Captain, R.A.,
Brigade-Major,
34th. Divisional Artillery.

13th. November, 1918.

Distribution:-

152 Bde.	34 Div. "G"
160 Bde.	II Corps R.A.
D.A.C.	War Diary
D.T.M.O.	File
S.C.R.A.	

No. 1 Coy Train

BmRA

34 D.A., OO/45a.

Reference 3 4th. Divisional Artillery Operation Order No. 45;

Para. 2; after "ROLLEGHEM" insert "BELLEGHEM , LE CHAT CABt."

-o-o-o-o-o-o-o-o-o-o-o-

R.A. H. Q. will close at MOORSEELE, and re-open at WATTRIPONT (TOURNAI Sheet, G.4.58.75) at 12.00 on November 15th., 1918.

Captain, R.A.,
Brigade-Major,
34th. Divisional Artillery.

14th. November, 1918.

6775

MINUTES OF SECOND CORPS CONFERENCE,

held 10 am., 13th. November,
1918.

---

1. The Second and Fourth British Armies will advance Eastwards about November 17th. The Cavalry Corps will precede the Infantry Corps. The IInd. Corps will advance as follows:-

1st. Line, 29th. Divn. on the Right, 41st. Divn. on the left,
2nd. Line, 34th. ,, ,, 9th. ,, ,,

Each Division will have an Army Field Artillery Brigade affiliated to it. Heavy Artillery will follow in rear.

2. The 9th. and 34th. Divisions will start moving forward into their concentration areas in accordance with IInd. Corps Order No. 303, on 14th. November.

3. (a) On the march, the ammunition to be carried by the men will be reduced to 60 rounds. Steel hats and box respirators will be carried.
(b) Precautions for protection will have to be taken, first-line Divisions throwing out advance guards.

4. The use of cable will be reduced to a minimum, communication being established normally by D.R. Head-quarters must be established on or quite near main roads.

5. All students undergoing courses have been ordered to rejoin their Divisions at once. Reception Camps will be temporarily disbanded.

6. Units will march closed up, the spaces laid down in Field Service Regulations being adhered to only.

7. The Commander-in-Chief wishes the following points to receive special attention at the end of the march forward, and where possible during the march forward:-

Battalion and R.A. Brigade Messes; if possible one lorry will be provided for these.
Sergeants' Messes, Recreation Rooms and Canteens for the men.
Ceremonial Parades for the benefit of the troops, and to impress the inhabitants.

8. Leave will remain on its present basis.

9. The Censorship will be abolished.
Secret documents will be reduced to a minimum.

WD

<u>AMENDMENT</u>. <u>G/773/a</u>.

MINUTES OF SECOND CORPS CONFERENCE,

held 10 a.m., 13th. November, 1918.

Reference this Office G/773, please make following correction:-

Para. 9. For "Abolished" read "Modified."

Serial No.	Unit	From.	To.	Route	Remarks.
Col.No.	1	2	3	4	5
1.	101 Bde.Group.	COYGHEM Area	ANSEROEUL ARC AINIERES LA BACOTTERIE	Any Roads North of DOTTIGNIES-ESPIERRES Road - HELCHIN Bridge.	To be East of SCHELDT by 11.00
2.	102 Bde.Group.	BELLEGHEM Area	CELLES POTTES REJET MOULEUX BASSE PLAINE	Any roads North of DOTTIGNIES-ESPIERRES Road - HELCHIN Bridge.	Not to cross SCHELDT before 11.00
3.	103 Bde.Group.	ROLLEGHEM	MOLEMBAIX HERINNES CAVRINNES	DOTTIGNIES - ESPIERRES - WARCOING Bridge.	
4.	R.A.Group.	MOORSEELE	COYGHEM St.GENOIS	WEVELGHEM - LAUWE - ROLLEGHEM.	
5.	Div.H.Q.Group.	MOORSEELE	WATTRIPONT		

- All Mechanical Transport will cross SCHELDT by HELCHIN Bridge. -

Copy No. 9

14-11-1918.

34th DIVISION OPERATION ORDER No 303.

Reference Map - TOURNAI - 1/100,000.

1. The 34th Division will continue its march tomorrow November 15th in accordance with the table overleaf.

2. Divisional H.Q. will close at MOORSEELE at 10 a.m. and re-open at WATTRIPONT at 12 noon.

3 ACKNOWLEDGE.

for Lieut-Colonel, G.S.,
34th Division.

Issued by D.R. at 2 p.m

DISTRIBUTION:-

Copies Nos.	
1 & 2	File
3 & 4	War Diary.
5	G.O.C.
6	101st Infantry Brigade
7	102nd " "
8	103rd " "
9	C.R.A.
10	C.R.E.
11	2/4th Somerset L.I.
12	34th Bn. M.G.Corps
13	Signal Coy.
14	"Q"
15	A.D.M.S.
16	D.A.P.M.
17	34th Div. Train
18	S.S.O.
19	D.A.D.O.S.
20	Camp Commandant
21	D.G.O.
22	D.A.D.V.S.
23	44th Mob.Vet.Sec.
24	34th M.T.Coy.
25-26	II Corps
27	9th Division.
28	29th "

SECRET.

Reference Maps,
Sheets 29 and 37,
1:40,000.

34th. DIVISIONAL ARTILLERY OPERATION ORDER No. 46.

o-o-o-o-o-o-o-o-o-o-o-o-o-o-o-o-o-o-o-o-o-o-o-o-o-o-o-

1. The 34th. Divisional Artillery will move on October 16th., to the area ARC AINIERES - ANVAING - FRASNES (less area occupied by 74th. D.H.Q.) - BUSSENAT.

2. 152nd. Bde., R.F.A., will cross the SCHELDT at HELCHIN (Sheet 37, C.5.b), crossing not to commence before 11.00, and move to the ARC AINIERES area via D.20.b - CELLES (not to be entered till the tail of the 102nd. Infantry Brigade is clear) D.24.b. - E.13.d - E.28.a.

3. 160th. Bde., R.F.A., will cross the SCHELDT at WARCOING (Sheet 37 C.20.d), the crossing not to commence before 10.30, and move to FRASNES - BUSSENAT area, via I.6.a - D.26.a - J.10.b - VELAINES - POTTELLES FOREST - ELLIGNIES-LES-FRASNES.

4. The D.A.C. will follow the same routes as the 152nd. Bde., crossing of the SCHELDT not to commence before 12.00.

5. No. 1 Coy., Divisional Train, will follow in rear of 160th. Bde.

6. D.A. Units please ACKNOWLEDGE.

Captain, R.A.,
Brigade-Major,
34th. Divisional Artillery.

14th. November, 1918.

DISTRIBUTION:-

152 Bde. — R.A. II Corps
160 Bde. — S.C.R.A.
34 D.A.C. — S.C.R.A.
No. 1 Coy. Train, — War Diary ✓
34 Div. "G" — File

MARCH TABLE to accompany 34th Division Operation Order No. 304

Serial No.	Unit	From	To	ROUTE	Remarks
Col.No	1	2	3	4	5
1.	101st Bde Group	ANSEROEUL - ARC AINIERES Area	ELLEZELLES, GROS CHENE, CROISISSART, CONTREPRE, BOURLIQUET, TOMBELLE	Any road South of WATRIPONT RENAIX Road and North of a line from FRASNES - FOREST. ANSEROEUL - WATRIPONT - RENAIX Road East of the 16th milestone can be used after 10.30 at which hour the tail of the 30th Div. column proceeding to ESCANAFFLES will be clear.	To be East of RENAIX - ELLIGNIES Road by 12.30.
2	102nd Bde. Group	CELLES, POTTES Area	RIGANDRIE MONT d'ELLEZELLES HAUFAUX, HARIVE RENAIX (S. of WATRIPONT - ELLEZELLES Road)	CELLES - ANSEROEUL - RENAIX. Not to pass 16th milestone S.W of ANSEROEUL before 11.00 and to be clear of CELLES by 11.00.	
3	103rd Bde Group	HERRINNES HOLEMBAIX Area	ARABIE, CROISETTE, DERGNEAU, BIEST.	CELLES, ANSEROEUL, WATRIPONT. Not to enter CELLES before 11.00 and tail of column to be clear of village by 12.00.	Accommodation for 1 Bn. 103rd Bde. will be allotted in RENAIX under Div. arrangements
4	34th Div. Arty. Group	COYENHEM, ST. GENOIS Area	BUISSENAL FRASNES (less accommodation occupied by 74th Div. H.Q.) ELLIGNIES ANVAING DELBART, CARNOIS ARC AINIERES, AINIERES	Any route S. of a line due East from CELLES. Not to enter CELLES before tail of 103rd Bde. is clear. Cross WARCOING bridge after 10.30 and HELCHIN bridge after 11.00.	

NOTE: All lorries of Inf.Bde. Groups should be East of ANSEROEUL by 10.00. Lorries of R.A. Group not to pass CELLES before 13.00.

Copy No. 22

S.

15th November 1918.

34th DIVISION OPERATION ORDER NO.304.

1. The Division will move on the 16th instant in accordance with the March Table overleaf.

2. ACKNOWLEDGE.

Issued by D.R.at 0800.

Lieut.Colonel, G.S.
34th Division.

DISTRIBUTION.

Copies Nos.1-2 File.
3-4 War Diary.
5 G.O.C.
6 101st Infantry Brigade.
7 102 nd Infantry Brigade.
8 103rd Infantry Brigade.
9 C.R.A.
10 C.R.E.
11 2/4th Somerset L.I.
12 34th Bn.M.G.Corps.
13 Signal Coy.
14 [illegible]
15 A.D.M.S.
16 D.A.P.M.
17 34th Div.Train.
18 S.S.O.
19 D.A.D.O.S.
20 Camp Commandant.
21 D.G.O.
22 D.A.D.V.S.
23 44 Mob.Vet.Section.
24 34th M.T.Coy .
25 -26 II Corps.
27 9th Division.
28 29th Division.
29 34th Div.Reception Camp.

P.T.O.

S E C R E T
****
Copy No. 9

34th DIVISION

AMENDMENT No. 1 to OPERATION ORDER No. 305

17-11-18

Reference March Table 'A' :

1. Amend Column 5 as under :-

101st Brigade Group not to pass cross-roads West of LAHAMAIDE before 09.00.

102nd Brigade Group not to enter ELLEZELLES before 09.30

103rd Brigade Group

(a) Not to enter ELLEZELLES before 09.00, being clear by 09.30
Not to pass cross-roads 48th kilometre-stone 1 mile North of WODECQ before 11.00.

(b) To be East of FRASNES by 11.00.

R.A. Group not to enter FRASNES before 11.00.

2. Lorries. Add one hour to the restrictions laid down.

3. Acknowledge by bearer.

Issued by D.R. at 1930

for Lieut. Colonel, G.S.
34th Division.

-- Distribution --

Copies Nos. 1 & 2 File
3 & 4 War Diary
5 G.O.C.
6 101st Inf. Bde.
7 102nd " "
8 103rd " "
9 C.R.A.
10 Signal Coy.
11 "Q"
12 A.D.M.S.
13 D.A.P.M.
14 Div. Train.
15 Camp Commandant
16) 17) IInd Corps
18 29th Division
19 9th Division.

34th Div. Arty. No. 1817/A.

O.C., 152nd Brigade R.F.A.
O.C., 160th Brigade R.F.A.
O.C., 3 4th D.A.C. (For information)

AF VIII a

REDUCTION OF BATTERIES TO FOUR GUNS.

1. The 34th Divisional Artillery will be reduced to a four gun basis by withdrawing one Section of guns or hows. from each battery.

2. Existing deficiences in personnel in four gun batteries will be made up from the third section in each case, provided that sufficient personnel is left in the third section to look after horses and equipment.

The minimum of personnel to be sent away is one driver per two horses, one gunner per vehicle, and one N.C.O. per sub-section.

3 . The residues of the personnel, horses and equipment of the third section will be transferred to XIX Corps, and will be prepared to move westwards on 17th inst. to a place to be notified later.

4. The establishment of officers of the Divisional Artillery is unchanged, and G.H.Q. has authorised an additional 16 Officers to be retained as surplus.

No Officers will therefore be sent away with the sections unless specially detailed from this office.

5. 152nd Brigade will transfer one Air-recuperator gun complete to 160th Brigade on morning of 17th inst in exchange for Spring-recuperator gun.

Details of exchange to be arranged between Brigades.

No air-recuperator guns will be sent away under any circumstances.

Two batteries of 160th F.A. Brigade will then be equipped with 4 air-recuperators.

I ndents for special stores are to be submitted to D.A.D.O.S., forthwith.

6. It is understood that these third sections are to be disbanded.

Nominal Rolls will be sent with each Brigade details and the postings to XIX Corps shewn in current A.F.B.213, quoting R.A. II Corps wire X/461 dated 15-11-18, as authority.

7. Report early on 17th inst. deficiences by ranks (18-pdr. or 4.5" How.) after third section have been drawn from.

Sd,. A. BEAL,
Captain.
Staff Captain.
34th Divisional Artillery.

15th Novr. 1918.

COPY.

War Diary

App IX

34th Division.

G.14 15

113th Army Bde R.F.A. will be attached to 34th Div. from 16th Nov. (incl) and will march on the 16th Nov to 34th Div. area AAA Routes available (a) OBIGIES - MOURCOURT - VELAINES - CORDES AAA (b) CELIES thence WATTRIPONT or ARC AINIERES AAA 34th Div will notify 113th army Bde through 2nd Corps exact location of billets AAA ACKNOWLEDGE

FROM 2nd Corps
TIME 14.40

(Sgd) J.P.DUKE
Major G.S.

C.R.A.
Signal Coy
"Q"

G.545.

For information.

The 113th Brigade R.F.A. will be billeted in ANVAING Area.

J Hacker

Major G.S.
34th Division.

ADDENDUM No. 1.

All times of heads of columns passing starting points in Appendix to 34th. Div. Arty. O.O.47 will have one hour added to them.

Captain, R.A.,
Brigade-Major,
34th. Divisional Artillery.

17th. Novr. 1918.

To 113 Bde AFA
152 Bde RFA
160 Bde RFA
34 D A C
D.T.M.O.
S.C.R.A.
34 Div G
No; 1 Coy Train
R.A. II Corps

Copy No...........

[illegible]th. Divisional Artillery Operation Order No. 47

Ref. Map 1/10[illegible],
Sheets [illegible].

1[illegible]th. Novr. 19[illegible].

1. The [illegible]th. Divisional Artillery and 11[illegible]th. Army Brigade R.F.A. will march on November 1[illegible]th. to the area [illegible] - LAHA[illegible] - [illegible]CHIEN - [illegible] as per march table attached.

2. Allotment of billeting areas will be notified later.

3. R.A.H.Q. will move on the same day from [illegible] to L[illegible].

4. R.A. Units please ACKNOWLEDGE by bearer.

Captain. R.A.
Brigade Major.
[illegible]th. Division Artillery.

Copies to 11[illegible]th. A.F.A. Brigade.
1[illegible]nd. R.F.A. Brigade.
1[illegible]th. " "
[illegible]th. D.A.C.
[illegible].C.R.A.
[illegible]th. Division "G"
IInd. Corps R.A.

MARCH TABLE "A" To accompany 34th Division Operation Order No.305. S E C R E T Copy No. 9

Serial No.	Unit.	Present Area	New Area.	Route.	Remarks.
Col.No.	1	2	3	4	5
1.	101 Bde.Group.	ELLEZELLES LA VIEILLE MAISON	PAPIGNIES ISIERES	Any route as far as cross roads 1 mile East of LAHAMAIDE thence via SCAUBECQ - WANNEBECQ - PAPIGNIES. Tail of column to be clear of above cross roads by 10.00.	Units crossing DENDRES can use bridge at LOCK E. of PAPIGNIES or iron bridge ½M N.W.of ISIERES.
2.	102 Bde.Group.	RENAIX	FLOBECQ WODECQ	ELLEZELLES - FLOBECQ and ELLEZELLES - WODECQ Roads. Units to be off the ELLEZELLES - FLOBECQ and ELLEZELLES - WODECQ - MARTOYAU Roads by 11.30 in order to allow 103 Bde to march through.	ELLEZELLES not to be entered before 08.00 and to be cleared by 10.00.
3.	103 Bde.Group.	St.SAUVEUR RENAIX	OGY OSTICHES WANNEBECQ	RENAIX - ELLEZELLES - FLOBECQ - OGY Road. ELLEZELLES - WODECQ - SCAUBECQ Road. St.SAUVEUR - thence any road to FRASNE - LAHAMAIDE Road to be East of FRASNES by 10.00.	Not to enter ELLEZELLES before 10.00.
4.	34th Div.Arty. Group.	ANVAING ARC AINIERES	LAHAMAIDE OEUDEGHIEN	FRASNES - LAHAMAIDE.	Not to enter FRASNES before 1000.
5.	Div.H.Q.Group.	WATTRIPONT	LESSINES		

All lorries of Bde.Groups to be East of Roman Road LAHAMAIDE - FLOBECQ by 08.00.
Lorries of 34th Div.Arty Group to be clear of FRASNES by 09.00.
Lorries crossing DENDRE to proceed via LESSINES.

App XI

S E C R E T

34th. DIVISIONAL ARTILLERY OPERATION ORDER NO. [illegible]

Ref: Maps, 1:100,000, TOURNAI & BRUSSELS.

1. In accordance with the terms of the armistice, the occupied portions of FRANCE, BELGIUM and LUXEMBOURG are to be evacuated by the enemy by 26th. November, 1918.

The country as far as the German Frontier has been divided into three zones, and the enemy has been instructed to be clear of each zone on the day preceding the commencement of the march of the Cavalry into that zone, i.e., two days before it is entered by the leading divisions of the IInd. Corps.

2. The Second Army, consisting of the Cavalry Corps (less one division), IInd., IIIrd., XXIInd. and Canadian Corps, will begin its advance to the German frontier on 17th. November, 1918.

The Cavalry Corps will cover the advance and be followed by the Canadian Corps on the right and the IInd. Corps on the left, one day's march in rear.

The IIIrd. and XXIInd. Corps will follow at a later date.

3. On 17th. November, the Cavalry Corps will advance through the present outpost line.

4. On the 18th. November, the IInd. Corps will begin its march and will move in the following order:-

1st. Echelon, 41st. Division on the left,
29th. Division on the right.
2nd. Echelon, 9th. Division on the left,
34th. Division on the right.
3rd. Echelon, IInd. Corps Heavy Artillery Group.

5. The various stages of the advance of the 34th. Division and the divisional area on each day are shewn on Map X which will be issued shortly to Brigades.

The date written over each area indicates the date on which that area will be reached. A two days' halt will take place in areas A and E. This is indicated by two dates on the map.

A tracing shewing the division of areas into Group sub-areas will be issued with each march table.

Captain,
Brigade-Major, R.A.,
34th. Divisional Artillery.

17th. November, 1918.

34th. Div.Arty. No. G.784.

App XIII

O.C., 113th. (Army) Bde., R.F.A.,
O.C., 152nd. Bde., R.F.A.,
O.C., 160th. Bde., R.F.A.,
O.C., 3'th. D.A.C.,
O.C., No. 1 Coy., Div. Train.

Owing to difficulties of surply, the 34th. Division will probably remaih in its present area for a week instead of continuing theadvance. on 21st. November.

Captain, R.A.
Brigade-Major,
34th. Divisional Artillery.

19th. November, 1918.

App XII

S E C R E T

Ref: Map, Sh. 38.
Scale 1:40,000.

34th. DIVISIONAL ARTILLERY LOCATION STATEMENT.

R.A., H.Q., LESSINES, 13, Rue Cesar Depret, C.16.d.4.6.

115th. (Army) Brigade, R.F.A., H.Q., ... B.25.d.5.4.
A/115, ... A.30.b.9.7.
B/115, ... B.19.central.
D/115, ... A.30.d.9.5.
B.A.C., ... B.19.a.3.5.

152nd. Bde. R.F.A., H.Q., ... G.12.b.8.0.
A/152, ... H.7.b.3.5.
B/152, ... H.7.d.8.0.
C/152, ... G.6.c.5.3.
D/152, ... H.7.a.8.0.

160th. Bde., R.F.A., H.Q., ... B.26.d.0.7.
A/160, ... B.27.c.7.1.
B/160, ... B.26.a.9.8.
C/160, ... B.26.c.6.5.
D/160, ... B.27.b.8.2.

34th. Divisional Ammunition Column, H.Q., H.14.b.3.7.
No. 1 Section, H.14.b.2.5.
No. 2 Section, H.20.b.9.8.
S.A.A. Section, H.20.d.9.9.

X and Y Batteries, 34th. Trench Mortars, STOCQ.

No. 1 Coy., 34th. Divisional Train, ... G.11.d.8.9.

19th. November, 1918.

[signature]
Captain, R.A.,
Brigade-Major,
34th. Divisional Artillery.

Army Form C. 2118.

WAR DIARY

Instructions regarding War Diaries and Intelligence Summaries are contained in F. S. Regs., Part II. and the Staff Manual respectively. Title pages will be prepared in manuscript.

H.Q.R.A., 34th. Division ~~or~~ for the month of DECEMBER 1918.
~~INTELLIGENCE SUMMARY~~
(Erase heading not required.)

Page 1.

VII 36

Place	Date	Hour	Summary of Events and Information	Remarks and references to Appendices
			(Reference Sheets TOURNAI - BRUSSELS - NAMUR 1/100,000)	
LESSINES	1918 Dec 1st.		H.Q.R.A. remained at LESSINES.	
SOIGNIES	12th.		H.Q.R.A. moved to SOIGNIES. Brigades and D.A.C. marched to the area of OLLIGNIES BASSILLY and BOIS de LESSINES..........	App. 1.
do	14th.		Brigades and D.A.C. marched to the area of SOIGNIES HORRUES and NEUSART..........	App. 11.
COURCELLES	16th.		H.Q.R.A. moved to COURCELLES. Brigades and D.A.C. marched to the LA LOUVIERE area in accordance with March Table 34th. D.A. Operation Order No. 51..........	App. 111
do	17th.		34th. D.A. and 113th. Army Brigade RFA. moved to the ROUX area in accordance with ~~March Table~~ 34th. D.A. Operation Order No. 52..........	App. IV.
CHATELET	18th.		34th. D.A. and 113th. Army Brigade RFA. moved to the CHATELET area..........	App. V.
PROFONDEVILLE	19th.		H.Q.R.A. moved to PROFONDEVILLE. Brigades and D.A.C. marched to the final areas as under :- 152nd. Brigade RFA.......... at FRANIERE. 160th. Brigade RFA.......... at BOIS de VILLERS. 113th. Army Bde. RFA.......... at BAMBOIS. HAUT VENT. TRY AL HUTTE. GONOY MAISON..........	App. VI
do	31st.		H.Q.R.A. remained at PROFONDEVILLE.	

[signature]

Lieut. R.A.
for C.R.A., 34th. Division.

D. D. & L., London, E.C.
(A10266) Wt W5300/P713 750,000 2/18 Sch. 52 Forms/C2118/15.

War Diary

App I

Reference Map:-
Sheet 3G. 1/40,000.

34th DIVISIONAL ARTILLERY OPERATION ORDER No.48.

1. The 34th Divisional Artillery and the 113th (Army) Brigade R.F.A. will move on a day "B", to be notified later, in accordance with the attached march table.

2. Tracings showing the allotment of billeting areas to units have already been issued.

3. H.Q. 34th D.A. will move to SOIGNIES at 10.00 on "B" day.

4. D. A. units please ACKNOWLEDGE.

Captain,
Brigade Major R.A.,
34th Divisional Artillery.

8th December 1918.

Distribution.

113th Bde. R.F.A.
152nd Bde. R.F.A.
160th Bde. R.F.A.
34th D.A.C.
D.T.M.O.
No.1.Coy. 34th Div. Train.
S.C.R.A.
34th Division "G".
X Corps R.A.

1. Serial No.	2. Unit.	3. From.	4. To.	5. Starting Point.	6 Time.	7. Route.	8. Remarks.
1.	113th Bde. R.F.A. & B.A.C.	ROME.	OLLIGNIES	LAHAMAIDE Church	10.45	LAHAMAIDE-LESSINES.	Head of column not to reach road junction ¼ mile W of LESSINES before 12.00
2.	152nd Bde. R.F.A.	OEUDEGHIEN	OLLIGNIES.	OEUDGHIEN Church.	10.00	OSTICHES-WANNEBECQ -PAPIGNIES-LOCK No.3.-OLLIGNIES.	Head of column not to reach LESSINES - GHISLENGHIEN road before 12.00 or until the tail of 102nd Bde. Group is clear.
3.	160th Bde. R.F.A.	LAHAMAIDE	BASSILLY	X Roads B.28.b.	10.30.	LESSINES-BOIS de LESSINES-BASSILLY.	Head of column not to reach road junction ¼ mile W of LESSINES before 11.30.
4.	34th D.A.C.	STOCQ	BOIS de LESSINES.	X Roads H.15.c.	11.00	OSTICHES-WANNEBECQ -PAPIGNIES-LOCK No.3.-OLLIGNIES-BOIS de LESSINES.	Head of column not to reach LESSINES-GHISLENGHIEN road before 13.00
5.	X & Y T.M.Bs.	As	for 34th D.A.C.				
6.	No.1.Coy. Div.Train.	OEUDEGHIEN	STOQUOI			OSTICHES-WANNEBECQ -PAPIGNIES-LOCK No. 3.-OLLIGNIES-STOCQUOI.	To follow in rear of 152nd Brigade R.F.A.

War Diary

App II

Reference Map.
Sheet 38. 1/40,000.

34th DIVISIONAL ARTILLERY OPERATION ORDER No. 49.

1. The 34th Divisional Artillery will move in accordance with the attached March Table on D day 12th inst to the SOIGNIES - HORRUES area.

2. A tracing showing allotment of areas to units has already been sent out.

3. The MONS - SOIGNIES Road is reserved for D.H.Q.

4. The Eastern side of the SOIGNIES - HAL Road is inclusive to 152nd Bde. R.F.A.
The Western side of the SOIGNIES - HAL Road is inclusive to the 113th Bde. R.F.A.

5. The area round the road junction in X.4.d. is reserved for No.1.Coy. Train.

6. The area S.E. of the MONS - HAL Road is exclusive to the Divisional Artillery.

7. D.A. units please acknowledge.

Captain,
Brigade Major R.A.,
34th Divisional Artillery.

11th December 1918.

DISTRIBUTION.

113th Bde. R.F.A.
152nd Bde..R.F.A.
160th Bde. R.F.A.
34th D.A.C.
No.1.Coy. Train.
S.C.R.A.
34th Divn. "G".
X Corps R.A.

Serial No.	Unit.	From.	To.	Starting Point.	Time.	Route.	Remarks.
1.	113th Bde R.F.A. & B.A.C.	OLLIGNIES	SOIGNIES.	GHISLENGHIEN Station.	09.30	GHISLENGHIEN -SOIGNIES.	Head of column not to pass road junction ½ mile S.W. of SILLY before 10.15
2.	152nd Bde. R.F.A.	OLLIGNIES	SOIGNIES	GHISLENGHIEN STATION.	10.00	GHISLENGHIEN -SOIGNIES.	
3.	160th Bde R.F.A.	BASSILLY	HORRUES	X roads K.13.c.	10.45	SILLY - HORRUES.	Head of column not to pass road junction ½ mile S.W. of SILLY before 11.15
4.	34th I.A.C. X & Y T.M.Bs.	BOIS de LESSINES.	NEUSART	Road junction J.4.a.8.5.	11.00	BOURLON-SILLY.	
5.	No.1.Coy. Train.	STOQUOI	SOIGNIES.	Road junction. J.21.b.9.5.	12.00	SILLY.	

Apt III

S E C R E T.

Copy No. 10

34th. DIVISIONAL ARTILLERY OPERATION ORDER NO. 51.

Ref: Maps BRUSSELS) 1/100.000.
NAMUR)

15th. Decr. 1918.

1. 34th. D.A. O.O. No. 50 is cancelled.

2. On F day, 16th. inst, 34th. Divisional Artillery and 113th. Brigade RFA. will march to the LA LOUVIERE area in accordance with the attached March Table.

3. The allotment of billeting areas is shown on the map circulated to units.

4. D.A. Units please ACKNOWLEDGE.

Captain,
Brigade Major.R.A.
34th. Divisional Artillery.

Copy No:
1. 113th. Bde. RFA.
2. 152nd. " "
3. 160th. " "
4. 34th. D.A.C.
5. No. 1 Coy. Train.
6. C.C.R.A.
7. 34th. Divn. "G".
8. File.
9-10. War Diary.

MARCH TABLE attached to 34th. D.A. O.O. No. 51 d/ 15-12-18.

1.	2.	3.	4.	5.	6.	7.	8.
Serial No.	Unit	From	To	Starting Point	Time	Route	Remarks.
1.	113th. Bde RFA. & B.A.C.	GONDREGNIES	LA LOUVIERE	Road junction ½ mile North of SOIGNIES	09.20.	SOIGNIES ROEULX HOUDENG.	
2.	152nd. Bde. RFA.	THORICOURT	LA LOUVIERE	do	10.00.	do	
3.	160th. Bde. RFA.	HORRUES	LA LOUVIERE	do	09.00.	do	Head of Column not to pass HAUTE FOLIE X Roads before 10.00 or till the Divl. HQ transport is clear.
4.	34th. D.A.C. X & Y T.M.Bs.	LONGPONT	HOUDENG AIMERIES	do	10.20.	do	
5.	No. 1 Coy. Train.	HORRUES	LA LOUVIERE	do	10.40.	do	

App IV

SECRET.

Copy No...

34th. DIVISIONAL ARTILLERY OPERATION ORDER No. 52.

Ref: Maps NAMUR 1/100,000.

16th.Decr. 1918.

1. On G day 17th. inst. the 34th. D.A. and 113th. Bde. RFA will move to the ROUX area as per March Table "G" attached.

2. Billeting parties will report to the S.C.R.A. at COURCELLES (40 Rue Antoine GARNIERE (near Maison Communal)) at 10.00 on the 17th. inst for allotment of areas.

3. 113th. Bde. RFA. will allot accommodation in SOUVRET for No. 1 Coy. Divisional Train.

4. Units will march closed up to the distances laid down in Fourth Army G.S. 128.

5. Halts other than the 10 minute halts laid down before every clockhour will not be made without orders from this office between Starting Points and destination.

6. A D.R. to be shown locations of H.Q. 160th. Bde. and D.A.C. will be met by guides at ROUX Station at 15-00.
A D.R. to be shown location of H.Q. 113th. Bde. will be met by a guide at SOUVRET Church at 14.00.
152nd. Bde. will notify this office of location of H.Q. by orderly as soon as possible.

7. D.A. Units please ACKNOWLEDGE. by Bearer.

Captain,
Brigade Major.R.A.
34th. Divisional Artillery.

Copies to:

113th. Bde. RFA.
152nd. " "
160th. " "
34th. D.A.C.
No. 1 Coy. Train.
34th. Div. "G".
S.C.R.A.
War Diary.
File.

MARCH TABLE "G" attached to 34th. D.A. O.O No. 52.

Serial No.	Unit	From	To	Starting Point	Time	Route	Remarks.
1.	113th. Bde.RFA & B.A.C.	LA LOUVIERE	SOUVRET	Road junction ½ mile East of E in BAUME.	09.00	LA HESTRE-CHAPELLE LES HERLAI MONT - TRAZEGNIES	Head of Col. to pass TRAZEGNIES at 11-30
2.	152nd. Bde.RFA	do	COURCELLES	do		do	To follow in rear of 113th
3.	160th. Bde.RFA.	do	ROUX	do		do	To follow in rear of 152nd.
4.	34th. D.A.C. X & Y T.M.Bs.	HOUDENG AIMERIES	LAGASSE GOHISSART	do		do	To follow in rear of 160th.
5.	No. 1 Coy. Train.	LA LOUVIERE	SOUVRET	do		do	To follow in rear of D.A.C.

Lorries to be off March Route by 09.00

War Diary

App V

S E C R E T.

34th. DIVISIONAL ARTILLERY OPERATION ORDER NO. 53.

Ref: Map NAMUR 1/100,000. 16-12-18

1. On H day 18th. inst. the 34th. D.A. and 113th. Bde. RFA will move to the CHATELET area as per March Table "H" attached.

2. Billeting parties will report to the S.C.R.A. on the 17th inst. for definite allotment of areas at H.Q.R.A. 40 Rue ANTOINE CARNIERE (near Maison Communal) COURCELLES.

3. Units will march closed up to the distances laid down in Fourth Army G.S. 128.

4. A bicycle orderly will be sent by all units to report to an N.C.O. from this office the location of their H.Q.
This N.C.O. will be at the Railway Bridge on CHATELET - GILLY Road ~~XXXXX~~ 200 yards N of the R. SAMBRE in CHATELET at 15.00.

5. D.A. Units please ACKNOWLEDGE by Bearer.

[signature]
Captain,
Brigade Major.R.A.
34th. Divisional Artillery.

Copies to:
113th. Bde. RFA.
152nd. Bde. RFA.
160th. Bde. RFA.
34th. D.A.C.
No. 1 Coy. Train.
S.C.R.A.
War Diary.
File.

MARCH TABLE "H" to 34th D.A.,O.O. No.58.

Serial No.	Unit.	From.	To.	Starting Point.	Time.	Route.	Remarks.
1.	113th Bde. R.F.A. & B.A.C.	SOUVRET	MONTIGNIES Sur SAMBRE.	Road junction ¼ mile south of 1st "L"		LODELINCART - GILLY.	To follow 152nd Bde. R.F.A.
2.	152nd Bde. R.F.A.	COURCELLES	PONT de LOUP.	in LODELINSART.			To follow 160th Bde. R.F.A.
3.	160th Bde. R.F.A.	ROUX.	Portion of CHATELET N of R. SAMBRE.	do	10.30		Head of Column to reach GILLY at 11. Road from MONCEAU sur SAMBRE to CHARLEROI not to b used by units.movi to starting Point.
4.	D.A.C. & X & Y T.M. Btys.	LAGASSE	CHATELINEAU	do			To follow 113th Bde. R.F.A.
5.	No.1.Coy. Train.	SOUVRET	CHAMBRY	do			To follow D.A.C.

Lorries to be off march route by 02.15.

App VI

34th. DIVISIONAL ARTILLERY OPERATION ORDER NO. 54.

Ref: Map NAMUR 1/100,000. 17th. Decr. 1918.

1. The 34th. Divisional Artillery and 113th. Brigade RFA. will continue its march into the final area on "I" day 19th. inst in accordance with March Table "I" attached.

2. H.Q.R.A. will move from CHATELET to PROFONDEVILLE.

3. D.A. Units please ACKNOWLEDGE.

Captain,
Brigade Major.R.A.
34th. Divisional Artillery.

Copies to:
113th. Bde. RFA.
152nd. Bde. RFA.
160th. Bde. RFA.
34th. D.A.C.
No. 1 Coy. Train.
S.C.R.A. .
War Diary.
File.

MARCH TABLE "I" attached to 34th. D .A. O.O. No. 54 d/17-12-18.

Col. No.	1	2	3	4	5	6	7	8
Serial No.	Unit.	From.	To.	Starting Point.	Time.	Route.	Remarks.	Billets allott by -
1.	113th Bde & B.A.C.	MONTIGNIES sur SAMBRE	BAMBOIS HAUT VENT TRY AL HUTTE GONOY MAISON.	Road junction ½ mile West of C in CHATELET.	In rear of 152 Bde.	CHATELET - PRESLES - VITRIVAL FOSSE - thence most direct route to destination.	Head of Col. to reach VITRIVAL by 11.00	102nd. I.B.
2.	152nd. Bde. RFA.	PONT de LOUP	FRANIERE		In rear of 160 Bde.			101st. I.B.
3.	160th. Bde. RFA.	CHAMBRE	BOIS de VILLIERS		09.00.			103rd. I.B.
4.	34th. D.A.C. X & Y T.M.Bs.	CHATELINEAU	ST. GERARD		In rear of 113 Bde.			102nd. I.B.
5.	No. 1 Coy. Train.	CHAMBRE	RIVIERE		In rear of D.A.C.			C.R.E.

Army Form C. 2118.

WAR DIARY
or
~~INTELLIGENCE SUMMARY~~.

H.Q.R.A., 34th. Division.

Instructions regarding War Diaries and Intelligence Summaries are contained in F. S. Regs., Part II. and the Staff Manual respectively. Title pages will be prepared in manuscript.

for the Month of JANUARY 1919.

(*Erase heading not required.*)

Place	Date	Hour	Summary of Events and Information	Remarks and references to Appendices
	Jany.			
PROFONDEVILLE	1st. to 25th.		H.Q.R.A. remained at PROFONDEVILLE (NAMUR Sheet 1/100,000)	
SIEGBURG	27th.		34th. Divisional Artillery relieved the 2nd. Canadian Divisional Artillery in the COLOGNE Bridgehead.	
			H.Q.R.A. established at SIEGBURG. Vide 34th. Divisional Artillery Administrative Instructions No. 1	App. 1.
	28th.		Re-organization of the Xth. Corps Sector of the COLOGNE Bridgehead, vide..................	App. 11.
			[signature] Lieut.R.A. for C.R.A., 34th. Division.	

D. D. & L., London, E.C.
(A10266) Wt W5300/P713 750,000 2/18 Sch. 52 Forms/C2118/16.

Army Form C. 2118.

WAR DIARY
or
INTELLIGENCE SUMMARY

(Erase heading not required.)

Instructions regarding War Diaries and Intelligence Summaries are contained in F. S. Regs., Part II. and the Staff Manual respectively. Title pages will be prepared in manuscript.

H.Q.R.A., 34th. Division. Month of FEBRUARY 1919.

Vol 38

Place	Date	Hour	Summary of Events and Information	Remarks and references to Appendices
	1919			
SIEGBURG	Feb. 3rd.		113th. Army Brigade RFA. moved from RAMERSDORF Area to WAHN Barracks)	Appendix 1.
	4th.		160th. Brigade RFA. moved from BEUEL Area to SIEGBURG.)	
			Locations - February 28th. C.R.A. SIEGBURG, Munition Factory, LUISENSTRASSE. 152nd. Brigade RFA. SIEGBURG. 160th. Brigade RFA. SIEGBURG 113th. Army Brigade RFA. WAHN Barracks. 34th. D.A.C. ZUNDORF.	

C. Thompson
Lieut.R.A.
for C.R.A., 34th. Division.

D. D. & L., London, E.C.
(A10266) Wt W5300/P713 750,000 2/18 Sch. 52 Forms/C2118/16.

EASTERN DIVISIONAL ARTILLERY.

Instructions regarding War Diaries and Intelligence Summaries are contained in F. S. Regs., Part II. and the Staff Manual respectively. Title pages will be prepared in manuscript.

WAR DIARY for MARCH 1919.
or
INTELLIGENCE SUMMARY.
(Erase heading not required.)

Army Form C. 2118.

Vol 39

Place	Date	Hour	Summary of Events and Information	Remarks and references to Appendices
SIEGBERG GERAMNY	March 1919.		NIL	

[signature] Lieut. R.A.,
for C.R.A. EASTERN DIVISIOB.

D. D. & L., London, E.C.
(A10266) Wt W5300/P713 750,000 2/18 Sch. 52 Forms/C2118/16.

EASTERN DIVISIONAL ARTILLERY. Headquarters.

WAR DIARY APRIL 1919.
or
INTELLIGENCE SUMMARY.
(Erase heading not required.)

Army Form C. 2118.

Instructions regarding War Diaries and Intelligence Summaries are contained in F. S. Regs., Part II. and the Staff Manual respectively. Title pages will be prepared in manuscript.

Place	Date	Hour	Summary of Events and Information	Remarks and references to Appendices
SIEGBURG. GERMANY.	APRIL 5th.		C.R.A. and Brigade Major.R.A. reconnoitre Southern edge of the Perimeter.	
	9th.		" " " " " Northern " " " "	
	20th to 3rd. May		Major E.F. BUDDEN proceeds on 14 days Leave to England. Captain A. BEAL.MC.RA., discharged the duties of the Brigade Major, during absence of Major BUDDEN.	

[signature] Lieut.R.A.
R.O., R.A., EASTERN DIVISION.

D. D. & L., London, E.C.
(A10266) Wt W5300/P713 750,000 2/18 Sch. 52 Forms/C2118/16.

EASTERN DIVISIONAL ARTILLERY. HEADQUARTERS. **WAR DIARY** *or* **INTELLIGENCE SUMMARY.** MAY 1919.

Army Form C. 2118.

Instructions regarding War Diaries and Intelligence Summaries are contained in F. S. Regs., Part II. and the Staff Manual respectively. Title pages will be prepared in manuscript.

(Erase heading not required.)

Place	Date	Hour	Summary of Events and Information	Remarks and references to Appendices
	1919.			
SIEGBURG.	May 4th.		Captain. A. BEAL. MC. Staff Captain. R.A.. demobilised. Captain W. HOLDEN. RFA. appointed Staff Captain R.A. vice Capt A.BEAL.	
	5th.		A and D Batteries 160th Bde.RFA. moved from SIEGBURG (GESCHOSS FABRIK) to WAHN Barracks.	
	11th to 24th.		Brigadier General W.H. KAY. DSO. proceeds on leave to England., during his absense Lieut Colonel W. KINNEAR, DSO. 152nd Bde.RFA. assumed temporary command., of this Divisional Artillery.	
	30.		Permission having been given to the Germans to hold a meeting and demonstration in SIEGBURG, One Section of Howitzers from D Battery 152nd Bde.RFA. were held in readiness in case of disturbance.	

[signature] Lieut.R.A.
R.O.,R.A. EASTERN DIVISION.

D. D. & L., London, E.C.
(A10266) Wt W5300/P713 750,000 2/18 Sch. 52 Forms/C2118/16.

Eastern Divisional Artillery. Headquarters. **WAR DIARY** *or* **INTELLIGENCE SUMMARY.** (*Erase heading not required.*) June 1919. R.A.

Army Form C. 2118.

Instructions regarding War Diaries and Intelligence Summaries are contained in F. S. Regs., Part II. and the Staff Manual respectively. Title pages will be prepared in manuscript.

Place	Date 1919.	Hour	Summary of Events and Information	Remarks and references to Appendices
SIEGBURG. Germany	June 18th	and 19th.	Owing to the delay by the Germans in signing the "TREATY OF PEACE" The Artillery Brigades concentrated in Areas shown below, in accordance with Instructions received from Eastern Div. Headquarters.	

152nd Brigade. R.F.A.) SELINGENTHAL.(near) Map Ref. B.72.39
Nos 1 and S.A.A. Section D.A.C.) " " " " B.755.395.

160th Bde.H.Q.	SIEGBURG.	B.25.38.
"A" Battery 160th Bde.	DONRATH.	W.42.09.
"B" " " "	LOHMAR.	B.25.92.
"C" " " "	"	B.25.92.
"D" " " "	DONRATH.	W.42.09.
No.2 Section D.A.C.	LOHMAR.	B.25.92.

The following Appendices are attached.

EASTERN DIVISIONAL ARTILLERY INSTRUCTIONS FOR AN ADVANCE. NO. 2. dated 26th May 1919.
" " " " " " " " 3. " 1st June 1919.(with March Table attached)
" " " " " " " " 4. " 17th June 1919.
" " " " " " " " 5. " 17th June 1919.

[illegible]
[illegible] R.A., ~~EASTERN DIVISION~~.

D. D. & L., London, E.C. Sch. 52 Forms/C2118/16.

Sheet 8

Army Form C. 2118.

WAR DIARY
or
INTELLIGENCE SUMMARY.

(Erase heading not required.)

Instructions regarding War Diaries and Intelligence Summaries are contained in F. S. Regs., Part II. and the Staff Manual respectively. Title pages will be prepared in manuscript.

Place	Date	Hour	Summary of Events and Information	Remarks and references to Appendices
	1919			
SIEGBURG. Germany	June	28th	Information was received by Wireless that the "Treaty of PEACE" was signed.	
		30th	The G.O.C. EASTERN DIVISION Inspected 152nd Brigade R.F.A. at HENNEF 09.30 hours.	
		30th	160th Brigade RFA. moved from LOHMAR and DONRATH to WAHN Barracks in readiness for the forthcoming Practice on WAHN Artillery Ranges.	

[signature] Lieut.R.A.
Staff Lieut.R.A.
EASTERN DIVISIONAL ARTILLERY.

Instructions regarding War Diaries and Intelligence Summaries are contained in F. S. Regs., Part II. and the Staff Manual respectively. Title pages will be prepared in manuscript.

WAR DIARY
or
INTELLIGENCE SUMMARY.
(Erase heading not required.)

Army Form C. 2118.

Place	Date	Hour	Summary of Events and Information	Remarks and references to Appendices
SIEGBURG.	2-7-19		R.A.,H.Q. moved to WAHN for practice.	
	2-7-19 to 17-7-19		Practice camp out at WAHN.	
	3-7-19.		General Holiday to celebrate the Signing of Peace.	
	18-7-19		Returned to former billets at SIEGBURG.	

[signature]
Lieut. R.A.
R.O.,R.A.
Eastern Division.

D. D. & L., London, E.C.
(A10266) Wt W5300/P713 750,000 2/18 Sch. 52 Forms/C2118/16.

www.ingramcontent.com/pod-product-compliance
Lightning Source LLC
Chambersburg PA
CBHW080817010526
44111CB00015B/2569

* 9 7 8 1 4 7 4 5 1 6 8 3 9 *